Colonels in Blue—
Missouri and the Western
States and Territories

ALSO BY ROGER D. HUNT
AND FROM McFARLAND

*Colonels in Blue—Illinois, Iowa,
Minnesota and Wisconsin* (2017)

*Colonels in Blue—Indiana,
Kentucky and Tennessee* (2014)

*Colonels in Blue—Michigan,
Ohio and West Virginia* (2011)

Colonels in Blue— Missouri and the Western States and Territories
A Civil War Biographical Dictionary

Roger D. Hunt

McFarland & Company, Inc., Publishers
Jefferson, North Carolina

ISBN (print) 978-1-4766-7589-3
ISBN (ebook) 978-1-4766-3685-6

Library of Congress and British Library
cataloguing data are available

© 2019 Roger D. Hunt. All rights reserved

No part of this book may be reproduced or transmitted in any form or by any means, electronic or mechanical, including photocopying or recording, or by any information storage and retrieval system, without permission in writing from the publisher.

Front cover images from left: Charles Ransford Jennison (J.P. Marshall & Co., 40 Delaware St., Leavenworth, KS); Theodore Meumann (Brown & Scholten, Artists, 82 North Fourth St., St. Louis, MO); George E. Waring, Jr. (all images Roger D. Hunt Collection, USAMHI)

Printed in the United States of America

*McFarland & Company, Inc., Publishers
Box 611, Jefferson, North Carolina 28640
www.mcfarlandpub.com*

In memory of David F. Zullo,
Civil War bibliophile and friend (1942–2018)

David F. Zullo.

Table of Contents

Acknowledgments ix
Introduction 1

Missouri
Regiments 3
Biographies 18

Arkansas
Regiments 143
Biographies 143

California
Regiments 148
Biographies 149

Colorado Territory
Regiments 156
Biographies 156

Kansas
Regiments 162
Biographies 165

Louisiana
Regiments 197
Biographies 197

Nebraska Territory
Regiments 204
Biographies 204

Nevada Territory
Regiments 207
Biographies 207

New Mexico Territory
Regiments 209
Biographies 210

Oregon
Regiments 213
Biographies 213

Texas
Regiments 216
Biographies 216

Washington Territory
Regiments 218
Biographies 218

Bibliography 221
Index 237

Acknowledgments

Although I appreciate the contributions of all of the individuals in the following list, I want to mention a few individuals whose contributions to this volume have been especially noteworthy. Dennis Hood has been generous in providing images from his outstanding Missouri collection. Jeff Patrick has been equally generous in providing images from the collections at Wilson's Creek National Battlefield. The late Richard Baumgartner, Everitt Bowles, Rick Carlile, Henry Deeks, and Steve Meadow have always been helpful in providing elusive photographs and valuable information. Ron Coddington has been especially active in supporting my efforts. Roberta Fairburn and Jan Perone have been especially helpful in supporting my research activities at the Abraham Lincoln Presidential Library & Museum. Randy Hackenburg, Dr. Richard Sommers and the late Mike Winey have provided ready access to the unparalleled photo archives of the U.S. Army Military History Institute during the past 40 years. Alan Aimone has been equally hospitable in providing access to the outstanding collections at the U.S. Military Academy Library.

John Abney, Iron County Historical Society, Ironton, MO
Jill M. Abraham, National Archives, Washington, D.C.
Alan C. Aimone, U.S. Military Academy Library, West Point, NY
Gil Barrett, New Bern, NC
Richard A. Baumgartner, Huntington, WV
Randy Beck, St. Charles, MO
Bruce P. Bonfield, Naples, FL
Jaime Ellyn Bourassa, Missouri Historical Society, St. Louis, MO
Everitt Bowles, Woodstock, GA
Mike Brackin, Winterville, NC
Rick Brown, Leesburg, VA
Paul J. Brzozowski, Fairfield, CT
Denell Burks, Vacaville, CA
David L. Callihan, Harrisburg, PA
Richard F. Carlile, Dayton, OH
Allen Cebula, Mooresville, IN
Ronald S. Coddington, Arlington, VA
Matthew Cowan, Oregon Historical Society, Portland, OR
Janet D. Curtis, Nesbit, MS
Henry Deeks, Ashburnham, MA
Thomas P. Dixon, Sheridan, WY
Dennis Edelin, National Archives, Washington, DC
Elizabeth E. Engel, State Historical Society of Missouri, Columbia, MO
Jerry Everts, Lambertville, MI
Roberta Fairburn, Abraham Lincoln Presidential Library, Springfield, IL
David D. Finney, Carmel, IN
James C. Frasca, Croton, OH
Perry M. Frohne, Oshkosh, WI
Sarah Gilmor, Hart Research Library, History Colorado, Denver, CO
Randy Hackenburg, Boiling Springs, PA
Pete Hakel, Rockville, MD
Rudy M. Hanson, Warsaw, IN
Thomas Harris, New York, NY
Terre Heydari, DeGolyer Library, Southern Methodist University, Dallas, TX
Michael A. Hogle, Okemos, MI
Dennis Hood, Bolivar, MO
Angela Hoover, Chicago History Museum, Chicago, IL
Craig T. Johnson, New Freedom, PA
Lawrence T. Jones III, Austin, TX
Wayne Jorgenson, Eden Prairie, MN
Alan Jutzi, The Huntington Library, San Marino, CA
Michael Kraus, Pittsburgh, PA
John W. Kuhl, Pittstown, NJ
Mary Beth Linné, National Archives, Washington, D.C.
Donald J. Litznerski, Mishawaka, IN
Robert F. MacAvoy, Clark, NJ
Vann R. Martin, Kingston, TN
Michael J. McAfee, Newburgh, NY
William McFarland, Topeka, KS
Edward McGuire, New York State Library, Albany, NY
Marcus S. McLemore, Poland, OH
Sarah T. McNeive, Topeka, KS
Steven J. Meadow, Midland, MI
Mike Medhurst, North Liberty, IA
Dan Miles, Clinton, MO
Mary-Jo Miller, Nebraska State Historical Society, Lincoln, NE

Acknowledgments

Tom Molocea, North Lima, OH
Jim Mundie, Kenner, LA
Douglas R. Niermeyer, Webster Groves, MO
Olaf, Berkeley, CA
Ronn Palm, Kittanning, PA
Linell Palo, Carrollton, TX
Jeffrey L. Patrick, Wilson's Creek National Battlefield, Republic, MO
Jan Perone, Abraham Lincoln Presidential Library, Springfield, IL
Nicholas P. Picerno, Bridgewater, VA
Becki Plunkett, State Historical Society of Iowa, Des Moines, IA
Brad and Donna Pruden, Marietta, GA
Jim Quinlan, Alexandria, VA
Mary Beth Revels, St. Joseph (MO) Public Library
Jeffrey I. Richman, Brooklyn, NY
Kathy Ridge, Andrew County (MO) Museum & Historical Society
Mary Robbins, Kent Library, Southeast Missouri State University, Cape Girardeau, MO
Brian Robertson, Butler Center for Arkansas Studies, Little Rock, AR
Stephen B. Rogers, Ithaca, NY
Paul Russinoff, Baltimore, MD
Steve Saathoff, Franklin Grove, IL
Angela Schad, Hagley Museum and Library, Wilmington, DE
Alan J. Sessarego, Gettysburg, PA
Sandra Sheldon, Edmond, OK
Nancy Sherbert, Kansas State Historical Society, Topeka, KS
Dr. Richard J. Sommers, Carlisle, PA
Megan Spainhour, Tennessee State Library and Archives, Nashville, TN
Geoffery Stark, University of Arkansas Libraries, Fayetteville, AR
Marc and Beth Storch, DeForest, WI
Larry M. Strayer, Urbana, OH
Karl E. Sundstrom, North Riverside, IL
David W. Taylor, Sylvania, OH
Ann Toplovich, Tennessee Historical Society, Nashville, TN
Ken C. Turner, Ellwood City, PA
Michael W. Waskul, Ypsilanti, MI
Michael Wells, Kansas City Public Library, Kansas City, MO
Michael J. Winey, Mechanicsburg, PA
Richard A. Wolfe, Bridgeport, WV
Bridget Wood, Arkansas State Archives, Little Rock, AR
Robert J. Younger, Dayton, OH
Buck Zaidel, Cromwell, CT
Ray Zielin, Orland Park, IL
Dave Zullo, Lake Monticello, VA

I am also indebted to the staffs of the following libraries for their capable assistance:

Abraham Lincoln Presidential Library & Museum, Springfield, IL
Chicago History Museum, Chicago, IL
Civil War Library & Museum, Philadelphia, PA
Colorado Historical Society, Denver, CO
Connecticut State Library, Hartford, CT
Family History Library, Salt Lake City, UT
The Huntington Library, San Marino, CA
Indiana Historical Society, Indianapolis, IN
Indiana State Library, Indianapolis, IN
Institute of Texan Cultures, University of Texas at San Antonio, TX
Kansas State Historical Society, Topeka, KS
Library of Congress, Washington, D.C.
Milwaukee Public Library, Milwaukee, WI
Minnesota Historical Society, St. Paul, MN
Missouri Historical Society, St. Louis, MO
National Archives, Washington, D.C.
National Society Daughters of the American Revolution, Washington, D.C.
New England Historic Genealogical Society, Boston, MA
New York Genealogical and Biographical Society, New York, NY
The New-York Historical Society, New York, NY
New York State Library, Albany, NY
Oakland Public Library, Oakland, CA
Ohio Genealogical Society, Mansfield, OH
Ohio Historical Society, Columbus, OH
Oregon Historical Society, Portland, OR
Rutherford B. Hayes Presidential Center, Fremont, OH
San Diego Public Library, San Diego, CA
Schaffer Library, Union College, Schenectady, NY
The Sheridan Libraries, The Johns Hopkins University, Baltimore, MD
Spokane Public Library, Spokane, WA
State Historical Society of Iowa, Des Moines, IA
State Historical Society of Iowa, Iowa City, IA
State Historical Society of Missouri, Columbia, MO
Tacoma Public Library, Tacoma, WA
Tennessee State Library and Archives, Nashville, TN
U.S. Army Military History Institute, Carlisle, PA
U.S. Military Academy Library, West Point, NY
Washington State Historical Society, Tacoma, WA
Western Reserve Historical Society, Cleveland, OH
Wisconsin Historical Society, Madison, WI

Introduction

At the beginning of the Civil War the Regular Army of the United States numbered only 1,098 officers and 15,304 enlisted men. Faced with this shortage of manpower in suppressing the escalating rebellion, President Abraham Lincoln issued a call for 75,000 militia for three months' service on April 15, 1861, and then a call for 500,000 volunteers for three years' service on July 22, 1861. These calls for troops and others issued later in the war specified that the various state governors would appoint the commanding officers of the regiments raised in their states.

Patriotic fervor throughout the Northern states resulted in spirited competition to complete the organization of regiments to meet the state quotas. In most cases the prospective commanders of these regiments were prominent citizens whose military background (if any) consisted of service in a local militia organization. In general the early war Union army colonels were known more for their patriotic enthusiasm than for their military competence. Many of them were more successful in convincing their fellow townsmen to enlist than they were in actually leading them into battle. Fortunately for the Union cause, the colonels who stayed in the service eventually acquired the necessary military skills or were replaced by subordinates who proved their capabilities on the field of battle.

This book is the seventh in a series of books containing photographs and biographical sketches of that diverse group of motivated citizens who attained the rank of colonel in the Union army, but failed to win promotion to brigadier general or brevet brigadier general. This volume presents the colonels who commanded regiments from Missouri and the Western states and territories (Arkansas, California, Colorado, Kansas, Louisiana, Nebraska, Nevada, New Mexico, Oregon, Texas, and Washington). Preceding the photographs and biographical sketches for each state is a breakdown by regiment of all the colonels who commanded regiments from that state, with the name of each colonel being followed by the dates of his service. Included in this breakdown are the colonels who were promoted beyond the rank of colonel, with their final rank indicated in bold letters. Those indicated as attaining the rank of brigadier general are covered in the book *Generals in Blue*, by Ezra J. Warner, while those attaining the rank of brevet brigadier general are covered in the book *Brevet Brigadier Generals in Blue*, by Roger D. Hunt and Jack R. Brown.

Some explanatory notes are necessary concerning the content of the biographical sketches:

(1.) The date associated with each rank may be the date when the colonel was commissioned or appointed or the date when he was mustered at that rank. Generally, the date of muster was used whenever available. The reader should be aware that these dates were often adjusted or corrected by the War Department during and after the war, so that any hope of providing totally consistent dates is virtually impossible.
(2.) When the word "Colonel" is italicized, this indicates that the colonel was commissioned as colonel but never mustered as such.
(3.) The following abbreviations are used in the text:

AAG	Assistant Adjutant General
ACM	Assistant Commissary of Musters
ACP	Appointment, Commission, and Personal
ADC	Aide-de-Camp
AGO	Adjutant General's Office
AIG	Assistant Inspector General
aka	also known as
AQM	Assistant Quartermaster
BG	Brigadier General
Brig.	Brigadier
Bvt.	Brevet
Capt.	Captain
Cav.	Cavalry
CB	Commission Branch
Co.	County or Company

Col.	Colonel	Regt.	Regiment
CSA	Confederate States Army	RQM	Regimental Quartermaster
CT	Colored Troops	SM	State Militia
DOW	Died of Wounds	Twp.	Township
EMM	Enrolled Missouri Militia	U.S.	United States
GAR	Grand Army of the Republic	USA	United States Army
Gen.	General	USAMHI	United States Army Military History Institute
GSW	Gun Shot Wound		
KIA	Killed in Action	USCT	United States Colored Troops
Lt.	Lieutenant	USMA	United States Military Academy
MOLLUS	Military Order of the Loyal Legion of the United States	USV	United States Volunteers
		Vol.	Volume
NHDVS	National Home for Disabled Volunteer Soldiers	VRC	Veteran Reserve Corps
		VS	Volunteer Service

Missouri

Regiments

Benton Cadets
Henry C. De Ahna	Aug. 3, 1861	Dismissed Sept. 2, 1861
Louis H. Marshall	Sept. 24, 1861	Mustered out Jan. 8, 1862

Benton County Home Guards
Henry Imhauser   July 21, 1861   Discharged Sept. 13, 1861

Black Hawk Cavalry
William Bishop   Aug. 15, 1861   To 7th MO Cav. Feb. 20, 1862

Cass County Home Guards Cavalry
Andrew G. Newgent   Aug. 1, 1861   Mustered out Feb. 28, 1862

Cole County Home Guards
Allen P. Richardson   June 17, 1861   Discharged Oct. 1, 1861

Dallas County Home Guards
William B. Edwards   June 24, 1861   Discharged Aug. 11, 1861

Franklin County Home Guards
James W. Owens   June 13, 1861   Discharged Sept. 13, 1861

Gasconade County Battalion Home Guards
James A. Matthews   June 8, 1861   Discharged Sept. 4, 1861

Gentry County Home Guards
Manlove Cranor   Aug. 1, 1861   Discharged Oct. 17, 1861

Harrison County Home Guards
Henry O. Nevill   Sept. 3, 1861   Discharged Sept. 23, 1861

Johnson County Home Guards
Jacob Knaus		Superseded by James D. Eads
James D. Eads	May 1, 1861	Discharged Oct. 30, 1861

Kimball's Regiment, Six Months Militia
Thomas F. Kimball   Nov. 28, 1861   Mustered out April 2, 1862

Lawrence County Home Guards
James C. Martin   June 16, 1861   Discharged Sept. 1, 1861

Militia of Central and St. Louis Townships
Norman J. Colman   April 21, 1864   To 85th EMM May 28, 1864

Missouri Regiments

Nodaway County Home Guards
William J.W. Bickett   July 5, 1861   Discharged Oct. 2, 1861

Osage County Home Guards
Joseph W. McClurg   July 18, 1861   Discharged Dec. 20, 1861

Phelps' Regiment Infantry
John S. Phelps   Dec. 19, 1861   Mustered out May 13, 1862, **Brig. Gen., USV**

Pike County Home Guards
George W. Anderson   July 17, 1861   Discharged Sept. 3, 1861

Richardson's Regiment, Six Months Militia
Allen P. Richardson   Oct. 1, 1861   Mustered out Dec. 18, 1861

Stone County Home Guards
Asa G. Smith   June 6, 1861   Discharged Nov. 6, 1861

Webster County Home Guards
Noah H. Hampton   July 6, 1861   Discharged Aug. 18, 1861

1st Cavalry
Calvin A. Ellis	Sept. 6, 1861	Mustered out April 2, 1862
John F. Ritter	June 18, 1862	Resigned Dec. 5, 1864
Milton H. Brawner	Feb. 22, 1865	Not mustered
John J. Joslyn	April 13, 1865	Mustered out July 8, 1865

1st State Militia Cavalry
James H.B. McFerran   March 31, 1862   Mustered out Feb. 11, 1865

2nd Cavalry
Lewis Merrill   Aug. 23, 1861   Mustered out Sept. 19, 1865, **Bvt. Brig. Gen., USV**

2nd State Militia Cavalry
John McNeil	June 30, 1862	Promoted **Brig. Gen., USV,** March 8, 1863
John B. Rogers	May 26, 1863	Mustered out March 1, 1865

3rd Cavalry
John M. Glover	Sept. 4, 1861	Resigned March 13, 1864
John H. Reed	June 6, 1865	Mustered out June 14, 1865

3rd State Militia Cavalry
Walter King   April 24, 1862   Mustered out Feb. 15, 1863

3rd State Militia Cavalry (designation of regiment changed from 10th State Militia Cavalry, Feb. 2, 1863)
Edwin J. Smart	May 5, 1862	Resigned May 23, 1863
Richard G. Woodson	May 25, 1863	Commission vacated Feb. 27, 1864

4th Cavalry
George E. Waring, Jr.   Jan. 9, 1862   Mustered out Oct. 24, 1864

4th State Militia Cavalry
George H. Hall   April 28, 1862   Mustered out Sept. 1, 1864

5th Cavalry
Joseph Nemett   Feb. 14, 1862   Mustered out Dec. 4, 1862

5th State Militia Cavalry
William R. Penick   March 17, 1862   Mustered out June 22, 1863

5th State Militia Cavalry (designation of regiment changed from 13th State Militia Cavalry, Feb. 2, 1863)
Albert Sigel   May 19, 1862   Mustered out Jan. 7, 1865

6th Cavalry
T. Clark Wright   Feb. 14, 1862   Discharged Sept. 16, 1863

6th State Militia Cavalry
Edwin C. Catherwood   April 30, 1862   To 13th MO Cavalry, Nov. 25, 1864

7th Cavalry
Daniel Huston, Jr.   Feb. 22, 1862   Mustered out Dec. 30, 1864

7th State Militia Cavalry
John F. Philips   May 1, 1862   Mustered out March 18, 1865

8th Cavalry
Washington F. Geiger   Aug. 10, 1862   Mustered out July 20, 1865

8th State Militia Cavalry
Joseph W. McClurg   June 25, 1862   Resigned Dec. 22, 1862
Joseph J. Gravely   March 30, 1863   Mustered out March 20, 1865

9th Cavalry (consolidated with the 10th MO Cavalry, Dec. 4, 1862)

9th State Militia Cavalry
Odon Guitar   May 3, 1862   Mustered out June 30, 1863
John F. Williams   July 13, 1863   Mustered out Feb. 11, 1865

10th Cavalry
Florence M. Cornyn   Dec. 19, 1862   Killed Aug. 10, 1863

10th State Militia Cavalry (designation of regiment changed to 3rd State Militia Cavalry, Feb. 2, 1863)
Edwin J. Smart   May 5, 1862   Resigned May 23, 1863

11th Cavalry
William D. Wood   Dec. 14, 1863   Resigned April 8, 1865, **Bvt. Brig. Gen, USV**
James F. Dwight   May 9, 1865   Mustered out July 27, 1865

11th State Militia Cavalry
Henry S. Lipscomb   May 6, 1862   Discharged July 18, 1862

12th Cavalry
Oliver Wells   March 21, 1864   Resigned Dec. 2, 1865
Richard H. Brown   Jan. 24, 1866   Mustered out April 9, 1866

12th State Militia Cavalry
Albert Jackson   May 14, 1862   Commission vacated Sept. 10, 1862

13th Cavalry
Edwin C. Catherwood   Nov. 25, 1864   Resigned June 20, 1865
Austin A. King, Jr.   July 10, 1865   Mustered out Jan. 11, 1866

13th State Militia Cavalry (designation of regiment changed to 5th State Militia Cavalry, Feb. 2, 1863)
Albert Sigel   May 19, 1862   Mustered out Jan. 7, 1865

14th Cavalry (regiment failed to complete organization)

14th State Militia Cavalry
John M. Richardson   May 26, 1862   Mustered out March 5, 1863

15th Cavalry
John D. Allen   Nov. 1, 1863   Mustered out July 1, 1865

16th Cavalry
John F. McMahan   March 22, 1865   Mustered out July 1, 1865

1st Light Artillery (designation of regiment changed from 1st Infantry, Sept. 1, 1861)
Francis P. Blair, Jr.   April 26, 1861   Promoted **Brig. Gen., USV,** Aug. 7, 1862
John V.D. DuBois   Aug. 7, 1862   Resigned Oct. 14, 1862
Warren L. Lothrop   Oct. 1, 1862   Mustered out July 29, 1865

2nd Light Artillery
Henry Almstedt   Nov. 8, 1861   Resigned Aug. 27, 1863
Nelson Cole   Feb. 27, 1864   Mustered out Nov. 30, 1865

Engineer Regiment of the West (designation of regiment changed to 1st MO Engineers upon consolidation with 25th MO Infantry, Dec. 28, 1863)
Josiah W. Bissell   July 26, 1861   Resigned June 2, 1863
Henry Flad   Oct. 17, 1863   Mustered out Nov. 18, 1864

1st Engineers
Henry Flad   Oct. 17, 1863   Mustered out Nov. 18, 1864
Eben M. Hill   June 10, 1865   Mustered out July 22, 1865

1st Enrolled Militia
William P. Fenn   Oct. 11, 1862   Commission vacated March 12, 1865

1st Infantry (designation of regiment changed to 1st Light Artillery, Sept. 1, 1861)
Francis P. Blair, Jr.   April 26, 1861   Promoted **Brig. Gen., USV,** Aug. 7, 1862

1st Northeast Home Guards
William Bishop   June 10, 1861   To Black Hawk Cav. Aug. 15, 1861

Missouri Regiments

1st Northeast Infantry (designation of regiment changed to 21st MO Infantry upon consolidation with 2nd Northeast MO Infantry, Feb. 1, 1862)
David Moore　　　　　　Oct. 25, 1861　　　　　Mustered out Feb. 11, 1865, **Bvt. Brig. Gen., USV**

1st Provisional Enrolled Militia
Joseph B. Douglass　　　Temporary service

1st St. Louis City Guards
Charles A. Fritz　　　　Oct. 4, 1864

1st State Militia Infantry
John B. Gray　　　　　　March 1, 1862　　　　　Resigned March 18, 1863
John F. Tyler　　　　　March 18, 1863　　　　　Dismissed Jan. 13, 1865

1st U.S. Reserve Corps (3 months)
Henry Almstedt　　　　　May 7, 1861　　　　　　Mustered out Aug. 20, 1861

1st U.S. Reserve Corps
Robert J. Rombauer　　　Sept. 12, 1861　　　　Mustered out Oct. 6, 1862

2nd Enrolled Militia
Edward Stafford　　　　Sept. 23, 1862　　　　Commission vacated March 12, 1865

2nd Infantry (3 months)
Henry Boernstein　　　　May 14, 1861　　　　　Mustered out July 30, 1861

2nd Infantry
Frederick Schaefer　　　Sept. 10, 1861　　　　KIA Dec. 31, 1862
Bernard Laibold　　　　Jan. 8, 1863　　　　　Mustered out Dec. 8, 1864

2nd Northeast Infantry (designation of regiment changed to 21st MO Infantry upon consolidation with 1st Northeast MO Infantry, Feb. 1, 1862)
Humphrey M. Woodyard　Oct. 5, 1861　　　　　To 21st MO Infantry, Feb. 1, 1862

2nd Provisional Enrolled Militia
Edward A. Kutzner　　　Temporary service

2nd St. Louis City Guards
Charles G. Stifel　　　Oct. 4, 1864

2nd U.S. Reserve Corps (3 months)
Herrmann F. Kallmann　　May 7, 1861　　　　　Mustered out Aug. 16, 1861

2nd U.S. Reserve Corps
Herrmann F. Kallmann　　Sept. 20, 1861　　　　Mustered out Sept. 10, 1862

3rd Enrolled Militia
Nicholas Schittner　　　Sept. 30, 1862　　　　Commission vacated Oct. 23, 1863
Adolph E. Hugo　　　　　Oct. 28, 1863　　　　Resigned June 18, 1864
Henry F. Vahlkamp　　　July 22, 1864　　　　Commission vacated March 12, 1865

3rd Infantry (3 months)
Franz Sigel　　　　　　May 4, 1861　　　　　Promoted **Brig. Gen., USV,** May 17, 1861

3rd Infantry
Henry Ramming	Sept. 21, 1861	Discharged Jan. 18, 1862
Isaac F. Shepard	Jan. 18, 1862	Promoted **Brig. Gen., USV,** Nov. 16, 1863
Theodore Meumann	Nov. 17, 1863	Mustered out Nov. 23, 1864

3rd Militia (Dallmeyer's Battalion)
James A. Matthews	Sept. 8, 1861	Resigned Nov. 26, 1861

3rd Provisional Enrolled Militia
William Heren	Temporary service
Bennett Pike	Temporary service

3rd St. Louis City Guards
Herman T. Hesse	Oct. 5, 1864

3rd U.S. Reserve Corps (3 months)
John McNeil	May 8, 1861	Mustered out Aug. 17, 1861, **Brig. Gen., USV**

3rd U.S. Reserve Corps
Charles A. Fritz	Oct. 27, 1861	Discharged Jan. 18, 1862

4th Enrolled Militia
Christian D. Wolff	Oct. 18, 1862	Promoted BG, EMM Oct. 1, 1864

4th Infantry (3 months)
Nicholas Schittner	May 5, 1861	Mustered out July 31, 1861

4th Infantry
Charles A. Fritz	Jan. 18, 1862	Declined
Robert Hundhausen	Jan. 18, 1862	Mustered out Feb. 1, 1863

4th Provisional Enrolled Militia
John B. Hale	Temporary service
John H. Shanklin	Temporary service

4th St. Louis City Guards
Eugene C. Harrington	Oct. 5, 1864

4th U.S. Reserve Corps (3 months)
B. Gratz Brown	May 8, 1861	Mustered out Aug. 19, 1861

5th Enrolled Militia
Ferdinand T.L. Boyle	Sept. 24, 1862	Resigned May 2, 1864
Louis Duestrow	June 1, 1864	Commission vacated March 12, 1865

5th Infantry (3 months)
Charles E. Salomon	May 18, 1861	Mustered out Aug. 26, 1861, **Bvt. Brig. Gen., USV**

5th Infantry
August H. Poten	May 27, 1862	Resigned Oct. 22, 1862
Samuel A. Foster	Oct. 23, 1862	Mustered out Nov. 22, 1862

5th Provisional Enrolled Militia
Henry Neill Temporary service

5th State Militia (6 months)
Thomas J.C. Fagg Sept. 4, 1861 Mustered out Feb. 5, 1862

5th U.S. Reserve Corps (3 months)
Charles G. Stifel May 11, 1861 Mustered out Sept. 3, 1861

5th U.S. Reserve Corps
Charles G. Stifel Aug. 28, 1861 Discharged Nov. 1, 1861

6th Enrolled Militia
Thomas Richeson Sept. 24, 1862 Resigned Jan. 21, 1863
Henry C. Marston April 27, 1863 Resigned Sept. 14, 1863
Tony Niederwieser May 23, 1864 Commission vacated March 12, 1865

6th Infantry
Peter E. Bland June 29, 1861 Resigned Aug. 31, 1862
Peter E. Bland Oct. 22, 1862 Discharged Dec. 22, 1862
James H. Blood Jan. 1, 1863 Resigned April 2, 1864
Delos Van Deusen May 2, 1865 Mustered out Aug. 17, 1865

6th Provisional Enrolled Militia
Henry Sheppard Temporary service
Fidelio S. Jones Temporary service

6th State Militia (6 months)
Manlove Cranor Oct. 1, 1861 Mustered out Feb. 13, 1862

7th Enrolled Militia
George E. Leighton Sept. 23, 1862 Resigned Dec. 25, 1863
Edward C. Pike Jan. 13, 1864 Promoted BG, EMM Mar. 29, 1864
George F. Meyers April 30, 1864 Promoted BG, EMM Oct. 1, 1864
Henry F.C. Kleinschmidt Oct. 1, 1864 Commission vacated March 12, 1865

7th Infantry
John D. Stevenson June 1, 1861 Promoted **Brig. Gen., USV,** April 17, 1863
William S. Oliver April 17, 1863 Mustered out July 18, 1864

7th Provisional Enrolled Militia
John D. Allen Temporary service

8th Enrolled Militia
John Knapp Sept. 22, 1862 Resigned Sept. 14, 1863
William L. Catherwood April 30, 1864 Resigned Jan. 5, 1865

8th Infantry
Morgan L. Smith July 4, 1861 Promoted **Brig. Gen., USV,** July 16, 1862
Giles A. Smith Aug. 8, 1862 Promoted **Brig. Gen., USV,** Aug. 4, 1863
David C. Coleman Sept. 1, 1863 Mustered out July 12, 1864

8th Provisional Enrolled Militia
William H. McLane   Temporary service

9th Enrolled Militia
John M. Krum	Oct. 1, 1862	Resigned Sept. 14, 1863
Henry H. Catherwood	Sept. 15, 1863	
Edward Morrison	Date unknown	

9th Infantry (designation of regiment changed to 59th IL Infantry, March 20, 1862)
John C. Kelton   Sept. 19, 1861   Resigned March 1, 1862, **Bvt. Brig. Gen., USV**

9th Provisional Enrolled Militia
Thomas L. Crawford   Temporary service

10th Enrolled Militia
Ephraim H.E. Jameson	Sept. 24, 1862	Resigned Sept. 23, 1863
Henry Hildenbrand	March 28, 1864	Commission vacated March 12, 1865

10th Infantry
Chester Harding, Jr.	Aug. 15, 1861	Resigned Dec. 1, 1861, **Bvt. Brig. Gen., USV**
George R. Todd	Dec. 1, 1861	Discharged April 9, 1862
Samuel A. Holmes	April 9, 1862	Resigned June 10, 1863
Francis C. Deimling	June 11, 1863	Mustered out Aug. 24, 1864

10th Provisional Enrolled Militia
Christian D. Wolff   Temporary service

11th Enrolled Militia
William Cuddy	Sept. 17, 1862	Resigned July 3, 1863
James Coff	April 30, 1864	Commission vacated March 12, 1865

11th Infantry
David Bayles	Aug. 6, 1861	Discharged Sept. 30, 1861
Joseph B. Plummer	Sept. 25, 1861	Promoted **Brig. Gen., USV,** Oct. 22, 1861
Joseph A. Mower	May 3, 1862	Promoted **Brig. Gen., USV,** April 14, 1863
Andrew J. Weber	May 15, 1863	DOW June 30, 1863
William L. Barnum	July 1, 1863	Mustered out Aug. 15, 1864
Eli Bowyer	May 22, 1865	Mustered out Jan. 15, 1866, **Bvt. Brig. Gen., USV**

11th Provisional Enrolled Militia
John Knapp	Temporary service
Henry H. Catherwood	Temporary service

12th Enrolled Militia
William Bailey   Oct. 9, 1862

12th Infantry
Peter J. Osterhaus	Dec. 19, 1861	Promoted **Brig. Gen., USV,** June 9, 1862
Hugo Wangelin	July 20, 1862	Mustered out Oct. 17, 1864, **Bvt. Brig. Gen., USV**

13th Enrolled Militia
Brainard M. Million	Sept. 24, 1862	Resigned April 13, 1864
John B. de Narcy	July 11, 1864	Dismissed Dec. 29, 1864

13th Infantry (regiment failed to complete organization)
Everett Peabody   Sept. 1, 1861   Discharged Oct. 26, 1861

13th Infantry (designation of regiment changed to 22nd OH Infantry, July 7, 1862)
Crafts J. Wright   Aug. 3, 1861   Resigned Sept. 9, 1862

14th Enrolled Militia
Julian Bates   Sept. 3, 1861

14th Home Guards
Robert White   Sept. 1, 1861   Discharged Oct. 19, 1861

14th Infantry (designation of regiment changed to 66th IL Infantry, Nov. 20, 1862)
Patrick E. Burke   June 24, 1862   DOW May 20, 1864

15th Enrolled Militia
George Rinkel, Jr.   May 14, 1863   Resigned April 21, 1864

15th Infantry
Francis J. Joliat   Sept. 22, 1861   Resigned Nov. 26, 1862
Joseph Conrad   Nov. 29, 1862   Mustered out Feb, 3, 1866, **Bvt. Brig. Gen., USV**

15th U.S. Reserve Corps (Polk County Home Guards)
James W. Johnson   July 6, 1861   Discharged Dec. 6, 1861

16th Enrolled Militia
Marinus W. Warne   Sept. 17, 1862   Commission vacated April 12, 1864

16th Infantry (regiment failed to complete organization)

17th Enrolled Militia
Charles L. Tucker   Sept. 17, 1862   Commission vacated April 12, 1864

17th Infantry
Franz P. Hassendeubel   Dec. 19, 1861   DOW July 17, 1863
John F. Cramer   July 18, 1863   Committed suicide May 2, 1864

18th Infantry
W. James Morgan   Nov. 14, 1861   Mustered out April 15, 1862
Madison Miller   April 16, 1862   Resigned March 15, 1864, **Bvt. Brig. Gen., USV**
Charles S. Sheldon   Dec. 24, 1864   Mustered out July 18, 1865, **Bvt. Brig. Gen., USV**

19th Enrolled Militia
Thomas Scott   April 21, 1863   Commission vacated April 16, 1864

19th Infantry (regiment failed to complete organization)

20th Enrolled Militia
Philip A.C. Stremmel   Feb. 5, 1863

20th Infantry (regiment failed to complete organization)

21st Infantry (consolidated with 10th MO Infantry, Dec. 1, 1861)
Aaron Brown   Sept. 27, 1861   To 10th MO Infantry, Dec. 1, 1861

21st Infantry (formed by consolidation of 1st Northeast MO Infantry with 2nd Northeast MO Infantry, Feb. 1, 1862)
David Moore	Oct. 25, 1861	Mustered out Feb. 11, 1865, **Bvt. Brig. Gen., USV**
James J. Lyon	Aug. 17, 1865	Resigned Aug. 7, 1865
Joseph G. Best	Sept. 30, 1865	Mustered out April 19, 1866

22nd Enrolled Militia
Thomas Miller, Jr.   Oct. 29, 1862   Commission vacated April 12, 1864

22nd Infantry
John D. Foster   Aug. 26, 1861   Resigned Sept. 3, 1862

23rd Enrolled Militia
George R. Taylor   Sept. 11, 1862   Commission vacated April 12, 1864

23rd Infantry
Jacob T. Tindall	Aug. 26, 1861	KIA April 6, 1862
William P. Robinson	June 7, 1862	Mustered out Sept. 22, 1864

24th Enrolled Militia
Adelbert R. Buffington   Sept. 10, 1862   Commission vacated July 15, 1863

24th Infantry
Sempronius H. Boyd	Aug. 2, 1861	Resigned April 18, 1863
James K. Mills	April 22, 1863	Resigned Nov. 26, 1864, **Bvt. Brig. Gen., USV**

25th Enrolled Militia
John Severance	Sept. 8, 1862	Resigned April 22, 1863
John Scott	Sept. 29, 1863	Regiment disbanded Nov. 1, 1863

25th Infantry (designation of regiment changed to 1st MO Engineers upon consolidation with Engineer Regiment of the West, Dec. 28, 1863)
Everett Peabody	Nov. 1, 1861	KIA April 6, 1862
Chester Harding, Jr.	June 14, 1862	Resigned Feb. 3, 1864, **Bvt. Brig. Gen., USV**

26th Enrolled Militia
James W. Johnson	Sept. 1, 1862	Resigned March 28, 1864
Adam C. Mitchell	May 28, 1864	Relieved from duty Nov. 19, 1864

26th Infantry
George B. Boomer	Jan. 20, 1862	KIA May 22, 1863
Benjamin D. Dean	May 28, 1863	Mustered out Jan. 9, 1865

27th Enrolled Militia
Benjamin Emmons, Jr.	Sept. 20, 1862	Resigned Aug. 17, 1863
Arnold Krekel	Oct. 4, 1864	Commission vacated March 12, 1865

27th Infantry
Thomas Curley   Jan. 10, 1863   Mustered out June 13, 1865, **Bvt. Brig. Gen., USV**

28th Enrolled Militia

Lebbeus Zevely   Sept. 11, 1862   Commission vacated March 12, 1865

28th Infantry (regiment failed to complete organization)

29th Enrolled Militia

Edward A. Kutzner   Sept. 27, 1862   Commission vacated Oct. 24, 1863
William W. Purmort   April 30, 1864   Relieved from duty Nov. 25, 1864

29th Infantry

John S. Cavender   Oct. 18, 1862   Resigned Feb. 19, 1863, **Bvt. Brig. Gen., USV**
James Peckham   Feb. 20, 1863   Mustered out March 9, 1864
Joseph S. Gage   March 10, 1864   Mustered out June 12, 1865, **Bvt. Brig. Gen., USV**

30th Enrolled Militia

John H. Shanklin   Aug. 21, 1862   Commission vacated March 12, 1865

30th Infantry

Bernard G. Farrar   Oct. 29, 1862   To 6 U.S.C.H.A., Jan. 21, 1864, **Bvt. Brig. Gen., USV**

31st Enrolled Militia

Manlove Cranor   Sept. 11, 1862   Commission vacated March 12, 1865

31st Infantry

Thomas C. Fletcher   Oct. 7, 1862   Resigned June 16, 1864, **Bvt. Brig. Gen., USV**

32nd Enrolled Militia

Samuel H. Melcher   Aug. 30, 1862   Resigned Oct. 17, 1862
Thomas J. Whitely   Oct. 17, 1862   Resigned April 1, 1864
Philip R. Van Frank   April 30, 1864   Resigned Oct. 4, 1864
William H. Evens   Oct. 7, 1864   Commission vacated March 12, 1865

32nd Infantry

Francis H. Manter   Dec. 9, 1862   Died June 13, 1864
Abraham J. Seay   June 12, 1865   Mustered out July 18, 1865

33rd Enrolled Militia

William S. Brown   Sept. 15, 1862   Commission vacated March 12, 1865

33rd Infantry

Clinton B. Fisk   Sept. 5, 1862   Promoted **Brig. Gen., USV,** Nov. 24, 1862
William A. Pile   Dec. 23, 1862   Promoted **Brig. Gen., USV,** Dec. 26, 1863
William H. Heath   Dec. 22, 1863   Mustered out Aug. 10, 1865

34th Enrolled Militia

James O. Sitton   Sept. 7, 1862   Resigned June 10, 1864
Rudolph von Poser   Aug. 6, 1864   Commission vacated March 12, 1865

34th Infantry (regiment failed to complete organization)

Otto Schadt   Sept. 6, 1862

35th Enrolled Militia
William E. Moberly   Sept. 6, 1862   Commission vacated March 12, 1865

35th Infantry
Samuel A. Foster   Dec. 3, 1862   Resigned July 20, 1863

36th Enrolled Militia
William J.W. Bickett   Aug. 16, 1862   Commission vacated Nov. 1, 1863
Berryman K. Davis   Sept. 24, 1863   Commission vacated March 12, 1865

36th Infantry (regiment failed to complete organization)

37th Enrolled Militia
Charles W. Parker   Sept. 9, 1862   Commission vacated March 12, 1865

37th Infantry (regiment failed to complete organization)

38th Enrolled Militia
John T.K. Hayward   Sept. 2, 1862   Commission vacated March 12, 1865

38th Infantry (regiment failed to complete organization)

39th Enrolled Militia
James A. Price   Sept. 10, 1862   Commission vacated Sept. 30, 1863

39th Infantry
Edward A. Kutzner   Jan. 14, 1865   Mustered out March 14, 1865

40th Enrolled Militia
Robert R. Spedden   Sept. 10, 1862   Resigned June 7, 1864
John D. Crawford   June 13, 1864   Commission vacated March 12, 1865

40th Infantry
Samuel A. Holmes   Sept. 8, 1864   Mustered out Aug. 8, 1865

41st Enrolled Militia
William Heren   Sept. 9, 1862   Dismissed Oct. 7, 1863
Harrison B. Branch   Oct. 7, 1863   Commission vacated Nov. 1, 1863
Harrison B. Branch   Dec. 3, 1863

41st Infantry
Joseph Weydemeyer   Sept. 17, 1864   Mustered out July 11, 1865

42nd Enrolled Militia
Thomas L. Crawford   Sept. 15, 1862   Promoted BG, EMM Oct. 23, 1862
John Pound   June 10, 1863   Relieved from duty Nov. 30, 1863
Matthew M. Flesh   April 30, 1864   Commission vacated March 12, 1865

42nd Infantry
William Forbes   Nov. 2, 1864   Mustered out March 22, 1865

43rd Enrolled Militia
Franklin W. Hickox Sept. 24, 1862 Commission vacated March 12, 1865

43rd Infantry
Chester Harding, Jr. Sept. 22, 1864 Mustered out June 30, 1865, **Bvt. Brig. Gen., USV**

44th Enrolled Militia
William B. Rogers Aug. 29, 1862 Resigned Sept. 8, 1864

44th Infantry
Robert C. Bradshaw Sept. 29, 1864 Mustered out Aug. 15, 1865, **Bvt. Brig. Gen., USV**

45th Enrolled Militia
William A. Shelton Sept. 27, 1862 Commission vacated March 12, 1865

45th Infantry (regiment not entitled to a colonel since it never attained full strength)

46th Enrolled Militia
Thomas J. Bartholow Sept. 27, 1862 Promoted BG, EMM, Dec. 15, 1862
Clark H. Green Dec. 16, 1862 Commission vacated July 28, 1864

46th Infantry
Robert W. Fyan Nov. 14, 1864 Mustered out March 7, 1865

47th Enrolled Militia
Hervey A. Massey Sept. 18, 1862 Resigned Nov. 13, 1862
John D. Brutsche March 23, 1863 To 8 MO SM Cavalry Nov. 1, 1863
Thompson J. Kelly Sept. 16, 1864 Commission vacated March 12, 1865

47th Infantry
Thomas C. Fletcher Sept. 17, 1864 Resigned Nov. 18, 1864, **Bvt. Brig. Gen., USV**
Amos W. Maupin Nov. 25, 1864 Mustered out April 18, 1865

48th Enrolled Militia
James H. Moss Sept. 29, 1862 To 82 EMM Dec. 25, 1863

48th Infantry
Wells H. Blodgett Nov. 22, 1864 Mustered out June 29, 1865

49th Enrolled Militia
George W. Anderson Aug. 13, 1862 Commission vacated March 12, 1865

49th Infantry
David P. Dyer Feb. 9, 1865 Mustered out Aug. 5, 1865

50th Enrolled Militia
Samuel M. Wirt Aug. 29, 1862 Resigned Jan. 18, 1865

50th Infantry
David Murphy June 27, 1865 Mustered out July 15, 1865

Missouri Regiments

51st Enrolled Militia
Adam J. Barr	Oct.1, 1862	To 44 MO Infantry, Sept. 28, 1864

51st Infantry
David Moore	May 1, 1865	Mustered out Aug. 31, 1865, **Bvt. Brig. Gen., USV**

52nd Enrolled Militia
William Pope	Oct. 4, 1862	Resigned April 28, 1863
David W. Wear	June 10, 1863	To 45 MO Infantry Sept. 29, 1864

53rd Enrolled Militia
Orwin C. Tinker	Oct. 16, 1862	Commission vacated March 12, 1865

54th Enrolled Militia
Daniel Q. Gale	Aug. 15, 1862	Commission vacated Sept. 22, 1863
George Krumsick	Sept. 22, 1863	Commission vacated Sept. 29, 1864
Daniel Q. Gale	Sept. 29, 1864	Commission vacated March 12, 1865

55th Enrolled Militia
Amos W. Maupin	Nov. 15, 1862	Commission vacated Sept. 22, 1863
August Krumsick	Sept. 22, 1863	Commission vacated March 12, 1865

56th Enrolled Militia
William H. McLane	Oct. 4, 1862	Commission vacated March 12, 1865

57th Enrolled Militia
David J. Heaston	Oct. 15, 1862	Resigned June 3, 1863
James M. Nevill	June 3, 1863	Resigned Oct. 26, 1863
William G. Lewis	March 15, 1864	Resigned Sept. 22, 1864

58th Enrolled Militia
Bennett Pike	Nov. 1, 1862	Commission vacated March 12, 1865

59th Enrolled Militia
John E. Hutton	Sept. 2, 1862	
Frederick Morsey	Aug. 6, 1864	Commission vacated March 12, 1865

60th Enrolled Militia
Asa C. Marvin	Oct. 13, 1862	Commission vacated March 12, 1865

61st Enrolled Militia
Joseph B. Douglass	Oct. 21, 1862	Promoted BG, EMM Sept. 1, 1863
Lewis P. Miller	Sept. 25, 1863	To 48 MO Infantry Dec. 6, 1864

62nd Enrolled Militia
Reuben J. Eberman	Sept. 3, 1862	Commission vacated March 12, 1865

63rd Enrolled Militia
John E. Davis	Nov. 13, 1862	Commission vacated Oct. 13, 1863
Isaac S. Warmoth	Oct. 13, 1863	Commission vacated March 12, 1865

64th Enrolled Militia
Robert M. Brewer	Oct. 27, 1862	Commission vacated March 12, 1865

65th Enrolled Militia
John B. Hale						Nov. 3, 1862				Commission vacated March 12, 1865

66th Enrolled Militia
Oliver P. Phillips					Oct. 19, 1862				Commission vacated March 12, 1865

67th Enrolled Militia
Walter L. Lovelace				Aug. 13, 1862				Resigned Nov. 8, 1862
James G. Kettle					Dec. 11, 1862				Commission vacated Sept. 24, 1863
Cornelius H. Canfield			Sept. 24, 1863				Commission vacated March 12, 1865

68th Enrolled Militia
James Lindsay					Nov. 20, 1862				Dismissed Nov. 2, 1863
William Lawson					March 17, 1864			Commission revoked Mar. 18, 1864
John W. Emerson				March 21, 1864			Commission vacated March 12, 1865

69th Enrolled Militia
William M. Reading				Aug. 26, 1862				Dismissed Oct. 13, 1863
James T. Howland				Oct. 21, 1863				Commission revoked Feb. 11, 1865
William M. Reading				Feb. 11, 1865				Commission vacated March 12, 1865

70th Enrolled Militia
William B. Okeson				Sept. 10, 1862				Commission vacated March 12, 1865

71st Enrolled Militia
Henry Neill						Aug. 20, 1862				Resigned June 7, 1864

72nd Enrolled Militia
Colley B. Holland					Aug. 16, 1862				Promoted BG, EMM Oct. 27, 1862
Henry Sheppard					Nov. 11, 1862				Resigned Sept. 30, 1863
Fidelio S. Jones					Oct. 1, 1863				Resigned Jan. 22, 1864
John S. Phelps					June 25, 1864				Commission vacated Mar. 12, 1865, **Brig. Gen., USV**

73rd Enrolled Militia
Ratcliff B. Palmer					Aug. 31, 1862				Commission vacated March 12, 1865

74th Enrolled Militia
Marcus Boyd					Aug. 16, 1862				Resigned (date unknown)

75th Enrolled Militia
Robert Bailey, Jr.					Oct. 14, 1862				To 67th USCT March 28, 1864

76th Enrolled Militia
John D. Allen					Jan. 1, 1863				Commission revoked Nov. 1, 1863

77th Enrolled Militia
Kersey Coates					Dec. 30, 1862				Commission vacated March 12, 1865

78th Enrolled Militia
Franklin Leavenworth			April 24, 1863				Commission vacated March 12, 1865

79th Enrolled Militia
Henry J. Deal					June 29, 1863				Commission vacated March 12, 1865

80th Enrolled Militia

Louis J. Rankin	Sept. 28, 1863	Resigned Dec. 8, 1864
Carman A. Newcomb	Dec. 31, 1864	Commission vacated March 12, 1865

81st Enrolled Militia

John Scott	Dec. 8, 1863	Commission vacated March 12, 1865

82nd Enrolled Militia

James H. Moss	Dec. 25, 1863	Promoted BG, EMM Mar. 18, 1864
Nathaniel Grant	April 4, 1864	Commission vacated March 12, 1865

83rd Enrolled Militia

John C. Porter	May 3, 1864	Relieved from duty Sept. 19, 1864

84th Enrolled Militia

William H. Pulsifer	May 11, 1864	Relieved from duty Sept. 19, 1864

85th Enrolled Militia

William J.A. Smith	May 28, 1864	Commission vacated March 12, 1865

86th Enrolled Militia

John D. Foster	June 28, 1864	Commission vacated March 12, 1865

87th Enrolled Militia

Thomas Harbine	July 13, 1864	Declined
Robert C. Bradshaw	July 15, 1864	To 44th MO Infantry Sept. 29, 1864, **Bvt. Brig. Gen., USV**
James W. Strong	Oct. 6, 1864	Commission vacated March 12, 1865

88th Enrolled Militia

Edward Russell	July 14, 1864	Commission vacated March 12, 1865

Biographies

John Daugherty Allen

1 Lieutenant, Co. E, Lawrence County Regiment, MO Home Guards, June 16, 1861. Discharged Aug. 10, 1861. Colonel, 76 Enrolled MO Militia, Jan. 1, 1863. Commission revoked, Nov. 1, 1863. Colonel, 7 Provisional Enrolled MO Militia, April 1, 1863. Colonel, 15 MO Cavalry, Dec. 3, 1864, with rank from Nov. 1, 1863. Commanded District of Southwest Missouri, Department of the Missouri, June 10–July 1, 1865. Honorably mustered out, July 1, 1865. Battle honors: Shelby's Raid in Arkansas and Missouri (Neosho).

Born: July 23, 1818, Callaway Co., MO
Died: Aug. 14, 1898 Verona, MO
Occupation: Farmer
Offices/Honors: Surveyor, Lawrence Co., MO, 1845–46. Sheriff, Lawrence Co., MO, 1854–56.
Miscellaneous: Resided Mount Vernon, Lawrence Co., MO; Carthage, Jasper Co., MO, 1870–78; Golden City, Barton Co., MO; and Verona, Lawrence Co., MO
Buried: Spanish Fort Cemetery, near Hoberg, Lawrence Co., MO
References: *History of Newton, Lawrence, Barry and McDonald Counties, Missouri.* Chicago, IL, 1888. Obituary, *Mount Vernon Fountain & Journal*, Aug. 18, 1898. Pension File and Military Service File, National Archives. Ward L. Schrantz, compiler. *Jasper County, Missouri, in the Civil War.* Carthage, MO, 1923.

Henry Almstedt

Colonel, 1 U.S. Reserve Corps, MO Infantry (3 months), May 7, 1861. Honorably mustered out, Aug. 20, 1861. Colonel, 2 MO Light Artillery, Nov. 8, 1861. Commanded Post of St. Louis, District of St. Louis, Department of the Missouri, Oct. 20, 1862–April 21, 1863, and May 25–Aug.

10, 1863. Feeling "in honor bound to resign my position" due to the muster out of a portion of his regiment and its reorganization, he resigned Aug. 27, 1863. Additional Paymaster, USV, April 20, 1864. Honorably mustered out, Jan. 1, 1868. Bvt. Lieutenant Colonel, USV, May 1, 1867, for faithful and meritorious services in the Pay Department. Battle honors: Price's Missouri Expedition.

Born: April 15 (or March 24, tombstone), 1817 Hanover, Germany

Died: Nov. 21, 1884 Fenton, St. Louis Co., MO

Other Wars: Mexican War (1 Lieutenant, Adjutant, St. Louis Legion, MO Infantry, 2 Lieutenant, 12 U.S. Infantry, and Bvt. 1 Lieutenant, USA, Aug. 20, 1847, for gallant and meritorious conduct in the battles of Contreras and Churubusco, Mexico)

Occupation: Clerk (1860), drayman (1864), U.S. Storekeeper (1870), distiller (1877), and stairbuilder (1881)

Miscellaneous: Resided St. Louis, MO

Buried: Bellefontaine Cemetery, St. Louis, MO (Block 42, Lot 1941)

Henry Almstedt (Library of Congress [LC-DIG-cwpb-04714]).

References: Obituary, *St. Louis Post-Dispatch*, Nov. 24, 1884. Military Service File, National Archives. Letters Received, Commission Branch, Adjutant General's Office, File A202(CB)1867, National Archives. Letters Received, Adjutant General's Office, File 63(A)1847, National Archives. Louis S. Gerteis. *The Civil War in Missouri: A Military History*. Columbia, MO, 2012. Robert J. Rombauer. *The Union Cause in St. Louis in 1861: An Historical Sketch*. St. Louis, MO, 1909. William C. Winter. *The Civil War in St. Louis: A Guided Tour*. St. Louis, MO, 1994. Henry Almstedt Papers, 1846–1939 (A0022), Missouri History Museum Archives, St. Louis, MO.

George Washington Anderson

Captain, Co. A, Pike County Regiment, MO Home Guards, June 12, 1861. Colonel, Pike County Regiment, MO Home Guards, July 17, 1861. Discharged Sept. 3, 1861. Colonel, 49 Enrolled MO Militia, Aug. 13, 1862. Commission vacated, March 12, 1865.

Born: May 22, 1832, Jefferson Co., TN

Died: Feb. 26, 1902 Rhea Springs, TN

Education: Attended Franklin College, near Nashville, TN

Occupation: Lawyer

Offices/Honors: Missouri House of Representatives, 1858–60. U.S. House of Representatives, 1865–69.

Miscellaneous: Resided Louisiana, Pike Co., MO; and St. Louis, MO, after 1875

Buried: Leuty Cemetery, near Spring City, Rhea Co., TN

References: *The History of Pike County, Missouri*. Des Moines, IA, 1883. James L. Harrison, compiler. *Biographical Directory of the American Congress, 1774–1949*. Washington, D.C., 1950. William H. Barnes. *The Fortieth Congress of the United States: Historical and Biographical*. New York City, NY, 1870. William M. Paxton. *The Marshall Family*. Cincinnati, OH, 1885. Obituary, *St. Louis Post-Dispatch*, March 3, 1902. Obituary, *St. Louis Republic*, March 4, 1902. Clayton Keith. *Military History of Pike County, Missouri*. Louisiana, MO, 1915.

Robert Bailey, Jr.

1 Lieutenant, Co. I, St. Charles County Regiment, MO Home Guards, June 18, 1861. Captain, Co. I, St. Charles County Regiment, MO Home Guards, July 11, 1861. Discharged Aug. 7, 1861. Captain, Co. I, 75 Enrolled MO Militia,

Sept. 7, 1862. Colonel, 75 Enrolled MO Militia, Oct. 14, 1862. Captain, Co. D, 67 USCT, March 28, 1864.
  Born: 1837? Pond Fort, St. Charles Co., MO
  Died: May 17, 1864, Port Hudson, LA (typhoid fever)
  Occupation: Lawyer
  Miscellaneous: Resided Dardenne, St. Charles Co., MO
  Buried: Old Dardenne Cemetery, Dardenne, MO
  References: Pension File and Military Service File, National Archives. Letters Received, Colored Troops Branch, Adjutant General's Office, File B370(CT)1864, National Archives. *Annual Report of the Adjutant General of the State of Missouri, December 31, 1863.* Jefferson City, MO, 1864. www.findagrave.com.

William Bailey

Colonel, 12 Enrolled MO Militia, Oct. 9, 1862. Major, Additional Paymaster, USV, May 28, 1864. Honorably mustered out, July 31, 1865.
  Born: July 25, 1837, New York City, NY
  Died: April 24, 1903, New York City, NY
  Occupation: Railroad president
  Miscellaneous: Resided St. Louis, MO, to 1892; Tacoma, Pierce Co., WA, 1892–1901; and New York City, NY
  Buried: Marble Cemetery Vault, New York City, NY
  References: Pension File, National Archives. Obituary, *Tacoma Daily Ledger*, April 25–26, 1903. Obituary, *St. Louis Post-Dispatch*, April 30, 1903. Obituary, *New York Times*, April 27, 1903. T.A. Busbey, editor. *The Biographical Directory of the Railway Officials of America.* Chicago, IL, 1893. *Annual Report of the Adjutant General of the State of Missouri, December 31, 1863.* Jefferson City, MO, 1864.

William Lewis Barnum

Captain, Co. I, 11 MO Infantry, July 30, 1861. Shell wound right foot, Corinth, MS, Oct. 4, 1862. Acting AAG, Staff of Brig. Gen. Mason Brayman, Nov. 16, 1862–April 30, 1863. Lieutenant Colonel, 11 MO Infantry, May 15, 1863. *Colonel*, 11 MO Infantry, July 1, 1863. Honorably mustered out, Aug. 15, 1864. Battle honors: Corinth, Operations on the Mississippi Central Railroad (Jackson), Vicksburg Campaign, Meridian Expedition.

William Lewis Barnum (T.L. Rivers, Photographer, S.E. Cor. 4th & Olive Sts., St. Louis, Missouri; Courtesy of Dennis Hood, D.V.M.).

William Lewis Barnum, post-war (*Memorials of Deceased Companions of the Commandery of the State of Illinois MOLLUS, from January 1, 1912, to December 31, 1922.* Chicago, 1923).

  Born: Aug. 24, 1829 Newark, NJ
  Died: May 28, 1921, Chicago, IL
  Occupation: Merchant and land agent before war. Fire insurance executive after war.
  Miscellaneous: Resided Springfield, Sangamon Co., IL, to 1866; and Chicago, IL, after 1866

Buried: Oak Ridge Cemetery, Springfield, IL (Block 10, Lot 215)
References: *Memorials of Deceased Companions of the Commandery of the State of Illinois MOLLUS, from Jan. 1, 1912 to Dec. 31, 1922*. Chicago, IL, 1923. *The Union Army*. Illinois Edition. Vol. 8. Madison, WI, 1908. Obituary Circular, Whole No. 986, Illinois MOLLUS. Obituary, *Chicago Daily Tribune*, May 29, 1921. Dennis W. Belcher. *The 11th Missouri Volunteer Infantry in the Civil War: A History and Roster*. Jefferson, NC, 2011. Pension File and Military Service File, National Archives. Letters Received, Volunteer Service Branch, Adjutant General's Office, File I387(VS)1862, National Archives.

Adam Johnston Barr

Colonel, 51 Enrolled MO Militia, Oct. 1, 1862. Lieutenant Colonel, 44 MO Infantry, Sept. 28, 1864. Suffering from "chronic inflammation of stomach and bowels," he was honorably discharged, May 15, 1865, "on account of his services being no longer required and physical disability." Battle honors: Franklin, Nashville.
Born: July 4, 1828, Bethlehem, PA
Died: May 26, 1898, Kansas City, MO

Education: Attended Eclectic Medical Institute, Cincinnati, OH
Occupation: Physician before war. Lawyer and circuit court clerk after war.
Offices/Honors: Missouri House of Representatives, 1862–64. Missouri Constitutional Convention, 1865.
Miscellaneous: Resided Richmond, Ray Co., MO, to 1884; and Kansas City, MO, after 1884
Buried: Forest Hill Cemetery, Kansas City, MO (Block 38, Lot 83)
References: *The United States Biographical Dictionary and Portrait Gallery of Eminent and Self-Made Men*. Missouri Volume. New York, Chicago, St. Louis, and Kansas City, 1878. *History of Ray County, Missouri*. St. Louis, MO, 1881. Obituary, *Kansas City Journal*, May 27, 1898. Obituary, *Kansas City Star*, May 26, 1898. Pension File and Military Service File, National Archives. Letters Received, Volunteer Service Branch, Adjutant General's Office, File B1607(VS)1865, National Archives. *Annual Report of the Adjutant General of the State of Missouri, December 31, 1863*. Jefferson City, MO, 1864.

Thomas Jeremiah Bartholow

Colonel, 46 Enrolled MO Militia, Sept. 27, 1862. Brig. Gen., Enrolled MO Militia, Dec. 15, 1862. Resigned Aug. 31, 1863.
Born: Jan. 31, 1826 Cooksville, MD
Died: May 19, 1879, St. Louis, MO

Adam Johnston Barr (courtesy Missouri Historical Society, St. Louis [P0487-1152]).

Thomas Jeremiah Bartholow (Troxell & Brother, Photographers, S.W. cor. of 4th and Locust Sts., St. Louis, Missouri; author's photograph).

Other Wars: Mexican War (Sergeant, Co. G, 1 MO Mounted Infantry)

Occupation: Merchant and tobacco manufacturer before war. Banker after war.

Miscellaneous: Resided Glasgow, Howard Co., MO, before war; and St. Louis, MO, after war

Buried: Washington Cemetery, Glasgow, MO

References: Logan U. Reavis. *Saint Louis: The Future Great City of the World.* Biographical Edition. St. Louis, MO, 1875. Obituary, *St. Louis Post-Dispatch*, May 19, 1879. Obituary, *St. Louis Globe-Democrat*, May 20, 1879. *Annual Report of the Adjutant General of the State of Missouri, December 31, 1863.* Jefferson City, MO, 1864.

Julian Bates

Colonel, 14 Enrolled MO Militia, Sept. 3, 1862. Surgeon, Board of Enrollment, 1st District of Missouri, June 2, 1863. Honorably discharged, May 30, 1865.

Born: Jan. 7, 1833 St. Louis, MO

Died: July 20, 1902, St. Louis, MO

Education: Graduated University of Pennsylvania Medical School, Philadelphia, PA, 1855

Occupation: Physician

Miscellaneous: Resided St. Louis, MO. Son of U.S. Attorney General Edward Bates. Brother-in-law of Colonel Richard G. Woodson (3 MO State Militia Cavalry).

Buried: Bellefontaine Cemetery, St. Louis, MO (Blocks 222–223, Lot 1315, Space 12)

References: William Hyde and Howard L. Conard, editors. *Encyclopedia of the History of St. Louis.* New York, Louisville, and St. Louis, 1899. Obituary, *St. Louis Globe Democrat*, July 22, 1902. Obituary, *St. Louis Post-Dispatch*, July 21, 1902. J. Thomas Scharf. *History of Saint Louis City and County.* Philadelphia, PA, 1883. Ewing Jordan, compiler. *University of Pennsylvania Men Who Served in the Civil War, 1861–1865: Department of Medicine, Classes 1816–1862.* Philadelphia, PA, 1915.

David Bayles

Captain, Co. A, 1 Battalion Rifles, MO Infantry, May 11, 1861. Colonel, 11 MO Infantry, Aug. 6, 1861. Apparently unaware that Bayles had been mustered as colonel when the prospective colonel, Rufus Saxton, declined the position, Major Gen. John C. Fremont ordered Captain Joseph B. Plummer to take command, superseding Bayles, Sept. 28, 1861. Although Bayles appealed his case and received an order reinstating him, May 15, 1862, he was unable to rejoin his regiment due to sickness and the reinstatement order was revoked, Jan. 23, 1863, after his death. An order was finally issued, July 17, 1871, honorably discharging him, to date Sept. 30, 1861.

Born: 1819? OH

Died: Dec. 18, 1862 St. Louis, MO (cirrhosis of the liver)

Other Wars: Mexican War (Sergeant, Co. B, 1 Regiment St. Louis Legion, MO Infantry)

Occupation: Collector of Water Rates, City of St. Louis

Offices/Honors: Confirmed by the U.S. Senate, March 27, 1861, as U.S. Marshal for the Territory of Nevada, he did not take office because he "failed to qualify"

Miscellaneous: Resided St. Louis, MO. Nephew of Colonel Jesse Bayles (4 KY Cavalry).

Buried: Sappington Cemetery, Crestwood, St. Louis Co., MO (family marker only)

References: Obituary, *Daily Missouri Democrat*, Dec. 20, 1862. Obituary, *Daily Missouri Republican*, Dec. 20, 1862. Pension File and Military Service File, National Archives. Letters Received, Volunteer Service Branch, Adjutant General's Office, File B403(VS)1862, National Archives. Dennis W. Belcher. *The 11th Missouri Volunteer Infantry in the Civil War: A History and Roster.* Jefferson, NC, 2011. John C. Bayles and G. H. Bayles. *Jesse Bayles: A Partial List of his Descendants.* Morgantown, WV, 1944.

Joseph Gibson Best

Private, Co. I, 21 MO Infantry, Oct. 25, 1861. Sergeant Major, 21 MO Infantry, Feb. 1, 1862. 1 Lieutenant, Co. I, 21 MO Infantry, June 16, 1862. Captain, Co. I, 21 MO Infantry, July 17, 1862. Major, 21 MO Infantry, June 15, 1865. Lieutenant Colonel, 21 MO Infantry, Aug. 17, 1865. Colonel, 21 MO Infantry, Sept. 30, 1865. Honorably mustered out, April 19, 1866. Battle honors: Shiloh, Corinth, Tupelo, Nashville, Mobile Campaign (Fort Blakely).

Born: May 8, 1838, County Monaghan, Ireland

Died: Aug. 6, 1887 Memphis, MO (fatally injured in carriage accident)

Occupation: Bricklayer and bookkeeper

Offices/Honors: County court clerk, 1883–87

Miscellaneous: Resided Quincy, Adams Co., IL; and Memphis, Scotland Co., MO. Son-in-law of Bvt. Brig. Gen. David Moore.

Buried: Memphis Cemetery, Memphis, MO (Section 1, Row 27)

Joseph Gibson Best (State Historical Society of Missouri, Photograph Collection [Dr. Leslie Anders, P0365, 019404]).

References: *History of Lewis, Clark, Knox and Scotland Counties, Missouri.* St. Louis and Chicago, 1887. Obituary, *Memphis Reveille*, Aug. 11, 1887. Pension File and Military Service File, National Archives. Letters Received, Volunteer Service Branch, Adjutant General's Office, File B103(VS)1866, National Archives. Leslie Anders. *The Twenty-first Missouri: From Home Guard to Union Regiment.* Westport, CT, 1975. www.findagrave.com.

William Joseph Winterton Bickett

Colonel, Nodaway County Regiment, MO Home Guards, July 5, 1861. Discharged, Oct. 2, 1861. Colonel, 36 Enrolled MO Militia, Aug. 16, 1862. Assistant Surgeon, 41 Enrolled MO Militia, June 1, 1863. Assistant Surgeon, 3 Provisional Enrolled MO Militia, June 6, 1863. Relieved from duty as surgeon, Oct. 19, 1863. Commission vacated, Nov. 1, 1863.

Born: July 5, 1820, KY
Died: Feb. 23, 1869 Helena, MT
Occupation: Physician
Offices/Honors: Nodaway County Treasurer, 1860–62. Postmaster, Maryville, MO, 1858–64.
Miscellaneous: Resided Maryville, Nodaway Co., MO; and Helena, MT
Buried: Forestvale Cemetery, Helena, MT (Valleyview Section, Lot 137)

References: Pension File, National Archives. Joaquin Miller. *An Illustrated History of the State of Montana.* Chicago, IL, 1894. *The History of Nodaway County, Missouri.* St. Joseph, MO, 1882. *Annual Report of the Adjutant General of the State of Missouri, December 31, 1863.* Jefferson City, MO, 1864.

William Bishop

Colonel, 1 Northeast MO Home Guards, June 10, 1861. Colonel, Black Hawk Cavalry, MO Volunteers, Aug. 15, 1861. While on trial by court martial on frivolous charges in Feb. 1862, he learned that his regiment, never at full strength, had been consolidated with other units to form the 7 MO Cavalry. Lieutenant Colonel, 7 MO Cavalry, Feb. 20, 1862. Denied a leave of absence after being acquitted of all court-martial charges and reacting to the degradation of his demotion, he left the regiment, resulting in his immediate discharge, April 3, 1862.

Born: March 24, 1817, Martinsburg, VA (now WV)
Died: May 2, 1879, Clark City, MO
Occupation: Merchant and speculator before war. Druggist after war.
Offices/Honors: Missouri State Treasurer, 1864–68

William Bishop (State Historical Society of Iowa, Des Moines).

Miscellaneous: Resided Alexandria, Clark Co., MO

Buried: Kahoka Cemetery, Kahoka, Clark Co., MO

References: William Garrett Piston, "The Bishops and the Black Hawks: Ambition and Family in Raising a Volunteer Regiment in Civil War Missouri," *Missouri Historical Review*, Vol. 110, No. 3 (April 2016). Pension File and Military Service File, National Archives. Letters Received, Volunteer Service Branch, Adjutant General's Office, File B817 1/2 (VS)1862, National Archives. William Bishop Papers, 1839–1891 (C3894), State Historical Society of Missouri-Columbia. Leslie Anders. *The Twenty-first Missouri: From Home Guard to Union Regiment*. Westport, CT, 1975. Thomas P. Lowry. *Tarnished Eagles: The Courts-Martial of Fifty Union Colonels and Lieutenant Colonels*. Mechanicsburg, PA, 1997. Court-martial Case Files, 1809–1894, File II-883, National Archives. Obituary, *Clark County Democrat*, May 3, 1879.

Josiah Wolcott Bissell

Brigade Quartermaster, U.S. Reserve Corps, MO Volunteers, May 8–11, 1861. Acting AAG, U.S. Reserve Corps, MO Volunteers, May 11–28, 1861. AAG, U.S. Reserve Corps, MO Volunteers, May 28, 1861. Colonel, Engineer Regiment of the West, July 26, 1861. Nominated as Brig. Gen., USV, April 23, 1862. Nomination tabled by U.S. Senate, July 16, 1862. Although he received numerous accolades for his engineering work, his tyrannical manner made him the frequent target of charges (never proven) preferred by disgruntled subordinates. Described as an "incoragibly (sic) gassy man" by Major Gen. Grant, who suspected him of leaking military information to the Memphis press in April 1863, he was "mustered out of the service of the United States for absence from his post without proper authority and general insubordination" to date May 21, 1863. Not wishing "to quit the army with any implied stigma on my name," he protested his unjustified discharge and submitted his resignation, which was accepted to date June 2, 1863. Battle honors: Island No. 10, Siege of Corinth, Vicksburg Campaign.

Born: May 12, 1818, Rochester, NY

Died: Nov. 30, 1891 Pittsburgh, PA

Occupation: Banker, architect, and civil engineer before war. After the war he devised a system for abstracting and recording real estate titles, which he introduced in numerous cities.

Miscellaneous: Resided Rochester, Monroe Co., NY; Minneapolis, MN; and Pittsburgh, PA. Brother of Colonel George P. Bissell (25 CT Infantry).

Buried: Mount Hope Cemetery, Rochester, NY (Section A, Lot 38)

Josiah Wolcott Bissell (Massachusetts MOLLUS Collection, USAMHI [Vol. 69, p. 3402]).

Josiah Wolcott Bissell, post-war (William A. Neal. *An Illustrated History of the Missouri Engineer and the 25th Infantry Regiments*. Chicago, Illinois, 1889).

References: William A. Neal. *An Illustrated History of the Missouri Engineer and the 25th Infantry Regiments*. Chicago, IL, 1889. Obituary Circular, Whole No. 97, Minnesota MOLLUS. Obituary, *Rochester Democrat and Chronicle*, Dec. 5, 1891. Obituary, *Pittsburgh Dispatch*, Dec. 3, 1891. William F. Peck. *Landmarks of Monroe County, New York*. Boston, MA, 1895. Military Service File, National Archives. John Y. Simon, editor. *The Papers of Ulysses S. Grant*. Vol. 8: April 1–July 6, 1863. Carbondale, IL, 1979. Edward Hooker. *The Descendants of Rev. Thomas Hooker, Hartford, Connecticut, 1586–1908*. Rochester, NY, 1909.

Peter Edward Bland

Colonel, 6 MO Infantry, June 29, 1861. Commanded Post of Pilot Knob (MO), Western Department, July–Sept. 1861. Commanded Post of Jefferson City, District of Central Missouri, Department of the Mississippi, April–May 1862. Resigned Aug. 31, 1862, since "my health has been precarious and of late it has so declined as to render me useless to the service." Recommissioned as colonel, Sept. 29, 1862, and mustered in, Oct. 22, 1862. Accused of "physical disability, incompetency, and incapacity to command" by a clique of mutinous officers (including Lieutenant Colonel James H. Blood), he was discharged upon adverse report of a Board of Examination, Dec. 22, 1862. Upon appeal to President Lincoln and review of his case by Judge Advocate General Joseph Holt, his discharge upon adverse report was revoked, April 20, 1864, and he was honorably discharged on account of physical disability to date Dec. 22, 1862. Battle honors: Siege of Corinth.

Born: March 29, 1824, St. Charles Co., MO
Died: April 8, 1885, St. Louis, MO
Education: Attended Illinois College, Jacksonville, IL. Graduated Methodist College, St. Charles, MO, 1846.
Occupation: Lawyer
Miscellaneous: Resided St. Louis, MO; and Memphis, Shelby Co., TN, 1864–67
Buried: Bellefontaine Cemetery, St. Louis, MO (Block 58, Lot 1843, unmarked)
References: Logan U. Reavis. *Saint Louis: The Future Great City of the World*. Centennial Edition. St. Louis, MO, 1876. David W. Dillard. *The Union Post Commanders at Pilot Knob, 1861–1865*. Ironton, MO, 2013. *The Bench and Bar of St. Louis, Kansas City, Jefferson City, and Other Missouri Cities*. St. Louis and Chicago, 1884. Military Service File, National Archives. Letters Received, Volunteer Service Branch, Adjutant General's Office, File M2118(VS)1862, National Archives. Obituary, *St. Louis Post-Dispatch*, April 9, 1885. Obituary, *St. Louis Globe-Democrat*, April 9, 1885. J. Thomas Scharf. *History of Saint Louis City and County*. Philadelphia, PA, 1883.

Wells Howard Blodgett

1 Lieutenant, Co. D, 37 IL Infantry, Aug. 15, 1861. Acting ADC, Staff of Brig. Gen. Egbert B. Brown, District of Southwest Missouri, Department of the Missouri, Aug. 1862–Feb. 1863. Captain, Co. D, 37 IL Infantry, Jan. 1, 1863. Major, Judge Advocate, Army of the Frontier, March 10, 1863. Commission vacated, July 14, 1863. Lieutenant Colonel, 48 MO Infantry, Sept. 23, 1864. Colonel, 48 MO Infantry, Nov. 22, 1864. Commanded Post of Columbia, TN, Jan. 1865. Honorably mustered out, June 29, 1865. Battle honors: Pea Ridge, Prairie Grove, Newtonia.

Born: Jan. 29, 1839 Downers Grove, IL
Died: May 8, 1929, St. Louis, MO
Education: Attended Wheaton (IL) College and Rock River Seminary, Mount Morris, IL
Occupation: Lawyer
Offices/Honors: Medal of Honor, Newtonia, MO, Sept. 30, 1862. "With a single orderly, captured an armed picket of eight men and marched them in as prisoners." Missouri House of Representatives, 1867–69. Missouri Senate, 1869–73.

Wells Howard Blodgett (courtesy Missouri Historical Society, St. Louis [P0233-2665]).

Wells Howard Blodgett, 1893 (Rosch, 1208 Olive Street, St. Louis, Missouri; courtesy Missouri Historical Society, St. Louis [P0233-2666]).

Miscellaneous: Resided Chicago, IL; Warrensburg, Johnson Co., MO, 1865–73; and St. Louis, MO, 1873–1929.

Buried: Bellefontaine Cemetery, St. Louis, MO (Block 67, Lot 2947)

References: William Hyde and Howard L. Conard, editors. *Encyclopedia of the History of St. Louis.* New York, Louisville, and St. Louis, 1899. *The Biographical Dictionary and Portrait Gallery of Representative Men of Chicago, St. Louis and the World's Columbian Exposition.* Chicago and New York, 1893. *The United States Biographical Dictionary and Portrait Gallery of Eminent and Self-Made Men.* Missouri Volume. New York, Chicago, St. Louis, and Kansas City, 1878. *St. Louis The Fourth City Pictorial and Biographical Deluxe Supplement.* St. Louis and Chicago, 1909. Obituary, *St. Louis Post-Dispatch,* May 8, 1929. Pension File and Military Service File, National Archives. Letters Received, Commission Branch, Adjutant General's Office, File B115(CB)1863, National Archives. Edwin A. Blodgett. *Ten Generations of Blodgetts in America.* Barre, VT, 1969. Michael A. Mullins. *The Fremont Rifles: A History of the 37th Illinois Veteran Volunteer Infantry.* Wilmington, NC, 1990.

James Harvey Blood

Lieutenant Colonel, 6 MO Infantry, June 13, 1861. Commanded Post of Tipton, MO, March– April 1862. GSW left breast, Chickasaw Bluffs, MS, Dec. 29, 1862. Colonel, 6 MO Infantry, Jan. 1, 1863. Commanded 1 Brigade, 2 Division, 15 Army Corps, Army of the Tennessee, July 20–Sept. 10, 1863. Resigned April 2, 1864, since "the original term of three years for which I entered the service expires June 1st 1864, beyond which time circumstances connected with the regiment as well as personal considerations do not allow me to think of remaining." Lieutenant Colonel, 5 St. Louis City Guards, Oct. 6, 1864. Battle honors: Chickasaw Bluffs, Arkansas Post, Vicksburg Campaign.

Born: Dec. 29, 1833 Dudley, MA

Died: Dec. 29, 1885 Akantin, Ghana, West Africa

Occupation: Railroad executive, journalist, and writer

Offices/Honors: St. Louis City Auditor, 1865–66

Miscellaneous: Resided St. Louis, MO, to 1866; New York City, NY; Auburn, Androscoggin Co., ME; and Akantin, Ghana, West Africa. An ardent spiritualist, he became the common-law husband and mentor of pioneer suffragist and presidential candidate, Victoria Claflin Woodhull.

Buried: Green-Wood Cemetery, Brooklyn, NY (Section 193, Lot 25770)

James Harvey Blood, 1866 (Thomas M. Easterly; courtesy Missouri Historical Society, St. Louis [N17206]).

James Harvey Blood, post-war (author's photograph).

James Harvey Blood, post-war (National Archives [BA-476]).

References: Pension File and Military Service File, National Archives. Mary Gabriel. *Notorious Victoria: The Life of Victoria Woodhull, Uncensored*. Chapel Hill, NC, 1998. Emanie N. Sachs. *The Terrible Siren: Victoria Woodhull,* *1838–1927*. New York City, NY, 1928. Dolores A. Kilgo. *Likeness and Landscape: Thomas M. Easterly and the Art of the Daguerreotype*. St. Louis, MO, 1994. Roger Deane Harris. *The Story of the Bloods*. Boston, MA, 1960. "Sudden Departure of the City Auditor for South America," *Daily Missouri Republican*, June 25, 1866. *The War of the Rebellion: A Compilation of the Official Records of the Union and Confederate Armies*. (Vol. 41, Part 3, pp. 657, 753). Washington, D.C., 1893.

Henry Boernstein

Colonel, 2 MO Infantry (3 months), May 14, 1861. Honorably mustered out, July 30, 1861.

Born: Nov. 4, 1805 Hamburg, Germany

Died: Sept. 10, 1892 Vienna, Austria

Occupation: Journalist and theatrical director

Offices/Honors: U.S. Consul, Bremen, Germany, 1861–66

Miscellaneous: Resided St. Louis, MO; and Vienna, Austria

Buried: Matzleinsdorfer Protestant Cemetery, Vienna, Austria (unmarked)

Henry Boernstein (Robert J. Rombauer. *The Union Cause in St. Louis in 1861: An Historical Sketch*. St. Louis, Missouri, 1909).

Henry Boernstein, 1873 (courtesy Missouri Historical Society, St. Louis [N11677]).

References: Henry Boernstein. *Memoirs of a Nobody: The Missouri Years of an Austrian Radical, 1849–1866.* Translated and edited by Steven Rowan. St. Louis, MO, 1997. Lawrence O. Christensen, William E. Foley, Gary R. Kremer, and Kenneth H. Winn, editors. *Dictionary of Missouri Biography.* Columbia, MO, 1999. Alfred Vagts, "Heinrich Boernstein, Ex- and Repatriate," *Bulletin of the Missouri Historical Society*, Vol. 12, No. 2 (Jan. 1956). J. Thomas Scharf. *History of Saint Louis City and County.* Philadelphia, PA, 1883. Robert J. Rombauer. *The Union Cause in St. Louis in 1861: An Historical Sketch.* St. Louis, MO, 1909. Richard Edwards and Merna Hopewell. *Edwards's Great West and Her Commercial Metropolis, Embracing a General View of the West, and a Complete History of St. Louis.* St. Louis, MO, 1860. Adolf E. Zucker, editor. *The Forty-Eighters: Political Refugees of the German Revolution of 1848.* New York City, NY, 1950. Pension File and Military Service File, National Archives.

George Boardman Boomer

Colonel, 26 MO Infantry, Jan. 20, 1862. GSW right shoulder, left thigh and back, Iuka, MS, Sept. 19, 1862. Commanded 3 Brigade, 7 Division, 13 Army Corps, Army of the Tennessee, Nov. 1–Dec. 18, 1862. Commanded 3 Brigade, 7 Division, 17 Army Corps, Army of the Tennessee, Feb. 12–May 22, 1863. GSW head, Vicksburg, MS, May 22, 1863. Battle honors: Iuka, Champion's Hill, Vicksburg Campaign.

Born: July 26, 1832, Sutton, MA

George Boardman Boomer (Massachusetts MOLLUS Collection, USAMHI [Vol. 5, p. 224]).

George Boardman Boomer (Relief Portrait, Vicksburg National Military Park).

Died: May 22, 1863, KIA Vicksburg, MS
Education: Attended Worcester (MA) Academy
Occupation: Railroad contractor/bridge builder and farmer
Miscellaneous: Resided St. Louis, MO; and Crawford Twp., Osage Co., MO. Although Major Gen. Grant recommended Boomer's promotion to Brig. Gen. in Jan. 1863, no action was taken on the recommendation. There is also no evidence that the brevet of brigadier general was conferred on him. Nevertheless he was, after death, frequently referred to as General Boomer.
Buried: Rural Cemetery, Worcester, MA
References: Mary Amelia Stone. *Memoir of George Boardman Boomer*. Boston, MA, 1864. Benjamin D. Dean. *Recollections of the 26th Missouri Infantry in the War for the Union*. Lamar, MO, 1892. Obituary, *Massachusetts Weekly Spy*, June 17, 1863. "Funeral of Gen. Boomer," *Massachusetts Weekly Spy*, July 1, 1863. "Gen. Boomer," *Worcester National Aegis*, July 4, 1863. Abijah P. Marvin. *History of Worcester in the War of the Rebellion*. Worcester, MA, 1870. Military Service File, National Archives. Letters Received, Appointment, Commission and Personal Branch, Adjutant General's Office, File 3688(ACP)1891, National Archives. John Y. Simon, editor. *The Papers of Ulysses S. Grant*. Vol. 7: December 9, 1862–March 31, 1863. Carbondale, IL, 1979.

Marcus Boyd

Lieutenant Colonel, Greene County Regiment, MO Home Guards, June 11, 1861. Discharged Aug. 17, 1861. Colonel, 74 Enrolled MO Militia, Aug. 16, 1862. Resigned (date unknown). Battle honors: Marmaduke's Expedition into Missouri (Springfield).
Born: July 27, 1803, Williamson Co., TN
Died: Nov. 30, 1866 Springfield, MO
Occupation: Lawyer and farmer
Offices/Honors: Missouri House of Representatives, 1854–56 and 1858–62. Grand Master of the Grand Lodge A.F. & A.M. of Missouri, 1859. Postmaster of Springfield, MO, 1866.
Miscellaneous: Resided Springfield, Greene Co., MO. Father of Colonel Sempronius H. Boyd (24 MO Infantry).
Buried: Hazelwood Cemetery, Springfield, MO (Lot 81)
References: Howard L. Conard, editor. *Encyclopedia of the History of Missouri*. New York, Louisville, and St. Louis, 1901. *An Illustrated Historical Atlas Map of Greene County, Missouri*. Philadelphia, PA, 1876. "The Late Hon. Marcus Boyd," *Daily Missouri Republican*, Dec. 22, 1866. Obituary, *Daily Missouri Republican*, Dec. 10, 1866. *Biographies and Engravings of Grand Masters, Grand Treasurers and Grand Secretaries of the Grand Lodge of Missouri*. St. Louis, MO, 1901. *History of Greene County, Missouri*. St. Louis, MO, 1883. Military Service File, National Archives.

Sempronius Hamilton Boyd

Major, Greene County Regiment, MO Home Guards, June 11, 1861. Discharged, Aug. 2, 1861. Colonel, 24 MO Infantry, Aug. 2, 1861. Commanded Post of Rolla, District of Central Missouri, Department of the Mississippi, March–July 1862. Commanded Post of Greenville, St. Louis Division, District of Missouri, Department of the Mississippi, Aug.–Sept. 1862. Commanded Post of Pilot Knob, District of St. Louis, Department of the Missouri, Oct. 1862. Commanded 2 Division, Army of Southeast Missouri, Department of the Missouri, Oct. 1862–Jan. 1863. Commanded District of Rolla, Department of the Missouri, March 1863. Resigned April 18, 1863, to take seat in U.S. House of Representatives. Battle honors: Pitman's Ferry.
Born: May 28, 1828, Williamson Co., TN
Died: June 22, 1894, Ant's Creek, Stone Co., MO

Sempronius Hamilton Boyd (Wilson's Creek National Battlefield [WICR 11508]).

Sempronius Hamilton Boyd (Brady-Handy Photograph Collection, Library of Congress [LC-DIG-cwpbh-02397]).

Sempronius Hamilton Boyd (Brady's National Photographic Portrait Gallery, No. 352 Pennsylvania Ave., Washington, D.C.; courtesy of Dennis Hood, D.V.M.).

Sempronius Hamilton Boyd (Brady's National Photographic Portrait Gallery, No. 352 Pennsylvania Ave., Washington, D.C.; courtesy Olaf).

Occupation: Lawyer

Offices/Honors: U.S. House of Representatives, 1863–65, 1869–71. U.S. Minister to Siam, 1890–92.

Miscellaneous: Resided Springfield, Greene Co., MO. Son of Colonel Marcus Boyd (74 Enrolled MO Militia).

Buried: Hazelwood Cemetery, Springfield, MO (Lot 81)

References: *The United States Biographical Dictionary and Portrait Gallery of Eminent and Self-Made Men*. Missouri Volume. New York, Chicago, St. Louis, and Kansas City, 1878. J. Randall Houp. *The 24th Missouri Volunteer Infantry: Lyon Legion*. Alma, AR, 1997. Pension File and Military Service File, National Archives. *History of Greene County, Missouri*. St. Louis, MO, 1883. *Pictorial and Genealogical Record of Greene County, Missouri*. Chicago, IL, 1893. *An Illustrated Historical Atlas Map of Greene County, Missouri*. Philadelphia, PA, 1876. William Horatio Barnes. *History of Congress. The Forty-First Congress of the United States, 1869–1871*. New York City, NY, 1872. James L. Harrison, compiler. *Biographical Directory of the American Congress, 1774–1949*. Washington, D.C., 1950. Letters Received, Volunteer Service Branch, Adjutant General's Office, File B1196(VS)1864, National Archives. David W. Dillard. *The Union Post Commanders at Pilot Knob, 1861–1865*. Ironton, MO, 2013.

Ferdinand Thomas Lee Boyle

Colonel, 5 Enrolled MO Militia, Sept. 24, 1862. Resigned May 2, 1864.

Born: July 6, 1820, Ringwood, Hampshire, England

Died: Dec. 2, 1906 Brooklyn, NY
Occupation: Portrait painter and art professor
Miscellaneous: Resided St. Louis, MO, 1855–66; and Brooklyn, NY, after 1866. Subjects of his portraits included General Ulysses S. Grant, Charles Dickens, Senator Thomas Hart Benton, and General Francis Preston Blair, Jr.
Buried: Green-Wood Cemetery, Brooklyn, NY (Section 8, Lot 9993)
References: Henry R. Stiles, editor. *The Civil, Political, Professional and Ecclesiastical History and Commercial and Industrial Record of the County of Kings and the City of Brooklyn, N.Y.* New York City, NY, 1884. David B. Dearinger, editor. *Paintings and Sculpture in the Collection of the National Academy of Design.* Volume 1, 1826–1925. Manchester, VT, 2004. George C. Groce and David H. Wallace. *The New-York Historical Society's Dictionary of Artists in America, 1564–1860.* New Haven and London, 1957. Obituary, *Brooklyn Daily Eagle*, Dec. 3, 1906. Obituary, *New York Times*, Dec. 4, 1906. Letters Received, Colored Troops Branch, Adjutant General's Office, File B200(CT)1863, National Archives. https://americangallery19th.wordpress.com/category/-boyle-ferdinand-t-l/.

Harrison Bell Branch

Colonel, 41 Enrolled MO Militia, Oct. 7, 1863. Commission vacated, Nov. 1, 1863. Recommissioned as Colonel, Enrolled MO Militia, Dec. 3, 1863.
Born: Aug. 21, 1824 Buckingham Co., VA
Died: Aug. 29, 1892 St. Joseph, MO
Occupation: Lawyer
Offices/Honors: Superintendent of Indian Affairs, 1862–64. Postmaster, Kansas City, MO, 1866–67.
Miscellaneous: Resided St. Joseph, Buchanan Co., MO; and Kansas City, MO
Buried: Mount Mora Cemetery, St. Joseph, MO (Section L, Block 28, Lot 4)
References: Obituary, *St. Joseph Herald*, Aug. 30, 1892. Benjamin H. Branch, Jr. *The Branch, Harris, Jarvis and Chinn Book: A Family Outline.* Ann Arbor, MI, 1963. William M. Paxton. *Annals of Platte County, Missouri, from Its Exploration Down to June 1, 1897.* Kansas City, MO, 1897. *Portrait and Biographical Record of Buchanan and Clinton Counties, Missouri.* Chicago, IL, 1893. Obituary, *Kansas City Star*, Aug. 30, 1892.

Milton Hale Brawner

Captain, Co. A, Black Horse Cavalry, MO Volunteers, July 5, 1861. Captain, Co. A, 7 MO Cavalry, March 14, 1862. GSW side, Lone Jack, MO, Aug. 16, 1862. Major, 7 MO Cavalry, Dec. 19, 1862. Commanded 1 Brigade, Cavalry Division, 7 Army Corps, Department of Arkansas, Jan. 24–Feb. 1, 1865. Upon the consolidation of the 7 MO Cavalry with the 1 MO Cavalry, Major Gen. Joseph J. Reynolds ordered Major Brawner to take command as *Colonel*, 1 MO Cavalry, Feb. 22, 1865, despite the seniority of Lt. Col. John J. Joslyn, then commanding the regiment. Mustered as Lieutenant Colonel, 1 MO Cavalry, May 9, 1865, following the muster of John J. Joslyn as colonel. Commanded Separate Dismounted Cavalry Brigade, 7 Army Corps, Department of Arkansas, June 10–July 12, 1865. Honorably mustered out, Sept. 2, 1865. Battle honors: Lone Jack, Prairie Grove, Princeton (AR).
Born: Dec. 15, 1834 Fauquier Co., VA
Died: Dec. 16, 1866 Warsaw, IL
Occupation: Dentist
Offices/Honors: Postmaster, Warsaw, IL, 1866
Miscellaneous: Resided Warsaw, Hancock Co., IL
Buried: Oakland Cemetery, Warsaw, IL (Block 3, Lot 2)

Milton Hale Brawner (State Historical Society of Iowa, Des Moines).

Milton Hale Brawner (State Historical Society of Iowa, Des Moines).

Milton Hale Brawner (Troxell & Brother, St. Louis, Missouri; courtesy Tennessee Historical Society and Tennessee State Library and Archives [Nichols-Britt Collection, 34965]).

References: Obituary, *Warsaw Public Record*, Dec. 28, 1866. Military Service File, National Archives. Letters Received, Volunteer Service Branch, Adjutant General's Office, Files B1662(VS)1864 and B1857(VS)1865, National Archives. Howard N. Monnett, editor, "A Yankee Cavalryman Views the Battle of Prairie Grove," *Arkansas Historical Quarterly*, Vol. 21, No. 4 (Winter 1962).

Robert Milton Brewer

Colonel, 64 Enrolled MO Militia, Oct. 27, 1862. Commission vacated, March 12, 1865.
Born: Sept. 27, 1820 Spencer Co., KY
Died: Oct. 20, 1894 Brewer, MO
Occupation: Farmer and county court judge
Offices/Honors: Missouri House of Representatives, 1862–66, 1879–81
Miscellaneous: Resided Perryville, Perry Co., MO; and Brewer, Perry Co., MO
Buried: Mount Hope Cemetery, Perryville, MO (Row 31, Monument 30)
References: Timothy J. O'Rourke. *Maryland Catholics on the Frontier: The Missouri and Texas Settlements*. Parsons, KS, 1980. *History of Southeast Missouri*. Chicago, IL, 1888. *The Centennial History of Perry County, Missouri, 1821–1921*. Perryville, MO, 1984.

Aaron Brown

Lieutenant Colonel, 21 MO Infantry, Sept. 7, 1861. *Colonel*, 21 MO Infantry, Sept. 27, 1861. Major, 10 MO Infantry, Dec. 1, 1861, upon consolidation of 21 MO Infantry with 10 MO Infantry. Discharged April 9, 1862, having been reported upon adversely by a Board of Examination, which found him "totally ignorant of even the simplest principles of tactics."
Born: 1811? VA
Died: Feb. 13, 1875 St. Louis, MO
Occupation: Jeweler and watchmaker
Miscellaneous: Resided Rolla, Phelps Co., MO; and St. Louis, MO. Had a long career as a thief and scoundrel. His real name was James W. Gilmour, but after killing two men in a Virginia gambling house in 1853, he fled to Alabama and changed his name. He then drifted from place to place, leaving a trail of deceit in his wake. Along the way he married four wives, including a fifteen-year-old as his last wife.
Buried: Bellefontaine Cemetery, St. Louis, MO (Block 217, Lot F, Grave 769, unmarked)
References: Pension File and Military Service

File, National Archives. "Old Aaron Brown: The Story of his Checkered Life Told By One of his Wives," *Rolla Weekly Herald*, March 11, 1875. "Aaron Brown's Wives," *St. Louis Post-Dispatch*, March 5, 1875. Letters Received, Volunteer Service Branch, Adjutant General's Office, Files M445(VS)1862 and B358(VS)1870, National Archives. Obituary, *Daily Missouri Democrat*, Feb. 14, 1875. Death Notice, St. Louis Republican, Feb. 15, 1875. *Annual Report of the Adjutant General of the State of Missouri, December 31, 1863*. Jefferson City, MO, 1864.

Benjamin Gratz Brown

Colonel, 4 U.S. Reserve Corps, MO Infantry (3 months), May 8, 1861. Honorably mustered out, Aug. 19, 1861. Volunteer ADC, Staff of Major Gen. William S. Rosecrans, commanding St. Louis City Guard, Sept. 27–Oct. 12, 1864.

Born: May 28, 1826, Lexington, KY

Died: Dec. 13, 1885 Kirkwood, MO

Education: Attended Transylvania University, Lexington, KY. Graduated Yale University, New Haven, CT, 1847. Graduated University of Louisville (KY) Law School, 1849.

Occupation: Lawyer

Offices/Honors: Missouri House of Representatives, 1852–58. U.S. Senate, 1863–67. Governor of Missouri, 1871–73. Vice Presidential candidate for Liberal Republican party in 1872 election.

Benjamin Gratz Brown (Frederick Hill Meserve. Historical Portraits, a Part of the Collection of Americana of Frederick Hill Meserve. New York City, 1913-1915; courtesy New York State Library, Manuscripts and Special Collections).

Benjamin Gratz Brown (Brady's National Photographic Portrait Gallery, Washington, D.C.; James Wadsworth Family Papers, Library of Congress [LC-MSS-44297-33-052]).

Benjamin Gratz Brown, post-war (Massachusetts MOLLUS Collection, USAMHI [Vol. 22, p. 1063L]).

Miscellaneous: Resided St. Louis, MO; and Kirkwood, St. Louis Co., MO. Half-brother of Colonel John Mason Brown (45 KY Infantry).

Buried: Oak Hill Cemetery, Kirkwood, MO (Section I, Block 35, Lot 153/410)

References: Allen Johnson and Dumas Malone, editors. *Dictionary of American Biography*. New York City, NY, 1964. Lawrence O. Christensen, William E. Foley, Gary R. Kremer, and Kenneth H. Winn, editors. *Dictionary of Missouri Biography*. Columbia, MO, 1999. *The United States Biographical Dictionary and Portrait Gallery of Eminent and Self-Made Men*. Missouri Volume. New York, Chicago, St. Louis, and Kansas City, 1878. Walter B. Davis and Daniel S. Durrie. *An Illustrated History of Missouri*. St. Louis, MO, 1876. Norma L. Peterson. *Freedom and Franchise: The Political Career of B. Gratz Brown*. Columbia, MO, 1965. Howard L. Conard, editor. *Encyclopedia of the History of Missouri*. New York, Louisville, and St. Louis, 1901. Obituary, *St. Louis Post-Dispatch*, Dec. 14, 1885. Military Service File, National Archives.

Richard Hardy Brown

Private, Co. D, 5 U.S. Reserve Corps, MO Infantry (3 months), June 15, 1861. Honorably mustered out, Aug. 31, 1861. 1 Lieutenant, Co. D, 14 MO Home Guards, Aug. 5, 1861. Taken prisoner and paroled, Lexington, MO, Sept. 19, 1861. Honorably discharged, Oct. 19, 1861. Captain, Co. K, 23 MO Infantry, Dec. 22, 1861. GSW both thighs, Shiloh, TN, April 6, 1862. Provost Marshal, Benton Barracks, MO, Aug.–Dec. 1862 and Feb.–March 1863. Honorably mustered out, Jan. 4, 1864. Major, 12 MO Cavalry, Jan. 5, 1864. Lieutenant Colonel, 12 MO Cavalry, March 21, 1864. Commanded 1 Brigade, 5 Division, Cavalry Corps, Military Division of the Mississippi, Feb. 3–8, 1865. Assumed command of the Post of Omaha (NE), Department of the Missouri, July 13, 1865. Complaints by the Mayor of Omaha of his "unnecessary twaddle and egotism in relation to his power and his arbitrary trespasses upon property belonging to citizens" resulted in his reassignment to command of Fort Cottonwood, NE, Sept. 24, 1865. Commanded Post of Fort Sedgwick, CO, Oct. 23–Dec. 31, 1865. *Colonel*, 12 MO Cavalry, Jan. 24, 1866. Honorably mustered out, April 9, 1866. Battle honors: Lexington (MO), Shiloh, Shelby's Raid in Arkansas and Missouri, Expedition from LaGrange, TN, to Oxford. MS (Tallahatchie River), Nashville.

Born: April 13, 1832, Salford, Lancashire, England

Richard Hardy Brown (Courtesy Missouri Historical Society, St. Louis [P0233-2813]).

Richard Hardy Brown, 1897 (Genelli, 923 Olive Street, St. Louis, Missouri; Courtesy Missouri Historical Society, St. Louis [P0233-2814]).

Died: Aug. 14, 1900 Edgebrook, St. Louis Co., MO

Occupation: Engaged in stove and hardware business. Appointed Captain, 10 U.S. Cavalry, Oct. 19, 1866, but failed to pass a satisfactory examination before the Board of Cavalry Examination. Later foreman in Missouri Pacific Railroad car shops.

Miscellaneous: Resided St. Louis, MO

Buried: Jefferson Barracks National Cemetery, St. Louis, MO (Section OPS1, Grave 2170A)

References: Obituary Circular, Whole No. 213, Missouri MOLLUS. Pension File and Military Service File, National Archives. Letters Received, Commission Branch, Adjutant General's Office, File B1219(CB)1866, National Archives. Obituary, *St. Louis Post-Dispatch*, Aug. 16, 1900. *Report of the Proceedings of the Society of the Army of the Tennessee at the Thirty-Third Meeting*. Cincinnati, OH, 1902.

William Smith Brown

Colonel, 33 Enrolled MO Militia, Sept. 15, 1862. Commission vacated, March 12, 1865. Battle honors: Operations in Western Missouri (Union Mills).

Born: Sept. 16, 1824 (Nov. 6, 1826 on gravestone) Preble Co., OH

Died: June 12, 1906, Daviess Co., MO

Occupation: Physician and farmer

Miscellaneous: Resided Bethany, Harrison Co., MO; and Grand River Twp., Daviess Co., MO

Buried: Scotland Cemetery, near Jameson, Daviess Co., MO

References: *History of Daviess County, Missouri*. Kansas City, MO, 1882. www.findagrave.com.

John D. Brutsche

Lieutenant Colonel, 47 Enrolled MO Militia, Sept. 18, 1862. Colonel, 47 Enrolled MO Militia, March 23, 1863. Lieutenant Colonel, 9 Provisional Enrolled MO Militia, July 1, 1863. Lieutenant Colonel, 8 MO State Militia Cavalry, Nov. 1, 1863. Commanded Post of Lebanon (MO), District of Southwest Missouri, Department of the Missouri, Jan.–Feb. 1864. Commanded Post of Springfield (MO), District of Southwest Missouri, Department of the Missouri, April 1864. Provost Marshal, District of Southwest Missouri, Department of the Missouri, May 1864–March 1865. Acting AAG, Staff of Brig. Gen. John B. Sanborn, District of Southwest Missouri, Sept.–Oct. 1864. Honorably mustered out, May 5, 1865. Battle honors: Shelby's Raid in Arkansas and Missouri, Price's Missouri Expedition.

Born: March 1833 Philadelphia, PA

Died: March 26, 1907, Leavenworth, KS

John D. Brutsche (Missouri Valley Special Collections, Kansas City Public Library, Kansas City, Missouri).

Occupation: Dry goods merchant and railway express agent

Miscellaneous: Resided Camden Co., MO (1863); Springfield, Greene Co., MO (1870); St. Louis, MO (1878); and Pierce City, Lawrence Co., MO (1890)

Buried: Leavenworth National Cemetery, Leavenworth, KS (Section 22, Row 4, Grave 3153)

References: Pension File and Military Service File, National Archives. Obituary, *Leavenworth Times*, March 28, 1907. Historical Register of National Homes for Disabled Volunteer Soldiers, 1866–1938, National Archives. www.findagrave.com.

Adelbert Rinaldo Buffington

2 Lieutenant, Ordnance, May 14, 1861. 1 Lieutenant, Ordnance, July 22, 1861. Lieutenant Colonel, 24 Enrolled MO Militia, Aug. 27, 1862. Colonel, 24 Enrolled MO Militia, Sept. 10, 1862. Commission vacated, July 15, 1863. Commanded Wheeling (WV) Ordnance Depot, Oct. 25, 1862–Sept. 12, 1863. Captain, Ordnance, March 3, 1863. Commanded New York Arsenal, July 13, 1864–Sept. 1865. Commanded Baton Rouge (LA) Arsenal, Sept. 14, 1865–Aug. 15, 1866. Bvt. Major, USA, March 13, 1865, for faithful and meritorious services in the Ordnance Department.

Born: Nov. 22, 1837 Wheeling, WV

Adelbert Rinaldo Buffington, West Point Cadet, Class of May 1861 (USAMHI [RG25S-West Point Album-1861.30]).

Adelbert Rinaldo Buffington, post-war (National Archives, Letters Received, Commission Branch, Adjutant General's Office [File B1220(CB)1863]).

Died: July 10, 1922, Madison, NJ
Education: Graduated U.S. Military Academy, West Point, NY, May 1861
Occupation: Regular Army (Brig. Gen., Chief of Ordnance, April 5, 1899; retired Nov. 22, 1901). Originator of various improvements in ordnance and methods of manufacturing small arms.
Buried: Arlington National Cemetery, Arlington, VA (Section 3, Lot 3939)
References: *Fifty-third Annual Report of the Association of Graduates of the United States Military Academy.* Saginaw, MI, 1922. Mary Elizabeth Sergent. *They Lie Forgotten: The United States Military Academy, 1856–1861, Together with a Class Album for the Class of May 1861.* Middletown, NY, 1986. George W. Cullum. *Biographical Register of the Officers and Graduates of the U.S. Military Academy.* Third Edition. Boston, MA, 1891. Obituary, *Morristown Daily Record*, July 11, 1922. Letters Received, Commission Branch, Adjutant General's Office, File B1220(CB)1863, National Archives. Obituary, *New York Times*, July 11, 1922.

Patrick Emmet Burke

1 Lieutenant, 13 U.S. Infantry, May 14, 1861. Captain, Co. K, 1 MO Infantry (3 months), May 18, 1861. Captain, Co. K, 1 MO Infantry (3 years), June 11, 1861. Unit designation changed to Battery K, 1 MO Light Artillery, Sept. 1, 1861. Captain, 14 U.S. Infantry, Oct. 24, 1861. Colonel, Western Sharpshooters, 14 MO Infantry, June 24, 1862. Commanded Post of Corinth, MS, Oct. 1862. Designation of regiment changed to 66 IL Infantry, Nov. 20, 1862. Commanded Camp Davies, District of Corinth, Nov. 1862–Oct. 1863. Commanded 2 Brigade, 2 Division, Left Wing, 16 Army Corps, Army of the Tennessee, April 22–May 16, 1864. GSW left leg (amputated), Rome Crossroads, GA, May 16, 1864. Bvt. Major, USA, May 14, 1864, for gallant and meritorious services in the battle of Resaca, GA. Battle honors: Wilson's Creek, Corinth, Atlanta Campaign (Resaca, Rome Crossroads).
Born: 1830? County Tipperary, Ireland
Died: May 20, 1864, DOW Resaca, GA
Education: Graduated St. Mary's of the Barrens Seminary, Perryville, MO, 1848
Occupation: Lawyer
Offices/Honors: Missouri House of Representatives, 1856–58
Miscellaneous: Resided St. Louis, MO

Patrick Emmet Burke (Armstead & White, Artists, Corinth, Missouri; Steve Saathoff collection).

Patrick Emmet Burke (Ray Zielin collection).

Patrick Emmet Burke (N. Brown, Photographer, S.E. Corner Fourth & Pine Streets, Opposite Planters' House, St. Louis, Missouri; courtesy Steve Meadow).

Buried: Calvary Cemetery, St. Louis, MO (Section 7, Lot 80)
References: Obituary, *Daily Missouri Republican*, June 7, 1864. Pension File and Military Service File, National Archives. Letters Received, Adjutant General's Office, File B356(AGO)1861, National Archives. Lorenzo A. Barker. *Military History (Michigan Boys) Company D, 66th Illinois, Birge's Western Sharpshooters in the Civil War, 1861–1865.* Huntington, WV, 1994.

Cornelius H. Canfield

Colonel, 67 Enrolled MO Militia, Sept. 24, 1863. Commission vacated, March 12, 1865. Battle honors: Price's Missouri Expedition.
Born: June 5, 1812, Genesee Co., NY
Died: Nov. 1, 1872 Batavia, NY
Education: Attended Cazenovia (NY) Seminary
Occupation: Lawyer
Miscellaneous: Resided Buffalo, NY; and Wellsville, Montgomery Co., MO, after 1858
Buried: Burial place unknown
References: Obituary, *Batavia Republican Advocate*, Nov. 7, 1872. *Descendants of Thomas Canfield and Matthew Camfield*. Hillsboro, KS,

2006. *First Fifty Years of Cazenovia Seminary, 1825–1875.* Cazenovia, NY, 1877.

Edwin Church Catherwood

Lieutenant Colonel, 6 MO State Militia Cavalry, March 22, 1862. Colonel, 6 MO State Militia Cavalry, April 30, 1862. Commanded Post of Warrensburg (MO), Central District of Missouri, Department of the Missouri, Dec. 1862–Feb. 1863. Commanded Post of Springfield (MO), District of Southwest Missouri, Department of the Missouri, Dec. 1863 and June 1864. Colonel, 13 MO Cavalry, Nov. 25, 1864. Commanded District of Rolla (MO), Department of the Missouri, Dec. 1864 and March 1865. Desiring "to return to private life," he resigned June 20, 1865. Battle honors: Pineville (MO), Shelby's Raid in Arkansas and Missouri, Price's Missouri Expedition (Independence, Mine Creek).

Born: Nov. 1835 New York City, NY
Died: Nov. 7, 1897 Oconomowoc, WI
Occupation: Wholesale liquor merchant before war. Commission merchant after war, with mining interests in Nevada, Arizona, and Lower California.
Miscellaneous: Resided St. Louis, MO, before war; New York City, NY (1870); San Francisco, CA, 1871–81; and Oconomowoc, Waukesha Co., WI, after 1881. Brother of Colonel Henry H. Catherwood (9 Enrolled MO Militia) and Colonel William L. Catherwood (8 Enrolled MO Militia).
Buried: Bellefontaine Cemetery, St. Louis, MO (Blocks 111–112, Lot 86)
References: Obituary, *Oconomowoc Free Press*, Nov. 13, 1897. Military Service File, National Archives. Letters Received, Volunteer Service Branch, Adjutant General's Office, File C1953(VS)1863, National Archives. Letters Received, Commission Branch, Adjutant General's Office, File C1154(CB)1863, National Archives. Obituary, *Chicago Inter Ocean*, Nov. 11, 1897. Richard E. Lingenfelter. *Death Valley & the Amargosa: A Land of Illusion.* Berkeley, CA, 1986.

Henry Hamilton Catherwood

Major, 9 Enrolled MO Militia, Oct. 1, 1862. Lieutenant Colonel, 9 Enrolled MO Militia, Oct. 15, 1862. Colonel, 9 Enrolled MO Militia, Sept. 15, 1863. Temporary service as Colonel, 11 Provisional Enrolled MO Militia.

Born: 1837 NY
Died: Aug. 31, 1872 Indianapolis, IN
Education: Attended St. Louis (MO) University
Occupation: Superintendent of street railway
Miscellaneous: Resided St. Louis, MO; and Indianapolis, IN. Brother of Colonel Edwin C. Catherwood (13 MO Cavalry) and Colonel William L. Catherwood (8 Enrolled MO Militia).
Buried: Crown Hill Cemetery, Indianapolis, IN (Section 38, Lot 1)
References: Obituary, *Indianapolis Journal*, Sept. 2, 1872. Death Notice, *Indianapolis Daily Sentinel*, Sept. 2, 1872. Jane E. Darlington, "Burials, 1870–1892, St. Paul's Episcopal Church, Indianapolis, IN," *The Hoosier Genealogist*, Vol. 35, No. 1 (March 1995). *Report of the Adjutant General State of Missouri, 1915–1916.* Jefferson City, MO, 1916.

William Lane Catherwood

Captain, Co. D, 8 Enrolled MO Militia, Sept. 20, 1862. Major, 8 Enrolled MO Militia, May 19, 1863. Colonel, 8 Enrolled MO Militia, April 30, 1864. Resigned Jan. 5, 1865.
Born: Nov. 25, 1825 NY

Edwin Church Catherwood (Brown & Scholten, Artists, 82 North Fourth Street, St. Louis, Missouri; Courtesy Missouri Historical Society, St. Louis [P0084-0107]).

Died: May 31, 1895, Chicago, IL
Occupation: Capitalist with interests in Nevada silver mining
Miscellaneous: Resided St. Louis, MO, before war; New York City, NY (1867, 1875); Nashotah, Waukesha Co., WI; and Chicago, IL. Brother of Colonel Edwin C. Catherwood (13 MO Cavalry) and Colonel Henry H. Catherwood (9 Enrolled MO Militia).
Buried: Bellefontaine Cemetery, St. Louis, MO (Blocks 111–112, Lot 86)
References: William L. Catherwood Papers, 1859–1873 (C3799), State Historical Society of Missouri-Columbia. Obituary, *St. Louis Globe-Democrat*, June 2, 1895. Death notice, *Chicago Daily Tribune,* June 1, 1895.

Kersey Coates

Colonel, 77 Enrolled MO Militia, Dec. 30, 1862 Commanded Post of Kansas City (MO), Army of the Border, Oct. 1864. Commission vacated, March 12, 1865. Battle honors: Price's Missouri Expedition (Westport).
Born: Sept. 15, 1823 Sadsbury, Lancaster Co., PA
Died: April 24, 1887, Kansas City, MO
Education: Attended Phillips Academy, Andover, MA

Kersey Coates, post-war (Laura Coates Reed, editor. *In Memoriam Sarah Walter Chandler Coates*. Kansas City, Missouri, 1898).

Occupation: Lawyer, banker, and railroad president
Miscellaneous: Resided Kansas City, MO
Buried: Elmwood Cemetery, Kansas City, MO (Block C, Lot 95)
References: *The United States Biographical Dictionary and Portrait Gallery of Eminent and Self-Made Men*. Missouri Volume. New York, Chicago, St. Louis, and Kansas City, 1878. Laura C. Reed, editor. *In Memoriam: Sarah Walter Chandler Coates*. Kansas City, MO, 1898. Henry Hall, editor. *America's Successful Men of Affairs*. New York City, NY, 1895. Obituary, *Kansas City Times,* April 25, 1887. Wilda Sandy. *Here Lies Kansas City*. Kansas City, MO, 1984. William Garrett Piston and Thomas P. Sweeney. *Portraits of Conflict: A Photographic History of Missouri in the Civil War*. Fayetteville, AR, 2009.

James Coff

Major, 11 Enrolled MO Militia, Sept. 17, 1862. Lieutenant Colonel, 11 Enrolled MO Militia, June 17, 1863. Colonel, 11 Enrolled MO Militia, April 30, 1864. Relieved from active service, July 2, 1864. Commission vacated, March 12, 1865.
Born: Oct. 15, 1833 Canada
Died: Oct. 21, 1909 St. Louis, MO
Occupation: Merchant and deputy county marshal. Later U.S. Internal Revenue Storekeeper.

Kersey Coates, pre-war (Wilson's Creek National Battlefield [WICR 30358]).

Miscellaneous: Resided St. Louis, MO
Buried: Calvary Cemetery, St. Louis, MO (Section 13, Lot 34, unmarked)
References: Pension File, National Archives. Death notice, *St. Louis Post-Dispatch*, Oct. 22, 1909.

Nelson Cole

Captain, Co. A, 5 MO Infantry (3 months), May 9, 1861. Captain, Co. E, 1 MO Infantry, June 10, 1861. GSW jaw, Wilson's Creek, MO, Aug. 10, 1861. Captain, Battery E, 1 MO Light Artillery, Sept. 1, 1861. Chief of Ordnance and Artillery, Staff of Major Gen. John M. Schofield and Major Gen. Francis J. Herron, Army of the Frontier, Department of the Missouri, Sept. 26, 1862–June 3, 1863. Major, 1 MO Light Artillery, Aug. 12, 1863. Chief of Artillery, Staff of Major Gen. John M. Schofield, Major Gen. William S. Rosecrans, and Major Gen. Grenville M. Dodge, Department of the Missouri. Aug. 1863–May 1865. Lieutenant Colonel, 2 MO Light Artillery, Oct. 5, 1863. Colonel, 2 MO Light Artillery, Feb. 27, 1864. Temporarily assigned as Chief of Staff, Staff of Major Gen. Alfred Pleasanton, Provisional Cavalry Division, Department of the Missouri, Oct. 1864. Honorably mustered out, Nov. 30, 1865. Battle honors: Wilson's Creek, Shelby's Raid in Arkansas and Missouri, Vicksburg Campaign, Price's Missouri Expedition (Big Blue, Mine Creek), Powder River Indian Expedition.

Nelson Cole, as Brig. Gen., USV, 1898 (Obituary Circular, Whole No. 193, Missouri MOLLUS).

Born: Nov. 18, 1833 Rhinebeck, NY
Died: July 31, 1899, St. Louis, MO
Other Wars: Spanish-American War (Brig. Gen., USV, May 28, 1898. Honorably discharged, Mar. 8, 1899)
Occupation: Planing mill operator and lumber merchant
Miscellaneous: Resided St. Louis, MO
Buried: Bellefontaine Cemetery, St. Louis, MO (Block 160, Lot 2532)
References: William Hyde and Howard L. Conard, editors. *Encyclopedia of the History of St. Louis*. New York, Louisville, and St. Louis, 1899. Pension File and Military Service File, National Archives. Walter B. Stevens. *St. Louis The Fourth City, 1764–1909*. St. Louis and Chicago, 1909. Obituary Circular, Whole No. 193, Missouri MOLLUS. Obituary, *St. Louis Post-Dispatch*, Aug. 1, 1899. *Report of the Proceedings of the Society of the Army of the Tennessee at the Thirty-First Meeting*. Cincinnati, OH, 1900.

Nelson Cole (courtesy Missouri Historical Society, St. Louis [P0084-0114]).

David Crockett Coleman

1 Lieutenant, Adjutant, 8 MO Infantry, July 4, 1861. Acting AAG, Staff of Colonel Morgan L. Smith, 1 Brigade, 5 Division, Army of the Tennessee, May 1862. Lieutenant Colonel, 8 MO Infantry, Aug. 16, 1862. GSW left leg and

hand, Vicksburg, MS, May 22, 1863. *Colonel*, 8 MO Infantry, Sept. 1, 1863. Commanded 1 Brigade, 2 Division, 15 Army Corps, Army of the Tennessee, Jan. 1–Feb. 21, 1864. Honorably mustered out, July 12, 1864. Brig. Gen., Enrolled MO Militia, Sept. 29, 1864. Commanded 1 Military District, Enrolled MO Militia. Commission vacated, March 12, 1865. Battle honors: Siege of Corinth, Chickasaw Bluffs, Arkansas Post, Steele's Bayou Expedition, Vicksburg Campaign.

Born: Dec. 23, 1825 Canonsburg, PA
Died: Aug. 16, 1909 St. Louis, MO
Other Wars: Mexican War (Corporal, Co. K, 5 IN Infantry)
Occupation: Grocer (1860); clerk of county court (1870); superintendent, North St. Louis post office (1880); deputy collector, U.S. Internal Revenue, 1891–93; and bailiff in U.S. courts, 1899–1908
Miscellaneous: Resided St. Louis, MO
Buried: Bellefontaine Cemetery, St. Louis, MO (Blocks 78–79–87–88, Lot 945)
References: Obituary Circular, Whole No. 357, Missouri MOLLUS. Obituary, *St. Louis Post-Dispatch*, Aug. 16, 1909. Pension File and Military Service File, National Archives.

David Crockett Coleman, post-war (Obituary Circular, Whole No. 357, Missouri MOLLUS).

Norman Jay Colman

Colonel, Militia of Central and St. Louis Townships, April 21, 1864. Lieutenant Colonel, 85 Enrolled MO Militia, May 28, 1864. Commission vacated, March 12, 1865.

Born: May 16, 1827, near Richfield Springs, NY
Died: Nov. 3, 1911 On train, near Centralia, MO
Education: Graduated University of Louisville (KY) Law School, 1849
Occupation: Agriculturist and journalist
Offices/Honors: Missouri House of Representatives, 1867–69. Lieutenant Governor of Missouri, 1875–77. U.S. Secretary of Agriculture, 1889.
Miscellaneous: Resided St. Louis, MO
Buried: Bellefontaine Cemetery, St. Louis, MO (Block 3, Lot 4025)
References: Allen Johnson and Dumas Malone, editors. *Dictionary of American Biography*. New York City, NY, 1964. Howard L. Conard, editor. *Encyclopedia of the History of Missouri*. New York, Louisville, and St. Louis, 1901. William Hyde and Howard L. Conard, editors. *Encyclopedia of the History of St. Louis*. New York, Louisville, and St. Louis, 1899. Walter B. Davis and Daniel S. Durrie. *An Illustrated History of Missouri*. St. Louis, MO, 1876. J.

David Crockett Coleman (Mansfield & Cornwell, Photographers, St. Louis, Missouri; author's photograph).

Thomas Scharf. *History of Saint Louis City and County*. Philadelphia, PA, 1883. John W. Leonard, editor. *The Book of St. Louisans*. St. Louis, MO, 1906. "Special Order No. 6, Headquarters First Military District, E.M.M.," *Daily Missouri Republican*, April 22, 1864. Obituary, *St. Louis Post-Dispatch*, Nov. 3, 1911.

Florence M. Cornyn

Surgeon, 1 MO Infantry (3 months), April 26, 1861. Surgeon, 1 MO Infantry (3 years), June 12, 1861. Surgeon, 1 MO Light Artillery, Sept. 1, 1861. Discharged for promotion, Oct. 9, 1862. Colonel, 10 MO Cavalry, Dec. 19, 1862. Commanded Cavalry Brigade, 2 Division, 16 Army Corps, Army of the Tennessee, March 3–June 9, 1863. Commanded 3 Cavalry Brigade, Left Wing, 16 Army Corps Army of the Tennessee, June 9–July 13, 1863. Battle honors: Wilson's Creek, Shiloh, Tuscumbia, Expeditions to Courtland, AL, and Tupelo, MS, (King's Creek), Expedition from Corinth (MS) to Florence (AL), Iuka (July 7, 1863).

Born: Aug. 3, 1829 Bridgeport, OH
Died: Aug. 10, 1863 Corinth, MS (Killed by Lieutenant Colonel William D. Bowen)
Education: M.D., University of New York, 1852
Occupation: Physician
Miscellaneous: Resided St. Louis, MO. Although Lieutenant Colonel Bowen was acquitted by court-martial on the charge of murder, "the homicide being justifiable," he was dismissed, Oct. 14, 1863, when Major Gen. Stephen A. Hurlbut disapproved the findings of the court.

Norman Jay Colman (Walter B. Davis and Daniel S. Durrie. *An Illustrated History of Missouri Comprising Its Early Record, and Civil, Political, and Military History from the First Exploration to the Present Time*. St. Louis, Missouri, 1876).

Norman Jay Colman, post-war (Howard L. Conard, editor. *Encyclopedia of the History of Missouri*. New York, Louisville, and St. Louis, 1901).

Florence M. Cornyn (G.W. Armstead, Artist, Corinth, Mississippi; Wilson's Creek National Battlefield [WICR 11506]).

Florence M. Cornyn (G.W. Armstead, Artist, Corinth, Mississippi; Courtesy James C. Frasca).

Buried: Calvary Cemetery, St. Louis, MO (Section 3, Lot 237)

References: William Hyde and Howard L. Conard, editors. *Encyclopedia of the History of St. Louis*. New York, Louisville, and St. Louis, 1899. Howard L. Conard, editor. *Encyclopedia of the History of Missouri*. New York, Louisville, and St. Louis, 1901. Pension File and Military Service File, National Archives. Charles K. Mills. *Harvest of Barren Regrets: The Army Career of Frederick William Benteen, 1834–1898*. Glendale, CA, 1985. Court-martial Case Files, 1809–1894, File MM-1304, National Archives. Letters Received, Volunteer Service Branch, Adjutant General's Office, File B2186(VS)1863, National Archives. "The Death of Colonel Cornyn," *Daily Missouri Republican*, Aug. 17, 1863. "The Killing of Colonel Cornyn," *Daily Missouri Democrat*, Aug. 19, 1863.

John Frederick Cramer

Captain, Co. A, 3 MO Infantry (3 months), May 27, 1861. Honorably mustered out, Sept. 3, 1861. Lieutenant Colonel, 17 MO Infantry, Dec. 19, 1861. *Colonel*, 17 MO Infantry, July 18, 1863. Battle honors: Carthage (MO), Searcy Landing (AR), Vicksburg Campaign, Chattanooga-Ringgold Campaign (Ringgold Gap).

Born: April 18, 1830, Eschwege, Hesse, Germany

Died: May 2, 1864, Bellefonte, Jackson Co., AL (Committed suicide by shooting himself with a revolver during temporary insanity)

Occupation: Dry goods merchant

Miscellaneous: Resided St. Louis, MO

Buried: Possibly Western Evangelical Lutheran Cemetery, St. Louis, MO (His daughter, Louisa, buried there in Sept. 1867)

References: William Hyde and Howard L. Conard, editors. *Encyclopedia of the History of St. Louis*. New York, Louisville, and St. Louis, 1899. Pension File and Military Service File, National Archives. Obituary, *Daily Missouri Republican*, May 5, 1864. Death notice, *Daily Missouri Democrat*, May 5, 1864.

Manlove Cranor

Colonel, Gentry County Regiment, MO Home Guards, Aug. 1, 1861. Discharged, Oct. 17, 1861. Colonel, 6 MO State Militia (6 months), Oct. 1, 1861. Honorably mustered out, Feb. 13, 1862. Colonel, 31 Enrolled MO Militia, Sept. 11, 1862. Commission vacated, March 12, 1865.

Born: April 28, 1815, Wayne Co., IN

Died: Sept. 24, 1883 Jackson Twp., Gentry Co., MO

Occupation: Farmer and stock raiser

Miscellaneous: Resided Island City and Albany, Jackson Twp., Gentry Co., MO; and Maryville, Nodaway Co., MO, 1876–77

Buried: Cranor Cemetery, Jackson Twp., Gentry Co., MO

References: *The United States Biographical Dictionary and Portrait Gallery of Eminent and Self-Made Men*. Missouri Volume. New York, Chicago, St. Louis, and Kansas City, 1878. Carmeta P. Robertson. *Gentry County, MO, the Civil War, 1861–1865: Fighters & Survivors*. Ozark, MO, 1994. Pension File and Military Service File, National Archives.

John Daniel Crawford

Captain, Co. C, 40 Enrolled MO Militia, Aug. 18, 1862. Temporary service as Captain, Co. K, 5 Provisional Enrolled MO Militia. Colonel, 40 Enrolled MO Militia, June 13, 1864. Commanded Post of Sedalia, MO, Oct. 1864. Commission vacated, March 12, 1865. Battle honors: Price's Missouri Expedition.

Born: March 1, 1838, Pettis Co., MO

Died: Dec. 20, 1908 Sedalia, MO

Education: Attended William Jewell College, Liberty, MO

Occupation: Farmer, stock raiser, and real estate agent

Offices/Honors: Pettis County Recorder, 1871–79. Mayor of Sedalia (MO), 1888–90.

John Daniel Crawford, post-war (*Portrait and Biographical Record of Johnson and Pettis Counties, Missouri.* Chicago, Illinois, 1895).

Miscellaneous: Resided Sedalia, Pettis Co., MO
Buried: Crown Hill Cemetery, Sedalia, MO (Section 7A, Lot 11)
References: Howard L. Conard, editor. *Encyclopedia of the History of Missouri*. New York, Louisville, and St. Louis, 1901. *History of Pettis County, Missouri.* N.p., 1882. *Portrait and Biographical Record of Johnson and Pettis Counties, Missouri.* Chicago, IL, 1895. Obituary, *Missouri Historical Review.* Vol. 3, No. 3 (April 1909). Obituary, *Sedalia Daily Capital*, Dec. 22, 1908.

Thomas L. Crawford

Captain, Co. I, 42 Enrolled MO Militia, Aug. 23, 1862. Colonel, 42 Enrolled MO Militia, Sept. 15, 1862. Brig. Gen., Enrolled MO Militia, Oct. 23, 1862. Commanded 2 Military District, Enrolled MO Militia, Dec. 1863–Jan. 1864. Temporary service as Colonel, 9 Provisional Enrolled MO Militia.
Born: 1828? TN
Died: Prior to 1878
Occupation: Merchant
Miscellaneous: Resided Jefferson City, Cole Co., MO (1850, 1860, and 1870)
Buried: Possibly Woodland-Old City Cemetery, Jefferson City, MO, where his widow, Mary, was buried, March 1, 1880
References: www.ancestry.com.

William Cuddy

Private, Co. D, 3 U.S. Reserve Corps, MO Infantry (3 months), May 8, 1861. Honorably discharged, Aug. 8, 1861. Colonel, 11 Enrolled MO Militia, Sept. 17, 1862. Resigned July 3, 1863.
Born: 1833? England
Died: Jan. 10, 1871 St. Louis, MO
Occupation: Newspaper publisher before war. U.S. Internal Revenue Assessor after war.
Offices/Honors: Surveyor General of Public Lands, District of Illinois and Missouri, 1861–64
Miscellaneous: Resided St. Louis, MO; and Carondelet Twp., St. Louis Co., MO
Buried: Calvary Cemetery, St. Louis, MO (Section 13, Lot 85)
References: Obituary, *Daily Missouri Democrat*, Jan. 11, 1871. Death notice, *Missouri Republican*, Jan. 11, 1871. www.ancestry.com.

Berryman Kenchin Davis

1 Lieutenant, Adjutant, 36 Enrolled MO Militia, Aug. 16, 1862. Colonel, 36 Enrolled MO Militia, Sept. 24, 1863. Commission vacated, March 12, 1865. Major, 43 MO Infantry, Oct. 15, 1864. Taken prisoner, Glasgow, MO, Oct. 15, 1864. Paroled Oct. 16, 1864. Commanded Post of Independence (MO), District of North Missouri, Department of the Missouri, Feb.–March 1865. Commanded 4 Sub-District, District of Central Missouri, Department of the Missouri, April 1865. Honorably mustered out, June 30, 1865. Battle honors: Price's Missouri Expedition (Glasgow).
Born: April 23, 1839, Pettis Co., MO
Died: Nov. 16, 1876 Maryville, MO
Occupation: Lawyer
Miscellaneous: Resided Maryville, Nodaway Co., MO
Buried: Oak Hill Cemetery, Maryville, MO
References: *The History of Nodaway County, Missouri.* St. Joseph, MO, 1882. Obituary, *Nodaway Democrat*, Nov. 23, 1876. Martha L. Cooper. *The Civil War and Nodaway County, Missouri: A Border County in a Border State.* Signal Mountain, TN, 1989. Pension File and Military Service File, National Archives.

John E. Davis

Colonel, 63 Enrolled MO Militia, Nov. 13, 1862. Commission vacated, Oct. 13, 1863.
Born: 1807? VA
Died: Date and place of death unknown
Occupation: Carpenter

Miscellaneous: Resided Steelville, Crawford Co., MO
Buried: Place of burial unknown
References: *History of Franklin, Jefferson, Washington, Crawford & Gasconade Counties, Missouri.* Chicago, IL, 1888. www.ancestry.com.

Henry Charles De Ahna

Colonel, IN Legion, July 22, 1861. Ordered to serve on the staff of Major Gen. John C. Fremont, Department of the West, he was appointed, Aug. 3, 1861, Colonel of the select regiment of infantry known as the Fremont Guard (later renamed the Benton Cadets), MO Infantry. Frustrated by his difficulty in personally accessing Fremont, he violently forced his way past the sentinels at Fremont's headquarters, resulting in his court-martial and dismissal, Sept. 2, 1861, for "conduct unbecoming an officer and a gentleman." Upon review of the case, he was restored to his command, Oct. 7, 1861, when it was decided that the lesser charge of "conduct to the prejudice of good order and military discipline" would have been more appropriate. He was, however, unable to resume command of his regiment due to the appointment of Louis H. Marshall as colonel in his absence. Nominated as Brig. Gen., USV, March 11, 1862, but rejected by the U.S. Senate, April 25, 1862, possibly through the influence of Major Gen. Henry W. Halleck, who commented, in a telegram to Senator Milton S. Latham, "I would rather trust my dinner to a hungry dog than give such a responsible position to a foreign adventurer of this stamp. I have not the least doubt he would take pay on either side and fight on none."
Born: 1823? Bavaria
Died: Oct. 13, 1891 New York City, NY
Other Wars: Lieutenant Colonel of Engineers, Staff of Major Gen. Giuseppe Garibaldi of Italy
Occupation: Civil engineer and U.S. government appointee
Offices/Honors: U.S. Collector of Customs, Sitka, Alaska, 1877. Special timber agent, U.S. General Land Office, 1882–85.
Miscellaneous: Resided Washington, D.C.; New York City, NY; and Carson City, NV
Buried: Cypress Hills National Cemetery, Brooklyn, NY (Officers' Section West, Grave 33)
References: Pension File and Military Service File, National Archives. Obituary, *New York Times*, Oct. 18, 1891. Letters Received, Volunteer Service Branch, Adjutant General's Office, File D122(VS)1862, National Archives. Thomas P. Lowry. *Tarnished Eagles: The Courts-Martial of Fifty Union Colonels and Lieutenant Colonels.* Mechanicsburg, PA, 1997. Pamela Herr and Mary Lee Spence, editors. *The Letters of Jessie Benton Fremont.* Urbana, IL, 1993. David Donald, editor. *Inside Lincoln's Cabinet: The Civil War Diaries of Salmon P. Chase.* New York, London, and Toronto, 1954. Obituary, *St. Louis Republic*, Oct. 15, 1891. Obituary, *Baltimore Sun*, Oct. 24, 1891. "De Ahna's Disgrace," *Daily Illinois State Register*, Oct. 11, 1878. Court-martial Case Files, 1809–1894, File II-408, National Archives. "Report No. 124 (Colonel H.C. De Ahna), June 21, 1864," *Reports of Committees of the House of Representatives, Made During the First Session Thirty-Eighth Congress, 1863–64.* Washington, D.C., 1864.

Henry J. Deal

Colonel, 79 Enrolled MO Militia, June 29, 1863. Commission vacated, March 12, 1865.
Born: Dec. 1, 1829 Oxford, Adams Co., PA
Died: Nov. 19, 1891 Charleston, MO
Occupation: Railroad and levee contractor and farmer
Offices/Honors: Missouri Senate, 1862–68. Missouri House of Representatives, 1877–79, 1881–83.
Miscellaneous: Resided Charleston, Mississippi Co., MO. Name at birth was Henry J. Diehl.
Buried: Oak Grove Cemetery, Charleston, MO (Section 2)

Henry J. Deal (author's photograph).

References: *History of Southeast Missouri.* Chicago, IL, 1888. Robert S. Douglass. *History of Southeast Missouri.* Chicago and New York, 1912. Obituary, *Charleston Daily Enterprise,* Nov. 21, 1891. Betty F. Powell. *History of Mississippi County, Missouri, Beginning Through 1972.* Independence, MO, 1975. Harry A. Diehl. *The Diehl-Deal-Dill-Dale Families of America. Volume 1. Diehl Families of York and Adams Counties, Pennsylvania.* Wilmington, DE, 1989. Walter B. Stevens. *Missouri: The Center State, 1821–1915.* Chicago and St. Louis, 1915. Chancy R. Barns, editor. *The Commonwealth of Missouri: A Centennial Record.* St. Louis, MO, 1877. *History of Cumberland and Adams Counties, Pennsylvania.* Chicago, IL, 1886.

Benjamin Devor Dean

Sergeant, Co. B, Franklin County Regiment, MO Home Guards, June 11, 1861. Discharged Sept. 11, 1861. Captain, Co. F, 26 MO Infantry, Dec. 17, 1861. GSW right ankle, Iuka, MS, Sept. 19, 1862. Colonel, 26 MO Infantry, May 28, 1863. Commanded 3 Brigade, 7 Division, 17 Army Corps, Army of the Tennessee, July 27–Aug. 28, 1863. Commanded 3 Brigade, 2 Division, 17 Army Corps, Army of the Tennessee, Nov. 25, 1863. Commanded 3 Brigade, 3 Division, 15 Army Corps, Army of the Tennessee, May 15–31, 1864 and July 25–Aug. 6, 1864. Commanded Post of Kingston, GA, July–Oct. 1864. Honorably mustered out, Jan. 9, 1865. Battle honors: Iuka, Vicksburg Campaign, Chattanooga-Ringgold Campaign (Missionary Ridge), Atlanta Campaign, Savannah Campaign.

Born: Oct. 7, 1828 Greenville, OH
Died: Nov. 2, 1908 Lamar, MO
Occupation: Dentist, clothing merchant, and farmer
Offices/Honors: Franklin County (MO) Treasurer, 1872–76
Miscellaneous: Resided Union, Franklin Co., MO, 1865–77; Sedalia, Pettis Co., MO, 1877–88; Lebanon, Laclede Co., MO, 1888–91; and Lamar, Barton Co., MO, 1891–1908
Buried: Lake Cemetery, Lamar, MO
References: Benjamin D. Dean. *Recollections of the 26th Missouri Infantry in the War for the Union.* Lamar, MO, 1892. *History of Pettis County, Missouri.* N.p., 1882. Walter B. Davis and Daniel S. Durrie. *An Illustrated History of Missouri.* St. Louis, MO, 1876. Obituary, *Lamar Democrat,* Nov. 5, 1908. Pension File and Military Service File, National Archives.

Benjamin Devor Dean (A.J. Fox, Artist, Cor. Fourth and Olive Sts., St, Louis, Missouri; Wilson's Creek National Battlefield [WICR 11660]).

Benjamin Devor Dean, post-war (Walter B. Davis and Daniel S. Durrie. *An Illustrated History of Missouri Comprising Its Early Record, and Civil, Political, and Military History from the First Exploration to the Present Time.* St. Louis, Missouri, 1876).

Francis Christopher Deimling

Private, Co. K, 3 U.S. Reserve Corps, MO Infantry (3 months), May 8, 1861. Discharged Aug. 8, 1861. 1 Lieutenant, Adjutant, 10 MO Infantry, Aug. 15, 1861. Major, 10 MO Infantry, Oct. 27, 1862. Colonel, 10 MO Infantry, June 11, 1863. Commanded 2 Brigade, 2 Division, 17 Army Corps, Army of the Tennessee, Nov. 25, 1863. Honorably mustered out, Aug. 24, 1864. Battle honors: Iuka, Corinth, Raymond, Jackson, Champion's Hill, Vicksburg Campaign, Chattanooga-Ringgold Campaign (Missionary Ridge).

Born: Sept. 13, 1835 Philadelphia, PA
Died: Jan. 2, 1887 Virginia City, MT
Education: Attended Philadelphia Central High School. Graduated University of Pennsylvania Law School, Philadelphia, PA, 1857.
Occupation: Lawyer
Offices/Honors: Postmaster, Virginia City, MT, 1872–80
Miscellaneous: Resided Philadelphia, PA, to 1858; St. Louis, MO, 1858–65; and Virginia City, Madison Co., MT, 1865–87
Buried: Virginia City Cemetery, Virginia City, MT

Francis Christopher Deimling, post-war (USAMHI [RG641S-MOLLUS-PA4.5]).

References: *Report of the Proceedings of the Society of the Army of the Tennessee, at the Twentieth Meeting.* Cincinnati, OH, 1893. Pension File and Military Service File, National Archives. Marcus O. Frost. *Regimental History of the Tenth Missouri Volunteer Infantry.* Topeka, KS, 1892. W.J. Maxwell, compiler. *General Alumni Catalogue of the University of Pennsylvania.* Philadelphia, PA, 1917. Records of the Commandery of Pennsylvania, MOLLUS, 1865–1935, Vol. 16, Microfilm Series LM047, Record Group 200, National Archives. *Pioneer Trails and Trials: Madison County, 1863–1920.* Great Falls, MT, 1976.

John Bardorman de Narcy

Lieutenant Colonel, 13 Enrolled MO Militia, Sept. 24, 1862. Colonel, 13 Enrolled MO Militia, July 11, 1864. Dismissed Dec. 29, 1864, for "conduct unbecoming an officer, using seditious language, and cowardice." Upon further examination of the evidence in the case, Governor Thomas C. Fletcher revoked his dismissal, Feb. 27, 1865. Battle honors: Price's Missouri Expedition.

Born: 1812? France
Died: Sept. 21, 1869 St. Louis, MO
Occupation: Chemist and varnish manufacturer
Miscellaneous: Resided St. Louis, MO

Francis Christopher Deimling (F. Gutekunst, Photographer, 704 & 706 Arch St., Philadelphia, Pennsylvania; Courtesy Paul J. Brzozowski).

Buried: Holy Trinity Catholic Cemetery (no longer in existence), St. Louis, MO

References: Obituary, *Daily Missouri Democrat*, Sept. 23, 1869. Obituary, *Missouri Republican*, Sept. 23, 1869. "General Order No. 26, Headquarters 1st Military District, E.M.M.," *Daily Missouri Republican*, Jan. 1, 1865. "Communication from Officers of the 13th E.M.M.," *Daily Missouri Democrat*, April 4, 1865. *The Miscellaneous Documents of the House of Representatives for the First Session of the Fortieth Congress, 1867*. Washington, D.C., 1868. www.ancestry.com.

Joseph Beeler Douglass

Colonel, 61 Enrolled MO Militia, Oct. 21, 1862. Colonel, 1 Provisional Enrolled MO Militia, March 16, 1863. Brig. Gen., Enrolled MO Militia, Sept. 1, 1863. Commanded 8 Military District, Enrolled MO Militia. Commission vacated, March 12, 1865. Battle honors: Price's Missouri Expedition.

Born: Nov. 12, 1819 Boyle Co., KY

Died: Aug. 20, 1898 Columbia, MO

Occupation: Farmer, county sheriff, and county clerk before war. Engaged in nursery business after war, also acting as general agent of the horticultural department, University of Missouri.

Offices/Honors: Sheriff, Boone Co., MO, 1850–54. Missouri House of Representatives, 1856–58. County Clerk, Boone Co., MO, 1860–67.

Joseph Beeler Douglass and his wife, Nancy (USAMHI, uncataloged image)

Miscellaneous: Resided Columbia, Boone Co., MO

Buried: Columbia Cemetery, Columbia, MO (Old Cemetery, Lot 4)

References: *History of Boone County, Missouri*. St. Louis, MO, 1882. Obituary, *Missouri Herald*, Aug. 26, 1898. Pension File, National Archives.

John Van Deusen DuBois

1 Lieutenant, U.S. Mounted Riflemen, May 13, 1861. 1 Lieutenant, 3 U.S. Cavalry, Aug. 3, 1861. Major, 1 MO Light Artillery, Sept. 1, 1861. Colonel, Additional ADC, USV, Feb. 19, 1862. Captain, 3 U.S. Cavalry, Feb. 21, 1862. Chief of Artillery, Staff of Major Gen. Henry W. Halleck, Department of the Missouri, Feb. 21–March 11, 1862. Chief of Artillery, Staff of Major Gen. Henry W. Halleck, Department of the Mississippi, March 11–July 11, 1862. Colonel, 1 MO Light Artillery, Aug. 7, 1862. Resigned Oct. 14, 1862. Commanded 3 Brigade, 2 Division, Army of West Tennessee, Oct. 4–14, 1862. Nominated Brig. Gen., USV, Jan. 19, 1863, to rank from Nov. 29, 1862. Nomination as Brig. Gen., USV, withdrawn Feb. 12, 1863. Chief of

Joseph Beeler Douglass (courtesy Robert J. Younger).

Cavalry, Staff of Major Gen. John M. Schofield and Major Gen. William S. Rosecrans, Department of the Missouri, Sept. 29, 1863–Sept. 25, 1864. Chief of Staff, Staff of Major Gen. William S. Rosecrans, Department of the Missouri, Sept. 25–Dec. 7, 1864. Inspector General, Staff of Major Gen. Grenville M. Dodge, Department of the Missouri, Dec. 9, 1864–Aug. 5, 1865. Inspector General, Staff of Major Gen. John Pope, Department of the Missouri, Aug. 5, 1865–Feb. 9, 1866. He initially accepted brevets of captain, major, and lieutenant colonel, but becoming aware of the post-war proliferation of brevets, he withdrew his acceptance of these brevets, July 5, 1867, dissatisfied with the inadequate recognition of his war-time services as compared with others. Battle honors: Wilson's Creek, Farmington, Iuka, Corinth, Price's Missouri Expedition.

Born: Aug. 7, 1833 Livingston, Columbia Co., NY
Died: July 31, 1879, Hudson, NY
Education: Graduated U.S. Military Academy, West Point, NY, 1855
Occupation: Regular Army (Major, 3 U.S. Cavalry, retired May 17, 1876)
Miscellaneous: Resided Hudson, Columbia Co., NY
Buried: Rhinebeck Cemetery, Rhinebeck, NY

References: *Eleventh Annual Reunion of the Association of the Graduates of the U.S. Military Academy at West Point, NY.* East Saginaw, MI, 1880. George W. Cullum. *Biographical Register of the Officers and Graduates of the U.S. Military Academy.* Third Edition. Boston, MA, 1891. William Heidgerd. *The American Descendants of Chretien Du Bois of Wicres, France.* Part 7. New Paltz, NY, 1973. Jared C. Lobdell, editor, "The Civil War Journal and Letters of Colonel John Van Deusen Du Bois, April 12, 1861 to October 16, 1862," *Missouri Historical Review*, Vol. 60, No. 4 (July 1966) and Vol. 61, No. 1 (Oct. 1966). Letters Received, Commission Branch, Adjutant General's Office, File R390(CB)1870, National Archives. Military Service File, National Archives. Obituary, *New York Times*, Aug. 1, 1879. Obituary, Circular No. 8, Series of 1879–80, New York MOLLUS. Obituary, *Poughkeepsie Daily Eagle,* Aug. 1, 1879.

Louis Duestrow

1 Lieutenant, Co. I, 3 U.S. Reserve Corps, MO Infantry (3 months), May 8, 1861. Honorably mustered out, Aug. 18, 1861. Major, 5 Enrolled MO Militia, Oct. 31, 1862. Colonel, 5 Enrolled MO Militia, June 1, 1864. Commission vacated, March 12, 1865.

Born: July 16, 1832, Mayence, Germany

John Van Deusen DuBois (Nichols & Bro's Photographic Gallery, No. 60 N. 4th Street, St. Louis, Missouri; courtesy Marcus S. McLemore).

Louis Duestrow, post-war (*American Biography, A New Cyclopedia.* Vol. 10. New York City, New York, 1922).

Died: March 7, 1892, St. Louis, MO
Occupation: Fire insurance executive
Miscellaneous: Resided St. Louis, MO
Buried: Bellefontaine Cemetery, St. Louis, MO (Blocks 116–117, Lot 1570)
References: William Hyde and Howard L. Conard, editors. *Encyclopedia of the History of St. Louis.* New York, Louisville, and St. Louis, 1899. *American Biography: A New Cyclopedia.* Vol. 10. New York City, NY, 1922. Obituary, *St. Louis Post-Dispatch*, March 8, 1892. Military Service File, National Archives.

James Fowler Dwight

Battalion Adjutant, 4 MO Cavalry, Sept. 25, 1861. 1 Lieutenant, Adjutant, 4 MO Cavalry, Jan. 1, 1862. Captain, Co. F, 4 MO Cavalry, Feb. 21, 1862. Major, 4 MO Cavalry, Oct. 14, 1862. Resigned Nov. 4, 1862, since "I desire that Captain (Benjamin C.) Ludlow, who is a personal friend of mine and a most excellent soldier, should take the place which I wish to vacate." Captain, Co. F, 4 MO Cavalry, Nov. 6, 1862. Assistant Provost Marshal General, Staff of Major Gen. Samuel R. Curtis, Department of the Missouri, Nov. 1862–June 1863. Assistant Inspector General, Staff of Major Gen. John M. Schofield and Major Gen. William S. Rosecrans, Department of the Missouri, June 1863–April 1864. Major, 11 MO Cavalry, April 8, 1864. Acting Provost Marshal, Staff of Brig. Gen. Clinton B. Fisk, District of North Missouri, Department of the Missouri, April–June 1864. Acting Assistant Inspector General and Chief of Staff, Staff of Brig. Gen. Eugene A. Carr, District of Little Rock, Department of Arkansas, July–Oct. 1864. Acting Assistant Inspector General, Staff of Brig. Gen. Joseph R. West, Cavalry Division, 7 Army Corps, Department of Arkansas, Jan.–Feb. 1865. Lieutenant Colonel, 11 MO Cavalry, March 14, 1865. *Colonel*, 11 MO Cavalry, May 9, 1865. Honorably mustered out, July 27, 1865.

Born: Jan. 30, 1830 Westfield, MA
Died: Sept. 22, 1899 Stockbridge, MA
Education: Attended Williston Seminary, Easthampton, MA. Graduated Williams College, Williamstown, MA, 1849. Attended Harvard University Law School, Cambridge, MA.
Occupation: Lawyer
Miscellaneous: Resided New York City, NY; and Stockbridge, Berkshire Co., MA. First cousin of Colonel Charles C. Dwight (160 NY Infantry).
Buried: Stockbridge Cemetery, Stockbridge, MA

James Fowler Dwight (Massachusetts MOLLUS Collection, USAMHI [Vol. 130, p. 6663L]).

Captain James Fowler Dwight (left) and Captain Benjamin Chambers Ludlow (right) (courtesy Henry Deeks).

References: Benjamin W. Dwight. *The History of the Descendants of John Dwight of Dedham, Massachusetts.* New York City, NY, 1874. L. Hasbrouck von Sahler, "The Dwights of Stockbridge," *The New York Genealogical and Biographical Record,* Vol. 33, No. 1 (Jan. 1902). Obituary, *New York Times,* Sept. 23, 1899. Benjamin W. Dwight. *The History of the Descendants of Elder John Strong of Northampton, Massachusetts.* Albany, NY, 1871. Letters Received, Volunteer Service Branch, Adjutant General's Office, File D209(VS)1865, National Archives. Military Service File, National Archives. Obituary Circular, Whole No. 221, District of Columbia MOLLUS.

David Patterson Dyer

Private, Co. B, Pike County Regiment, MO Home Guards, June 17, 1861. Honorably mustered out, Sept. 2, 1861. Lieutenant Colonel, 49 MO Infantry, Sept. 20, 1864. Provost Marshal, District of North Missouri, Department of the Missouri, Nov. 10–23, 1864. Colonel, 49 MO Infantry, Feb. 9, 1865. Honorably mustered out, Aug. 5, 1865. Battle honors: Price's Missouri Expedition, Mobile Campaign.

Born: Feb. 12, 1838 Henry Co., VA
Died: April 29, 1924, St. Louis, MO
Education: Attended St. Charles (MO) College

David Patterson Dyer (pre-war) (courtesy Missouri Historical Society, St. Louis [P0249-0991]).

David Patterson Dyer, U.S. House of Representatives, 1869 (Brady's National Photographic Portrait Galleries, 627 Pennsylvania Avenue, Washington, D.C.; author's photograph).

Occupation: Lawyer and judge
Offices/Honors: Missouri House of Representatives, 1862–65. U.S. House of Representatives, 1869–71. Judge, U.S. District Court, Eastern District of Missouri, 1907–24.
Miscellaneous: Resided Louisiana, Pike Co., MO, to 1875; and St. Louis, MO, after 1875
Buried: Bellefontaine Cemetery, St. Louis, MO (Block 269, Lot 5549)
References: David P. Dyer. *Autobiography and Reminiscences.* St. Louis, MO, 1922. Obituary, *St. Louis Post-Dispatch,* April 29, 1924. *The United States Biographical Dictionary and Portrait Gallery of Eminent and Self-Made Men.* Missouri Volume. New York, Chicago, St. Louis, and Kansas City, 1878. *The History of Pike County, Missouri.* Des Moines, IA, 1883. J. Thomas Scharf. *History of Saint Louis City and County.* Philadelphia, PA, 1883. William Horatio Barnes. *History of Congress. The Forty-First Congress of the United States, 1869–1871.* New York City, NY, 1872. Pension File and Military Service File, National Archives. Clayton Keith. *Military History of Pike County, Missouri.* Louisiana, MO, 1915. Letters Received, Volunteer Service Branch, Adjutant General's Office, File H2771(VS)1864, National Archives. Letters Received, Commission Branch, Adjutant General's Office, File D791(CB)1865, National Archives.

James Douglas Eads

Colonel, Johnson County Regiment, MO Home Guards, May 1, 1861. Discharged Oct. 30, 1861. Lieutenant Colonel, 27 MO Mounted Infantry, Oct. 30, 1861. Honorably mustered out, Jan. 27, 1862. Captain, Co. M, 1 MO State Militia Cavalry, Jan. 5, 1864. Commanded Post of Lexington (MO), Department of the Missouri, Oct. 1864. Sentenced, March 17, 1865, to be dismissed upon charges of cowardice and misbehavior before the enemy, he was instead returned to duty when Brig. Gen. John McNeil disapproved the sentence with the remark, "The record not only shows a perfect failure of evidence to sustain the charges…, but gives to the whole case the appearance of an attempt to persecute and blast the character of a brave, efficient, and valuable officer." Honorably mustered out, July 12, 1865. Battle honors: Lexington, Kingsville, Price's Missouri Expedition (Lexington).

Born: Sept. 14, 1813 Monroe Co., VA (now WV)
Died: June 10, 1871, Warrensburg, MO
Other Wars: Mexican War (Private, Stapp's Independent Co., IL Mounted Volunteers)
Occupation: Physician and newspaper editor before war. Hotel proprietor after war.
Offices/Honors: Iowa Superintendent of Public Instruction, 1854–56 (removed from office due to improper handling of school funds)
Miscellaneous: Resided Macomb, McDonough Co., IL; Fort Madison, Lee Co., IA; St. Louis, MO; and Warrensburg, Johnson Co., MO
Buried: Sunset Hill Cemetery, Warrensburg, MO
References: Obituary, *Missouri Republican*, June 13, 1871. Pension File and Military Service File, National Archives. Obituary, *Warrensburg Standard*, June 15, 1871. George S. Grover, "Civil War in Missouri," *Missouri Historical Review*, Vol. 8, No. 1 (Oct. 1913). Letters Received, Volunteer Service Branch, Adjutant General's Office, Files M79(VS)1862 and E410(VS)1863, National Archives. *The History of Johnson County, Missouri*. Kansas City, MO, 1881. Benjamin F. Gue. *History of Iowa from the Earliest Times to the Beginning of the Twentieth Century*. New York City, NY, 1903. Court-martial Case Files, 1809–1894, File MM-1781, National Archives.

Reuben Jacob Eberman

Colonel, 62 Enrolled MO Militia, Sept. 3, 1862. Commission vacated, March 12, 1865.
Born: Nov. 27, 1824 Lancaster, PA
Died: Sept. 15, 1903 Macon, MO
Occupation: Lawyer
Miscellaneous: Resided Wooster, Wayne Co., OH, to 1859; and Macon, Macon Co., MO, after 1859
Buried: Oakwood Cemetery, Macon, MO
References: *History of Randolph and Macon Counties, Missouri*. St. Louis, MO, 1884. *The Bench and Bar of St. Louis, Kansas City, Jefferson City, and Other Missouri Cities*. St. Louis and Chicago, 1884. Pension File, National Archives. Obituary, *Macon Republican*, Sept. 19, 1903.

William Brewer Edwards

Colonel, Dallas County Regiment, MO Home Guards, June 24, 1861. Discharged Aug. 11, 1861.
Born: April 8, 1810, Robertson Co., TN
Died: Aug. 19, 1878 Newtonia, MO
Other Wars: Indian Wars (Sergeant, Co. A, 1 U.S. Dragoons, 1833–35)
Occupation: Farmer and mill operator
Offices/Honors: Missouri House of Representatives, 1842–46, 1856–60. Missouri Senate, 1862–64.
Miscellaneous: Resided Buffalo, Dallas Co., MO; Garnett, Anderson Co., KS; and Newtonia, Newton Co., MO
Buried: Possibly Village Cemetery, Newtonia, MO
References: Pension File, National Archives. Obituary, *Neosho Times*, Aug. 29, 1878. *History of Laclede, Camden, Dallas, Webster, Wright, Texas, Pulaski, Phelps and Dent Counties, Missouri*. Chicago, IL, 1889.

Calvin A. Ellis

Colonel, 1 MO Cavalry, Sept. 6, 1861. Acting upon numerous allegations against Ellis, including absence without proper authority, giving of illegal and unauthorized orders, appropriating captured horses and other government property to his own use, falsification of muster rolls, and "keeping in camp a woman (his wife, Mary, known as Madame Blanche, a fortune teller) of reputed bad character, who was continually insulting and abusing officers who had too much self-respect to make court to her," Major Gen. Henry W. Halleck, with approval from the Assistant Secretary of War, mustered Ellis out of service, effective April 2, 1862, thereby relieving the army of a "most inefficient and troublesome, if not guilty, man." Battle honors: Pea Ridge.

Calvin A. Ellis (Charles D. Fredricks & Co., "Specialite," 587 Broadway, New York; courtesy Henry Deeks).

Born: 1823? or 1827? Tioga Co., PA
Died: Aug. 11, 1895 (according to grave marker)
Other Wars: Enlisted Co. E, 2 U.S. Artillery, Jan. 1, 1845. Deserted March 15, 1845. Later saw service as Texas Ranger (according to July 1861 letter of recommendation urging acceptance of his regiment).
Occupation: Railroad overseer
Miscellaneous: Resided Cincinnati, OH, before war; Chester, Middlesex Co., CT; Marysville, Marshall Co., KS; and Bremen, Marshall Co., KS, after war. See (Mary A. Gardner Holland, compiler. *Our Army Nurses*. Boston, MA, 1895) for an account by Mary A. Ellis of her services in "raising the regiment and caring for the sick."
Buried: Marysville City Cemetery, Marysville, KS (Section G, Block 8, Lot 11)
References: Pension File and Military Service File, National Archives. Letters Received, Volunteer Service Branch, Adjutant General's Office, File M896(VS)1862, National Archives. Letters Received by the Secretary of War, Irregular Series, File E31(July 1861), National Archives. Michael E. Banasik, editor. *Missouri in 1861: The Civil War Letters of Franc B. Wilkie, Newspaper Correspondent*. Iowa City, IA, 2001.

Obituary of Mary A. Ellis, *Indianapolis News*, Oct. 28, 1897.

John Wesley Emerson

Colonel, 68 Enrolled MO Militia, March 21, 1864. Commission vacated, March 12, 1865. Private, Co. E, 47 MO Infantry, Sept. 5, 1864. Major, 47 MO Infantry, Oct. 10, 1864. Honorably mustered out, April 14, 1865. Battle honors: Price's Missouri Expedition (Pilot Knob).
Born: July 26, 1830, Pepperell, MA
Died: June 20, 1899, Ironton, MO
Education: Graduated University of Michigan Law School, Ann Arbor, MI, 1862
Occupation: Lawyer, judge, and capitalist
Offices/Honors: Circuit Court Judge, 1863. U.S. Marshal, Eastern District of MO, 1887–90
Miscellaneous: Resided Ironton, Iron Co., MO. Founder of the Emerson Electric Company. His fascination with General U.S. Grant and his early-war connection with Ironton resulted in his "Grant's Life in the West and His Mississippi Valley Campaigns," published serially by *The Midland Monthly*, beginning in October 1896.
Buried: Masonic Cemetery, Ironton, MO

John Wesley Emerson, post-war (courtesy Missouri Historical Society, St. Louis [P0233-2627]).

References: *Past and Present: A History of Iron County, Missouri, 1857–1994.* Marceline, MO, 1995. Lawrence O. Christensen, William E. Foley, Gary R. Kremer, and Kenneth H. Winn, editors. *Dictionary of Missouri Biography.* Columbia, MO, 1999. Obituary Circular, Whole No. 195, Missouri MOLLUS. *History of Southeast Missouri.* Chicago, IL, 1888. Howard L. Conard, editor. *Encyclopedia of the History of Missouri.* New York, Louisville, and St. Louis, 1901. Obituary, *Iron County Register*, June 22, 1899. Military Service File, National Archives. Letters Received, Volunteer Service Branch, Adjutant General's Office, File M1434(VS)1864, National Archives.

Benjamin Emmons, Jr.

Colonel, 27 Enrolled MO Militia, Sept. 20, 1862. Resigned Aug. 17, 1863.
  Born: 1810 Cottleville, St. Charles Co., MO
  Died: Aug. 31, 1885 Leadville, CO
  Occupation: Lawyer
  Offices/Honors: Circuit Court Clerk, 1848–65 and 1883–85. Postmaster, St. Charles, MO, 1881–83.
  Miscellaneous: Resided St. Charles, St. Charles Co., MO
  Buried: St. Charles Borromeo Catholic Cemetery, St. Charles, MO
  References: *Portrait and Biographical Record of St. Charles, Lincoln and Warren Counties, Missouri.* Chicago, IL, 1895. *History of St. Charles, Montgomery and Warren Counties, Missouri.* St. Louis, MO, 1885. Obituary, *St. Charles Cosmos*, Sept. 2 and 9, 1885.

William Henry Evens

Captain, Co. C, 31 MO Infantry, Aug. 28, 1862. Shell wound right shoulder, Chickasaw Bluffs, MS, Dec. 29, 1862. Suffering from chronic diarrhea, he resigned Aug. 10, 1863, since "I have every reason to believe … that I will not be able to recover my health in this climate." Captain, Co. F, 32 Enrolled MO Militia, May 18, 1864. Colonel, 32 Enrolled MO Militia, Oct. 7, 1864. Commission vacated, March 12, 1865. Battle honors: Chickasaw Bluffs, Vicksburg Campaign.
  Born: Dec. 11, 1839 Washington Co., MO
  Died: Dec. 18, 1934 Festus, MO
  Occupation: Clerk before war. Lumber merchant and flour miller after war.
  Offices/Honors: Missouri House of Representatives, 1911–13 and 1915–21

William Henry Evens, post-war (John L. Sullivan, compiler. *Official Manual of the State of Missouri for the Years 1919-1920.* Jefferson City, Missouri, 1920).

  Miscellaneous: Resided Hopewell, Washington Co., MO; and Festus, Jefferson Co., MO. Brother-in-law of Colonel Philip R. Van Frank (32 Enrolled MO Militia).
  Buried: Hopewell Cemetery, Hopewell, MO
  References: Obituary, *Potosi Independent-Journal*, Dec. 27, 1934. Pension File and Military Service File, National Archives. *History of Franklin, Jefferson, Washington, Crawford and Gasconade Counties, Missouri.* Chicago, IL, 1888. John L. Sullivan, compiler. *Official Manual of the State of Missouri for the Years 1919–1920.* Jefferson City, MO, 1920. Gary L. Scheel. *Rain, Mud & Swamps: 31st Missouri Volunteer Infantry Regiment: Marching Through the South During the Civil War with General William T. Sherman.* Pacific, MO, 1998.

Thomas James Clark Fagg

Private, Co. A, Pike County Regiment, MO Home Guards, June 12, 1861. Discharged Sept. 3, 1861. Colonel, 5 MO State Militia (6 months), Sept. 4, 1861. Honorably mustered out, Feb. 5, 1862.
  Born: July 15, 1822, Albemarle Co., VA
  Died: Oct. 26, 1914 St. Louis, MO

Thomas James Clark Fagg, post-war (*The Illinois College Alumni Fund Association: Book of Memorial Memberships.* **Centennial Edition, 1829-1929. Jacksonville, Illinois, 1929**).

Education: Graduated Illinois College, Jacksonville, IL, 1842
Occupation: Lawyer and judge
Offices/Honors: Missouri House of Representatives, 1854–56 and 1858–60. Circuit Court Judge, 1862–66. Judge, Missouri Supreme Court, 1866–69, described as "a man of some learning, more native talent, and an immense capacity for yawning and whittling." Postmaster, Louisiana, MO, 1898–1909.
Miscellaneous: Resided Louisiana, Pike Co., MO; and St. Louis, MO
Buried: Riverview Cemetery, Louisiana, MO (Old Cemetery, Lot 135)
References: Howard L. Conard, editor. *Encyclopedia of the History of Missouri.* New York, Louisville, and St. Louis, 1901. *Portrait and Biographical Record of Marion, Ralls and Pike Counties, Missouri.* Chicago, IL, 1895. *The History of Pike County, Missouri.* Des Moines, IA, 1883. *The Illinois College Alumni Fund Association: Book of Memorial Memberships.* Centennial Edition, 1829–1929. Jacksonville, IL, 1929. *History of Lincoln County, Missouri, From the Earliest Time to the Present.* Chicago, IL, 1888. Clayton Keith. *Military History of Pike County, Missouri.* Louisiana, MO, 1915. Obituary, *St. Louis Post-Dispatch*, Oct. 27, 1914. "Successor to Judge Lovelace," *Daily Missouri Republican,* Oct. 17, 1866. "Partners of Many Years," *St. Louis Globe-Democrat,* Nov. 13, 1902.

William P. Fenn

Colonel, 1 Enrolled MO Militia, Oct. 11, 1862. Commission vacated, March 12, 1865. Battle honors: Price's Missouri Expedition.
Born: 1818? OH
Died: March 27, 1873, St. Louis, MO
Occupation: Farmer and dairyman before war. Lime manufacturer after war.
Offices/Honors: Missouri House of Representatives, 1864–66. Chief of Metropolitan Police, St. Louis, MO, 1866–68.
Miscellaneous: Resided Carondelet, St. Louis Co., MO; and St. Louis, MO
Buried: Bellefontaine Cemetery, St. Louis, MO (Block 73, Lot 523, unmarked)
References: Obituary, *Daily Missouri Democrat,* March 28, 1873. Allen E. Wagner. *Good Order and Safety: A History of the St. Louis Metropolitan Police, 1861–1906.* St. Louis, MO, 2008. Death notice, *Missouri Republican,* March 28, 1873. www.ancestry.com.

Henry Flad

Private, Co. F, 3 U.S. Reserve Corps, MO Infantry (3 months), June 15, 1861. Honorably mustered out, Aug. 17, 1861. Captain, Co. B, Engineer Regiment of the West, Nov. 12, 1861. Major, Engineer Regiment of the West, Nov. 17, 1862. Lieutenant Colonel, Engineer Regiment of the West, July 30, 1863. Colonel, Engineer Regiment of the West, Oct. 17, 1863. Designation of regiment changed to 1 MO Engineers upon consolidation with 25 MO Infantry, Dec. 28, 1863. Honorably mustered out, Nov. 18, 1864. Battle honors: Island No. 10, Vicksburg Campaign.
Born: July 30, 1824, Rennhoff, near Heidelberg, Baden, Germany
Died: June 20, 1898, Pittsburgh, PA
Education: Graduated University of Munich (Germany), 1846
Other Wars: Commanded company of engineers during German Revolution of 1848
Occupation: Civil engineer and inventor
Miscellaneous: Resided Arcadia, Iron Co., MO, before war; and St. Louis, MO, after war. Collaborated with James B. Eads in the construction of the celebrated Eads bridge across the Mississippi River, 1868–74.

Henry Flad (Morse's Gallery of the Cumberland, 25 Cedar Street, Opposite the Commercial Hotel, Nashville, Tennessee; Henry Flad Papers Collection, circa 1855-1978, Special Collections and Archives, Southeast Missouri State University).

Henry Flad, post-war (Courtesy Missouri Historical Society, St. Louis [N37216]).

Buried: Originally Hillcrest Abbey Mausoleum, St. Louis, MO (Tier 1, Niche 19). Cremains removed, Oct. 13, 1920, to Bellefontaine Cemetery, St. Louis, MO (Blocks 54–194, Lot 5547).

References: Allen Johnson and Dumas Malone, editors. *Dictionary of American Biography*. New York City, NY, 1964. Obituary Circular, Whole No. 182, Missouri MOLLUS. William Hyde and Howard L. Conard, editors. *Encyclopedia of the History of St. Louis*. New York, Louisville, and St. Louis, 1899. Obituary, *St. Louis Post-Dispatch*, June 21, 1898. William A. Neal. *An Illustrated History of the Missouri Engineer and the 25th Infantry Regiments*. Chicago, IL, 1889. Pension File and Military Service File, National Archives. J. Thomas Scharf. *History of Saint Louis City and County*. Philadelphia, PA, 1883. Adolf E. Zucker, editor. *The Forty-Eighters: Political Refugees of the German Revolution of 1848*. New York City, NY, 1950. Douglas Niermeyer, "Colonel Henry Flad, 1st MO Eng. USV," http://home.usmo.com/~momollus/CiCmtg/Flad.htm.

Matthew Martin Flesh

Captain, Co. I, 42 Enrolled MO Militia, Sept. 22, 1862. Temporary service as Captain, Co. E, 9 Provisional Enrolled MO Militia. Colonel, 42 Enrolled MO Militia, April 30, 1864. Commission vacated, March 12, 1865.

Born: March 20, 1835, Prussia
Died: Jan. 1, 1904 St. Louis, MO

Henry Flad (seated center, with fellow soldiers) (Peplow & Balch, Artists, Star Gallery, 221 Main St., Memphis, Tennessee; Henry Flad Papers Collection, circa 1855-1978, Special Collections and Archives, Southeast Missouri State University).

Occupation: Sign and house painter
Miscellaneous: Resided Jefferson City, Cole Co., MO, before war; and St. Louis, MO, after war
Buried: Bellefontaine Cemetery, St. Louis, MO (Block 11, Lot 3846)
References: Obituary, *St. Louis Republic*, Jan. 2, 1904. Obituary, *St. Louis Globe-Democrat*, Jan. 2, 1904. Obituary, *St. Louis Post-Dispatch*, Jan. 2, 1904. www.ancestry.com.

William Forbes

Captain, Co. E, 22 MO Infantry, Dec. 1, 1861. Captain, Co. K, 10 MO Infantry, July 20, 1862. GSW right shoulder, Corinth, MS, Oct. 4, 1862. Resigned Aug. 7, 1863, since "what property I possess in real estate is in danger of being lost without my immediate personal attention." Colonel, 42 MO Infantry, Nov. 2, 1864. Commanded Post of Fort Donelson (TN), District of Tennessee, Department of the Cumberland, Dec. 1864. Commanded Post of Tullahoma (TN), District of Tennessee, Department of the Cumberland, Jan.–March 1865. Honorably mustered out, March 22, 1865. Battle honors: Corinth, Price's Missouri Expedition.
Born: Sept. 22, 1827 Camden, NJ
Died: July 28, 1882, Macon, MO
Occupation: Carpenter and builder
Offices/Honors: Sheriff, Macon County, MO, 1866–68. Postmaster, Macon, MO, 1870–73.

William Forbes (George Wells, Photographer, Rollins Street, Macon, Missouri; Roger D. Hunt Collection, USAMHI [RG98S-CWP160.60]).

Miscellaneous: Resided Callao, Macon Co., MO, before war; and Macon, Macon Co., MO, after war
Buried: Oakwood Cemetery, Macon, MO
References: Obituary, *Macon Republican*, Aug. 3, 1882. Pension File and Military Service File, National Archives. *History of Randolph and Macon Counties, Missouri*. St. Louis, MO, 1884. Marcus O. Frost. *Regimental History of the Tenth Missouri Volunteer Infantry*. Topeka, KS, 1892.

John Daniel Foster

Authorized as colonel by Major Gen. John C. Fremont, Aug. 26, 1861, to raise 22 MO Infantry. *Lieutenant Colonel*, 22 MO Infantry, Dec. 28, 1861. Lieutenant Colonel, 10 MO Infantry, July 21, 1862. Not allowed to complete the organization of the 22 MO Infantry due to the transfer of multiple companies to other regiments and finally consolidation with the 10 MO Infantry, he submitted his resignation, July 29, 1862, accepted to date Sept. 3, 1862, "because I consider my treatment has been unjust—not right—degrading and humiliating so much so that I am not willing to serve under existing circumstances." Colonel, 86 Enrolled MO Militia, June 28, 1864. Commission vacated, March 12, 1865. Battle honors: Iuka.
Born: Aug. 20, 1829 Clark Co., KY
Died: Aug. 12, 1890 Commerce, MO
Other Wars: Mexican War (2 Lieutenant, Co. D, 4 IL Infantry)
Occupation: Lawyer and judge
Offices/Honors: Circuit Court Judge, 1880–86
Miscellaneous: Resided Kirksville, Adair Co., MO, before war; and Commerce, Scott Co., MO, after war
Buried: Anderson Cemetery, Commerce, MO
References: Obituary, *St. Louis Globe-Democrat*, Aug. 13, 1890. *History of Southeast Missouri*. Chicago, IL, 1888. Obituary, *St. Louis Post-Dispatch*, Aug. 17, 1890. Letters Received, Volunteer Service Branch, Adjutant General's Office, File F204(VS)1862, National Archives. Pension File and Military Service File, National Archives. Marcus O. Frost. *Regimental History of the Tenth Missouri Volunteer Infantry*. Topeka, KS, 1892.

Samuel Augustus Foster

1 Lieutenant, 6 U.S. Infantry, May 14, 1861. Acting AAG, Staff of Brig. Gen. George Sykes, 2 Division, 5 Army Corps, Army of the Potomac, Feb. 28–Aug. 7, 1862. Colonel, 5 MO Infantry, Oct. 23, 1862. Honorably mustered out,

Nov. 22, 1862. Colonel, 35 MO Infantry, Dec. 3, 1862. With various charges pending against him, including "Using disloyal and treasonous language against the President" and "Behaving in an ungentlemanly manner towards his superior officer," he submitted his resignation, April 30, 1863, "being unequal to the fatigues of the field in this climate ... and having been appointed captain, commissary of subsistence, USA, and ordered to report as soon as practicable." Commanded 1 Brigade, 13 Division, 13 Army Corps, District of Eastern Arkansas, Department of the Tennessee, May 25–June 12, 1863. The Court-Martial verdict of dismissal on the pending charges was disapproved by Brig. Gen. Frederick Salomon due to insufficient evidence, June 29, 1863, and his resignation was accepted to date July 20, 1863. Captain, Commissary of Subsistence, USA, Feb. 9, 1863. Bvt. Captain, USA, June 27, 1862, for gallant and meritorious services at the battle of Gaines' Mill, VA. Bvt. Major, USA, March 13, 1865, for faithful and meritorious services during the war. Battle honors: Virginia Peninsular Campaign (Gaines' Mill, Malvern Hill).

Samuel Augustus Foster (Frederick Hill Meserve. Historical Portraits, a Part of the Collection of Americana of Frederick Hill Meserve. New York City, 1913-1915; courtesy New York State Library, Manuscripts and Special Collections).

Born: Aug. 31, 1836 Winthrop, ME
Died: Feb. 3, 1871 San Francisco, CA
Education: Graduated U.S. Military Academy, West Point, NY, 1860
Occupation: Regular Army (Captain, Commissary of Subsistence, died Feb. 2, 1871)
Miscellaneous: Resided St. Louis, MO
Buried: Bellefontaine Cemetery, St. Louis, MO (Blocks 111–120, Lot 67)
References: Frederick Clifton Pierce. *Foster Genealogy: Being the Record of the Posterity of Reginald Foster.* Chicago, IL, 1899. George W. Cullum. *Biographical Register of the Officers and Graduates of the U.S. Military Academy.* Third Edition. Boston, MA, 1891. Pension File and Military Service File, National Archives. Obituary, *Daily Missouri Democrat,* Feb. 15 and 17, 1871. Obituary, *San Francisco Chronicle,* Feb. 7, 1871. Letters Received, Volunteer Service Branch, Adjutant General's Office, File F300(VS)1863, National Archives. *The Association of the Graduates of the United States Military Academy. Annual Reunion, June 17th, 1871.* New York City, NY, 1871. Letters Received, Appointment, Commission and Personal Branch, Adjutant General's Office, File 830(ACP)1871, National Archives. Court-martial Case Files, 1809–1894, File NN-0357, National Archives.

Charles Augustus Fritz

Lieutenant Colonel, 3 U.S. Reserve Corps, MO Infantry (3 months), May 8, 1861. Honorably mustered out, Aug. 17, 1861. *Colonel,* 3 U.S. Reserve Corps, MO Infantry, Oct. 27, 1861. Declined appointment as Colonel, 4 MO Infantry, upon consolidation with Gasconade County Battalion, U.S. Reserve Corps, Jan. 18, 1862. *Colonel,* 1 St. Louis City Guards, Oct. 4, 1864. Assigned to command all St. Louis City Guard regiments, Oct. 14, 1864.

Born: July 7, 1824, Rheinpfalz, Bavaria
Died: Oct. 9, 1906 Freiburg, Baden, Germany
Other Wars: Mexican War (1 Sergeant, Co. H, 2 IL Infantry)
Occupation: Brewer
Miscellaneous: Resided St. Louis, MO
Buried: Burial place unknown
References: www.ancestry.com. Robert J. Rombauer. *The Union Cause in St. Louis in 1861: An Historical Sketch.* St. Louis, MO, 1909. *Annual Report of the Adjutant General of the State of Missouri, December 31, 1863.* Jefferson City, MO, 1864. Death notice, *St. Louis Post-Dispatch,* Oct. 10, 1906. *The War of the Rebellion: A Compilation*

of the *Official Records of the Union and Confederate Armies*. (Vol. 41, Part 3, pp. 611, 860). Washington, D.C., 1893.

Robert Washington Fyan

Lieutenant Colonel, Webster County Regiment, MO Home Guards, July 6, 1861. Discharged Aug. 18, 1861. Captain, Co. B, 24 MO Infantry, Aug. 20, 1861. Provost Marshal General, Army of Southeast Missouri, Nov.–Dec. 1862. Major, 24 MO Infantry, May 2, 1863. Commanded Post of Springfield (MO), District of Southwest Missouri, Department of the Missouri, Oct. 1864. Honorably mustered out, Nov. 13, 1864. Colonel, 46 MO Infantry, Nov. 14, 1864. Commanded Post of Springfield (MO), District of Southwest Missouri, Department of the Missouri, Nov. 1864–Feb. 1865. Honorably mustered out, March 7, 1865. Battle honors: Pea Ridge, Red River Campaign (Pleasant Hill, Yellow Bayou), Old River Lake, Tupelo, Price's Missouri Expedition.

Born: March 11, 1835, Bedford Springs, Bedford Co., PA

Died: July 28, 1896, Marshfield, MO

Education: Attended Mount Saint Mary's College, Emmitsburg, MD

Occupation: Lawyer and judge

Offices/Honors: Circuit Court Judge, 1866–83. U.S. House of Representatives, 1883–85 and 1891–95.

Miscellaneous: Resided Marshfield, Webster Co., MO

Buried: Lebanon Cemetery, Lebanon, Laclede Co., MO (Block 2)

References: J. Randall Houp. *The 24th Missouri Volunteer Infantry: Lyon Legion*. Alma, AR, 1997. *The United States Biographical Dictionary and Portrait Gallery of Eminent and Self-Made Men*. Missouri Volume. New York, Chicago, St. Louis, and Kansas City, 1878. Pension File and Military Service File, National Archives. James L. Harrison, compiler. *Biographical Directory of the American Congress, 1774–1949*. Washington, D.C., 1950. Obituary, *Hermitage Index*, Aug. 6, 1896. Obituary, *St. Louis Post-Dispatch*, July 29, 1896. *History of Laclede, Camden, Dallas, Webster, Wright, Texas, Pulaski, Phelps and Dent Counties, Missouri*. Chicago, IL, 1889.

Daniel Quinby Gale

Colonel, 54 Enrolled MO Militia, Aug. 15, 1862. Commission vacated, Sept. 22, 1863. Colonel, 54 Enrolled MO Militia, Sept. 29, 1864. Commanded Post of Franklin (MO), St. Louis District, Department of the Missouri, Oct.–Nov. 1864. Commission vacated, March 12, 1865. Battle Honors: Price's Missouri Expedition.

Born: Dec. 23, 1807 Amesbury, MA

Died: Jan. 7, 1894 Washington, MO

Occupation: Lawyer and judge

Offices/Honors: Postmaster, Washington, MO, 1840–57 and 1883–85. Circuit Court Judge, 1868–74.

Miscellaneous: Resided Washington, Franklin Co., MO

Buried: Wildey Odd Fellows Cemetery, Washington, MO

References: "Daniel Q. Gale, Washington's First Lawyer," *Washington Historical Society Newsletter*, Vol. 3, No. 16 (March 1994). *The Bench and Bar of St. Louis, Kansas City, Jefferson City, and Other Missouri Cities*. St. Louis and Chicago, 1884. Obituary, *Union Tribune-Republican*, Jan. 12, 1894. Pension File, National Archives. *History of Franklin, Jefferson, Washington, Crawford and Gasconade Counties, Missouri*. Chicago, IL, 1888. Henry C. Quinby. *Genealogical History of the Quinby (Quimby) Family in England and America*. New York City, NY, 1915.

Washington Franklin Geiger

Captain, Co. C, Phelps' Regt. MO Infantry, Sept. 23, 1861. Major, Phelps' Regiment, MO Infantry, Dec. 19, 1861. Honorably mustered out, May 13, 1862. Colonel, 8 MO Cavalry, Aug. 10, 1862. GSW left wrist, Prairie Grove, AR, Dec. 7, 1862. Commanded 2 Brigade, 3 Division, Army of the Frontier, Department of the Missouri, Dec. 1862–Feb. 1863. Commanded 3 Division, Army of the Frontier, Department of the Missouri, Feb.–June 1863. Commanded 1 Brigade, 1 Cavalry Division, Arkansas Expedition, Department of the Missouri, Aug. 1863 and Oct.–Nov. 1863. Commanded 2 Brigade, 1 Cavalry Division, 7 Army Corps, Department of Arkansas, Jan.–May 1864. Commanded Post of Devall's Bluff (AR), Department of Arkansas, March–June 1864. Commanded 3 Brigade, 2 Division, 7 Army Corps, District of Little Rock, Department of Arkansas, May–Sept. 1864. Commanded 3 Brigade, Cavalry Division, 7 Army Corps, District of Little Rock, Department of Arkansas, Sept. 1864–Jan. 1865. Commanded 2 Brigade, Cavalry Division, 7 Army Corps, Department of Arkansas, Jan.–March 1865. Commanded Separate

Dismounted Cavalry Brigade, 7 Army Corps, Department of Arkansas, March–May 1865. Honorably mustered out, July 20, 1865. Battle honors: Pea Ridge, Prairie Grove, Advance upon Little Rock (Bayou Fourche), Devall's Bluff (Ashley's Station).

Born: June 30, 1836, Holmes Co., OH
Died: Aug. 16, 1886 Springfield, MO
Occupation: Lawyer and judge
Offices/Honors: Circuit court judge, 1869–86
Miscellaneous: Resided Steelville, Crawford Co., MO, before war; and Springfield, Greene Co., MO, after war
Buried: Springfield National Cemetery, Springfield, MO (Section 22, Grave 1566)
References: Obituary, *Springfield Leader*, Aug. 16, 1886. *The United States Biographical Dictionary and Portrait Gallery of Eminent and Self-Made Men*. Missouri Volume. New York, Chicago, St. Louis, and Kansas City, 1878. *History of Greene County, Missouri*. St. Louis, MO, 1883. Pension File and Military Service File, National Archives. Letters Received, Volunteer Service Branch, Adjutant General's Office, File G398(VS)1862, National Archives. Jonathan Fairbanks and Clyde E. Tuck. *Past and Present of Greene County, Missouri*. Indianapolis, IN, 1915. David E. Casto. *Arkansas Late in the Civil War: The 8th Missouri Volunteer Cavalry, April 1864–July 1865*. Charleston, SC, 2013.

John Montgomery Glover

Colonel, 3 MO Cavalry, Sept. 4, 1861. Commanded District of Northeast Missouri, Department of the Mississippi, March–June 1862. Commanded Rolla Division, District of Missouri, Department of the Mississippi, June–Nov. 1862. Commanded District of Rolla (MO), Department of the Missouri, Nov. 1862–March 1863. Commanded Sub-District of Pilot Knob (MO), St. Louis District, Department of the Missouri, April 1863. Commanded 2 Brigade, 1 Cavalry Division, Department of the Missouri, June–Aug. 1863. Commanded 2 Brigade, 1 Cavalry Division, Arkansas Expedition, Department of the Missouri, Aug.–Nov. 1863. Resigned March 13, 1864, due to "chronic meningitis presenting an obstinate character after a treatment of over four months." Battle honors: Mount Zion Church, Marmaduke's Expedition into Missouri (Chalk Bluff), Advance upon Little Rock (Bayou Meto, Bayou Fourche).

Born: Sept. 4, 1824 Harrodsburg, Mercer Co., KY
Died: Nov. 11, 1891 near Newark, Knox Co., MO
Education: Attended Marion College, Philadelphia, MO
Occupation: Farmer and lawyer
Offices/Honors: Collector of Internal Revenue, 1866–67. U.S. House of Representatives, 1873–79.
Miscellaneous: Resided near Newark, Knox Co., MO; LaGrange, Lewis Co., MO; and Quincy, Adams Co., IL, after 1884

Washington Franklin Geiger (author's photograph).

John Montgomery Glover, post-war (Brady-Handy Photograph Collection, Library of Congress [LC-DIG-cwpbh-03587]).

John Montgomery Glover, post-war (Brady-Handy Photograph Collection, Library of Congress [LC-DIG-cwpbh-04074]).

Buried: Woodland Cemetery, Quincy, IL (Block 10, Lot 161)
References: Obituary, *Quincy Herald*, Nov. 12, 1891. Obituary, *Palmyra Spectator*, Nov. 19, 1891. *History of Lewis, Clark, Knox and Scotland Counties, Missouri*. St. Louis and Chicago, 1887. James L. Harrison, compiler. *Biographical Directory of the American Congress, 1774-1949*. Washington, D.C., 1950. Pension File and Military Service File, National Archives. A.W.M. Petty. *A History of the Third Missouri Cavalry: From Its Organization at Palmyra, Missouri, 1861, Up to November Sixth, 1864*. Little Rock, AR, 1865. Letters Received, Commission Branch, Adjutant General's Office, File G409(CB)1863, National Archives. Letters Received, Volunteer Service Branch, Adjutant General's Office, File G914(VS)1862, National Archives. Obituary, *Quincy Daily Journal*, Nov. 11, 1891. William Horatio Barnes. *The American Government. Biographies of Members of the House of Representatives of the Forty-Third Congress*. New York City, NY, 1874.

Nathaniel Grant

1 Lieutenant, Co. I, 82 Enrolled MO Militia, Sept. 24, 1863. Colonel, 82 Enrolled MO Militia, April 4, 1864. Commission vacated, March 12, 1865.
Born: Sept. 15, 1814 South Berwick, ME
Died: Feb. 17, 1887 Kansas City, MO
Occupation: Ordnance Agent, U.S. Ordnance Depot, Liberty, MO, 1846-61. Partner in a banking house after war.
Offices/Honors: City Comptroller, Kansas City, MO, 1880-87
Miscellaneous: Resided Liberty, Clay Co., MO; and Kansas City, MO, after 1868. Best known for surrendering the U.S. Ordnance Depot, Liberty, MO, upon its seizure by armed secessionists, April 20, 1861.
Buried: Elmwood Cemetery, Kansas City, MO (Block J, Lot 115)
References: Obituary, *Kansas City Times*, Feb. 18, 1887. Obituary, *Kansas City Star*, Feb. 17, 1887. Letters Received, Commission Branch, Adjutant General's Office, File G37(CB)1866, National Archives. *History of Clay and Platte Counties, Missouri*. St. Louis, MO, 1885.

Joseph Jackson Gravely

2 Lieutenant, Co. A, 8 MO State Militia Cavalry, Dec. 18, 1861. Captain, Co. D, 8 MO State Militia Cavalry, March 1, 1862. GSW Humansville, MO, March 26, 1862. Commanded Post of Sand Springs, District of Southwest Missouri, Department of the Missouri, Nov. 1862. Colonel, 8 MO State Militia Cavalry, March 30, 1863. Commanded Post of Lebanon (MO), District of Southwest Missouri, Department of the Missouri, Oct. 1863 and Jan.-Feb. 1864. Commanded Post of Springfield (MO), District of Southwest Missouri, Department of the Missouri, July-Aug. 1864 and Nov. 1864. Commanded Post of Neosho (MO), District of Southwest Missouri, Department of the Missouri, Aug. 1864. Commanded 3 Brigade, Provisional Cavalry Division, Department of the Missouri, Oct. 8-20, 1864. Commanded District of Southwest Missouri, Department of the Missouri, Dec. 9, 1864-Jan. 9, 1865. Honorably mustered out, March 20, 1865. Lieutenant Colonel, 14 MO Cavalry, April 12, 1865. Honorably mustered out, Oct. 26, 1865. Battle honors: Humansville, Montevallo, Shelby's Raid in Arkansas and Missouri, Price's Missouri Expedition (Big Blue, Marais des Cygnes, Mine Creek, Newtonia).
Born: Sept. 25, 1828 near Leatherwood, Henry Co., VA
Died: April 28, 1872, Stockton, MO
Occupation: Lawyer and school teacher
Offices/Honors: Virginia House of Delegates, 1853-54. Missouri Senate, 1862-66. U.S. House of Representatives, 1867-69. Lieutenant Governor of Missouri, 1871-72.
Miscellaneous: Resided Stockton, Cedar Co., MO

Joseph Jackson Gravely (State Historical Society of Missouri, Photograph Collection [Ralph Gravely Scrapbook, P0856, 856-01]).

John Burritt Gray (Hoelke & Benecke, Photographers, S.E. Cor., 4th and Market Sts., St. Louis, Missouri; courtesy Robert J. Younger).

Buried: Lindley Prairie Cemetery, near Bear Creek, Cedar Co., MO

References: *The American Annual Cyclopedia and Register of Important Events of the Year 1872*. New York City, NY, 1873. Obituary, *Quincy Whig*, May 3, 1872. Pension File and Military Service File, National Archives. James L. Harrison, compiler. *Biographical Directory of the American Congress, 1774–1949*. Washington, D.C., 1950. William H. Barnes. *The Fortieth Congress of the United States: Historical and Biographical*. New York City, NY, 1870. Lumir F. Buresh. *October 25th and the Battle of Mine Creek*. Kansas City, MO, 1977. Albert Griffen. *Biographical Register of the Members of the Twenty-Sixth General Assembly of the State of Missouri*. St. Louis, MO, 1872. Margaret C. Klein. *Joseph Gravely of Leatherwood*. Palm Coast, FL, 1984.

John Burritt Gray

Lieutenant Colonel, ADC and AIG, Staff of Brig. Gen. John M. Schofield, MO State Militia, Dec. 4, 1861. Colonel, 1 MO State Militia Infantry, March 1, 1862. Appointed Brig. Gen., Enrolled MO Militia, Aug. 21, 1862. Commanded Post of Pilot Knob, District of St. Louis, Department of Missouri, Nov. 1862–March 1863. Resigned as colonel, March 18, 1863. Adjutant General, State of Missouri, March 20, 1863–Jan. 12, 1865. Battle honors: Price's Missouri Expedition.

Born: June 25, 1831, Sheridan, NY

John Burritt Gray, post-war (Marcius D. Raymond. *Gray Genealogy, Being a Genealogical Record and History of the Descendants of John Gray, of Beverly, Mass*. Tarrytown, New York, 1887).

Died: June 6, 1896, Asheville, NC

Occupation: Wholesale dealer in hats and caps to 1880. Vice President of American Brake Company after 1880.

Miscellaneous: Resided St. Louis, MO; and Brooklyn, NY

Buried: Green-Wood Cemetery, Brooklyn, NY (Section P, Lot 22310)

References: David W. Dillard. *The Union Post Commanders at Pilot Knob, 1861–1865*. Ironton,

MO, 2013. Obituary Circular, Whole No. 529, New York MOLLUS. Marcius D. Raymond. *Gray Genealogy, Being a Genealogical Record and History of the Descendants of John Gray, of Beverly Mass.* Tarrytown, NY, 1887. Obituary, *New York Times,* June 9, 1896. "The Late General John B. Gray," *Railway Age,* Vol. 22, No. 1 (July 3, 1896). Obituary, *New York Tribune,* June 9, 1896. Military Service File, National Archives.

Clark Hall Green

Colonel, 46 Enrolled MO Militia, Dec. 16, 1862. Commission vacated, July 28, 1864. Deputy Provost Marshal, 8 District of Missouri, Oct. 7, 1863–Dec. 20, 1864. Taken prisoner and released, near Fayette, MO, July 9, 1864. GSW left arm, near Fayette, MO, July 9, 1864.

Born: Aug. 7, 1819 Cape Girardeau Co., MO
Died: Sept. 18, 1871 Macon, MO
Occupation: Newspaper editor
Offices/Honors: Missouri House of Representatives, 1864–66. Mayor, Macon, MO, 1866–67.
Miscellaneous: Resided Glasgow, Howard Co., MO; and Macon, Macon Co., MO, after 1865
Buried: Oakwood Cemetery, Macon, MO
References: Obituary, *Warrenton Banner,* Sept. 26, 1871. Pension File, National Archives. Obituary, *Macon Republican,* Sept. 19, 1871. Obituary, *Shelby County Herald,* Sept. 27, 1871. *History of Randolph and Macon Counties, Missouri.* St. Louis, MO, 1884.

Odon Guitar

Colonel, 9 MO State Militia Cavalry, May 3, 1862. Commanded Post of Jefferson City (MO), Department of the Missouri, June 1862. Commanded Post of Columbia (MO), Northeastern District of Missouri, Department of the Missouri, Nov. 1862. Commanded 7 Military District, State of Missouri, Jan. 1863. Nominated Brig. Gen., USV, Jan. 19, 1863, to rank from Nov. 29, 1862. Nomination as Brig. Gen., USV, withdrawn Feb. 12, 1863. Commanded District of Northeastern Missouri, Department of the Missouri, May–July 1863. Honorably mustered out as colonel, June 30, 1863. Appointed Brig. Gen., MO State Militia, June 27, 1863. Commanded District of North Missouri, Department of the Missouri, July 1863–April 1864. Commanded District of Rolla (MO), Department of the Missouri, April–Aug. 1864. Resigned Aug. 31, 1864. Battle honors: Moore's Mill, Pursuit of Poindexter in Missouri (Switzler's Mill, Compton's Ferry, Yellow Creek).

Odon Guitar (Nichols & Bro's, Photographic Gallery, No. 60 North Fourth St., St. Louis, Missouri; courtesy Robert J. Younger).

Odon Guitar (Walter B. Davis and Daniel S. Durrie. *An Illustrated History of Missouri Comprising Its Early Record, and Civil, Political, and Military History from the First Exploration to the Present Time.* **St. Louis, Missouri, 1876).**

Odon Guitar (courtesy Robert J. Younger).

Born: Aug. 31, 1825 Richmond, KY
Died: March 13, 1908, Columbia, MO
Education: Graduated University of Missouri, Columbia, MO, 1846
Other Wars: Mexican War (Private, Co. H, 1 MO Mounted Infantry)
Occupation: Lawyer
Offices/Honors: Missouri House of Representatives, 1854–56 and 1858–60
Miscellaneous: Resided Columbia, Boone Co., MO
Buried: Columbia Cemetery, Columbia, MO (Block A, Lot 5)
References: Lawrence O. Christensen, William E. Foley, Gary R. Kremer, and Kenneth H. Winn, editors. *Dictionary of Missouri Biography.* Columbia, MO, 1999. North T. Gentry, "General Odon Guitar," *Missouri Historical Review*, Vol. 22, No. 4 (July 1928). Walter B. Davis and Daniel S. Durrie. *An Illustrated History of Missouri.* St. Louis, MO, 1876. Obituary, *Sedalia Democrat,* March 15, 1908. *History of Boone County, Missouri.* St. Louis, MO, 1882. John Boyle, compiler. *Boyle Genealogy: John Boyle of Virginia and Kentucky.* St. Louis, MO, 1909. Pension File and Military Service File, National Archives. Odon Guitar Collection, 1836–1906 (C1007), State Historical Society of Missouri-Columbia.

John Blackwell Hale

Colonel, 65 Enrolled MO Militia, Nov. 3, 1862. Temporary service as Colonel, 4 Provisional Enrolled MO Militia. Commission vacated, March 12, 1865.
Born: Feb. 27, 1831 Brooke Co., VA (now WV)
Died: Feb. 1, 1905 Carrollton, MO
Occupation: Lawyer
Offices/Honors: Missouri House of Representatives, 1856–58. U.S. House of Representatives, 1885–87.
Miscellaneous: Resided Carrollton, Carroll Co., MO
Buried: Oak Hill Cemetery, Carrollton, MO
References: A.J.D. Stewart, editor. *The History of the Bench and Bar of Missouri.* St. Louis, MO, 1898. Ralph F. Lozier, "Memorial of John B. Hale," *Proceedings of the Twenty-Third Annual Meeting of the Missouri Bar Association.* Columbia, MO, 1905. James L. Harrison, compiler. *Biographical Directory of the American Congress, 1774–1949.* Washington, D.C., 1950. Obituary, *Moberly Evening Democrat,* Feb. 2, 1905. *History of Carroll County, Missouri.* St. Louis, MO, 1881. Obituary, *Kansas City Star,* Feb. 1, 1905.

George Henry Hall

Colonel, 4 MO State Militia Cavalry, April 28, 1862. Commanded 4 Brigade, MO State Militia, Sept. 1862. Commanded Post of Sedalia (MO), District of Central Missouri, Department of the Missouri, April–July 1863. Commanded Central District of Missouri, Department of the Missouri, Nov. 1863. Commanded 1 Sub-District, District of Central Missouri, Department of the Missouri, Jan.–May 1864. Commanded 1 and 2 Sub-Districts, District of Central Missouri, Department of the Missouri, June–July 1864. Honorably mustered out, Sept. 1, 1864. Brig. Gen., MO State Militia, Sept. 2, 1864. Resigned May 1, 1865. Battle honors: Newtonia, Marmaduke's Expedition into Missouri (Springfield), Shelby's Raid in Arkansas and Missouri.
Born: Jan. 5, 1825 Harper's Ferry, VA (now WV)
Died: March 4, 1897, Los Angeles, CA
Occupation: Railroad executive and lawyer
Offices/Honors: Postmaster, St. Joseph, MO, 1866–67. Mayor, St. Joseph, MO, 1868–70.
Miscellaneous: Resided St. Joseph, Buchanan Co., MO; and Deadwood, Lawrence Co., SD, 1877–91. Brother of Willard P. Hall, Governor of Missouri, 1864–65.
Buried: Evergreen Cemetery, Los Angeles, CA (Section F)

George Henry Hall (St. Joseph Public Library [V3Pic47Lozo]).

References: Pension File and Military Service File, National Archives. Christian L. Rutt, compiler. *The Daily News' History of Buchanan County and St. Joseph, Missouri, From the Time of the Platte Purchase to the End of the Year 1898.* St. Joseph, MO, 1898. Obituary, *Los Angeles Herald*, March 6, 1897. Letters Received, Volunteer Service Branch, Adjutant General's Office, File H2152(VS)1864, National Archives.

Noah H. Hampton

Colonel, Webster County Regiment, MO Home Guards, July 6, 1861. Discharged Aug. 18, 1861. Captain, Co. I, 74 Enrolled MO Militia, Aug. 15, 1862. Resigned March 3, 1863.

Born: 1820? Jackson Co., TN
Died: Dec. 22, 1889 Springfield, MO
Occupation: Physician
Offices/Honors: Postmaster, Mornington, Webster Co., MO, 1856–59. Elected to Missouri House of Representatives in 1872, but election successfully contested by D.R. Jameson.
Miscellaneous: Resided Marshfield, Webster Co., MO; and Springfield, Greene Co., MO
Buried: Marshfield Cemetery, Marshfield, MO (Section 1)
References: Obituary, *Springfield Daily Leader*, Dec. 23, 1889. Obituary, *Springfield Republican*, Dec. 24, 1889. Pension File and Military Service File, National Archives. *History of Laclede, Camden, Dallas, Webster, Wright, Texas, Pulaski, Phelps and Dent Counties, Missouri*. Chicago, IL, 1889.

Thomas Harbine, post-war (Albert Watkins. *History of Nebraska from the Earliest Explorations to the Present Time.* Lincoln, Nebraska, 1913).

Thomas Harbine

Lieutenant Colonel, 25 Enrolled MO Militia, Sept. 8, 1862. Temporary service as Lieutenant Colonel, 3 Provisional Enrolled MO Militia. Commission vacated, Nov. 1, 1863. Colonel, 87 Enrolled MO Militia, July 13, 1864. Declined.

Born: Dec. 15, 1820 Big Spring, Washington Co., MD
Died: Jan. 16, 1902 Tacoma, WA
Education: Attended Jefferson College, Canonsburg, PA; and Miami University, Oxford, OH
Occupation: Lawyer, railroad promoter, and banker
Offices/Honors: Mayor of St. Joseph, MO, 1862–64. County Collector, Buchanan Co., MO, 1864–66. Missouri Senate, 1867–71.
Miscellaneous: Resided Hagerstown, Washington Co., MD; St. Joseph, Buchanan Co., MO; Fairbury, Jefferson Co., NE; and Tacoma, Pierce Co., WA
Buried: Tacoma Cemetery, Tacoma, WA (Section 3, Block D, Lot 14)
References: Albert Watkins. *History of Nebraska from the Earliest Explorations to the Present Time.* Lincoln, NE, 1913. Obituary, *Tacoma Daily Ledger*, Jan. 17, 1902. Alfred T. Andreas. *History of the State of Nebraska*. Chicago, IL, 1882. Charles Dawson. *Pioneer Tales of the Oregon Trail and of Jefferson County.* Topeka, KS, 1912. Christian L. Rutt, compiler. *The Daily News' History of*

Buchanan County and St. Joseph, Missouri, From the Time of the Platte Purchase to the End of the Year 1898. St. Joseph, MO, 1898. "A Brief Autobiography of Thomas Harbine" (written in 1879), www.ancestry.com.

Eugene Clarence Harrington

Lieutenant Colonel, 11 Enrolled MO Militia, Sept. 17, 1862. Resigned June 11, 1863. *Colonel*, 4 St. Louis City Guards, Oct. 5, 1864.

Born: July 27, 1837, NY
Died: Oct. 27, 1894 St. Louis, MO
Education: Attended Columbia College, New York City, NY, and St. Louis (MO) University
Occupation: U.S. Government tobacco inspector (1865), after which he embarked in an unsuccessful general commission business (1870). Last 15 years held position in office of St. Louis Water Commissioner.
Miscellaneous: Resided St. Louis, MO
Buried: Bellefontaine Cemetery, St. Louis, MO (Block 41, Lot 424)
References: Obituary, *St. Louis Post-Dispatch*, Oct. 27, 1894. *The War of the Rebellion: A Compilation of the Official Records of the Union and Confederate Armies.* (Vol. 41, Part 3, pp. 635, 753). Washington, D.C., 1893. www.ancestry.com.

Franz Philipp Hassendeubel (J.A. Scholten, Photographer, South 5th St., Corner of Convent, No. 273, St. Louis, Missouri; Roger D. Hunt Collection, USAMHI [RG98S-CWP160.57]).

Franz Philipp Hassendeubel

Lieutenant Colonel, 3 MO Infantry (3 months), May 4, 1861. Discharged July 15, 1861. Colonel, 17 MO Infantry, Dec. 19, 1861. Commanded 1 Brigade, 3 Division, Army of the Southwest, Department of the Missouri, April–Oct. 1862. Commanded 3 Division, Army of the Southwest, Department of the Missouri, Oct. 1862. Shell wound chest, Vicksburg, MS, June 28, 1863. Battle honors: Carthage, Searcy Landing, Pea Ridge, Chickasaw Bayou, Arkansas Post, Vicksburg Campaign.

Born: Jan. 18, 1817 Germersheim, Rhineland-Palatinate, Germany
Died: July 17, 1863, DOW Vicksburg, MS
Other Wars: Mexican War (2 Lieutenant, Battery B, Clark's Battalion, MO Light Artillery, and Captain, Co. A, Santa Fe Battalion, MO Mounted Volunteers)
Occupation: Civil engineer
Miscellaneous: Resided St. Louis, MO
Buried: Bellefontaine Cemetery, St. Louis, MO (Block 35, Lot 1298)

Franz Philipp Hassendeubel (Klotter & Scherer, Photograph Art Gallery, 906 to 912 N. Sixth Street, St. Louis, Missouri; Roger D. Hunt Collection, USAMHI [RG98S-CWP160.58]).

References: *Roster and By-Laws of Col. Hassendeubel Post, No. 13, Department of Missouri, GAR.* St. Louis, MO, 1911. Myron J. Smith, Jr. *Civil War Biographies from the Western Waters.* Jefferson, NC, 2015. "Obsequies of Colonel Hassendeubel," *Daily Missouri Democrat*, July 31, 1863. Robert J. Rombauer. *The Union Cause in St. Louis in 1861: An Historical Sketch.* St. Louis, MO, 1909. Pension File and Military Service File, National Archives. Joseph G. Rosengarten. *The German Soldier in the Wars of the United States.* Second edition, revised and enlarged. Philadelphia, PA, 1890. Wilhelm Kaufmann. *The Germans in the American Civil War.* Translated by Steven Rowan and edited by Don Heinrich Tolzmann with Werner D. Mueller and Robert E. Ward. Carlisle, PA, 1999. Letters Received, Commission Branch, Adjutant General's Office, File H730(CB)1863, National Archives. Philip R. Hinderberger, "Colonel Franz Hassendeubel," http://www.17thmissouri.com/bio_hassendeubel.html.

John Thornton Kirkland Hayward

Colonel, 38 Enrolled MO Militia, Sept. 2, 1862. As Superintendent of the Hannibal & St. Joseph Railroad during the war, he was so successful with his schedules that his road became known as the "Old Reliable." Commanded Sub-District of Hannibal, District of North Missouri, Department of the Missouri, Aug. 1864–Jan. 1865. Commission vacated, March 12, 1865. Battle honors: Price's Missouri Expedition.

Born: Oct. 17, 1819 Plainfield, MA
Died: Nov. 18, 1901 Chicago, IL
Occupation: Civil engineer engaged in railroad construction. Wholesale grocer later in life.
Offices/Honors: Mayor, Bangor, ME, 1855–56. Missouri House of Representatives, 1869–71. Postmaster, Hannibal, MO, 1877–78. Mayor, Hannibal, MO, 1878.
Miscellaneous: Resided Bangor, Penobscot Co., ME, to 1857; Hannibal, Marion Co., MO, 1857–1885; St. Louis, MO, 1885–97; and Chicago, IL, 1897–1901.
Buried: Bellefontaine Cemetery, St. Louis, MO (Block 170, Lot 3605, family monument)
References: *Portrait and Biographical Record of Marion, Ralls, and Pike Counties, Missouri.* Chicago, IL, 1895. Obituary, *St. Louis Globe-Democrat*, Nov. 21, 1901. Obituary, *Chicago Daily Tribune*, Nov. 19, 1901. *History of Marion County, Missouri.* St. Louis, MO, 1884. *History of Penobscot County, Maine.* Cleveland, OH, 1882.

David Jackson Heaston, post-war (*History of Harrison and Mercer Counties, Missouri, from the Earliest Time to the Present.* **St. Louis and Chicago, 1888).**

David Jackson Heaston

Private, Co. D, Harrison County Regiment, MO Home Guards, Sept. 3, 1861. Discharged Sept. 23, 1861. Captain, Co. A, 57 Enrolled MO Militia, July 28, 1862. Colonel, 57 Enrolled MO Militia, Oct. 15, 1862. Resigned June 3, 1863.

Born: May 22, 1835, Champaign Co., OH
Died: July 21, 1902, Bethany, MO
Education: Attended Miami University, Oxford, OH. Attended Indiana Asbury (now DePauw) University, Greencastle, IN.
Occupation: Lawyer and newspaper editor
Offices/Honors: Probate Judge, 1861–62. Missouri Senate, 1879–83.
Miscellaneous: Resided Bethany, Harrison Co., MO
Buried: Miriam Cemetery, Bethany, MO (1st Addition, Block 16, Lot 4)
References: Walter Williams, editor. *A History of Northwest Missouri.* Chicago and New York, 1915. *History of Harrison and Mercer Counties, Missouri, From the Earliest Time to the Present.* St. Louis and Chicago, 1888. Obituary, *Bethany Democrat*, July 30, 1902. Obituary, *St. Louis Globe-Democrat*, July 22, 1902. A.J.D. Stewart, editor. *The History of the Bench and Bar of Missouri.* St. Louis, MO, 1898. George W. Wanamaker. *History of Harrison County, Missouri.* Topeka and Indianapolis, 1921.

William Henry Heath

Private, Co. K, 3 U.S. Reserve Corps, MO Infantry (3 months), May 8, 1861. Honorably mustered out, Aug. 8, 1861. 1 Lieutenant, Co. I, 18 IL Infantry, Dec. 10, 1861. Acting ACS, Staff of Brig. Gen. John A. McClernand, 1 Division, District of Cairo, Feb. 1862. 1 Lieutenant, Adjutant, 18 IL Infantry, Feb. 12, 1862. GSW spine, Shiloh, TN, April 6, 1862. Acting AAG, Staff of Brig. Gen. John A. Logan, 1 Brigade, 1 Division, District of West Tennessee, April–Aug. 1862. Major, 33 MO Infantry, Sept. 5, 1862. Lieutenant Colonel, 33 MO Infantry, Dec. 23, 1862. *Colonel*, 33 MO Infantry, Dec. 22, 1863. GSW left ear, Pleasant Hill, LA, April 9, 1864. Commanded 3 Brigade, 1 Division, 16 Army Corps, Military Division of West Mississippi, Feb. 4–March 2, 1865. Honorably mustered out, Aug. 10, 1865. Bvt. Colonel, USV, March 26, 1865, for faithful and meritorious services during the campaign against the city of Mobile and its defenses. Battle honors: Fort Henry, Fort Donelson, Shiloh, Helena, Meridian Expedition, Red River Campaign (Henderson's Hill, Pleasant Hill), Tupelo, Nashville, Mobile Campaign (Spanish Fort, Fort Blakely).

Born: July 21, 1840, near Wyoming, Stark Co., IL

Died: March 8, 1921, St. Louis, MO (from injuries received in street car accident)

Occupation: Bookkeeper and storekeeper

Miscellaneous: Resided St. Louis, MO, to 1889; Aspen, Pitkin Co., CO, 1889–95; St. Louis, MO, 1895–1921

William Henry Heath, post-war (F.W. Guerin; Courtesy Missouri Historical Society, St. Louis [P0083-0096]).

Buried: Oak Hill Cemetery, Kirkwood, St. Louis Co., MO (Section C, Block 37, Lot 26)

References: Pension File and Military Service File, National Archives. Obituary, *St. Louis Post-Dispatch*, March 9, 1921. Letters Received, Volunteer Service Branch, Adjutant General's Office, File F292(VS)1862, National Archives.

William Heren

Colonel, 41 Enrolled MO Militia, Sept. 9, 1862. Commanded District of Northwest Missouri, Department of the Missouri, June 1863. Temporary service as Colonel, 3 Provisional Enrolled MO Militia (relieved Aug. 17, 1863). Dismissed Oct. 7, 1863.

Born: Nov. 15, 1825 Zanesville, OH

Died: May 7, 1893, Savannah, MO

Occupation: Lawyer and judge

Offices/Honors: Missouri Senate, 1862–64. Circuit court judge, 1864–69.

Miscellaneous: Resided Savannah, Andrew Co., MO

Buried: Bennett Lane Cemetery, near Savannah, MO

References: *History of Andrew and DeKalb Counties, Missouri, from the Earliest Time to the Present.* St. Louis and Chicago, 1888. Howard L. Conard, editor. *Encyclopedia of the History of Missouri.* New York, Louisville, and St. Louis, 1901. *The Bench and Bar of St. Louis, Kansas*

William Henry Heath (Troxell & Brother, St. Louis, Missouri; Arkansas State Archives [G2665-05]).

City, Jefferson City, and Other Missouri Cities. St. Louis and Chicago, 1884. Obituary, *Savannah Reporter,* May 12, 1893. Pension File, National Archives.

Herman Theodor Hesse

Captain, Co. I, 1 U.S. Reserve Corps, MO Infantry (3 months), May 7, 1861. Honorably mustered out, Aug. 20, 1861. Captain, Co. E, 5 MO Cavalry, Sept. 30, 1861. Provost Marshal, Staff of Brig. Gen. Alexander Asboth, 2 Division, Army of the Southwest, Department of the Mississippi, March 1862. Resigned Aug. 9, 1862, "having been refused twenty days leave of absence, applied for in proper form, and seeing no prospect whatsoever to recover my much impaired health in the field." *Colonel*, 3 St. Louis City Guards, Oct. 5, 1864. Battle honors: Pea Ridge.

Born: May 30, 1822, Muhlhausen, Thuringen, Germany

Died: Sept. 27, 1900 St. Louis, MO

Occupation: Glass manufacturer before war. Bookkeeper after war.

Miscellaneous: Resided St. Louis, MO

Buried: Hillcrest Abbey Mausoleum, St. Louis, MO (Tier 2, Niche 222)

References: Pension File and Military Service File, National Archives. Obituary, *St. Louis Globe-Democrat*, Sept. 28, 1900. Herman T. Hesse Papers, 1851–1901 (A0692), Missouri History Museum Archives, St. Louis, MO.

Herman Theodor Hesse (Max Saettele's First National Photographic Gallery, No. 9 Carondelet Avenue, Opposite Park Avenue, St. Louis, Missouri; author's photograph).

Franklin Whiting Hickox

Captain, Co. A, 43 Enrolled MO Militia, Aug. 8, 1862. Colonel, 43 Enrolled MO Militia, Sept. 24, 1862. Commanded 1 Sub-District, District of Central Missouri, Department of the Missouri, Sept. 1864. Commission vacated, March 12, 1865. Battle honors: Shelby's Raid in Arkansas and Missouri, Price's Missouri Expedition.

Born: July 13, 1818, Boonville, MO

Died: Jan. 8, 1897 Medicine Lodge, KS

Occupation: Farmer, lumber merchant and coal mine operator

Offices/Honors: Missouri House of Representatives, 1854–56 and 1860–62. Missouri Senate, 1862–66. Kansas House of Representatives, 1891–93.

Miscellaneous: Resided California, Moniteau Co., MO (1860); Lamonte, Pettis Co., MO (1870); Wise Co., TX (1880); and Medicine Lodge, Barber Co., KS, after 1885

Buried: Lamonte Cemetery, Lamonte, MO

References: Obituary, *Barber County Index,* Jan. 13, 1897. Obituary, *Medicine Lodge Cresset,* Jan. 15, 1897. Charles N. Hickok. *The Hickok Genealogy: Descendants of William Hickocks of Farmington, Connecticut.* Rutland, VT, 1938. Obituary, *Clinton Daily Democrat,* Jan. 11, 1897. *The History of Pettis County, Missouri.* N.p., 1882. Edward E. Pixley and Franklin Hanford. *William Pixley of Hadley, Northampton, and Westfield, Mass. and Some of His Descendants.* Buffalo, NY, 1900. Pension File, National Archives.

Herman Theodor Hesse (Max Saettele's First National Photographic Gallery, No. 9 Carondelet Avenue, Opposite Park Avenue, St. Louis, Missouri; author's photograph).

Henry Hildenbrand

Captain, Co. A, 10 Enrolled MO Militia, Sept. 8, 1862. Major, 10 Enrolled MO Militia, June 27, 1863. Temporary service as Major, 11 Provisional Enrolled MO Militia. Colonel, 10 Enrolled MO Militia, March 28, 1864. Commission vacated, March 12, 1865.

Born: Oct. 17, 1824 Dettwiller, Bas-Rhin, Alsace, France

Died: Aug. 10, 1919 St. Louis, MO

Occupation: Saddler before war. Horse collar manufacturer after war.

Miscellaneous: Resided St. Louis, MO. Awarded a patent for an Improved Machine for Filling Horse Collars.

Buried: Bellefontaine Cemetery, St. Louis, MO (Block 209, Lot 1565, unmarked)

References: www.ancestry.com. Death notice, *St. Louis Post-Dispatch*, Aug. 11, 1919.

Eben Marvin Hill

Captain, Co. D, Engineer Regiment of the West, Oct. 3, 1861. Major, Engineer Regiment of the West, Aug. 1, 1863. Designation of regiment changed to 1 MO Engineers upon consolidation with 25 MO Infantry, Dec. 28, 1863. Lieutenant Colonel, I MO Engineers, June 1, 1865. *Colonel,* 1 MO Engineers, June 10, 1865. Honorably mustered out, July 22, 1865. Battle honors: Island No. 10, Vicksburg Campaign.

Eben Marvin Hill (William A. Neal. *An Illustrated History of the Missouri Engineer and the 25th Infantry Regiments.* Chicago, Illinois, 1889).

Born: March 11, 1828, Highgate, VT

Died: Aug. 19, 1904 Lawrence, KS

Occupation: Civil engineer and builder before war. Hardware clerk and farmer after war.

Offices/Honors: Postmaster, Appomattox, KS, 1891–94

Miscellaneous: Resided St. Louis, MO; Bethany, Jefferson Co., GA (1870); Hutchinson, Reno Co., KS, 1877–85; Appomattox, Grant Co., KS, 1885–95; and Lawrence, Douglas Co., KS, 1895–1904

Buried: Oak Hill Cemetery, Lawrence, KS (Section 10, Lot 79)

References: Sarah J.F. Hill. *Mrs. Hill's Journal—Civil War Reminiscences.* Edited by Mark M. Krug. Chicago, IL, 1980. Obituary, *Lawrence Daily Gazette*, Aug. 20, 1904. Obituary, *Lawrence Daily Journal*, Aug. 20, 1904. Pension File and Military Service File, National Archives. William A. Neal. *An Illustrated History of the Missouri Engineer and the 25th Infantry Regiments.* Chicago, IL, 1889.

Colley Blondville Holland

Captain, Capt. Holland's Co., MO Home Guards, June 7, 1861. Discharged Oct. 5, 1861. Captain, Co. D, Phelps' Regiment, MO Infantry, Oct. 17, 1861. Lieutenant Colonel, Phelps' Regiment, MO Infantry, Dec. 19, 1861. Commanded Post of Cassville (MO), Army of the Southwest, Department of the Mississippi, Feb.–May 1862. Honorably mustered out, May 13, 1862. Colonel, 72 Enrolled MO Militia, Aug. 16, 1862. Brig. Gen., Enrolled MO Militia, Oct. 27, 1862. Commanded 4 Military District, Enrolled MO Militia, District of Southwest Missouri, Department of the Missouri, Jan. 1863–Dec. 1864. Commission revoked, Jan. 12, 1865. Battle honors: Marmaduke's Expedition into Missouri (Springfield), Shelby's Raid in Arkansas and Missouri, Operations in Northwestern Arkansas.

Born: Aug. 24, 1816 Robertson Co., TN

Died: March 5, 1901, Springfield, MO

Other Wars: Florida Seminole War (Corporal, Capt. Henry's Co., 2 TN Mounted Infantry)

Occupation: Merchant tailor before war. Cotton manufacturer and banker after war.

Offices/Honors: Postmaster, Springfield, MO, 1852

Miscellaneous: Resided Springfield, Greene Co., MO

Buried: Hazelwood Cemetery, Springfield, MO (Lot 149)

Colley Blondville Holland, post-war (Howard L. Conard, editor. *Encyclopedia of the History of Missouri*. New York, Louisville and St. Louis, 1901).

References: Jonathan Fairbanks and Clyde E. Tuck. *Past and Present of Greene County, Missouri*. Indianapolis, IN, 1915. *The United States Biographical Dictionary and Portrait Gallery of Eminent and Self-Made Men*. Missouri Volume. New York, Chicago, St. Louis, Kansas City, 1878. Obituary, *Springfield Republican*, March 6, 1901. Howard L. Conard, editor. *Encyclopedia of the History of Missouri*. New York, Louisville, and St. Louis, 1901. *History of Greene County, Missouri*. St. Louis, MO, 1883. Obituary, *St. Louis Globe-Democrat*, March 7, 1901. Military Service File, National Archives.

Samuel Allison Holmes

Major, 10 MO Infantry, Aug. 15, 1861. Lieutenant Colonel, 10 MO Infantry, Dec. 1, 1861. Colonel, 10 MO Infantry, April 9, 1862. Commanded 2 Brigade, 3 Division, Army of the Mississippi, Oct. 3–26, 1862. Commanded 2 Brigade, 7 Division, 17 Army Corps, Army of the Tennessee, Feb.–June 1863. Resigned June 10, 1863, due to "chronic cystitis with also enlargement of the prostate gland ... causes of disability constantly aggravated by my stay in service and affecting my general health." Colonel, 40 MO Infantry, Sept. 8, 1864. Commanded 2 Brigade, 3 Division, 16 Army Corps, Military Division of West Mississippi, April 1865. Honorably mustered out, Aug. 8, 1865. Battle honors: Siege of Corinth, Iuka, Corinth, Port Gibson, Raymond, Jackson, Champion's Hill, Vicksburg Campaign, Nashville, Mobile Campaign.

Samuel Allison Holmes (Relief Portrait, Vicksburg National Military Park).

Born: Feb. 23, 1823 Springfield, VT
Died: Jan. 5, 1892 St. Louis, MO
Education: Attended Phillips Exeter Academy, Exeter, NH. Attended Dartmouth College, Hanover, NH.
Other Wars: Mexican War (1 Lieutenant, Adjutant, Easton's Battalion MO Infantry)
Occupation: Lawyer and judge
Miscellaneous: Resided St. Louis, MO
Buried: Concord Street Cemetery, Peterborough, NH
References: Pension File and Military Service File, National Archives. Leonard A. Morrison. *History of the Alison or Allison Family in Europe and America*. Boston, MA, 1893. Marcus O. Frost. *Regimental History of the Tenth Missouri Volunteer Infantry*. Topeka, KS, 1892. Obituary, *Peterborough Transcript*, Jan. 14, 1892. Albert Smith. *History of the Town of Peterborough, Hillsborough County, New Hampshire*. Boston, MA, 1876.

James T. Howland

Captain, Co. A, 3 MO Cavalry, Oct. 25, 1861. GSW right leg, Mount Zion, MO, Dec. 27, 1861. Major, 3 MO Cavalry, Feb. 3, 1863. Commanded Post of Pilot Knob, District of Southeastern Missouri, Department of the Missouri, June 1863.

Resigned July 21, 1863, since "my pecuniary affairs are in such a state as to demand my personal attention to them in order to save myself ... from the most serious loss." Colonel, 69 Enrolled MO Militia, Oct. 21, 1863. Commission revoked, Feb. 11, 1865. Battle honors: Mount Zion.
  Born: Sept. 3, 1823 Harrodsburg, KY
  Died: Feb. 27, 1910 LaGrange, MO
  Other Wars: Mexican War (Private, Co. C, 2 KY Infantry)
  Occupation: Carpenter
  Miscellaneous: Resided LaGrange, Lewis Co., MO
  Buried: LaGrange Memorial Cemetery, LaGrange, MO
  References: David W. Dillard. *The Union Post Commanders at Pilot Knob, 1861–1865*. Ironton, MO, 2013. Pension File and Military Service File, National Archives. Obituary, *LaGrange Weekly Indicator*, March 3, 1910. Obituary, *Quincy Daily Journal*, Feb. 28, 1910. *History of Lewis, Clark, Knox and Scotland Counties, Missouri*. St. Louis and Chicago, 1887.

Adolph E. Hugo

Major, 3 Enrolled MO Militia, Sept. 30, 1862. Colonel, 3 Enrolled MO Militia, Oct. 28, 1863. Resigned June 18, 1864.
  Born: 1826? Denmark
  Died: July 11, 1886, Ewing Twp., Mercer Co., NJ (New Jersey State Lunatic Asylum)
  Occupation: Accountant
  Miscellaneous: Resided St. Louis, MO; and Jersey City, Hudson Co., NJ. Served as Actuary for Washington University, St. Louis, MO, 1857–61.
  Buried: Bayview/New York Bay Cemetery, Jersey City, NJ
  References: Pension File, National Archives. "Adolph E. Hugo Insane," *New York Times*, July 6, 1885. Death Certificate. www.ancestry.com.

Robert Hundhausen

Captain, Co. I, 3 U.S. Reserve Corps, MO Infantry (3 months), May 8, 1861. Honorably mustered out, Aug. 18, 1861. Private, Co. D, 3 U.S. Reserve Corps, MO Infantry, Aug. 22, 1861. Major, 3 U.S. Reserve Corps, MO Infantry, Oct. 27, 1861. Colonel, 4 MO Infantry, Jan. 18, 1862. Commanded Post of Pacific City, (MO), District of St. Louis, Department of the Missouri, Nov. 1862. Honorably mustered out, Feb. 1, 1863. Additional Paymaster, USV, June 30, 1864. Resigned Aug. 4, 1865.

Robert Hundhausen (courtesy Missouri Historical Society, St. Louis [P0084-0012]).

Robert Hundhausen (Hinton's Photograph Gallery, 99 Camp Street, One door from Poydras, New Orleans, Louisiana; USAMHI [RG100S-Febiger Collection-p. 4-D]).

  Born: March 3, 1822, Neukirchen, near Cologne, Germany
  Died: April 10, 1872, Grays Summit, MO
  Other Wars: Mexican War (Private, Co. E, 1 MO Mounted Infantry)
  Occupation: Farmer and miller before war. Merchant after war.
  Offices/Honors: Postmaster, Grays Summit, MO, 1866–72

Miscellaneous: Resided Hermann, Gasconade Co., MO; and Grays Summit, Franklin Co., MO

Buried: City Cemetery, Pacific, Franklin Co., MO

References: Pension File and Military Service File, National Archives. *History of Franklin, Jefferson, Washington, Crawford and Gasconade Counties, Missouri.* Chicago, IL, 1888. Letters Received, Commission Branch, Adjutant General's Office, File H900(CB)1864, National Archives. "Colonel Robert Hundhausen (Gasconade County)," http://home.usmo.com/~momollus/GascCoCW/HunR.htm.

Daniel Huston, Jr.

Captain, 1 U.S. Infantry, Dec. 8, 1856. Colonel, 7 MO Cavalry, Feb. 22, 1862. Commanded Post of Lexington (MO), District of Central Missouri, Department of the Missouri, May–Aug. 1862. Commanded Post of Sedalia (MO), District of Central Missouri, Department of the Missouri, Aug.–Sept. 1862. Commanded 1 Brigade, 2 Division, Army of the Frontier, Department of the Missouri, Oct.–Dec. 1862 and Jan.–June 1863. Commanded 2 Division, Army of the Frontier, Department of the Missouri, Dec. 1862–Jan. 1863. Assistant Commissary of Musters, Department of the Missouri, May–Aug. 1863. Major, 11 U.S. Infantry, Aug. 1, 1863. President of Board for Examination of Applicants for Commissions in Colored Troops, St. Louis, MO, Aug. 1863–Jan. 1865. Honorably mustered out of volunteer service, Dec. 30, 1864. Commanded Boston Harbor and Massachusetts Seacoast Defenses, Department of the East, March–April 1865. Bvt. Major, USA, Aug. 10, 1861, for gallant and meritorious services in the battle of Wilson's Creek, MO. Bvt. Lieutenant Colonel, USA, July 4, 1863, for gallant and meritorious services during the siege of Vicksburg, MS. Bvt. Colonel, USA, March 13, 1865, for gallant and meritorious services during the war. Battle honors: Wilson's Creek, Prairie Grove, Vicksburg Campaign.

Born: Jan. 1825 Bangor, ME

Died: Dec. 2, 1884 Burlington, NJ

Education: Graduated U.S. Military Academy, West Point, NY, 1848

Occupation: Regular Army (Colonel, 5 U.S. Infantry, retired June 22, 1882)

Miscellaneous: Resided Zanesville, Muskingum Co., OH; and Burlington, Burlington Co., NJ

Buried: Arlington National Cemetery, Arlington, VA (Section 3, Lot 1969)

Daniel Huston, Jr. (W.L. Troxell, Photographer, S.W. Corner of Fourth and Locust Streets, St. Louis, Missouri; courtesy Tom Molocea).

Daniel Huston, Jr. (Anderson, 1311 Main Street, Richmond, Virginia; courtesy Steve Meadow).

References: Pension File and Military Service File, National Archives. Obituary, *Burlington Daily Enterprise*, Dec. 2, 1884. George W. Cullum. *Biographical Register of the Officers and Graduates of the U.S. Military Academy.*

Daniel Huston, Jr. (third from left, as Major, 11 U.S. Infantry, 1866, with, from left, Adjutant William H. Clapp, Quartermaster Oscar Hagen, and Assistant Surgeon John H. Frantz) (Anderson & Co's, Photographic Art Palace, 1311 Main Street, Opposite Mitchell & Tyler's, Richmond, Virginia; USAMHI [RG98S-CWP156.46]).

Third Edition. Boston, MA, 1891. *Sixteenth Annual Reunion of the Association of the Graduates of the U.S. Military Academy at West Point, NY*. East Saginaw, MI, 1885. Letters Received, Appointment, Commission and Personal Branch, Adjutant General's Office, File 663(ACP)1874, National Archives. Letters Received, Volunteer Service Branch, Adjutant General's Office, File H1369(VS)1864, National Archives.

John Edward Hutton

Colonel, 59 Enrolled MO Militia, Sept. 2, 1862.
Born: March 28, 1828, Polk Co., TN
Died: Dec. 28, 1893 Mexico, MO
Education: Graduated St. Louis Medical College, St. Louis, MO, 1860
Occupation: Physician before war and lawyer and newspaper editor after war
Offices/Honors: U.S. House of Representatives, 1885–89
Miscellaneous: Resided Warrenton, Warren Co., MO, before war; and Mexico, Audrain Co., MO, after war
Buried: Elmwood Cemetery, Mexico, MO
References: Obituary, *Mexico Intelligencer*, Jan. 4, 1894. Obituary, *Mexico Weekly Ledger*, Jan. 4, 1894. James L. Harrison, compiler. *Biographical Directory of the American Congress, 1774–1949*. Washington, D.C., 1950. Obituary, *St. Louis Post-Dispatch*, Dec. 29, 1893. *History of Audrain County, Missouri*. St. Louis, MO, 1884. *History of the St. Louis Medical College*. St. Louis, MO, 1898.

Henry Imhauser

2 Lieutenant, Co. F, Benton County Regiment, MO Home Guards, June 13, 1861. GSW neck, Cole Camp, MO, June 19, 1861. Colonel, Benton County Regiment, MO Home Guards, July 21, 1861. Discharged Sept. 13, 1861. Battle honors: Cole Camp.
Born: March 6, 1813, Altenkirchen, Rhineland-Palatinate, Germany
Died: Aug. 22, 1875 Pettis Co., MO
Occupation: Farmer
Miscellaneous: Resided Flat Creek Twp., Pettis Co., MO
Buried: St. John's Catholic Cemetery, Bahner, Pettis Co., MO
References: www.ancestry.com. www.findagrave.com. Military Service File, National Archives. Kathleen W. Miles. *Bitter Ground: The Civil War in Missouri's Golden Valley, Benton, Henry and St. Clair Counties*. Clinton, MO, 1971.

Albert Jackson

Colonel, 12 MO State Militia Cavalry, May 14, 1862. Commanded Post of Pilot Knob (MO), St. Louis Division, District of Missouri, Department of the Mississippi, June–July 1862. "Having been reported as incompetent by a Military Examining Board," his commission as colonel was vacated by order of Governor Hamilton R. Gamble, Sept. 10, 1862. Jackson was returned to duty with his regiment, Oct. 21, 1862, when the Secretary of War ruled that the Governor of Missouri did not have authority to discharge State Militia officers from the service of the United States Army. The authority controversy was finally referred to President Lincoln, who ordered, Dec. 28, 1862, "that His Excellency Governor Gamble may, in his discretion, remove from office all officers of the peculiar military force organized by him in Missouri." In response to this order Governor Gamble notified Jackson on Jan. 7, 1863 that his dismissal was confirmed, effective Sept. 10, 1862.
Born: 1811? NJ
Died: March 7, 1878, Jackson, MO
Occupation: Lawyer and judge
Offices/Honors: Circuit Court Judge, 1854–62 and 1865–69
Miscellaneous: Resided Greenville, Wayne Co., MO; and Jackson, Cape Girardeau Co., MO. Impeached in 1859 upon various charges of tyranny, oppression and favoritism, he was acquitted after a sixteen-day trial.
Buried: Burial place unknown
References: David W. Dillard. *The Union Post*

Commanders at Pilot Knob, 1861–1865. Ironton, MO, 2013. *History of Southeast Missouri*. Chicago, IL, 1888. William V. N. Bay. *Reminiscences of the Bench and Bar of Missouri*. St. Louis, MO, 1878. Obituary, *The Peoples' Tribune (Jefferson City, MO)*, March 20, 1878. Military Service File, National Archives. Letters Received, Volunteer Service Branch, Adjutant General's Office, Files J282(VS)1862 and T163(VS)1864, National Archives. Cletis R. Ellinghouse. *Old Wayne: A Brit's Memoir*. Philadelphia, PA, 2010. *Organization and Status of Missouri Troops (Union and Confederate) in Service During the Civil War*. Washington, D.C., 1902. Thomas J. Henderson. *Official Report of the Trial of the Hon. Albert Jackson, Judge of the Fifteenth Judicial Circuit, Before the Senate, Composing the High Court of Impeachment of the State of Missouri*. Jefferson City, MO, 1859.

Ephraim Hall Emery Jameson

Colonel, 10 Enrolled MO Militia, Sept. 24, 1862. Resigned Sept. 23, 1863.

Born: May 19, 1835, St. George, ME

Died: Oct. 12, 1907 Detroit, MI

Education: Attended New Hampton Literary and Theological Institution, Fairfax, VT. Received Doctor of Divinity degree, Central University of Iowa, Pella, IA, 1880.

Occupation: Newspaper reporter and editor to 1876; and Baptist clergyman after 1876

Ephraim Hall Emery Jameson, post-war (William Cathcart, editor. *The Baptist Encyclopedia*. Philadelphia, Pennsylvania, 1881).

Offices/Honors: Missouri House of Representatives, 1862–66. District Secretary of the American Baptist Missionary Society, 1890–1907.

Miscellaneous: Resided St. Louis, MO, to 1876; Omaha, Douglas Co., NE, 1876–81; Saginaw, Saginaw Co., MI, 1881–84; Lansing, Ingham Co., MI, 1884–90; and Detroit, MI, after 1890

Buried: Woodlawn Cemetery, Detroit, MI (Section 8, Lot 269, unmarked)

References: Ephraim O. Jameson. *The Jamesons in America, 1647–1900. Genealogical Records and Memoranda*. Concord, NH, 1901. Obituary, *Detroit Free Press*, Oct. 13, 1907. Obituary, *Detroit News Tribune*, Oct. 13, 1907. William Cathcart, editor. *The Baptist Encyclopaedia*. Philadelphia, PA, 1881. Obituary, *New York Times*, Oct. 14, 1907.

James W. Johnson

Colonel, 15 U.S. Reserve Corps, MO Infantry, July 6, 1861. Discharged Dec. 6, 1861. Colonel, 26 Enrolled MO Militia, Sept. 1, 1862. Resigned March 28, 1864.

Born: Aug. 24, 1811 VA (Age at death 77y, 4m, 11d, according to tombstone)

Died: Dec. 23, 1888 Bolivar, MO

Occupation: Farmer

Offices/Honors: Sheriff of Polk Co., MO, 1850–52

Miscellaneous: Resided Marion Twp., Polk Co., MO

Buried: Bolivar City Cemetery, Bolivar, MO

References: *History of Hickory, Polk, Cedar, Dade and Barton Counties, Missouri*. Chicago, IL, 1889. Military Service File, National Archives. www.ancestry.com.

Francis Joseph Joliat

Colonel, 15 MO Infantry, Sept. 22, 1861. Commanded 1 Brigade, 2 Division, Army of Southwest Missouri, Department of the Missouri, Feb. 1862. "Under treatment for weeks for bilious and intermittent fever with chronic diarrhea contracted in Mississippi and Tennessee," he resigned Nov. 26, 1862. Battle honors: Pea Ridge.

Born: March 14, 1821, Courtetelle, Delemont, Switzerland

Died: June 17, 1884, Chicago, IL

Occupation: School teacher before war. Liquor merchant and notary public after war.

Offices/Honors: Chancellor of the Belgian Consulate, Chicago, IL, in his final years

Miscellaneous: Resided Chicago, IL

Buried: Saint Boniface Cemetery, Chicago, IL

References: Pension File and Military Service File, National Archives. Obituary, *Chicago Inter Ocean*, June 18, 1884. Donald Allendorf. *Long Road to Liberty: The Odyssey of a German Regiment in the Yankee Army, The 15th Missouri Volunteer Infantry*. Kent, OH, 2006. Letters Received, Volunteer Service Branch, Adjutant General's Office, File J30(VS)1867, National Archives.

Fidelio Sharp Jones

Captain, Co. I, 72 Enrolled MO Militia, Aug. 15, 1862. Major, 72 Enrolled MO Militia, Aug. 17, 1862. Lieutenant Colonel, 72 Enrolled MO Militia, Nov. 11, 1862. Lieutenant Colonel, 6 Provisional Enrolled MO Militia, April 1, 1863. Colonel, 72 Enrolled MO Militia, Oct. 1, 1863. Colonel, 6 Provisional Enrolled MO Militia, Oct. 5, 1863. Resigned Jan. 22, 1864. Lieutenant Colonel, 72 Enrolled MO Militia, Sept. 28, 1864. Commission vacated, March 12, 1865. Battle honors: Marmaduke's Expedition into Missouri (Springfield), Shelby's Raid in Arkansas and Missouri.

Born: July 19, 1835, Tazewell, TN

Died: Dec. 3, 1898 Chula Vista, CA

Occupation: Merchant, farmer, live stock trader, and livery operator

Miscellaneous: Resided Springfield, Greene Co., MO; and Chula Vista, San Diego Co., CA

Buried: Mount Hope Cemetery, San Diego, CA (Division 1, Section 7, Lot 110)

Fidelio Sharp Jones, post-war (*History of Greene County, Missouri.* St. Louis, Missouri, 1883).

References: *History of Greene County, Missouri.* St. Louis, MO, 1883. Obituary, *Springfield Leader-Democrat*, Dec. 6, 1898. Pension File, National Archives.

John Jay Joslyn

Major, 1 MO Cavalry, Sept. 6, 1861. Lieutenant Colonel, 1 MO Cavalry, Oct. 14, 1863. Chief of Cavalry, District of Southeast Missouri, Department of the Missouri, Oct.–Dec. 1863. Chief of Cavalry, District of St. Louis, Department of the Missouri, Dec. 1863–Nov. 1864. Honorably mustered out, Sept. 8, 1864. Remustered as Lieutenant Colonel, 1 MO Cavalry, Dec. 29, 1864. Resigned Feb. 27, 1865, since "in the absence of any charges for incompetency, inefficiency, or dereliction of duty, a junior officer (Milton H. Brawner) has been placed in command immediately over me." Brig. Gen. Joseph R. West recommended acceptance of his resignation with the comment, "Lt. Col. Joslyn, during the command of his regiment for two months, has not exhibited such qualification as would induce me to recommend him for a colonelcy. He has also been imprudent and unofficerlike in his conduct." Commissioned as Colonel, 1 MO Cavalry, March 22, 1865, by Governor Thomas C. Fletcher, who recognized that the promotion of Major Brawner over Joslyn was unjust and contrary to the rules of the service. Mustered as Colonel, 1 MO Cavalry, April 13, 1865. Honorably mustered out, July 8, 1865. His muster as colonel was revoked upon muster out, being regarded as irregular since he was away from his command and physically unfitted for field service at the time of muster. The revocation of his muster was, however, declared void, May 12, 1897.

Born: Feb. 13, 1834 Ithaca, NY

Died: Sept. 3, 1931 Retsil, WA

Occupation: Traveling salesman before war. Merchant and bookkeeper after war.

Miscellaneous: Resided Cincinnati, OH, to 1872; Star City, Lincoln Co., AR, 1872–83; Chicago, IL, 1883–89; Spokane Falls, Spokane Co., WA, 1889–1931

Buried: Washington Veterans Home Cemetery, Retsil, WA

References: Pension File and Military Service File, National Archives. Letters Received, Volunteer Service Branch, Adjutant General's Office, File B1857(VS)1865, National Archives. Obituary, *Bremerton Daily News Searchlight*, Sept. 5, 1931. *Annual Report of the Adjutant General of Missouri for the Year Ending December 31, 1865.* Jefferson City, MO, 1866. Fay Hempstead. *Historical Review of Arkansas: Its Commerce, Industry and Modern Affairs. Chicago, IL, 1911.

Herrmann F. Kallmann

Colonel, 2 U.S. Reserve Corps, MO Infantry (3 months), May 7, 1861. Honorably mustered out, Aug. 16, 1861.Colonel, 2 U.S. Reserve Corps, MO Infantry, Sept. 20, 1861. Arrested on charges preferred by Lieutenant Colonel Herman Zakrzewski, he submitted his resignation, Jan. 7, 1862, since "my health has been much impaired." Major Gen. Samuel R. Curtis would not accept his resignation while prosecution of the charges was pending. Honorably mustered out, Sept. 10, 1862. 2 Lieutenant, Co. E, 40 MO Infantry, Aug. 10, 1864. Captain, Co. E, 40 MO Infantry, Sept. 5, 1864. Honorably mustered out, Aug. 8, 1865. Battle honors: Siege of Corinth.
Born: Jan. 12, 1823 Liegnitz, Silesia, Germany
Died: Nov. 1, 1904 Detroit, MI
Occupation: Railroad superintendent before war. Civil engineer after war.
Offices/Honors: U.S. Assistant Engineer in charge of River and Harbor Improvements, Detroit, MI, 1875-97
Miscellaneous: Resided St. Louis, MO, to 1875; Detroit, MI, after 1875

Herrmann F. Kallmann, post-war (Paul Leake. *History of Detroit: Chronicle of Its Progress, Its Industries, Its Institutions, and the People of the Fair City of the Straits.* Chicago and New York, 1912).

Buried: Woodlawn Cemetery, Detroit, MI (Section 14, Lot 176)
References: Paul Leake. *History of Detroit: Chronicle of Its Progress, Its Industries, Its Institutions, and the People of the Fair City of the Straits.* Chicago and New York, 1912. Pension File and Military Service File, National Archives. Obituary, *Detroit Free Press,* Nov. 2, 1904. Obituary, *Detroit News,* Nov. 2, 1904. Obituary Circular, Whole No. 310, Michigan MOLLUS. Letters Received, Volunteer Service Branch, Adjutant General's Office, File K650(VS)1865, National Archives. Wilhelm Kaufmann. *The Germans in the American Civil War.* Translated by Steven Rowan and edited by Don Heinrich Tolzmann with Werner D. Mueller and Robert E. Ward. Carlisle, PA, 1999.

Thompson J. Kelly

Colonel, 47 Enrolled MO Militia, Sept. 16, 1864. Commission vacated, March 12, 1865.
Born: June 30, 1819, Cooper Co., MO
Died: April 20, 1875, Camden Co., MO
Occupation: Farmer and lawyer
Offices/Honors: Camden County Court Clerk, 1850-68. Postmaster, Linn Creek, MO, 1854-56. Probate Judge, 1856-64. Missouri House of Representatives, 1873-75.
Miscellaneous: Resided Linn Creek, Camden Co., MO
Buried: Old Linn Creek Cemetery, near Linn Creek, MO
References: Obituary, *The Peoples' Tribune (Jefferson City, MO),* April 28, 1875. *History of Laclede, Camden, Dallas, Webster, Wright, Texas, Pulaski, Phelps and Dent Counties, Missouri.* Chicago, IL, 1889. John W. Pattison, compiler. *Biographical Sketches of the Officers and Members of the Twenty-Seventh General Assembly of Missouri.* Jefferson City, MO, 1874. www.findagrave.com.

James Gibson Kettle

Colonel, 67 Enrolled MO Militia, Dec. 11, 1862. Commission vacated, Sept. 24, 1863.
Born: Aug. 22, 1813 (Age at death, 84y, 8m, 29d, according to tombstone) Harper's Ferry, VA (now WV)
Died: Nov. 8, 1897 Callaway Co., MO
Occupation: Farmer
Offices/Honors: Postmaster, Prairie Fork, Montgomery Co., MO, 1879-87

James Gibson Kettle (private collection of Donald J. Litnerski, courtesy of Rudy M. Hanson).

Miscellaneous: Resided Bear Creek Twp., Montgomery Co., MO; Nine-Mile Prairie, Callaway Co., MO; and Woodland, Yolo County, CA (1890–93)
Buried: Mount Horeb Church Cemetery, near Mineola, Montgomery Co., MO
References: James M. Guinn. *History of the State of California and Biographical Record of the Sacramento Valley, California.* Chicago, IL, 1906. Pension File, National Archives. Obituary, *Montgomery Standard*, Nov. 12, 1897. www.findagrave.com. www.ancestry.com.

Thomas Fox Kimball

Colonel, Kimball's Regiment, Six Months MO Militia, Nov. 28, 1861. Honorably mustered out, April 2, 1862. Lieutenant Colonel, 35 MO Infantry, Sept. 30, 1862. Commanded Post of Jefferson City, Central District of Missouri, Department of the Missouri, Nov. 1862. Expecting to face charges for an unprovoked assault upon Major Joseph Penney, he resigned, Dec. 1, 1862, "feeling that my usefulness as an officer in the United States service has by force of circumstances been materially impaired and that my continuance in office ... will prove to be of vast injury to the regiment."
Born: 1827? KY
Died: Aug. 24, 1865 Yellowstone River, MT (murdered by Sioux Indians)
Occupation: Farmer
Miscellaneous: Resided Bedford, Taylor Co., IA
Buried: Burial place unknown
References: Pension File and Military Service File, National Archives. "Indian Murders on the Yellowstone," *The Montana Post (Virginia City, MT)*, Sept. 2, 1865. "Col. Kimball Killed by the Indians," *St. Joseph Morning Herald and Daily Tribune*, Nov. 26, 1865. Letters Received, Volunteer Service Branch, Adjutant General's Office, File K47(VS)1867, National Archives. *History of Taylor County, Iowa.* Des Moines, IA, 1881.

Austin Augustus King, Jr.

Private, Co. B, 3 MO State Militia Cavalry, Jan. 13, 1862. Captain, Co. D, 3 MO State Militia Cavalry, March 7, 1862. Honorably discharged, Feb. 28, 1863. Major, 6 MO State Militia Cavalry, April 12, 1863. Chief of Cavalry, Staff of Brig. Gen. John B. Sanborn, District of Southwest Missouri, Department of the Missouri, Jan.–July 1864. Lieutenant Colonel, 13 MO Cavalry, Sept. 19, 1864. Commanded Post of Glasgow (MO), District of North Missouri, Department of the Missouri, Sept. 1864. Acting ADC, Staff of Brig. Gen. Clinton B. Fisk, District of North Missouri, Department of the Missouri, Oct. 1864. Colonel, 13 MO Cavalry, July 10, 1865. Commanded Post of Fort Riley (KS), District of the Upper Arkansas, Sept. 1865. Commanded Post of Camp Wardwell (CO Territory), District of the Upper Arkansas, Oct. 1865. Honorably mustered out, Jan. 11, 1866. Battle honors: Marmaduke's Expedition into Missouri (Springfield), Shelby's Raid in Arkansas and Missouri (Humansville), Price's Missouri Expedition.
Born: Dec. 5, 1841 Richmond, MO
Died: May 30, 1886, St. Louis, MO
Education: Attended University of Missouri, Columbia, MO
Occupation: Lawyer and farmer
Miscellaneous: Resided Jefferson City, Cole Co., MO; Wyandotte, Wyandotte Co., KS (1880); and St. Louis, MO, 1881–86. Son of former Missouri Governor Austin A. King. Brother of Colonel Walter King (3 MO State Militia Cavalry). Brother-in-law of Colonel Allen P. Richardson (Cole County Regiment, MO Home Guards).
Buried: Originally Woodland-Old City Cemetery, Jefferson City, MO. Removed to Valhalla

Cemetery, Bel-Nor, St. Louis Co., MO, March 23, 1914 (Section 9, Lot 270).

References: Pension File and Military Service File, National Archives. Obituary, *Jefferson City Tribune*, June 2, 1886. *Annual Report of the Adjutant General of Missouri for the Year Ending December 31, 1865*. Jefferson City, MO, 1866. Douglas Niermeyer, "Colonel Austin Augustus King, Jr., 13th Missouri Cavalry," http://www.suvcw.org/mollus.art051.htm.

Walter King

Lieutenant Colonel, Grundy County (MO) Battalion, Six Months MO Militia, Oct. 14, 1861. Honorably mustered out, Feb. 2, 1862. Colonel, 3 MO State Militia Cavalry, April 24, 1862. Honorably mustered out, Feb. 15, 1863, upon consolidation of the regiment with 6 MO State Militia Cavalry and 7 MO State Militia Cavalry. Lieutenant Colonel, 4 MO State Militia Cavalry, March 20, 1863. Commanded Post of Lexington (MO), District of Central Missouri, Department of the Missouri, March–May 1863. While serving on court martial duty in St. Louis, Oct. 1863–Dec. 1864, he invented and promoted his "cavalry raiding equipment," which received the recommendation of General Grant. Honorably mustered out, April 20, 1865. Battle honors: Marmaduke's Expedition into Missouri (Springfield), Quantrill's Raid into Kansas and Pursuit by Union Forces.

Born: March 21, 1829, TN

Died: Feb. 1, 1885 St. Louis, MO

Education: Graduated University of Missouri, Columbia, MO, 1849

Other Wars: Mexican War (Private, Co. H, 1 MO Mounted Infantry)

Occupation: Lawyer

Offices/Honors: Missouri House of Representatives, 1858–60 and 1875–77. Circuit Court Judge, 1865–67 (impeached June 1867 for "instructing the grand jury ... to find no bills of indictment against Confederate soldiers ... for any crimes they might have committed while engaged in said service")

Miscellaneous: Resided Richmond, Ray Co., MO, to 1876; and St. Louis, MO, 1876–85. Son of former Missouri Governor Austin A. King. Brother of Colonel Austin A. King, Jr. (13 MO Cavalry). Brother-in-law of Colonel Allen P. Richardson (Cole County Regiment, MO Home Guards).

Buried: Richmond Cemetery, Richmond, MO

References: Obituary, *Richmond Democrat*, Feb. 5, 1885. Pension File and Military Service File, National Archives. Letters Received, Volunteer Service Branch, Adjutant General's Office, File K160(VS)1864, National Archives. Obituary, *Missouri Republican*, Feb. 4, 1885. Letters Received, Adjutant General's Office, File W2314(AGO)1864, National Archives. *The American Annual Cyclopedia and Register of Important Events of the Year 1867*. New York City, NY, 1868. *History of Ray County, Missouri*. St. Louis, MO, 1881.

Henry Frederick Conrad Kleinschmidt

Private, Co. A, 3 U.S. Reserve Corps, MO Infantry (3 months), May 8, 1861. Honorably mustered out, Aug. 18, 1861. Captain, Co. G, 7 Enrolled MO Militia, Sept. 4, 1862. Major, 7 Enrolled MO Militia, June 1, 1864. Colonel, 7 Enrolled MO Militia, Oct. 1, 1864. Commission vacated, March 12, 1865.

Born: July 3, 1832, Germany

Died: Nov. 30, 1900 Alameda, CA

Occupation: Bookkeeper

Miscellaneous: Resided St. Louis, MO, to 1878; Helena, Lewis and Clark County, MT, 1878–97; and Alameda, Alameda Co., CA, after 1897

Buried: Mountain View Cemetery, Oakland, CA (Plot 43, Lot 10)

References: Joaquin Miller. *An Illustrated History of the State of Montana*. Chicago, IL, 1894. Obituary, *Helena Independent*, Dec. 6, 1900. Death notice, *San Francisco Call*, Dec. 5, 1900. Pension File and Military Service File, National Archives.

John Knapp

Colonel, 8 Enrolled MO Militia, Sept. 22, 1862. Temporary service as Colonel, 11 Provisional Enrolled MO Militia. Resigned Sept. 14, 1863. Battle honors: Price's Missouri Expedition.

Born: June 20, 1816, New York City, NY

Died: Nov. 12, 1888 St. Louis, MO

Other Wars: Mexican War (Captain, Co. C, St. Louis Legion, MO Infantry)

Occupation: Newspaper publisher

Miscellaneous: Resided St. Louis, MO

Buried: Calvary Cemetery, St. Louis, MO (Section 1, Lot 46)

References: William Hyde and Howard L. Conard, editors. *Encyclopedia of the History of St. Louis*. New York, Louisville, and St. Louis, 1899. Obituary, *St. Louis Globe-Democrat*, Nov. 12, 1888. Howard L. Conard, editor. *Encyclopedia of the History of Missouri*. New York, Louisville, and St. Louis, 1901. J. Thomas Scharf. *History of Saint Louis City and County*. Philadelphia, PA, 1883. Walter B. Davis and Daniel S. Durrie. *An*

Illustrated History of Missouri. St. Louis, MO, 1876. Walter B. Stevens. *St. Louis The Fourth City, 1764–1909.* St. Louis and Chicago, 1909. Obituary, *St. Louis Post-Dispatch,* Nov. 12, 1888. William C. Winter. *The Civil War in St. Louis: A Guided Tour.* St. Louis, MO, 1994.

John Knapp, post-war (William Hyde and Howard L. Conard, editors. *Encyclopedia of the History of St. Louis.* New York, Louisville, and St. Louis, 1899).

John Knapp, post-war (Walter B. Stevens. *St. Louis, the Fourth City, 1764-1909.* St. Louis and Chicago, 1909).

Jacob Knaus

Colonel, Johnson County Regiment, MO Home Guards. Superseded by Colonel James D. Eads. Private, Co. E, 27 MO Mounted Infantry, Aug. 4, 1861. Taken prisoner, Lexington, MO, Sept. 20, 1861. Honorably mustered out, Jan. 27, 1862. Battle honors: Lexington.
Born: Oct. 27, 1810 Maysville, Mason Co., KY
Died: Nov. 12, 1902 Knob Noster, MO
Occupation: Farmer and blacksmith
Offices/Honors: County Court Judge, 1848–51
Miscellaneous: Resided Knob Noster, Johnson Co., MO
Buried: Knaus Cemetery, Knob Noster, MO
References: *Portrait and Biographical Record of Johnson and Pettis Counties, Missouri.* Chicago, IL, 1895. *The History of Johnson County, Missouri.* Kansas City, MO, 1881. Obituary, *Knob Noster Gem,* Nov. 21, 1902. Pension File and Military Service File, National Archives. Obituary, *St. Louis Globe-Democrat,* Nov. 14, 1902. George S. Grover, "Civil War in Missouri," *Missouri Historical Review,* Vol. 8, No. 1 (Oct. 1913).

Arnold Krekel

Major, Krekel's Battalion, U.S. Reserve Corps, MO Infantry, Aug. 12, 1861. Honorably mustered out, Jan. 10, 1862. Lieutenant Colonel, 1 Battalion, MO State Militia Cavalry, March 12, 1862. Commanded Post of Fulton (MO), Northeastern District of Missouri, Department of the Missouri, Nov. 1862. Honorably mustered out, Dec. 2, 1862. Colonel, 27 Enrolled MO Militia, Oct. 4, 1864. Commission vacated, March 12, 1865.
Born: March 12, 1815, near Langenfeld, Germany
Died: July 14, 1888, Kansas City, MO
Education: Attended St. Charles (MO) College
Occupation: Newspaper editor, lawyer, and judge
Offices/Honors: Missouri House of Representatives, 1852–54. President, Missouri Constitutional Convention, 1865. Judge, U.S. District Court, Western District of Missouri, 1865–88.
Miscellaneous: Resided St. Charles, St. Charles Co., MO; Jefferson City, Cole Co., MO, 1867–81; and Kansas City, MO, 1881–88
Buried: Oak Grove Cemetery, St. Charles, MO (Block 6, Lot 110)
References: Joan M. Juern. *More Than the Sum of His Parts: Arnold Krekel.* Augusta, MO, 1999. Lawrence O. Christensen, William E. Foley, Gary R. Kremer, and Kenneth H. Winn, editors.

Arnold Krekel, post-war (Walter B. Davis and Daniel S. Durrie. *An Illustrated History of Missouri Comprising Its Early Record, and Civil, Political, and Military History from the First Exploration to the Present Time.* St. Louis, Missouri, 1876).

Dictionary of Missouri Biography. Columbia, MO, 1999. Pension File and Military Service File, National Archives. Obituary, *Kansas City Times,* July 15, 1888. Walter B. Davis and Daniel S. Durrie. *An Illustrated History of Missouri.* St. Louis, MO, 1876. Theodore S. Case, editor. *History of Kansas City, Missouri.* Syracuse, NY, 1888. *History of St. Charles, Montgomery and Warren Counties, Missouri.* St. Louis, MO, 1885. *The Bench and Bar of St. Louis, Kansas City, Jefferson City, and Other Missouri Cities.* St. Louis and Chicago, 1884. Obituary, *Kansas City Star,* July 14, 1888. Obituary, *St. Louis Post-Dispatch,* July 15, 1888. Lawrence H. Larsen. *Federal Justice in Western Missouri: The Judges, The Cases, The Times.* Columbia, MO, 1994.

John Marshall Krum

Colonel, 9 Enrolled MO Militia, Oct. 1, 1862. Resigned Sept. 14, 1863.

Born: March 10, 1810, Hillsdale, NY
Died: Sept. 15, 1883 St. Louis, MO
Education: Attended Union College, Schenectady, NY
Occupation: Lawyer and judge
Offices/Honors: Mayor of Alton, IL, 1837. Circuit Court Judge, 1843–48. Mayor of St. Louis, MO, 1848–49.

Arnold Krekel, post-war (courtesy Missouri Historical Society, St. Louis [P0004-1020]).

John Marshall Krum (pre-war) (Richard Edwards and Merna Hopewell. *Edwards's Great West and Her Commercial Metropolis, Embracing a General View of the West, and a Complete History of St. Louis.* St. Louis, Missouri, 1860).

John Marshall Krum, post-war (Walter B. Stevens. *St. Louis, the Fourth City, 1764-1909*). St. Louis and Chicago, 1909).

Miscellaneous: Resided St. Louis, MO. Brother-in-law of Bvt. Brig. Gen. Chester Harding, Jr.
Buried: Bellefontaine Cemetery, St. Louis, MO (Block 30, Lot 307)
References: William Hyde and Howard L. Conard, editors. *Encyclopedia of the History of St. Louis*. New York, Louisville, and St. Louis, 1899. J. Thomas Scharf. *History of Saint Louis City and County*. Philadelphia, PA, 1883. Charles H. Cornwell. *St. Louis Mayors Brief Biographies*. St. Louis, MO, 1965. Richard Edwards and Merna Hopewell. *Edwards's Great West and Her Commercial Metropolis, Embracing a General View of the West, and a Complete History of St. Louis*. St. Louis, MO, 1860. Obituary, *St. Louis Post-Dispatch*, Sept. 17, 1883. Walter B. Stevens. *St. Louis The Fourth City, 1764–1909*. St. Louis and Chicago, 1909. Melvin G. Holli and Peter d'Alroy Jones, editors. *Biographical Dictionary of American Mayors, 1820–1980*. Westport, CT, 1981.

August Krumsick

Assistant Surgeon, 3 MO Infantry, Jan. 18, 1862. Taken prisoner, Searcy Landing, AR, May 19, 1862. Released July 15, 1862. Surgeon, 3 MO Infantry, July 23, 1862. Dismissed Jan. 24, 1863, for "intemperance, neglect of duty, and absence without leave." Colonel, 55 Enrolled MO Militia, Sept. 22, 1863. Commission vacated, March 12, 1865. Battle honors: Pea Ridge, Searcy Landing.
Born: 1830? Brunswick, Germany
Died: 1875
Occupation: Physician
Offices/Honors: Sheriff of Franklin Co., MO, 1863–64
Miscellaneous: Resided Washington, Franklin Co., MO; and Mound City, Pulaski Co., IL. Brother of Colonel George Krumsick (54 Enrolled MO Militia)
Buried: Burial place unknown
References: Military Service File, National Archives. Letters Received, Volunteer Service Branch, Adjutant General's Office, File K600(VS)1862, National Archives. "Estate of A. Krumsick," *Franklin County Record*, Sept. 2, 1875. *History of Franklin, Jefferson, Washington, Crawford and Gasconade Counties, Missouri*. Chicago, IL, 1888. Herman G. Kiel, compiler. *The Centennial Biographical Directory of Franklin County, Missouri*. Washington, D.C., 1925.

George Krumsick

Private, Battery B, Backof's Battalion, MO Light Artillery, May 18, 1861. 2 Lieutenant, Battery B, Backof's Battalion, MO Light Artillery, June 13, 1861. Honorably mustered out, Aug. 22, 1861. Captain, Co. A, 54 Enrolled MO Militia, Aug. 19, 1862. Colonel, 54 Enrolled MO Militia, Sept. 22, 1863. Commission vacated, Sept. 29, 1864.
Born: March 2, 1836, Brunswick, Germany
Died: Jan. 6, 1897 Washington, MO
Occupation: Brewer. Vice President of Anheuser-Busch Brewing Co. in later years.
Miscellaneous: Resided Washington, Franklin Co., MO; and St. Louis, MO. Brother of Colonel August Krumsick (55 Enrolled MO Militia).
Buried: Wildey Odd Fellows Cemetery, Washington, MO
References: Pension File and Military Service File, National Archives. Obituary, *St. Louis Globe-Democrat*, Jan. 7, 1897. Obituary, *Franklin County Tribune*, Jan. 15, 1897. Herman G. Kiel, compiler. *The Centennial Biographical Directory of Franklin County, Missouri*. Washington, D.C., 1925.

Edward Augustus Kutzner

Colonel, 29 Enrolled MO Militia, Sept. 27, 1862. Commission vacated, Oct. 24, 1863. Temporary service as Colonel, 2 Provisional Enrolled MO Militia, March 10, 1863. Relieved from duty,

Sept. 3, 1863. Lieutenant Colonel, 39 MO Infantry, Sept. 8, 1864. Commanded Post of Glasgow (MO), District of North Missouri, Department of the Missouri, Nov. 1864. Colonel, 39 MO Infantry, Jan. 14, 1865. Commanded Sub-District of Howard, District of North Missouri, Department of the Missouri, Jan.–March. 1865. Honorably mustered out, March 14, 1865. Battle honors: Price's Missouri Expedition (Centralia).

Born: Jan. 1, 1809 Sunbury, PA
Died: Jan. 17, 1900 Stanberry, MO
Occupation: Merchant and farmer
Offices/Honors: Postmaster, Minersville, PA, 1838–42
Miscellaneous: Resided Vernon Twp., Van Buren Co., IA, to 1861; Memphis, Scotland Co., MO, 1861–87; and Stanberry, Gentry Co., MO, after 1887
Buried: Memphis Cemetery, Memphis, MO
References: Obituary, *Memphis Reveille,* Jan. 25, 1900. Pension File and Military Service File, National Archives. Obituary, *The Stanberry Headlight,* Jan. 20, 1900. Letters Received, Volunteer Service Branch, Adjutant General's Office, File 4859(VS)1871, National Archives. *Genealogical and Biographical Annals of Northumberland County, Pennsylvania.* Chicago, IL, 1911.

Edward Augustus Kutzner (center, with Major Hiram Baxter, left, and Lt. Col. Samuel M. Wirt, right) (George P. Hall, Photographer, Nos. 63 and 65 N. Fourth St., St. Louis, Missouri; courtesy Steve Meadow).

Bernard Laibold

Major, 2 MO Infantry (3 months), May 14, 1861. Honorably mustered out, July 30, 1861. Lieutenant Colonel, 2 MO Infantry, Sept. 10, 1861. Commanded 2 Brigade, 5 Division, Army of the Mississippi, June 1–Sept. 4, 1862. Commanded 35 Brigade, 11 Division, 3 Army Corps, Army of the Ohio, Sept.–Oct. 1862. Commanded 2 Brigade, 3 Division, Right Wing, 14 Army Corps, Army of the Cumberland, Dec. 31, 1862–Jan. 9, 1863. Colonel, 2 MO Infantry, Jan. 8, 1863. Commanded 2 Brigade, 3 Division, 20 Army Corps, Army of the Cumberland, Jan. 9–Feb. 2, 1863 and March 3–Oct. 9, 1863. GSW left hand, Missionary Ridge, TN, Nov. 25, 1863. Commanded Post of Dalton (GA), District of the Etowah, Department of the Cumberland, May–Sept. 1864. Honorably mustered out, Dec. 8, 1864. Battle honors: Pea Ridge, Perryville, Stone's River, Tullahoma Campaign (Fairfield), Chickamauga, Missionary Ridge, Charleston (TN), Atlanta Campaign, Wheeler's Raid to North Georgia (Dalton), Price's Missouri Expedition.

Edward Augustus Kutzner (USAMHI [RG98S-CWP112.24]).

Bernard Laibold (The National Archives [BA-520]).

Bernard Laibold (*Minutes of the Twenty-Third Annual Reunion of the Survivors of the Seventy-Third Regiment Illinois Volunteer Infantry.* N.p., 1909).

Born: Aug. 20, 1827 Baden, Germany
Died: Nov. 17, 1882 St. Louis, MO
Other Wars: Mexican War (Corporal, Co. F, St. Louis Legion, MO Infantry, mustered in May 15, 1846 and deserted June 5, 1846)
Occupation: Saloonkeeper
Offices/Honors: Chief of Metropolitan Police, St. Louis, MO, 1865–66
Miscellaneous: Resided St. Louis, MO
Buried: Saint Matthew Cemetery, St. Louis, MO (Block 4, Lot 45)
References: William Hyde and Howard L. Conard, editors. *Encyclopedia of the History of St. Louis.* New York, Louisville, and St. Louis, 1899. Obituary, *St. Louis Globe-Democrat,* Nov. 18, 1882. Allen E. Wagner. *Good Order and Safety: A History of the St. Louis Metropolitan Police, 1861–1906.* St. Louis, MO, 2008. Pension File and Military Service File, National Archives. J. Thomas Scharf. *History of Saint Louis City and County.* Philadelphia, PA, 1883. Wilhelm Kaufmann. *The Germans in the American Civil War.* Translated by Steven Rowan and edited by Don Heinrich Tolzmann with Werner D. Mueller and Robert E. Ward. Carlisle, PA, 1999. Letters Received, Volunteer Service Branch, Adjutant General's Office, Files G24(VS)1862, L21(VS)1862, and B3265(VS)1864, National Archives. Letters Received, Commission Branch, Adjutant General's Office, File L702(CB)1864, National Archives. Obituary, *St. Louis Post-Dispatch,* Nov. 18, 1882.

William Lawson

Colonel, 68 Enrolled MO Militia, March 17, 1864. Commission revoked March 18, 1864.
Born: 1802? PA
Died: 1875? Ripley Co., MO?
Occupation: Farmer
Offices/Honors: Missouri House of Representatives, 1860–62 and 1864–71
Miscellaneous: Resided Old Mines, Union Twp., Washington Co., MO (1860); Cane Creek, Jackson Twp., Carter Co., MO (1870)
Buried: Burial place unknown
References: "Administrator's Sale," *Doniphan Prospect,* Aug. 13, 1875. www.ancestry.com.

Franklin Leavenworth

Colonel, 78 Enrolled MO Militia, April 24, 1863. Commission vacated, March 12, 1865.
Born: Sept. 13, 1828 Ste. Genevieve Co., MO
Died: Jan. 2, 1881 Ste. Genevieve, MO
Occupation: Millwright

Miscellaneous: Resided Ste. Genevieve, Ste. Genevieve Co., MO

Buried: Ste. Genevieve, MO (cemetery unknown)

References: Pension File, National Archives. Elias W. Leavenworth. *A Genealogy of the Leavenworth Family in the United States.* Syracuse, NY, 1873. Obituary, *Ste. Genevieve Fair Play*, Jan. 8, 1881.

George Eliot Leighton

1 Lieutenant, RQM, 3 U.S. Reserve Corps, MO Infantry (3 months), May 8, 1861. Honorably mustered out, Aug. 17, 1861. *Captain*, 19 MO Infantry, Sept. 23, 1861. Provost Marshal, District of St. Louis, Department of the Missouri, Nov. 1861–April 1863. Major, 12 MO State Militia Cavalry, April 14, 1862. Major, 5 MO State Militia Cavalry, March 11, 1863. Resigned April 20, 1863. Colonel, 7 Enrolled MO Militia, Sept. 23, 1862. Resigned Dec. 25, 1863.

Born: March 7, 1835, Cambridge, MA
Died: July 4, 1901, Monadnock, NH
Education: Attended Woodward College, Cincinnati, OH
Occupation: Lawyer and capitalist, devoting himself to his railway, iron manufacturing, and banking enterprises after 1874

Offices/Honors: President, Missouri Historical Society, St. Louis, MO, 1882–90

Miscellaneous: Resided Cincinnati, OH, to 1858; and St. Louis, MO, after 1858

Buried: Bellefontaine Cemetery, St. Louis, MO (Block 313, Lot 2793)

References: *The Biographical Dictionary and Portrait Gallery of Representative Men of Chicago, St. Louis and the World's Columbian Exposition.* Chicago and New York, 1893. Obituary Circular, Whole No. 231, Missouri MOLLUS. William Hyde and Howard L. Conard, editors. *Encyclopedia of the History of St. Louis.* New York, Louisville, and St. Louis, 1899. Obituary, *The St. Louis Republic*, July 5, 1901. Tristram F. Jordan. *Leighton Genealogy. An Account of the Descendants of Capt. William Leighton of Kittery, Maine.* Albany, NY, 1885. J. Thomas Scharf. *History of Saint Louis City and County.* Philadelphia, PA, 1883. *The National Cyclopedia of American Biography.* Vol. 4. New York City, NY, 1897. Obituary, *St. Louis Post-Dispatch*, July 4, 1901. Military Service File, National Archives.

William Grigsby Lewis

1 Lieutenant, Adjutant, 57 Enrolled MO Militia, Oct. 15, 1862. Resigned June 19, 1863. Colonel, 57 Enrolled MO Militia, March 15, 1864. Resigned Sept. 22, 1864.

Born: Dec. 9, 1826 Greenbrier Co., VA (now WV)
Died: Feb. 18, 1869 Bethany, MO
Occupation: Lawyer and judge
Offices/Honors: Probate Judge, 1853–57
Miscellaneous: Resided Bethany, Harrison Co., MO
Buried: Miriam Cemetery, Bethany, MO (Original Addition, Block 6, Lot 33)

References: *History of Harrison and Mercer Counties, Missouri, From the Earliest Time to the Present.* St. Louis and Chicago, 1888. Death notice, *Gallatin North Missourian*, March 4, 1869. "Death of Wm. G. Lewis, Action of the Gallatin Bar," *Gallatin North Missourian*, March 18, 1869.

James Lindsay

Colonel, 68 Enrolled MO Militia, Nov. 20, 1862. Dismissed Nov. 2, 1863. Battle honors: Fredericktown, Bloomfield, Marmaduke's Expedition into Missouri, Price's Missouri Expedition.

Born: Jan. 14, 1814 Orange Co., VA
Died: June 5, 1898, St. Louis, MO

George Eliot Leighton, post-war (William Hyde and Howard L. Conard, editors. *Encyclopedia of the History of St. Louis.* New York, Louisville, and St. Louis, 1899).

James Lindsay, post-war (courtesy Iron County Historical Society, Ironton, Missouri).

Occupation: Printer and newspaper publisher before war. U.S. Pension Agent and land agent after war.
Offices/Honors: Missouri House of Representatives, 1850–52. Missouri Senate, 1852–56. Register of U.S. Land Office, Ironton, MO, 1861–66. U.S. Pension Agent, St. Louis, MO, 1869–73.
Miscellaneous: Resided Fredericktown, Madison Co., MO, to 1856; Ironton, Iron Co., MO, 1856–69; and St. Louis, MO, after 1869
Buried: Masonic Cemetery, Ironton, MO
References: Obituary, *Iron County Register*, June 9, 1898. Obituary, *St. Louis Globe-Democrat*, June 7, 1898. Pension File, National Archives. *Past and Present: A History of Iron County, Missouri, 1857–1994*. Marceline, MO, 1995. Obituary, *St. Louis Post-Dispatch*, June 6, 1898.

Henry Stapleton Lipscomb

Colonel, 11 MO State Militia Cavalry, May 6, 1862. Judged "unfit for the service" for his inefficiency in permitting a body of marauders in Schuyler County (MO) to escape when they might have been destroyed, he was dismissed, July 18, 1862. Suspecting that "secret machinations of enemies" had induced Governor Gamble to dismiss him, Lipscomb demanded an investigation, which resulted in the revocation of his dismissal, Oct. 24, 1862. However, since his regiment had meanwhile been consolidated with the 2 MO State Militia Cavalry, he was not restored to command of his regiment. Battle honors: Cherry Grove.
Born: 1821 VA
Died: July 10, 1889, near Palmyra, MO
Occupation: Lawyer
Offices/Honors: Missouri House of Representatives, 1861–62
Miscellaneous: Resided Palmyra, Marion Co., MO; and St. Louis, MO, 1876–82
Buried: Old Palmyra Cemetery, Palmyra, MO (marker heavily damaged)
References: A.J.D. Stewart, editor. *The History of the Bench and Bar of Missouri*. St. Louis, MO, 1898. Pension File and Military Service File, National Archives. Letters Received, Volunteer Service Branch, Adjutant General's Office, Files L816(VS)1862 and M728(VS)1868, National Archives. *History of Marion County, Missouri*. St. Louis, MO, 1884. Obituary, *Marion County Herald*, July 11, 1889.

Warren Lane Lothrop

1 Lieutenant, 4 U.S. Artillery, Feb. 20, 1861. Captain, Co. A, 1 MO Infantry (3 months), April 22, 1861. Resigned May 25, 1861. Captain, AQM, USA, Aug. 3, 1861. Major, 1 MO Light Artillery, Sept. 1, 1861. Lieutenant Colonel, 1 MO Light Artillery, Feb. 19, 1862. Chief of Artillery, Staff of Major Gen. John Pope and Major Gen. William S. Rosecrans, Army of the Mississippi, March–Oct. 1862. Colonel, 1 MO Light Artillery, Oct. 1, 1862. Chief of Artillery, Staff of Brig. Gen. Charles S. Hamilton, Left Wing, Army of the Tennessee, Nov. 1862–Jan. 1863. Chief of Artillery and Ordnance, Staff of Major Gen. Stephen A. Hurlbut, 16 Army Corps, Army of the Tennessee, Feb. 1863–June 1864. Honorably mustered out of volunteer service, July 29, 1865. Bvt. Major, USA, March 14, 1862, for gallant and meritorious services in action at New Madrid, Missouri. Bvt. Lieutenant Colonel, USA, March 13, 1865, for gallant and meritorious services during the war. Battle honors: Boonville, Wilson's Creek, New Madrid, Island No. 10, Iuka, Corinth.
Born: July 5, 1823, Leeds, ME
Died: Oct. 31, 1866 Tallahassee, FL
Other Wars: Mexican War (Sergeant, Co. A, U.S. Engineers)
Occupation: Regular Army (Captain, AQM, died 1866)
Miscellaneous: Resided Auburn, Androscoggin Co., ME

Warren Lane Lothrop (Roger D. Hunt Collection, USAMHI [RG98S-CWP207.24]).

Warren Lane Lothrop (Peplow & Balch, Artists, Star Gallery, 221 Main St., Memphis, Tennessee; Roger D. Hunt Collection, USAMHI [RG98S-CWP207.25]).

Buried: Leeds Center Cemetery, Leeds, ME
References: John C. Stinchfield. *History of the Town of Leeds, Androscoggin County, Maine, From Its Settlement, June 10, 1780*. Lewiston, ME, 1901. Military Service File, National Archives. Letters Received, Commission Branch, Adjutant General's Office, File S1306(CB)1866, National Archives. Georgia D. Merrill, editor. *History of Androscoggin County, Maine*. Boston, MA, 1891.

Walter L. Lovelace

Colonel, 67 Enrolled MO Militia, Aug. 13, 1862. Resigned Nov. 8, 1862. Provost Marshal, 9 District of Missouri, Oct. 4, 1864. Resigned Dec. 13, 1864.
  Born: Oct. 1, 1831 Charlotte Co., VA
  Died: Aug. 5, 1866 Danville, MO
  Education: Attended University of Missouri, Columbia, MO
  Occupation: Lawyer and judge
  Offices/Honors: Missouri House of Representatives, 1862–65 (Speaker 1864–65). Judge, Missouri Supreme Court, 1865–66.
  Miscellaneous: Resided Danville, Montgomery Co., MO
  Buried: Fulkerson-Lovelace Cemetery, Danville, MO
  References: William V. N. Bay. *Reminiscences of the Bench and Bar of Missouri*. St. Louis, MO, 1878. Howard L. Conard, editor. *Encyclopedia of the History of Missouri*. New York, Louisville, and St. Louis, 1901. J. Thomas Scharf. *History of Saint Louis City and County*. Philadelphia, PA, 1883. Charles F. Ritter and Jon L. Wakelyn. *American Legislative Leaders, 1850–1910*. Westport, CT, 1989. Erroneous/premature obituary, *Daily Missouri Republican*, July 13, 1866. Obituary, *Daily Missouri Republican*, Aug. 7, 1866. "Looking Back. The Neglected Grave of Supreme Judge Lovelace Near Montgomery County's Capitol," *Montgomery Tribune*, Nov. 16, 1900.

James Jerome Lyon

Private, Co. B, 1 MI Infantry (3 months), June 4, 1861. Honorably mustered out, Aug. 7, 1861. 1 Sergeant, Co. H, 24 MO Infantry, Oct. 9, 1861. I Lieutenant, Co. H, 24 MO Infantry, Dec. 1, 1861. Captain, Co. H, 24 MO Infantry, July 1, 1862. Acting ADC, Staff of Colonel Sempronius H. Boyd, 2 Division, Army of Southeast Missouri, Department of the Missouri, Dec. 1862–Jan. 1863. Acting AAG, Staff of Colonel Robert R. Livingston, 2 Brigade, 2 Division, Army of Southeast Missouri, Department of the Missouri, Feb. 1863. Judge Advocate, Staff of Major Gen. Andrew J. Smith, Right Wing, 16 Army Corps, Army of the Tennessee, Feb.–Sept. 1864. Major, 24 MO Infantry, Oct. 1, 1864. Acting AIG, Staff of Major Gen. Andrew J. Smith, Right Wing, 16 Army

Corps, Army of the Tennessee, Oct. 1864–Feb. 1865. Transferred to 21 MO Infantry, Dec. 28, 1864. Acting AIG, Staff of Major Gen. Andrew J. Smith, 16 Army Corps, Military Division of West Mississippi, March–Aug. 1865. Lieutenant Colonel, 21 MO Infantry, June 1, 1865. *Colonel, 21 MO Infantry, Aug. 17, 1865.* Resigned Aug. 7, 1865, since "I have served the country faithfully in protecting its rights and honor, and I now ask of it the permission to take care of and defend my own." Battle honors: Pea Ridge, Red River Campaign (Pleasant Hill), Tupelo.

Born: July 22, 1837, West Pembroke, Genesee Co., NY

Died: Feb. 24, 1913 California Veterans' Home, Yountville., CA

Occupation: After several postwar years engaged in mining, he resumed his prewar career as a clerk and editor. For many years Assistant Weigher, U.S. Customs, San Francisco, CA.

Offices/Honors: Quartermaster and commissary, California Veterans' Home, 1898–1913

Miscellaneous: Resided Leslie, Ingham Co., MI, before war; Helena, Lewis and Clark Co., MT, 1866–73; San Francisco, CA, 1874–98; and California Veterans' Home, Yountville, CA, 1898–1913

Buried: California Veterans' Home Cemetery, Yountville, CA

James Jerome Lyon (Roger D. Hunt Collection, USAMHI [RG98S-CWP107.37]).

James Jerome Lyon (Wilson's Creek National Battlefield [WICR 11656]).

References: J. Randall Houp. *The 24th Missouri Volunteer Infantry: Lyon Legion.* Alma, AR, 1997. Pension File and Military Service File, National Archives. William H. Ward, editor. *Records of Members of the Grand Army of the Republic With a Complete Account of the Twentieth National Encampment.* San Francisco, CA, 1886. Obituary, *San Francisco Chronicle*, Feb. 25, 1913. Sidney E. Lyon, editor. *Lyon Memorial: Families of Connecticut and New Jersey.* Detroit, MI, 1907. Leslie Anders. *The Twenty-first Missouri: From Home Guard to Union Regiment.* Westport, CT, 1975. Obituary, *San Francisco Call*, Feb. 25, 1913.

Francis Howe Manter

1 Lieutenant, Co. H, 1 MO Infantry (3 months), April 25, 1861. 1 Lieutenant, Co. H, 1 MO Infantry (3 years), June 11, 1861. Captain, Co. A, 1 MO Infantry, Aug. 9, 1861. Designation of regiment changed to 1 MO Light Artillery, Sept. 1, 1861. Captain, Battery A, 1 MO Light Artillery, Sept. 24, 1861. Colonel, 32 MO Infantry, Dec. 9, 1862. Commanded 1 Brigade, 1 Division, 15 Army Corps, Army of the Tennessee, April–June 1863. Chief of Staff, Staff of Major Gen. Frederick Steele, 1 Division, 15 Army Corps, Army of the Tennessee, June–July 1863. Chief of Staff, Staff of Major Gen. Frederick Steele, Army of Arkansas, Department of the

Missouri, Aug.–Dec. 1863. Chief of Staff, Staff of Major Gen. Frederick Steele, 7 Army Corps, Department of Arkansas, Dec. 1863–June 1864. Battle honors: Wilson's Creek, Fredericktown, Cache River, Chickasaw Bayou, Arkansas Post, Vicksburg Campaign, Advance upon Little Rock (Bayou Meto, Bayou Fourche), Camden Expedition (Marks' Mills, Jenkins' Ferry).

Born: Dec. 31, 1824 Elyria, OH

Died: June 13, 1864, Little Rock, AR (died of injuries received when he was accidentally thrown from his horse)

Education: Attended Western Reserve College, Hudson, OH

Occupation: Lawyer

Miscellaneous: Resided Elyria, Lorain Co., OH; and St. Louis, MO

Buried: Ridgelawn Cemetery, Elyria, OH

References: *History of Lorain County, Ohio.* Philadelphia, PA, 1879. Pension File and Military Service File, National Archives. Obituary, *Elyria Independent Democrat*, June 29, 1864. Obituary, *Daily Missouri Republican*, June 26, 1864. William E. McLean. *The Forty-Third Regiment of Indiana Volunteers. An Historic Sketch of Its Career and Services.* Terre Haute, IN, 1903.

Francis Howe Manter (Brown's Gallery, Corner of Main & Markham Streets, Little Rock, Arkansas; Butler Center for Arkansas Studies, Central Arkansas Library System [Ebenezer S. Peake Civil War Collection, MSS 06-32]).

Letters Received, Commission Branch, Adjutant General's Office, File M814(CB)1863, National Archives. Obituary, *Daily Missouri Democrat*, June 24, 1864. James B. Thomas, "Down Through the Years in Elyria," *Elyria Chronicle Telegram*, July 24, 1951.

Louis Henry Marshall

Captain, 10 U.S. Infantry, Dec. 29, 1860. Colonel, Benton Cadets, MO Infantry, Sept. 24, 1861. Honorably mustered out of volunteer service, Jan. 8, 1862. Acting ADC, Staff of Major Gen. John Pope, Army of the Mississippi, Feb.–June 1862. Colonel, Additional ADC, Staff of Major Gen. John Pope, Army of Virginia (and Department of the Northwest), June 30, 1862–July 28, 1865. Mustering and Disbursing Officer, Department of the Northwest, Feb. 1863–July 1865. Major, 14 U.S. Infantry, Oct. 16, 1863. Bvt. Lieutenant Colonel, USA, March 13, 1865, for gallant and meritorious services during the war. Battle honors: New Madrid, Island No. 10, Siege of Corinth, Northern Virginia Campaign (Cedar Mountain, 2nd Bull Run).

Born: May 23, 1828, VA

Died: Oct. 8, 1891 Monrovia, CA

Education: Graduated U.S. Military Academy, West Point, NY, 1849

Francis Howe Manter (Abraham Lincoln Presidential Library & Museum, [ALPLM]).

Louis Henry Marshall (Brady's National Photographic Portrait Gallery, 352 Pennsylvania Avenue, Washington, D.C.; Frederick Hill Meserve. *Historical Portraits, a Part of the Collection of Americana of Frederick Hill Meserve.* New York City, 1913-1915; courtesy New York State Library, Manuscripts and Special Collections).

Occupation: Regular Army (Major, 23 U.S. Infantry, resigned Nov. 23, 1868). Rancher and claims collector and agent.
Miscellaneous: Resided Baltimore, MD, before war; Cucamonga, San Bernardino Co., CA; and Monrovia, Los Angeles Co., CA, after war. Nephew of CSA General Robert E. Lee, who told his daughter, "I could forgive [him] fighting against us, if he had not joined such a miscreant as Pope."
Buried: Evergreen Cemetery, Los Angeles, CA (Section G, Lot 250, unmarked)
References: William M. Paxton. *The Marshall Family.* Cincinnati, OH, 1885. Pension File and Military Service File, National Archives. Letters Received, Commission Branch, Adjutant General's Office, File M460(CB)1868, National Archives. George W. Cullum. *Biographical Register of the Officers and Graduates of the U.S. Military Academy.* Third Edition. Boston, MA, 1891. Death notice, Los Angeles Herald, Oct. 9, 1891. Gregory Michno. *The Deadliest Indian War in the West: The Snake Conflict, 1864-1868.* Caldwell, ID, 2007.

Henry Charles Marston

Major, 6 Enrolled MO Militia, Sept. 24, 1862. Colonel, 6 Enrolled MO Militia, April 27, 1863. Resigned Sept. 14, 1863. Commissioned Captain, AQM, USV, April 15, 1865. Commission canceled, Aug. 19, 1865.
Born: Oct. 21, 1835 Carlisle, England
Died: April 13, 1915, Clarens, Switzerland
Occupation: Commission merchant and steamboat agent before war; and U.S. Treasury Department clerk and U.S. foreign service officer after war
Offices/Honors: U.S. Consul, Port Louis, Mauritius, 1878-80. U.S. Consul, Malaga, Spain, 1880-90.
Miscellaneous: Resided St. Louis, MO; Washington, D.C. (1880); and Chicago, IL
Buried: Cremated Montoie Cemetery, Lausanne, Switzerland
References: Nathan W. Marston, compiler. *The Marston Genealogy in Two Parts.* South Lubec, ME, 1888. Letters Received, Commission Branch, Adjutant General's Office, File M167(CB)1865, National Archives. Henry L. Norton, "The Travels of the Marstons," *Journal of the Illinois State Historical Society,* Vol. 58, No. 3 (Autumn 1965). www.ancestry.com.

James C. Martin

Colonel, Lawrence County Regiment, MO Home Guards, June 16, 1861. Discharged Sept. 1, 1861.
Born: June 12, 1808, Circleville, OH
Died: May 2, 1882, Leon, KS
Occupation: Farmer
Miscellaneous: Resided Ozark Twp., Lawrence Co., MO; and Leon, Butler Co., KS
Buried: Leon Cemetery, Leon, KS
References: www.ancestry.com. www.findagrave.com. *History of Newton, Lawrence, Barry and McDonald Counties, Missouri.* Chicago, IL, 1888. Military Service File, National Archives.

Asa Crosby Marvin

1 Lieutenant, Battalion Adjutant, 7 MO State Militia Cavalry, May 1, 1862. Honorably mustered out, Oct. 1, 1862. Colonel, 60 Enrolled MO Militia, Oct. 13, 1862. Provost Marshal, 5 District of Missouri, June 2, 1863–Sept. 26, 1864. Commission vacated, March 12, 1865. Battle honors: Price's Missouri Expedition.

Born: Sept. 26, 1814 Alstead, NH
Died: Dec. 10, 1872 Sedalia, MO
Education: Graduated Norwich (VT) University, 1839
Occupation: Lawyer and railroad president
Offices/Honors: Missouri House of Representatives, 1846–48 and 1852–54. Register of U.S. Land Office, 1853–57. Missouri Senate, 1862–66 (President pro tem, 1864).
Miscellaneous: Resided Clinton, Henry Co., MO, before war; and Sedalia, Pettis Co., MO, after war
Buried: Crown Hill Cemetery, Sedalia, MO (Section 2, Lot 41)
References: William A. Ellis, editor. *History of Norwich University, 1819–1911, Her History, Her Graduates, Her Roll of Honor.* Montpelier, VT, 1911. Pension File and Military Service File, National Archives. Obituary, *Sedalia Daily Democrat*, Dec. 11, 1872. *The History of Pettis County, Missouri.* N.p., 1882. *The History of Henry and St. Clair Counties, Missouri.* St. Joseph, MO, 1883. A.J.D. Stewart, editor. *The History of the Bench and Bar of Missouri.* St. Louis, MO, 1898. George F. Marvin and William T.R. Marvin. *Descendants of Reinold and Matthew Marvin of Hartford, CT, 1638 and 1635, Sons of Edward Marvin of Great Bentley, England.* Boston, MA, 1904. Andrew N. Adams, editor. *A Genealogical History of Henry Adams of Braintree, Mass., and His Descendants.* Rutland, VT, 1898.

Hervey A. Massey

Colonel, 47 Enrolled MO Militia, Sept. 18, 1862. Resigned Nov. 13, 1862.
Born: Nov. 17, 1828 TN
Died: Jan. 7, 1872 Springfield, MO
Occupation: Merchant
Miscellaneous: Resided Linn Creek, Camden Co., MO; and Springfield, Greene Co., MO
Buried: Hazelwood Cemetery, Springfield, MO (Lot 365, unmarked)
References: Obituary, *Springfield Leader*, Jan. 11, 1872. Obituary, *Missouri Weekly Patriot*, Jan. 11, 1872. Military Service File, National Archives.

James Alpheus Matthews

Colonel, Gasconade County Battalion, MO Home Guards, June 8, 1861. Discharged Sept. 4, 1861. Colonel, 3 MO Militia (Dallmeyer's Battalion), Sept. 8, 1861. Resigned Nov. 26, 1861.
Born: Aug. 11, 1809 Franklin Co., TN
Died: Oct. 8, 1870 Owensville, MO
Occupation: Farmer
Offices/Honors: Missouri House of Representatives, 1844–46
Miscellaneous: Resided Owensville, Gasconade Co., MO
Buried: Matthews Family Cemetery, near Owensville, MO
References: *History of Franklin, Jefferson, Washington, Crawford, and Gasconade Counties, Missouri.* Chicago, IL, 1888. Pension File and Military Service File, National Archives. "James Alpheus Matthews (Gasconade County)," http://home.usmo.com/~momollus/GascCoCW/Matt.htm.

Amos W. Maupin

Captain, Co. B, Franklin County Regiment, MO Home Guards, June 11, 1861. Discharged Sept. 11, 1861. Colonel, 55 Enrolled MO Militia, Nov. 15, 1862. Commission vacated, Sept. 22, 1863. Lieutenant Colonel, 47 MO Infantry, Sept. 20, 1864. Commanded Post of Pilot Knob and 3 Sub-District, St. Louis District, Department of the Missouri, Oct. 31–Dec. 17, 1864. Colonel, 47 MO Infantry, Nov. 25, 1864. Declined appointment as Brig. Gen., 2 District, 2 Division, Missouri Militia, March 1865. Honorably mustered out, April 18, 1865. Battle honors: Price's Missouri Expedition (Pilot Knob).
Born: April 26, 1827, Franklin Co., MO
Died: July 1, 1900, Union, MO
Occupation: Blacksmith and wagon maker. Lawyer after 1872.
Offices/Honors: Sheriff of Franklin Co., MO, 1858–62. Clerk of Circuit Court, 1865–70.
Miscellaneous: Resided Union, Franklin Co., MO
Buried: Union Cemetery, Union, MO
References: *History of Franklin, Jefferson, Washington, Crawford and Gasconade Counties, Missouri.* Chicago, IL, 1888. David W. Dillard. *The Union Post Commanders at Pilot Knob, 1861–1865.* Ironton, MO, 2013. Military Service File, National Archives. Obituary, *St. Louis Globe-Democrat*, July 2, 1900. "Biographical Notes: Col. Amos W. Maupin," *Franklin County Tribune*, July 23, 1897. Herman G. Kiel, compiler. *The Centennial Biographical Directory of Franklin County, Missouri.* Washington, D.C., 1925. "Amos W. Maupin (1827 MO-1900 MO) Colonel of the 47th MO Infy USV," http://home.usmo.com/~momollus/FranCoCW/Maupin_a.htm.

Amos W. Maupin (courtesy Douglas R. Niermeyer, Missouri Commandery MOLLUS).

Joseph Washington McClurg

Colonel, Osage County Regiment, MO Home Guards, July 18, 1861. Discharged Dec. 20, 1861. Lieutenant Colonel, 8 MO State Militia Cavalry, March 1, 1862. Colonel, 8 MO State Militia Cavalry, June 25, 1862. Commanded Post of Linn Creek, Central District of Missouri, Department of the Mississippi, July–Sept. 1862. Commanded Post of Lebanon, District of Southwest Missouri, Department of the Missouri, Nov. 1862. Resigned Dec. 22, 1862 to take seat in U.S. Congress. Battle honors: Humansville.

Born: Feb. 22, 1818 St. Louis Co., MO

Died: Dec. 2, 1900 Lebanon, MO

Education: Attended Miami University, Oxford, OH

Occupation: Commission merchant and lead mining entrepreneur

Offices/Honors: U.S. House of Representatives, 1863–68. Governor of Missouri, 1869–71. Register, U.S. Land Office, 1889–93.

Miscellaneous: Resided Linn Creek, Camden Co., MO; and Lebanon, Laclede Co., MO, after 1885. First cousin of Bvt. Brig. Gen. Alexander C. McClurg.

Buried: Lebanon Cemetery, Lebanon, MO (Block 11)

References: Lynn Morrow, "Joseph Washington McClurg: Entrepreneur, Politician, Citizen," *Missouri Historical Review*, Vol. 78, No. 2 (Jan. 1984). Lawrence O. Christensen, William E. Foley, Gary R. Kremer, and Kenneth H. Winn, editors. *Dictionary of Missouri Biography*. Columbia, MO, 1999. Allen Johnson and Dumas Malone, editors. *Dictionary of American Biography*. New York City, NY, 1964. *Pictorial and Genealogical Record of Greene County, Missouri.* Chicago, IL, 1893. *History of Laclede, Camden, Dallas, Webster, Wright, Texas, Pulaski, Phelps and Dent Counties, Missouri.* Chicago, IL, 1889. Obituary, *St. Louis Post-Dispatch*, Dec. 3, 1900. "The Best Governor of Missouri Since the War is Said to be Dying," *Springfield Republican*, Jan. 18, 1900. William Horatio Barnes. *History of Congress: The Fortieth Congress of the United States, 1867–1869.* New York City, NY, 1871. James L. Harrison, compiler. *Biographical Directory of the American Congress, 1774–1949.* Washington, D.C., 1950. Pension File and Military Service File, National Archives. Letters Received, Volunteer Service Branch, Adjutant General's Office, File M407(VS)1863, National Archives.

Joseph Washington McClurg, post-war (William Horatio Barnes. *History of Congress: The Fortieth Congress of the United States, 1867–1869.* New York City, New York, 1871).

James Hamilton Bowles McFerran

Colonel, 1 MO State Militia Cavalry, March 31, 1862. Commanded Post of Lexington (MO), District of Missouri, Department of the Mississippi, Aug. 1862. Commanded Post of Lexington (MO), District of Central Missouri, Department of the Missouri, Sept. 1862–Feb. 1863. Commanded Post of Lexington (MO), District of the Border, Department of the Missouri, July–Aug. 1863. Commanded Post of Warrensburg (MO), District of Central Missouri, Department of the Missouri, Nov.–Dec. 1863. Commanded 3 Sub-District, District of Central Missouri, Department of the Missouri, Jan.–June 1864. Commanded 2 Sub-District, District of Central Missouri, Department of the Missouri, July and Sept. 1864. Charged by Major Gen. Alfred Pleasanton with "Misbehavior before the enemy" at Independence and "Disobedience of orders" and "Neglect of duty" at the Big Blue River, he was found not guilty by court-martial, Dec. 21, 1864. Honorably mustered out, Feb. 11, 1865. Battle honors: Price's Missouri Expedition (Independence, Big Blue).

Born: Sept. 17, 1819 Washington Co., MD
Died: Sept. 29, 1891 Colorado Springs, CO
Occupation: Lawyer, judge, and banker
Offices/Honors: Missouri House of Representatives, 1856–58. Missouri Senate, 1858–59. Circuit Court Judge, 1859–64.

Joseph Washington McClurg, post-war (Brady's National Photographic Portrait Gallery, Broadway & Tenth Street, New York; courtesy Olaf).

Joseph Washington McClurg, post-war (Brady-Handy Photograph Collection, Library of Congress [LC-DIG-cwpbh-01388]).

James Hamilton Bowles McFerran (courtesy Missouri Historical Society, St. Louis [X08588]).

Miscellaneous: Resided Gallatin, Daviess Co., MO; Chillicothe, Livingston Co., MO, 1867–73; and Colorado Springs, El Paso Co., CO, after 1873

Buried: Evergreen Cemetery, Colorado Springs, CO (Block 233, Lot 2)

References: *The History of Daviess County, Missouri.* Kansas City, MO, 1882. *History of the Arkansas Valley, Colorado.* Chicago, IL, 1881. Obituary, *St. Joseph Herald,* Oct. 14, 1891. Obituary, *Colorado Springs Gazette,* Sept. 30, 1891. Pension File and Military Service File, National Archives. Henry Clay McDougal. *Recollections, 1844–1909.* Kansas City, MO, 1910. Letters Received, Volunteer Service Branch, Adjutant General's Office, File M238(VS)1863, National Archives. *History of Harrison and Mercer Counties, Missouri, from the Earliest Time to the Present.* St. Louis and Chicago, 1888. Court-martial Case Files, 1809–1894, File LL-2942, National Archives.

William H. McLane

Colonel, 56 Enrolled MO Militia, Oct. 4, 1862. Commission vacated March 12, 1865. Temporary service as Colonel, 8 Provisional Enrolled MO Militia. Battle honors: Marmaduke's Expedition into Missouri, Price's Missouri Expedition.

Born: July 6, 1816, Cape Girardeau Co., MO
Died: Nov. 22, 1898 Clinton, MO
Occupation: Merchant and farmer
Offices/Honors: Missouri House of Representatives, 1854–56, 1862–66, and 1869–71
Miscellaneous: Resided Appleton, Cape Girardeau Co., MO, to 1866; and Clinton, Henry Co., MO, after 1866
Buried: Englewood Cemetery, Clinton, MO (Block 111, Lot 151)
References: *The History of Henry and St. Clair Counties, Missouri.* St. Joseph, MO, 1883. Pension File, National Archives. Kathleen W. Miles, compiler. *Annals of Henry County, Vol. 1, 1885–1900.* Clinton, MO, 1973. William H. McLane Papers, 1836–1893 (C1020), State Historical Society of Missouri-Columbia.

John Foster McMahan

Captain, Co. D, 74 Enrolled MO Militia, Aug. 16, 1862. Major, 74 Enrolled MO Militia, Dec. 20, 1862. Lieutenant Colonel, 72 MO Enrolled Militia, Oct. 1, 1863. Lieutenant Colonel, 16 MO Cavalry (originally 6 Provisional Enrolled MO Militia), Nov. 1, 1863. Commanded Post of Lebanon (MO), District of Southwest Missouri, Department of the Missouri, Jan.–April 1865. Colonel, 16 MO Cavalry, March 22, 1865. Commanded Post of Springfield (MO), District of Southwest Missouri, Department of the Missouri, April–June 1865. Honorably mustered out, July 1, 1865. Battle honors: Shelby's Raid in Arkansas and Missouri, Price's Missouri Expedition (Boonville, Big Blue).

Born: Nov. 24, 1826 Bedford Co., TN
Died: July 13, 1905, Seymour, MO
Other Wars: Mexican War (Private, Co. G, 3 MO Mounted Infantry)
Occupation: Farmer and stock dealer
Offices/Honors: Missouri House of Representatives, 1854–56 and 1875–77. Missouri Senate, 1881–85.
Miscellaneous: Resided Conway, Laclede Co., MO; and Union Twp., Webster Co., MO. Credited with naming Webster County and its county seat, Marshfield, in honor of Daniel Webster and his Marshfield, MA, home.
Buried: Seymour Masonic Cemetery, Seymour, MO (Section A)
References: *History of Laclede, Camden, Dallas, Webster, Wright, Texas, Pulaski, Phelps, and Dent Counties, Missouri.* Chicago, IL, 1889. Pension File and Military Service File, National Archives. Nettie W. Gorman. Obituaries from *The Marshfield Chronicle, Marshfield, Missouri.* Marshfield, MO, 1991. "Colonel John F. McMahan," *The Missouri Historical Review,* Vol. 29, No. 1 (Oct. 1934).

John Foster McMahan (courtesy of Linell Palo).

Samuel Henry Melcher

Assistant Surgeon, 5 MO Infantry (3 months), May 7, 1861. Honorably mustered out, Aug. 26, 1861. Major, Surgeon, Staff of Brig. Gen. John M. Schofield, MO State Militia, Dec. 4, 1861. Colonel, 32 Enrolled MO Militia, Aug. 30, 1862. Resigned as colonel, Oct. 17, 1862. Medical Director, District of Southwest Missouri and Army of the Frontier, Department of the Missouri, Oct. 1862–May 1863. Lieutenant Colonel, 6 MO State Militia Cavalry, May 28, 1863. Acting AIG, Staff of Major Gen. John M. Schofield (and later Major Gen. William S. Rosecrans), Department of the Missouri, May 1863–Aug. 1864. Acting ADC, Staff of Major Gen. Alfred Pleasanton, Provisional Cavalry Division, Department of the Missouri, Oct. 1864. Commanded Post of Jefferson City (MO), Department of the Missouri, Nov. 1864. Resigned Dec. 22, 1864, "having been in the service since May 7, 1861, … to the neglect of my private interests which require my attention." Battle honors: Wilson's Creek, Marmaduke's Expedition into Missouri (Springfield), Price's Missouri Expedition.

Born: Oct. 30, 1828 Gilmanton, NH
Died: Aug. 1, 1915 Chicago, IL
Education: Graduated Dartmouth Medical School, Hanover, NH, 1850
Occupation: Physician

Samuel Henry Melcher, post-war (*The Granite Monthly*. Old Series Vol. 48 (New Series, Vol. 11). Concord, New Hampshire, 1916).

Offices/Honors: Surgeon, U.S. Marine Hospital, St. Louis, MO, 1870–72

Miscellaneous: Resided Potosi, Washington Co., MO, before war; St. Louis, MO, 1870–73; Chicago, IL, 1873–83 and 1897–1915; and Crow Lake, Jerauld Co., SD

Buried: Oakwoods Cemetery, Chicago, IL (Oakwoods Mausoleum, Acacia Room, Niche B-9)

References: "Lieut. Col. Samuel H. Melcher, M.D., Physician, Patriot, Pioneer—A Worthy Son of the Granite State," *The Granite Monthly*, Vol. 48 (New Series, Vol. 11), 1916. *History of Greene County, Missouri*. St. Louis, MO, 1883. *Album of Genealogy and Biography Cook County, Illinois*. Chicago, IL, 1900. Obituary Circular, Whole No. 769, Illinois MOLLUS. *Memorials of Deceased Companions of the Commandery of the State of Illinois MOLLUS, from Jan. 1, 1912 to Dec. 31, 1922*. Chicago, IL, 1923. Niles J. Dunham. *A History of Jerauld County, South Dakota*. Wessington Springs, SD, 1910. Pension File and Military Service File, National Archives. Letters Received, Volunteer Service Branch, Adjutant General's Office, File M666(VS)1870, National Archives. Obituary, *Chicago Daily Tribune*, Aug. 3, 1915. "Missing In Action, The Memoirs of

Samuel Henry Melcher (*History of Greene County, Missouri*. St. Louis, Missouri, 1883).

Charles Woodbury Melcher, as told by Thomas P. Doherty," http://copland.udel.edu/~tdoherty/MissingInAction.pdf.

Theodore Meumann

Captain, Co. K, 3 MO Infantry (3 months), May 19, 1861. Honorably mustered out, Aug. 30, 1861. Captain, Co. E, 3 MO Infantry (3 years), Sept. 19, 1861. Major, 3 MO Infantry, May 26, 1862. Lieutenant Colonel, 3 MO Infantry, Sept. 1, 1862. *Colonel*, 3 MO Infantry, Nov. 17, 1863. Honorably mustered out, Nov. 23, 1864. Lieutenant Colonel, 15 MO Infantry, Jan. 27, 1865. Honorably mustered out, Dec. 25, 1865. Battle honors: Vicksburg Campaign, Jackson Campaign, Operations on the Memphis and Charleston Railroad (Cane Creek), Chattanooga-Ringgold Campaign (Lookout Mountain, Missionary Ridge), Atlanta Campaign (Resaca, Atlanta, Ezra Church).

Born: Aug. 5, 1828 Grossglogan, Prussia
Died: Nov. 23, 1887 East St. Louis, IL
Occupation: Bank cashier
Miscellaneous: Resided St. Louis, MO; and East St. Louis, IL
Buried: Bellefontaine Cemetery, St. Louis, MO (Blocks 163–164, Lots 2743–2744)

Theodore Meumann (Brown & Scholten, Artists, 82 North Fourth St., St. Louis, Missouri; author's photograph).

References: Obituary, *St. Louis Globe-Democrat,* Nov. 25, 1887. *Report of the Proceedings of the Society of the Army of the Tennessee, at the Twenty-First Meeting. Cincinnati, OH, 1893.* Obituary, *Missouri Republican,* Nov. 28, 1887. Wilhelm Kaufmann. *The Germans in the American Civil War.* Translated by Steven Rowan and edited by Don Heinrich Tolzmann with Werner D. Mueller and Robert E. Ward. Carlisle, PA, 1999. Military Service File, National Archives. Letters Received, Commission Branch, Adjutant General's Office, File M349(CB)1866, National Archives.

George Frederick Meyers

2 Lieutenant, Co. B, Rifle Battalion, 1 MO Infantry (3 months), May 19, 1861. 2 Lieutenant, Co. F, 1 MO Infantry (3 months), June 11, 1861. GSW hip, Wilson's Creek, MO, Aug. 10, 1861. Resigned Aug. 31, 1861. Captain, Co. A, 7 Enrolled MO Militia, Oct. 14, 1862. Lieutenant Colonel, 7 Enrolled MO Militia, Jan. 15, 1864. Colonel, 7 Enrolled MO Militia, April 30, 1864. Brig. Gen., Enrolled MO Militia, Oct. 1, 1864. Resigned Dec. 31, 1864. Battle honors: Wilson's Creek, Price's Missouri Expedition.

Born: March 28, 1839, Rock Island, IL
Died: Feb. 27, 1908 Cincinnati, OH
Occupation: Bookkeeper before war. Real estate agent after war.
Miscellaneous: Resided St. Louis, MO, to 1867; and Cincinnati, OH, after 1867
Buried: New St. Joseph Cemetery, Cincinnati, OH (Section 4, Range 3, Lot 1)
References: Obituary, *Cincinnati Enquirer,* Feb. 28, 1908. Pension File and Military Service File, National Archives. www.ancestry.com.

Lewis P. Miller

Captain, Co. A, 61 Enrolled MO Militia, Sept. 27, 1862. Major, 61 Enrolled MO Militia, Oct. 21, 1862. Colonel, 61 Enrolled MO Militia, Sept. 25, 1863. Temporary service as Major, 1 Provisional Enrolled MO Militia. Major, 48 MO Infantry, Dec. 6, 1864. Honorably mustered out, June 29, 1865.

Born: May 26, 1833, Newark, DE
Died: March 10, 1915, Bear Creek Twp., Montgomery Co., MO
Occupation: Merchant and miller
Miscellaneous: Resided Columbia, Boone Co., MO; and High Hill, Montgomery Co., MO
Buried: Mount Pleasant Cemetery, High Hill, MO (Section B, Row 2)

Lewis P. Miller (R. Goebel, Artist, St. Charles, Missouri; State Historical Society of Missouri, Photograph Collection [Victoria Branham, P0213, 213–20]).

References: Pension File and Military Service File, National Archives. Obituary, *Montgomery Standard*, March 19, 1915.

Thomas Miller, Jr.

Colonel, 22 Enrolled MO Militia, Oct. 29, 1862. Commission vacated, April 12, 1864.
   Born: Oct. 1833 Pittsburgh, PA
   Died: March 30, 1901, Pittsburgh, PA
   Occupation: Steamboat agent before war. Flour merchant and manufacturer of flour milling machinery after war.
   Miscellaneous: Resided St. Louis, MO; and Pittsburgh, PA, after 1891
   Buried: Bellefontaine Cemetery, St. Louis, MO (Blocks 74–83, Lot 610, unmarked)
   References: Obituary, *Pittsburgh Daily Post*, March 31, 1901. Samuel P. May. *The Descendants of Richard Sares (Sears) of Yarmouth, Mass., 1638–1888*. Albany, NY, 1890. www.ancestry.com.

Brainard M. Million

Colonel, 13 Enrolled MO Militia, Sept. 24, 1862. Resigned April 13, 1864.
   Born: 1836 or 1838 MO
   Died: May 17, 1883, St. Louis, MO
   Occupation: Merchant dealing in men's furnishings. Real estate agent after war.
   Buried: Bellefontaine Cemetery, St. Louis, MO (Blocks 165–167, Lot 1775)
   References: No obituary in *St. Louis Globe-Democrat*. Death notice only in *Missouri Republican*. www.ancestry.com.

Adam Clark Mitchell

Colonel, 26 Enrolled MO Militia, May 28, 1864. Relieved from duty, Nov. 19, 1864.
   Born: June 5, 1824, Blount Co., TN
   Died: March 25, 1905, Gail, Borden Co., TX
   Occupation: Farmer and Methodist minister
   Miscellaneous: Resided Marion Twp., Polk Co., MO; Shreveport, Caddo Co., LA, 1877–1901; and Gail, Borden Co., TX, 1901–05
   Buried: Gail Cemetery, Gail, TX
   References: www.ancestry.com. www.findagrave.com.

William Edward Moberly

Captain, Co. A, 35 Enrolled MO Militia, July 26, 1862. Lieutenant Colonel, 35 Enrolled MO Militia, Aug. 7, 1862. Colonel, 35 Enrolled MO Militia, Sept. 6, 1862. Commission vacated, March 12, 1865. Battle honors: Price's Missouri Expedition (Keytesville).
   Born: March 13, 1822, Garrard Co., KY
   Died: April 3, 1891, Cobden, IL
   Occupation: Lawyer, railroad president, and real estate agent
   Offices/Honors: Missouri House of Representatives, 1846–48
   Miscellaneous: Resided Brunswick, Chariton Co., MO, to 1864; St. Louis, MO, 1864–80; and Cobden, Union Co., IL, after 1880. City of Moberly, MO, named in his honor.
   Buried: Cobden Cemetery, Cobden, IL
   References: William H. Perrin, editor. *History of Alexander, Union, and Pulaski Counties, Illinois*. Chicago, IL, 1883. Pension File, National Archives. Obituary, *Jonesboro Gazette*, April 11, 1891.

William James Morgan

Colonel, 18 MO Infantry, Nov. 14, 1861. In Dec. 1861 he commanded Post of Weston (MO), Army of North Missouri, where his inflammatory actions included the burning of Platte City, MO, on Dec. 16, 1861. Although mustered as colonel, he was refused his commission as colonel by Acting Governor Willard P. Hall, who, believing him incompetent, persuaded Major General Halleck to assign Captain Madison Miller

(1 MO Light Artillery) to command of the regiment, Jan. 31, 1862. Despite his appeals for reinstatement, citing his sacrifices in raising the regiment and promising recommendations as to his ability and efficiency, he was mustered out, April 15, 1862. Given authority, June 30, 1862, to raise a regiment of cavalry in Arkansas, he was dishonorably discharged and the authority revoked, Nov. 18, 1862, for allowing his recruits to be employed for the benefit of cotton speculators in the search for and acquisition of cotton.

Born: June 3, 1817, New Rochelle, NY

Died: Nov. 17, 1871 Natchez, MS

Occupation: Merchant and farmer before war. Dry goods merchant and grocer after war.

Miscellaneous: Resided Wilmington, Clinton Co., OH; and Yellow Creek Twp., Chariton Co., MO, before war; and Natchez, Adams Co., MS, after war

Buried: City Cemetery, Natchez, MS (Plat 3, Lot 212)

William James Morgan (courtesy Janet D. Curtis).

References: Leslie Anders. *The Eighteenth Missouri.* Indianapolis, IN, 1968. Obituary, *Natchez Democrat*, Nov. 18, 1871. Death notice, *New York Herald*, Nov. 23, 1871. Letters Received, Volunteer Service Branch, Adjutant General's Office, File M1497(VS)1862, National Archives. Military Service File, National Archives. *The History of Clinton County, Ohio.* Chicago, IL, 1882. William M. Paxton. *Annals of Platte County, Missouri, from Its Exploration Down to June 1, 1897.* Kansas City, MO, 1897. Richard N. Current. *Lincoln's Loyalists: Union Soldiers from the Confederacy.* Boston, MA, 1992.

Edward Morrison

Captain, Co. B, 9 Enrolled MO Militia, Sept. 12, 1862. Major, 9 Enrolled MO Militia, Sept. 16, 1863. Colonel, 9 Enrolled MO Militia, date unknown.

Born: Feb. 11, 1828 Ireland

Died: April 6, 1904, Baldwin Co., AL

Occupation: Insurance agent

Miscellaneous: Resided St. Louis, MO; Wellsville, Montgomery Co., MO; and Marlow, Baldwin Co., AL

Buried: Timney South River Park Community Cemetery, Marlow AL

References: www.ancestry.com. www.findagrave.com. Alma J. Enloe Wheeler, compiler. *Montgomery County, Missouri, Newspaper Records for the Year 1904.* Shelbyville, MO, 1996. Obituary, *Mobile Register*, April 8, 1904.

Frederick Morsey

Lieutenant Colonel, 10 MO State Militia Cavalry, May 5, 1862. Commanded Post of Warrenton (MO), St. Louis Division, District of Missouri, Department of the Mississippi, May–June 1862. Designation of regiment changed to 3 MO State Militia Cavalry, Feb. 2, 1863. Resigned May 23, 1863. Colonel, 59 Enrolled MO Militia, Aug. 6, 1864. Relieved from active duty, Jan. 5, 1865. Commission vacated March 12, 1865. Battle honors: Marmaduke's Expedition into Missouri (Patterson).

Born: March 30, 1808, Celle, Hanover, Germany

Died: Oct. 13, 1875 Warrenton, MO

Occupation: Lawyer and civil engineer

Miscellaneous: Resided Warrenton, Warren Co., MO

Buried: City Cemetery, Warrenton, MO (Section 1, Square C, Block 2, Lot 5)

Frederick Morsey (*An Illustrated Historical Atlas of Warren County, Missouri*. Philadelphia, Pennsylvania, 1877).

References: *Portrait and Biographical Record of St. Charles, Lincoln and Warren Counties, Missouri.* Chicago, IL, 1895. *History of St. Charles, Montgomery and Warren Counties, Missouri.* St. Louis, MO, 1885. *The Bench and Bar of St. Louis, Kansas City, Jefferson City, and Other Missouri Cities.* St. Louis and Chicago, 1884. *An Illustrated Historical Atlas of Warren County, Missouri.* Philadelphia, PA, 1877. Obituary, *St. Louis Republican*, Oct. 28, 1875. Obituary, *St. Louis Globe-Democrat*, Oct. 22, 1875. Military Service File, National Archives.

James Hugh Moss

Captain, Co. E, 48 Enrolled MO Militia, Aug. 11, 1862. Colonel, 48 Enrolled MO Militia, Sept. 29, 1862. Commanded 1 Sub-District, 7 Military District, Enrolled MO Militia, Department of the Missouri, Sept. 1863–May 1864. Colonel, 82 Enrolled MO Militia, Dec. 25, 1863. Popularly known as Paw Paw Militia, the 82 Enrolled MO Militia, although composed of many Southern sympathizers, was effective in protecting the civilian population from thieves and bushwhackers. Accused of being a member of the Order of American Knights, a Southern subversive society, Colonel Moss received heavy criticism from Union authorities for actions viewed as reflecting a Southern bias. Brig. Gen., Enrolled MO Militia, March 18, 1864. Resigned May 12, 1864.
Born: July 24, 1824, Maysville, KY
Died: Sept. 13, 1873 Columbia, MO

James Hugh Moss, post-war (North Todd Gentry. *The Bench and Bar of Boone County, Missouri.* Columbia, Missouri, 1916).

Education: Graduated University of Missouri, Columbia, MO, 1844
Other Wars: Mexican War (2 Lieutenant, Co. C, 1 MO Mounted Infantry)
Occupation: Lawyer
Offices/Honors: Missouri House of Representatives, 1852–54
Miscellaneous: Resided Liberty, Clay Co., MO; and Columbia, Boone Co., MO. Brother-in-law of Senator John J. Crittenden of Kentucky.
Buried: Columbia Cemetery, Columbia, MO (Old Cemetery, Lot 188)
References: North Todd Gentry. *The Bench and Bar of Boone County, Missouri.* Columbia, MO, 1916. Obituary, *Liberty Tribune*, Sept. 26, 1873. Obituary, *Lexington Weekly Intelligencer*, Sept. 24, 1873. Howard L. Conard, editor. *Encyclopedia of the History of Missouri.* New York, Louisville, and St. Louis, 1901. Howard V. Canan, "The Missouri Paw Paw Militia of 1863–1864," *Missouri Historical Review*, Vol. 62, No. 4 (July 1968). *History of Clay and Platte Counties, Missouri.* St. Louis, MO, 1885. William M. Paxton. *Annals of Platte County, Missouri, from Its Exploration Down to June 1, 1897.* Kansas City, MO, 1897. Pension File, National Archives.

David Murphy

1 Lieutenant, Co. A, Rifle Battalion, 1 MO Infantry (3 months), May 8, 1861. 1 Lieutenant, Co. I, 1 MO Infantry (3 years), June 10, 1861.

GSW right knee, Wilson's Creek, MO, Aug. 10, 1861. Designation of regiment changed to 1 MO Light Artillery, Sept. 1, 1861. Captain, Battery F, 1 MO Light Artillery, Jan. 1, 1862. Major, 1 MO Light Artillery, March 19, 1863. Chief of Artillery, Army of the Frontier, Department of the Missouri, April–May 1863. Chief of Artillery, Herron's Division, 13 Army Corps, Department of the Tennessee, June–July 1863. Resigned July 10, 1863, since "the practice of attaching light batteries to brigades renders the services of a field officer unnecessary." 1 Lieutenant, Adjutant, 47 MO Infantry, Aug. 8, 1864. Acting ADC, Staff of Brig. Gen. Thomas Ewing, Jr., Sept.–Oct. 1864. Honorably mustered out, Oct. 28, 1864. Lieutenant Colonel, 50 MO Infantry, Oct. 29, 1864. Acting AIG, Staff of Brig. Gen. Thomas Ewing, Jr., St. Louis District, Department of the Missouri, Dec. 1864–March 1865. Colonel, 50 MO Infantry, June 27, 1865. Honorably mustered out, July 15, 1865. Battle honors: Wilson's Creek, Prairie Grove, Price's Missouri Expedition (Pilot Knob).

Born: Oct. 20, 1835 Woolwich, England
Died: April 11, 1916, San Diego, CA
Education: Graduated St. Louis Law School, 1871

David Murphy, post-war (William Hyde and Howard L. Conard, editors. *Encyclopedia of the History of St. Louis*. New York, Louisville, and St. Louis, 1899).

Occupation: Carpenter and school teacher before war. Lawyer and judge after war.

Offices/Honors: As Judge of the St. Louis Court of Criminal Correction, 1894–98, he acquired an unwelcome reputation for his controversial judicial conduct

Miscellaneous: Resided Union, Franklin Co., MO, to 1870; St. Louis, MO, 1870–1910; and San Diego, CA, 1910–16. Brother-in-law of Colonel James W. Owens (Franklin County Regiment, MO Home Guards).

Buried: Jefferson Barracks National Cemetery, St. Louis, MO (Section 4, Grave 12476)

References: Walter B. Stevens. *St. Louis The Fourth City, 1764–1909*. St. Louis and Chicago, 1909. William Hyde and Howard L. Conard, editors. *Encyclopedia of the History of St. Louis*. New York, Louisville, and St. Louis, 1899. Obituary, *St. Louis Post-Dispatch*, April 13, 1916. "Short History of David Murphy," *St. Louis Post-Dispatch*, Jan. 18, 1896. Clark Brown, "Incidents in the Life of Col. David Murphy," *Franklin County Tribune*, April 21, 1916. Pension File and Military Service File, National Archives. Letters Received, Volunteer Service Branch, Adjutant General's Office, File B488(VS)1863, National Archives. *History of Franklin, Jefferson, Washington, Crawford and Gasconade Counties, Missouri*. Chicago, IL, 1888.

David Murphy (courtesy Missouri Historical Society, St. Louis [P0004-1029]).

Henry Neill (courtesy Dan Miles)

Henry Neill

Colonel, 71 Enrolled MO Militia, Aug. 20, 1862. Temporary service as Colonel, 5 Provisional Enrolled MO Militia. Resigned June 7, 1864. Major, 1 MO State Militia Cavalry, March 12, 1864. Chief of Cavalry, Staff of Colonel John F. Philips, District of Central Missouri, Department of the Missouri, Dec. 1864–Feb. 1865. Honorably mustered out, Feb. 28, 1865. Battle honors: Quantrill's Raid into Kansas and Pursuit by Union Forces, Shelby's Raid in Arkansas and Missouri, Price's Missouri Expedition.
Born: April 8, 1828, Lee Co., VA
Died: Feb. 6, 1895 Warrensburg, MO
Occupation: Lawyer
Miscellaneous: Resided Lexington, Lafayette Co., MO, to 1867; and Warrensburg, Johnson Co., MO, after 1867
Buried: Sunset Hill Cemetery, Warrensburg, MO
References: *The History of Johnson County, Missouri*. Kansas City, MO, 1881. Obituary, *Lexington Weekly Intelligencer*, Feb. 16, 1895. Obituary, *Warrensburg Journal-Democrat*, Feb. 8, 1895. Pension File and Military Service File, National Archives. *History of Lafayette County, Missouri*. St. Louis, MO, 1881. William E. Crissey. *Warrensburg: A History With Folk Lore*. N.p., 1924.

Joseph Nemett

1 Lieutenant, Adjutant, 5 MO Infantry (3 months), May 18, 1861. Honorably mustered out, Aug. 26, 1861. Major, Benton Hussars (later 5 MO Cavalry), Dec. 17, 1861. Colonel, 5 MO Cavalry, Feb. 14, 1862. Honorably mustered out, Dec. 4, 1862, upon the consolidation of the 5 MO Cavalry with the 4 MO Cavalry. Battle honors: Wilson's Creek, Pea Ridge.
Born: March 31, 1809, Szeged (or Losonc), Hungary
Died: Jan. 21, 1881 Chicago, IL
Other Wars: Captain in Honved army during Hungarian War of Independence, 1848–49
Occupation: Served 18 years in Austrian army. Came to America with Louis Kossuth in 1851. Farrier and veterinary surgeon after war.
Miscellaneous: Resided St. Louis, MO, before war; and Chicago, IL, after war. Death certificate gives age as 65 years, 5 months.
Buried: Graceland Cemetery, Chicago, IL (Section P, Lot 152, unmarked)
References: Pension File and Military Service File, National Archives. Istvan Kornel Vida. *Hungarian Emigres in the American Civil War: A History and Biographical Dictionary*. Jefferson, NC, 2012. Edmund Vasvary. *Lincoln's Hungarian Heroes: The Participation of Hungarians in the Civil War, 1861–1865*. Washington, D.C., 1939. Eugene Pivany. *Hungarians in the American Civil War*. Cleveland, OH, 1913.

Henry O'Bannon Nevill

Colonel, Harrison County Regiment, MO Home Guards, Sept. 3, 1861. Discharged Sept. 23, 1861. Major, 3 MO State Militia Cavalry, April 5, 1862. Lieutenant Colonel, 3 MO State Militia Cavalry, May 13, 1862. Commanded Post of Cassville (MO), District of Southwest Missouri, Department of the Missouri, June 1862. Honorably mustered out, Feb. 15, 1863, upon consolidation of the regiment with 6 MO State Militia Cavalry and 7 MO State Militia Cavalry. Commissioned Lieutenant Colonel, 6 MO State Militia Cavalry, April 9, 1863. Did not report and commission annulled, May 1, 1863.
Born: June 25, 1815, Barren Co., KY
Died: Oct. 8, 1904 Ridgeway, MO
Other Wars: Mexican War (1 Lieutenant, Co. K, 4 KY Infantry)
Occupation: Farmer
Offices/Honors: Missouri House of Representatives, 1854–56
Miscellaneous: Resided Blythedale, Harrison

Co., MO; and Ridgeway, Harrison Co., MO. Twin brother of Colonel James M. Nevill (57 Enrolled MO Militia).

Buried: Cedar Hill Cemetery, Blythedale, MO
References: Pension File and Military Service File, National Archives. "The Oldest Twins," *Hazleton Plain Speaker*, Nov. 21, 1900. Obituary, *Bethany Democrat*, Oct. 13, 1904. Frances B. S. Hodges, compiler. *The Neville Family of England and the United States*. Wichita Falls, TX, 1964. "Missouri Twins Oldest in America," *St. Louis Post-Dispatch*, May 21, 1902. B. C. Holtzclaw. *The Genealogy of the Holtzclaw Family, 1540–1935*. Richmond, VA, 1936. George W. Wanamaker. *History of Harrison County, Missouri*. Topeka and Indianapolis, 1921. *History of Harrison and Mercer Counties, Missouri, From the Earliest Time to the Present*. St. Louis and Chicago, 1888.

James Morgan Nevill

Captain, Co. B, Harrison County Regiment, MO Home Guards, Sept. 3, 1861. Discharged Sept. 23, 1861. Captain, Co. B, Burris' Battalion, Six Months MO Militia, Oct. 5, 1861. Honorably discharged, March 14, 1862. Captain, Co. H, 57 Enrolled MO Militia, Aug. 5, 1862. Lieutenant Colonel, 57 Enrolled MO Militia, Oct. 15, 1862. Colonel, 57 Enrolled MO Militia, June 3, 1863. Resigned Oct. 26, 1863.

Born: June 25, 1815, Barren Co., KY
Died: Feb. 10, 1907 Bethany, MO
Occupation: Farmer
Offices/Honors: Missouri House of Representatives, 1858–60 and 1881–83
Miscellaneous: Resided Blythedale, Harrison Co., MO. Twin brother of Colonel Henry O. Nevill (Harrison County Regiment, MO Home Guards).
Buried: Cedar Hill Cemetery Blythedale, MO
References: Pension File, National Archives. Obituary, *Bethany Republican*, Feb. 14, 1907. Frances B. S. Hodges, compiler. *The Neville Family of England and the United States*. Wichita Falls, TX, 1964. "The Oldest Twins," *Hazleton Plain Speaker*, Nov. 21, 1900. "Missouri Twins Oldest in America," *St. Louis Post-Dispatch*, May 21, 1902. B. C. Holtzclaw. *The Genealogy of the Holtzclaw Family, 1540–1935*. Richmond, VA, 1936. George W. Wanamaker. *History of Harrison County, Missouri*. Topeka and Indianapolis, 1921.

Carman Adams Newcomb

Captain, Co. F, 3 IA Infantry, June 6, 1861. Resigned April 8, 1862, since "I am utterly unable to discharge the duties of my office," due to chronic rheumatism. Colonel, 80 Enrolled MO Militia, Dec. 31, 1864. Commission vacated, March 12, 1865.

Born: July 1, 1827, Mercer Co., PA
Died: April 6, 1902, St. Louis, MO

Carman Adams Newcomb (U.S. House of Representatives, 1867) (William Horatio Barnes. *History of Congress: The Fortieth Congress of the United States, 1867–1869*. **New York City, New York, 1871).**

Carman Adams Newcomb (U.S. House of Representatives, 1867) (Brady-Handy Photograph Collection, Library of Congress [LC-DIG-cwpbh-00298]).

Carman Adams Newcomb, post-war (Obituary Circular, Whole No. 246, Missouri MOLLUS).

Occupation: Lawyer and judge

Offices/Honors: County Judge, Fayette Co., IA, 1855–57. Missouri House of Representatives, 1864–66. U.S. House of Representatives, 1867–69. U.S. Marshal, Eastern District of Missouri, 1869–75.

Miscellaneous: Resided West Union, Fayette Co., IA; Vineland, Jefferson Co., MO; Kimmswick, Jefferson Co., MO; and St. Louis, MO

Buried: Hillcrest Abbey Mausoleum, St. Louis, MO (Tier 1, Niche 51)

References: *History of Franklin, Jefferson, Washington, Crawford and Gasconade Counties, Missouri*. Chicago, IL, 1888. Obituary Circular, Whole No. 246, Missouri MOLLUS. Obituary, *St. Louis Republic*, April 7, 1902. Pension File and Military Service File, National Archives. Obituary, *St. Louis Post-Dispatch*, April 7, 1902. William Horatio Barnes. *History of Congress: The Fortieth Congress of the United States, 1867–1869*. New York City, NY, 1871. George W. Fitch. *Past and Present of Fayette County, Iowa*. Indianapolis, IN, 1910. James L. Harrison, compiler. *Biographical Directory of the American Congress, 1774–1949*. Washington, D.C., 1950.

Andrew Gray Newgent

1 Lieutenant, RQM, Cass County Regiment, MO Home Guards Cavalry, July 7, 1861. Colonel, Cass County Regiment, MO Home Guards Cavalry, Aug. 1, 1861. Honorably mustered out, Feb. 28, 1862. Lieutenant Colonel, 2 Battalion MO State Militia Cavalry, April 14, 1862. Resigned Sept. 15, 1862.

Andrew Gray Newgent (Missouri Constitutional Convention, 1865) (courtesy Missouri Historical Society, St. Louis [P0487-1142]).

Born: Oct. 13, 1816 Clark Co., IN

Died: July 9, 1893, Independence, MO

Occupation: Merchant and Baptist preacher before war. Merchant, pension claim agent, and hotelkeeper after war.

Offices/Honors: Postmaster, Austin, MO, 1857–59. Missouri Constitutional Convention, 1865. Justice of Jackson County Court, 1865–66.

Miscellaneous: Resided Austin, Cass Co., MO, before war; and Kansas City, MO; Humboldt, Allen Co., KS; Rich Hill, Bates Co., MO; and Independence, Jackson Co., MO, after war

Buried: Union Cemetery, Kansas City, MO (Section 16, Lot 4)

References: *The United States Biographical Dictionary and Portrait Gallery of Eminent and Self-Made Men*. Missouri Volume. New York, Chicago, St. Louis, and Kansas City, 1878. Obituary, *Kansas City Star*, July 10, 1893. Pension File and Military Service File, National Archives. Letters Received, Volunteer Service Branch, Adjutant General's Office, File N8(VS)1868, National Archives. Tom A. Rafiner. *Caught Between Three Fires: Cass County, MO, Chaos, & Order No. 11, 1860–1865*. Bloomington, IN, 2010. Obituary, *Kansas City Times*, July 10, 1893. Alfred T. Andreas. *History of the State of Kansas*. Chicago, IL, 1883.

Tony Niederwieser

Captain, Co. C, 3 U.S. Reserve Corps, MO Infantry (3 months), May 8, 1861. Honorably mustered out, Aug. 18, 1861. Lieutenant Colonel, 6 Enrolled MO Militia, April 27, 1863. Temporary service as Lieutenant Colonel, 10 Provisional Enrolled MO Militia. Colonel, 6 Enrolled MO Militia, May 23, 1864. Commission vacated, March 12, 1865. Battle honors: Price's Missouri Expedition.
Born: April 8, 1828, Augsburg, Bavaria
Died: Jan. 25, 1918 St. Louis, MO
Occupation: Saloonkeeper
Miscellaneous: Resided St. Louis, MO; and St. James, Phelps Co., MO
Buried: Hillcrest Abbey Mausoleum, St. Louis, MO (Tier 2, Niche 257)
References: Pension File and Military Service File, National Archives. Obituary, *St. Louis Post-Dispatch*, Jan. 27, 1918. Robert J. Rombauer. *The Union Cause in St. Louis in 1861: An Historical Sketch*. St. Louis, MO, 1909. J. Thomas Scharf. *History of Saint Louis City and County*. Philadelphia, PA, 1883. "The Niederwieser Family," http://niederwieser-anton.blogspot.com/.

William Black Okeson

Colonel, 70 Enrolled MO Militia, Sept. 10, 1862. Commission vacated, March 12, 1865.
Born: Aug. 12, 1828 Tuscarora Valley, Juniata Co., PA
Died: Nov. 6, 1910 Chicago, IL
Education: Graduated Jefferson College, Canonsburg, PA, 1850
Occupation: Lawyer and farmer before war. Lawyer and real estate agent after war.
Miscellaneous: Resided Indian Creek, Monroe Co., MO, before war; and Wenona, LaSalle Co., IL; and Chicago, IL, after war
Buried: Wenona Community Cemetery, Wenona, IL
References: *Commemorative Biographical Encyclopedia of the Juniata Valley, Comprising the Counties of Huntingdon, Mifflin, Juniata, and Perry, Pennsylvania*. Chambersburg, PA, 1897. *Biographical and Historical Catalogue of Washington and Jefferson College*. Cincinnati, OH, 1889. Obituary, *Chicago Daily Tribune*, Nov. 7, 1910. Pension File, National Archives.

William Stockley Oliver

Captain, Co. B, 7 MO Infantry, June 26, 1861. Major, 7 MO Infantry, July 2, 1862. Lieutenant Colonel, 7 MO Infantry, Jan. 8, 1863. Colonel, 7 MO Infantry, April 17, 1863. Commanded the Steamer Tigress in the passage of the Vicksburg and Warrenton batteries by transports, April 22, 1863. GSW left foot, Bayou Pierre, MS, May 2, 1863. Honorably mustered out, July 18, 1864. Battle honors: Operations on the Mississippi Central Railroad, Corinth, Port Gibson (Bayou Pierre), Meridian Expedition.
Born: Oct. 27, 1836 Mobile, AL
Died: Aug. 14, 1896 Ensenada, Lower California, Mexico
Occupation: Merchant, contractor, furniture dealer, and fruit grower
Offices/Honors: Sheriff of Pulaski Co., AR, 1868–74 and 1880–82
Miscellaneous: Resided St. Louis, MO, before war; and Little Rock, Pulaski Co., AR; and Ensenada, Lower California, Mexico, after 1887. First cousin of Bvt. Brig. Gen. Paul A. Oliver.
Buried: Ensenada, Lower California, Mexico
References: *Report of the Proceedings of the Society of the Army of the Tennessee, at the Twenty-Eighth Meeting*. Cincinnati, OH, 1897. Horace E. Hayden, "The Oliver Family of New York, Delaware, and Pennsylvania," *New York Genealogical and Biographical Record*, Vol. 20, No. 1 (Jan. 1889). Pension File and Military Service File, National Archives. Obituary, *Daily Arkansas Gazette*, Aug. 19, 1896. Obituary, *San Diego Union*, Aug. 17, 1896. *Biographical and Historical Memoirs of Pulaski, Jefferson, Lonoke, Faulkner, Grant, Saline, Perry, Garland and Hot Spring Counties, Arkansas*. Chicago, Nashville and St. Louis, 1889.

James William Owens

Colonel, Franklin County Regiment, MO Home Guards, June 13, 1861. Discharged Sept. 13, 1861. Private, Co. D, 47 MO Infantry, Sept. 11, 1864. Honorably mustered out, March 30, 1865.
Born: Oct. 16, 1830 Union, Franklin Co., MO
Died: Nov. 20, 1871 Washington, MO
Education: Attended University of Missouri, Columbia, MO. Graduated University of Louisville (KY) Law School, 1856.
Occupation: Lawyer and judge
Offices/Honors: Missouri House of Representatives, 1858–62 and 1867. Circuit court judge, 1863–68. Missouri Constitutional Convention, 1865.
Miscellaneous: Resided Washington, Franklin Co., MO
Buried: Wildey Odd Fellows Cemetery, Washington, MO

James William Owens (Mansfield's City Gallery, Opp. entrance Planters' House, St. Louis, Missouri; author's photograph).

References: *History of Franklin, Jefferson, Washington, Crawford, and Gasconade Counties, Missouri.* Chicago, IL, 1888. Pension File and Military Service File, National Archives. Obituary, Albany Ledger, Dec. 7, 1871. Herman G. Kiel, compiler. *The Centennial Biographical Directory of Franklin County, Missouri.* Washington, D.C., 1925. www.findagrave.com.

Ratcliff Boone Palmer

Colonel, 73 Enrolled MO Militia, Aug. 31, 1862. Commission vacated March 12, 1865.
  Born: April 10, 1816, Pickens District, SC
  Died: July 25, 1896, near Hartville, MO
  Occupation: Lawyer and farmer
  Offices/Honors: Missouri House of Representatives, 1862–66 and 1879–81. Missouri Senate, 1871–75.
  Miscellaneous: Resided Hartville, Wright Co., MO
  Buried: Colonel Palmer Cemetery, near Hartville, MO
  References: *History and Families Wright County, Missouri, 1841–1991.* Paducah, KY, 1993. *History of Laclede, Camden, Dallas, Webster, Wright, Texas, Pulaski, Phelps, and Dent Counties, Missouri.* Chicago, IL, 1889. Albert Griffen. *Biographical Register of the Members of the Twenty-Sixth General Assembly of the State of Missouri.* St. Louis, MO, 1872. John W. Pattison, compiler. *Biographical Sketches of the Officers and Members of the Twenty-Seventh General Assembly of Missouri.* Jefferson City, MO, 1874.

Charles Wheeler Parker

Colonel, 37 Enrolled MO Militia, Sept. 9, 1862. Commission vacated, March 12, 1865.
  Born: March 21, 1831, Troy, MO
  Died: Aug. 4, 1901 St. Louis, MO
  Occupation: Dry goods merchant and bookkeeper
  Miscellaneous: Resided Troy, Lincoln Co., MO; and St. Louis, MO
  Buried: Troy City Cemetery, Troy, MO
  References: Obituary, *Warrenton Herald*, Aug. 14, 1901. Death notice, *St. Louis Globe-Democrat*, Aug. 5, 1901. *History of Lincoln County, Missouri, From the Earliest Time to the Present.* Chicago, IL, 1888. www.ancestry.com.

Everett Peabody

Major, 13 MO Infantry, June 13, 1861. Colonel, 13 MO Infantry, Sept. 1, 1861. GSW ankle, Lexington, MO, Sept. 19, 1861. Taken prisoner, Lexington, MO, Sept. 21, 1861. Paroled Sept. 25, 1861. The 13 MO Infantry never existed as a completed organization, the regiment being disbanded, Oct. 26, 1861, upon the discharge of the enlisted men captured at Lexington. Colonel, 25 MO Infantry, Nov. 1, 1861. Commanded 1 Brigade, 6 Division, Army of the Tennessee, March–April 1862. GSW head, Shiloh, TN, April 6, 1862. Battle honors: Siege of Lexington, Shiloh.
  Born: June 13, 1830, Springfield, MA
  Died: April 6, 1862, KIA Shiloh, TN

Everett Peabody (J. A. Scholten, No. 273 South 4th Street, Corner of Convent, St. Louis, Missouri; courtesy Henry Deeks).

Everett Peabody (Massachusetts MOLLUS Collection, USAMHI [Vol. 85, p. 4251L]).

Education: Attended University of Vermont, Burlington, VT. Graduated Harvard University, Cambridge, MA, 1849.
Occupation: Civil engineer
Miscellaneous: Resided St. Louis, MO; and St. Joseph, Buchanan Co., MO
Buried: Springfield Cemetery, Springfield, MA (Sweet Briar Path North, Lot 269)
References: Carlton L. Smith. *Peabody at Shiloh: A Short Study of Courage and Injustice.* Harvard, MA, 1983. Carlton L. Smith, "A Promising Son is Lost," *Civil War Times Illustrated,* Vol. 24, No.1 (March 1985). Thomas W. Higginson. *Harvard Memorial Biographies.* Cambridge, MA, 1866. William A. Neal. *An Illustrated History of the Missouri Engineer and the 25th Infantry Regiments.* Chicago, IL, 1889. "Obsequies of Col. Everett Peabody," *Springfield Daily Republican,* May 19, 1862. Timothy T. Isbell. *Shiloh and Corinth Sentinels of Stone.* Jackson, MS, 2007. Wiley Sword. *Shiloh: Bloody April.* New York City, NY, 1974. Military Service File, National Archives. Selim H. Peabody, compiler. *Peabody (Paybody, Pabody, Pabodie) Genealogy.* Boston, MA, 1909.

James Peckham

Lieutenant Colonel, 8 MO Infantry, July 4, 1861. Resigned Feb. 1, 1862, since "my private business is of such urgency as to demand my presence in Missouri." Lieutenant Colonel, 8 MO Infantry, March 4, 1862. Resigned June 1, 1862. Lieutenant Colonel, 29 MO Infantry, Sept. 6, 1862. Commanded Post of Cape Girardeau (MO), St. Louis District, Department of the Missouri, Sept. 1862. Acting AAG, Staff of Brig. Gen. Frank P. Blair, Jr., 1 Brigade, 1 Division, 15 Army Corps, Army of the Tennessee, Dec. 1862–April 1863. Colonel, 29 MO Infantry, Feb. 20, 1863. GSW left forearm, Vicksburg, MS, May 20, 1863. Chief Picket Officer, Staff of Major Gen. Frank P. Blair, Jr., Right Wing, 15 Army Corps, Army of the Tennessee, Oct. 1863. GSW right arm, Lookout Mountain, TN, Nov. 24, 1863. Honorably mustered out, March 9, 1864, "at his own request … on account of physical disability from wounds received in action." Battle honors: Shiloh, Siege of Corinth, Chickasaw Bluffs, Vicksburg Campaign, Jackson Campaign, Chattanooga-Ringgold Campaign (Lookout Mountain).
Born: 1830 NY
Died: June 1, 1869, Hot Springs, AR
Occupation: Newspaper editor, lawyer, and liquor inspector
Offices/Honors: Missouri House of Representatives, 1860–62
Miscellaneous: Resided St. Louis, MO. Author of *Gen. Nathaniel Lyon and Missouri in 1861. A Monograph of the Great Rebellion*, published in 1866.
Buried: Bellefontaine Cemetery, St. Louis, MO (Block 107, Lot 1540)
References: Pension File and Military Service File, National Archives. Obituary, *Missouri Republican,* June 4, 1869. J. Thomas Scharf. *History of Saint Louis City and County.* Philadelphia, PA, 1883. Edward S. Cooper. *John McDonald and the Whiskey Ring: From Thug to Grant's Inner Circle.* Madison, NJ, 2017. Thomas P. Lowry. *Tarnished Eagles: The Courts-Martial of Fifty Union Colonels and Lieutenant Colonels.* Mechanicsburg, PA, 1997. Letters Received, Volunteer Service Branch, Adjutant General's Office, File P463(VS)1864, National Archives. Stephen F. Peckham. *Peckham Genealogy: The English Ancestors and American Descendants of John Peckham of Newport, Rhode Island, 1630.* New York City, NY, 1922. "Union Colonel James Peckham Describes the Sacking of Jackson, Mississippi, Following Operations Against Vicksburg," *Blue & Gray Magazine,* Vol. 21, Issue 3 (Spring 2004). "The Late Lieut. Col. James Peckham," *Daily Missouri Democrat,* June 8, 1869. *Report of the Proceedings of the Society of the Army of the Tennessee, at the Fourth Annual Meeting.* Cincinnati, OH, 1877. H.E. Robinson, "Two Missouri Historians," *Missouri Historical Review,* Vol. 5, No. 3 (April 1911).

William Ridgeway Penick

Colonel, 5 MO State Militia Cavalry, March 17, 1862. Commanded Post of Independence (MO), District of Central Missouri, Department of the Missouri, Oct. 1862–May 1863. Honorably mustered out June 22, 1863. Brig. Gen., 1 District, 1 Division, Missouri Militia, Feb. 27–April 22, 1865.

Born: May 20, 1829, near Columbia, MO
Died: Dec. 4, 1891 St. Joseph, MO
Occupation: Wholesale druggist and bookseller
Offices/Honors: Mayor of St. Joseph, MO, 1864–66
Miscellaneous: Resided St. Joseph, Buchanan Co., MO. A Thirty-Second Degree Mason, he served as Grand Master of the Grand Lodge of Missouri Masons, 1861.
Buried: Mount Mora Cemetery, St. Joseph, MO
References: Christian L. Rutt, editor. *History of Buchanan County and the City of St. Joseph and Representative Citizens.* Chicago, IL, 1904. *The History of Buchanan County, Missouri.* St. Joseph, MO, 1881. Obituary, *St. Joseph Herald,* Dec. 5, 1891. Obituary, *St. Joseph Weekly Gazette,* Dec. 10, 1891. Pension File and Military Service File, National Archives. Letters Received, Volunteer Service Branch, Adjutant General's Office, File L232(VS)1863, National Archives. Lyman W. Penick. *The Penick Family: Descendants of Edward Penick/Penix/Pinix of St. Peter's Parish, New Kent County, Virginia.* Verona, VA, 1982. Ray V. Denslow. *Civil War and Masonry in Missouri.* St. Louis, MO, 1930.

William Ridgeway Penick, post-war (Christian L. Rutt, editor. *History of Buchanan County and the City of St. Joseph and Representative Citizens.* Chicago, Illinois, 1904).

William Ridgeway Penick, post-war (*The History of Buchanan County, Missouri.* St. Joseph, Missouri, 1881).

John Finis Philips

Colonel, 7 MO State Militia Cavalry, May 1, 1862. Commanded Post of Syracuse, Central Division, District of Missouri, Department of the Mississippi, June–July 1862. Commanded 2 Brigade, 3 Division, Army of the Frontier, Department of the Missouri, Oct. 1862. Commanded Post of Newtonia, District of Southwest Missouri, Department of the Missouri, Nov. 1862 and May–June 1863. Commanded Post of Greenfield, District of Southwest Missouri, Department of the Missouri, Jan.–May 1863. Commanded 3 Sub-District, District of Central Missouri, Department of the Missouri, Aug.–Dec. 1863. Commanded 2 Sub-District, District of Central Missouri, Department of the Missouri, Jan.–May 1864. Commanded Post of Warrensburg, District of Central Missouri, Department of the Missouri, Aug. 1864. Commanded 1 Brigade, Provisional Cavalry Division, Department of the Missouri, Oct. 1864. Commanded District of Central Missouri, Department of the Missouri, Nov. 1864–Feb. 1865. Honorably mustered out, March 18, 1865. Battle honors: Shelby's Raid in Arkansas and Missouri (Marshall), Price's Missouri Expedition (Big Blue, Mine Creek).

Born: Dec. 31, 1834 Thralls Prairie, Boone Co., MO
Died: March 13, 1919, Hot Springs, AR
Education: Attended University of Missouri, Columbia, MO. Graduated Centre College, Danville, KY, 1855.

John Finis Philips (Troxell & Brother, Photographers, S.W. Cor. 4th and Locust Streets, St. Louis, Missouri; Roger D. Hunt Collection, USAMHI [RG98S-CWP80.98]).

John Finis Philips (U.S. House of Representatives, 1875) (Brady-Handy Photograph Collection, Library of Congress [LC-DIG-cwpbh-04378]).

Occupation: Lawyer and judge
Offices/Honors: U.S. House of Representatives, 1875–77 and 1880–81. Judge, U.S. District Court, 1888–1910.
Miscellaneous: Resided Georgetown, Pettis Co., MO, to 1865; Sedalia, Pettis Co., MO, 1865–82; and Kansas City, MO, after 1882. Described as "Scholar, Jurist, Orator, Soldier" on his gravestone.
Buried: Mount Washington Cemetery, Independence, MO (Block 2, Lot 490)
References: Allen Johnson and Dumas Malone, editors. *Dictionary of American Biography*. New York City, NY, 1964. Obituary, *Kansas City Star*, March 13, 1919. "Philips, History Maker: Jurist Who Died Yesterday Helped Keep Missouri in Union," *Kansas City Star*, March 14, 1919. Howard L. Conard, editor. *Encyclopedia of the History of Missouri*. New York, Louisville, and St. Louis, 1901. *The United States Biographical Dictionary and Portrait Gallery of Eminent and Self-Made Men*. Missouri Volume. New York, Chicago, St. Louis, and Kansas City, 1878. Chancy R. Barns, editor. *The Commonwealth of Missouri: A Centennial Record*. St. Louis, MO, 1877. Pension File and Military Service File, National Archives. Letters Received, Commission Branch, Adjutant General's Office, File P910(CB)1865, National Archives. Lumir F. Buresh. *October 25th and the Battle of Mine Creek*. Kansas City, MO, 1977. Obituary Circular, Whole No. 542, Missouri MOLLUS. James L. Harrison, compiler. *Biographical Directory of the American Congress, 1774-1949*. Washington, D.C., 1950.

Oliver P. Phillips

Captain, Co. C, 1 MO State Militia Cavalry, Feb. 17, 1862. Resigned Aug. 20, 1862. Colonel, 66 Enrolled MO Militia, Oct. 19, 1862. Commission vacated, March 12, 1865.
Born: Feb. 26, 1816 Mercer Co., KY
Died: Jan. 29, 1892 Green Castle, MO
Occupation: Farmer
Offices/Honors: Sheriff, Sullivan Co., MO, 1860–64
Miscellaneous: Resided Milan, Sullivan Co., MO, to 1864; and Green Castle, Sullivan Co., MO, after 1864
Buried: Green Castle Cemetery, Green Castle, MO
References: *History of Adair, Sullivan, Putnam, and Schuyler Counties, Missouri*. Chicago, IL, 1888. Pension File and Military Service File, National Archives.

Bennett Pike

Sergeant, Co. A, Thompson's Battalion, Six Months MO Militia, Oct. 9, 1861. Honorably discharged, Feb. 11, 1862. Colonel, 58 Enrolled MO Militia, Nov. 1, 1862. Temporary service as Colonel, 3 Provisional Enrolled MO Militia, Aug. 17–Nov. 8, 1863. Commission vacated, March 12, 1865.

Born: Jan. 6, 1829 Cornish, ME
Died: July 25, 1892, Arcadia, MO
Education: Attended Bowdoin College, Brunswick, ME
Occupation: Lawyer and judge
Offices/Honors: Missouri House of Representatives, 1862–64. U.S. Attorney, Western District of Missouri, 1864–71. Circuit Court Judge, 1871–72.
Miscellaneous: Resided Rock Port, Atchison Co., MO, to 1864; St. Joseph, Buchanan Co., MO, 1864–79; and St. Louis, MO, after 1879. Played a leading role in the founding of Beatrice, Gage Co., NE, 1857–58.
Buried: Masonic Cemetery, Ironton, MO (unmarked?)
References: Hugh J. Dobbs. *History of Gage County, Nebraska*. Lincoln, NE, 1918. Obituary, *St. Joseph Weekly Herald*, July 28, 1892. Obituary, *St. Louis Globe-Democrat*, July 27, 1892. William F. Reed. *The Descendants of Thomas Durfee of Portsmouth, Rhode Island*. Washington, D.C., 1905. Obituary, *Iron County Register*, July 28, 1892. *General Catalogue of Bowdoin College and the Medical School of Maine: A Biographical Record of Alumni and Officers, 1794–1950*. Brunswick, ME, 1950. Pension File, National Archives.

Edward C. Pike

Lieutenant Colonel, 7 Enrolled MO Militia, Sept. 23, 1862. Colonel, 7 Enrolled MO Militia, Jan. 13, 1864. Brig. Gen., Enrolled MO Militia, March 29, 1864. Commanded First Military District, Enrolled MO Militia. Relieved from duty, Jan. 30, 1865. Battle honors: Price's Missouri Expedition.

Born: Dec. 7, 1823 Eastport, ME
Died: Sept. 21, 1904 Chatham, MA
Occupation: Wholesale druggist
Miscellaneous: Resided St. Louis, MO, to 1872; Eastport, Washington Co., ME; and Brookline, Norfolk Co., MA
Buried: Hillside Cemetery, Eastport, ME (East Side, Section B, Lot 135, unmarked)
References: Obituary, *Boston Evening Transcript*, Sept. 22, 1904. William H. Kilby, compiler. *Eastport and Passamaquoddy: A Collection of Historical and Biographical Sketches*. Eastport, ME, 1888.

Bennett Pike, post-war (Hugh J. Dobbs. *History of Gage County, Nebraska*. Lincoln, Nebraska, 1918).

Edward C. Pike (author's photograph).

Edward C. Pike (courtesy Lester S. Levy Collection of Sheet Music, Sheridan Libraries, Johns Hopkins University).

William Pope

Lieutenant Colonel, 52 Enrolled MO Militia, Oct. 1, 1862. Colonel, 52 Enrolled MO Militia, Oct. 4, 1862. Resigned April 28, 1863.
Born: July 21, 1808, Alford, Berkshire Co., MA
Died: June 15, 1884, Quincy, MI
Occupation: Farmer
Miscellaneous: Resided Clarks Fork, Cooper Co., MO; Otterville, Cooper Co., MO; and Quincy, Branch Co., MI
Buried: Lake View Cemetery, Quincy, MI (Old Cemetery, Lot 48)
References: www.ancestry.com. www.findagrave.com. Charles H. Pope. *A History of the Dorchester Pope Family, 1634–1888*. Boston, MA, 1888. William F. Johnson. *History of Cooper County, Missouri*. Topeka and Cleveland, 1919.

John Cooper Porter

1 Lieutenant, Co. A, 9 Enrolled MO Militia, Sept. 9, 1862. Colonel, 83 Enrolled MO Militia, May 3, 1864. Relieved from duty, Sept. 19, 1864.
Born: Feb. 6, 1825 Machias, ME
Died: Sept. 21, 1916 St. Louis, MO
Occupation: Capitalist, involved in printing, banking, railroad and mining enterprises

John Cooper Porter, post-war (James Cox, editor. *Notable St. Louisans in 1900*. St. Louis, Missouri, 1900).

Miscellaneous: Resided St. Louis, MO
Buried: Bellefontaine Cemetery, St. Louis, MO (Block 24, Lot 417)
References: Obituary, *St. Louis Globe-Democrat*, Sept. 22, 1916. Joseph W. Porter. *A Genealogy of the Descendants of Richard Porter, Who Settled at Weymouth, Mass., 1635, and Allied Families: Also, Some Account of the Descendants of John Porter, Who Settled at Hingham, Mass., 1635, and Salem, (Danvers) Mass., 1644*. Bangor, ME, 1878. Obituary, *St. Louis Post-Dispatch*, Sept. 22, 1916. James Cox, editor. *Notable St. Louisans in 1900*. St. Louis, MO, 1900.

Rudolph von Poser

1 Lieutenant, Light Battery C, 1 MO Artillery, U.S. Reserve Corps, Sept. 25, 1861. 1 Lieutenant, Battery M, 2 MO Light Artillery, Nov. 20, 1861. Resigned April 4, 1863, due to "chronic dysentery." Colonel, 34 Enrolled MO Militia, Aug. 6, 1864. Commission vacated, March 12, 1865. Battle honors: Price's Missouri Expedition.
Born: July 25, 1825, Prussia
Died: Nov. 21, 1900 Stony Hill, MO
Occupation: Farmer and surveyor
Offices/Honors: County surveyor, 1873–85
Miscellaneous: Resided Stony Hill, Gasconade Co., MO
Buried: St. James UCC Cemetery, near Stony Hill, MO

References: Pension File and Military Service File, National Archives. Obituary, *Hermann Advertiser-Courier*, Nov. 28, 1900. *History of Franklin, Jefferson, Washington, Crawford, and Gasconade Counties, Missouri*. Chicago, IL, 1888. Mark A. Lause. *Price's Lost Campaign: The 1864 Invasion of Missouri*. Columbia, MO, 2011. www.findagrave.com.

August Hero Poten

1 Lieutenant, Co. E, 3 MO Infantry (3 months), April 27, 1861. Honorably mustered out, Aug. 12, 1861. Major, 17 MO Infantry, Dec. 19, 1861. Colonel, 5 MO Infantry, May 27, 1862. Commanded Post of Sulphur Spring, Iron Mountain Railroad, St. Louis Division, District of Missouri, Department of the Mississippi, June–Sept. 1862. Embarrassed by the mutinous conduct of men of his regiment who expected to be mustered out upon the issuance of an order mustering out "so-called reserve regiments," he resigned Oct. 22, 1862, "on account of sickness." Major, 7 VRC, Sept. 1, 1863. Lieutenant Colonel, 7 VRC, Oct. 6, 1863. Assistant Commandant of Prisoners, Camp Chase, OH. "Having perfectly recovered from disabilities," he resigned, March 11, 1864, "to go once more into active service for my adopted flag and make room for real invalids." Battle honors: Carthage, Pea Ridge.

Born: Jan. 6, 1829 Aurich, Hanover, Germany
Died: April 14, 1883, St. Louis, MO
Education: Son of General von Poten of Hanover Army, he received a military education and served briefly as a lieutenant of cavalry

August Hero Poten (courtesy Missouri Historical Society, St. Louis [P0084-0014]).

Other Wars: Private, Co. K, 6 U.S. Infantry (May 1, 1853–March 29, 1855)
Occupation: Merchant before war. Farmer and insurance agent after war.
Miscellaneous: Resided St. Louis, MO; Columbus, Franklin Co., OH, 1865–68; Louisville, Jefferson Co., KY, 1872–76; Terre Haute, Vigo Co., IN, 1876–81
Buried: Bellefontaine Cemetery, St. Louis, MO (Block 199, Lot 304)
References: Pension File and Military Service File, National Archives. Obituary, *St. Louis Globe-Democrat*, April 17, 1883. Letters Received, Volunteer Service Branch, Adjutant General's Office, File 4084(VS)1871, National Archives. Wilhelm Kaufmann. *The Germans in the American Civil War*. Translated by Steven Rowan and edited by Don Heinrich Tolzmann with Werner D. Mueller and Robert E. Ward. Carlisle, PA, 1999.

John Pound

Lieutenant Colonel, Osage County Regiment, MO Home Guards, Oct. 3, 1861. Acting AAG, Staff of Brig. Gen. Thomas L. Price, commanding Post of Jefferson City (MO), Oct. 16, 1861. Captain, AAG, USV, Nov. 16, 1861. Discharged from Osage County Regiment, Dec. 6, 1861. Lieutenant Colonel, 14 MO State Militia Cavalry, May 26, 1862. Resigned commission as Captain, AAG, USV, Aug. 15, 1862. Commanded Post of Springfield, District of Southwest Missouri, Department of the Missouri, Aug.–Oct. 1862. Commanded Post of Ozark, District of Southwest Missouri, Department of the Missouri, Nov. 1862. Honorably mustered out, March 4, 1863, upon consolidation of regiment with several other state militia cavalry regiments. Colonel, 42 Enrolled MO Militia, June 10, 1863. Commanded Post of Jefferson City, District of Central Missouri, Department of the Missouri, June–Oct. 1863. Major, 9 Provisional Enrolled MO Militia, Sept. 16, 1863. Relieved from duty, Nov. 30, 1863. Captain, Co. F, 11 MO Cavalry, Dec. 8, 1863. Battle honors: Marmaduke's Expedition into Missouri (Springfield).

Born: 1820? Flushing, NY
Died: May 1, 1864, Batesville, AR (inflammation of the lungs)
Other Wars: Seminole War and Mexican War (Private, Co. E, 7 U.S. Infantry)
Occupation: Regular Army enlisted man (Musician, Co. E, 7 U.S. Infantry, Aug. 22, 1837; Principal Musician, 7 U.S. Infantry, Feb. 15, 1859; and Ordnance Sergeant, USA, Feb. 2, 1860)

Miscellaneous: Resided St. Louis, MO

Buried: Originally Batesville, AR (Supposedly removed to Fort Smith National Cemetery, Fort Smith, AR, but apparently without record of burial)

References: Pension File and Military Service File, National Archives. Obituary, *Daily Missouri Republican*, May 23, 1864. Letters Received, Adjutant General's Office, File P976(AGO)1862, National Archives. Martha & William Reamy, compilers. *Index to the Roll of Honor*. Baltimore, MD, 1995.

James Albert Price

Captain, Co. K, 18 MO Infantry, Feb. 18, 1862. GSW left ear, Shiloh, TN, April 6, 1862. Major, 18 MO Infantry, June 19, 1862. Resigned July 7, 1862, since "the unfortunate and helpless condition of my family renders it impossible for me to remain longer in the service of my country, which I love so much." Colonel, 39 Enrolled MO Militia, Sept. 10, 1862. Commission vacated, Sept. 30, 1863. Major, 16 KS Cavalry, Feb. 3, 1864. Resigned Oct. 7, 1864, since "I cannot in justice to myself remain in my present position," having been assured "that as soon as the regiment was organized, I would be commissioned as colonel of the same." Battle honors: Shiloh.

Born: Sept. 7, 1829 Bedford Co., VA

Died: Aug. 17, 1916 Weston, MO

Education: Attended Baltimore College of Dental Surgery

Occupation: Dentist

Offices/Honors: Postmaster, Weston, MO, 1877–85

Miscellaneous: Resided Weston, Platte Co., MO; and Savannah, Andrew Co., MO, 1896–1905

Buried: Laurel Hill Cemetery, Weston, MO

References: *History of Clay and Platte Counties, Missouri*. St. Louis, MO, 1885. Burton Lee Thorpe, "In Memoriam Dr. James Albert Price," *Western Dental Journal*, Vol. 30, No. 10 (Oct. 1916). Pension File and Military Service File, National Archives. William M. Paxton. *Annals of Platte County, Missouri, from Its Exploration Down to June 1, 1897*. Kansas City, MO, 1897. Leslie Anders. *The Eighteenth Missouri*. Indianapolis, IN, 1968. Obituary, *Leavenworth Times*, Aug. 18, 1916. Letters Received, Volunteer Service Branch, Adjutant General's Office, File P1714(VS)1864, National Archives. James A. Price, "Circular to the Citizens of Platte County, Missouri," *Weston Border Times*, Oct. 14, 1864.

James Albert Price, post-war (Burton Lee Thorpe, "In Memoriam Dr. James Albert Price," *Western Dental Journal*, Vol. 30, No. 10 [Oct. 1916]).

William Henry Pulsifer

1 Lieutenant, Co. A, 7 Enrolled MO Militia, March 27, 1863. Captain, Co. A, 7 Enrolled MO Militia, Feb. 8, 1864. Colonel, 84 Enrolled MO Militia, May 11, 1864. Relieved from duty, Sept. 19, 1864.

Born: Nov. 18, 1831 Boston, MA

Died: April 9, 1905, Washington, D.C.

Occupation: Provision dealer and commission merchant before war. White lead and oil manufacturer after war.

Miscellaneous: Resided Boston, MA, to 1858; St. Louis, MO, 1858–90; and Newton, Middlesex Co., MA, after 1890. Author of *Notes for a History of Lead and an Inquiry into the Development of the Manufacture of White Lead and Lead Oxides*, New York, 1888.

Buried: Newton Cemetery, Newton, MA (Section C, Lot 954)

References: "William Henry Pulsifer," *Transactions of the Academy of Science of St. Louis*. Vol. 15 (January-December 1905). St. Louis, MO, 1905. Oliver A. Roberts. *History of the Military Company of the Massachusetts Now Called the Ancient and Honorable Artillery Company of*

Massachusetts, 1637–1888. Vol. 3. Boston, MA, 1898. Death notice, *Washington Post*, April 11, 1905. Walter B. Stevens. St. Louis The Fourth City, 1764–1909. *St. Louis and Chicago, 1909.* J. Thomas Scharf. *History of Saint Louis City and County*. Philadelphia, PA, 1883.

William Wallace Purmort

Sergeant, Co. C, 1 Northeast MO Infantry, Oct. 25, 1861. 1 Sergeant, Co. C, 21 MO Infantry, Feb. 1, 1862. Honorably discharged, March 17, 1862, to accept appointment as county court clerk. Colonel, 29 Enrolled MO Militia, April 30, 1864. Relieved from duty, Nov. 25, 1864.

Born: Aug. 22, 1830 Jay, Essex Co., NY
Died: Nov. 17, 1902 Siboney, Kiowa Co., OK
Occupation: Farmer and merchant dealing in hardware and agricultural implements
Offices/Honors: County court clerk, 1862–65 and 1878–83
Miscellaneous: Resided Memphis, Scotland Co., MO
Buried: Memphis Cemetery, Memphis, MO (Section 3, Row 6)
References: Charles H. Purmort. *Purmort Genealogy, Consisting of Nineteen Generations, Nine in England, Ten in America*. Des Moines, IA, 1907. Obituary, *Memphis Reveille*, Nov. 27, 1902.

William Wallace Purmort, post-war (Charles H. Purmort. *Purmort Genealogy, Consisting of Nineteen Generations, Nine in England, Ten in America*. Des Moines, Iowa, 1907).

History of Lewis, Clark, Knox, and Scotland Counties, Missouri. St. Louis and Chicago, 1887. Pension File and Military Service File, National Archives. Leslie Anders. *The Twenty-first Missouri: From Home Guard to Union Regiment.* Westport, CT, 1975.

Henry Ramming

1 Lieutenant, Adjutant, 24 IL Infantry, June 16, 1861. *Colonel*, 3 MO Infantry, Sept. 21, 1861. Discharged Jan. 18, 1862, upon consolidation of the incomplete regiment with the 19 MO Infantry.

Born: May 4, 1822, Neimburg, Bohemia
Died: 1863 New Orleans, LA (unconfirmed report in 1870 Davenport newspaper)
Other Wars: German Revolution of 1848 (Captain in the Austrian army)
Occupation: Newspaper editor
Miscellaneous: Resided Davenport, Scott Co., IA
Buried: Burial place unknown
References: Frank I. Herriott, "The German Conference in the Deutsches Haus, Chicago, May 14–15, 1860," *Transactions of the Illinois State Historical Society for the Year 1928*. Springfield, IL, 1928. Letters Received, Volunteer Service Branch, Adjutant General's Office, File R77(VS)1861, National Archives. Military Service File, National Archives. Adolf E. Zucker, editor. *The Forty-Eighters: Political Refugees of the German Revolution of 1848*. New York City, NY, 1950. "Colonel Ramming," *Davenport Daily Democrat and News*, Sept. 11, 1861. Death report, *Daily Davenport Democrat*, Aug. 9, 1870. "Col. Ramming," *Davenport Der Demokrat*, Dec. 24, 1863. http://list.genealogy.net/mm/archiv/-hannover-l/2007-03/msg00354.html.

Louis James Rankin

Lieutenant Colonel, 80 Enrolled MO Militia, Sept. 11, 1863. Colonel, 80 Enrolled MO Militia, Sept. 28, 1863. Resigned Dec. 8, 1864. Battle honors: Price's Missouri Expedition.

Born: Nov. 16, 1811 Herculaneum, MO
Died: Aug. 10, 1897 De Soto, MO
Occupation: Dry goods merchant, real estate dealer, and bank president
Offices/Honors: County Treasurer, 1856–62. Postmaster, Hillsboro, MO, 1857–63.
Miscellaneous: Resided Hillsboro, Jefferson Co., MO; and De Soto, Jefferson Co., MO. Helped lay out town of De Soto, MO, in 1857. Brother-in-law

of Bvt. Brig. Gen. Thomas C. Fletcher and also of Bvt. Brig. Gen. Madison Miller.

Buried: City Cemetery, De Soto, MO

References: Obituary, *De Soto Press*, Aug. 14, 1897. Eddie Miller, "De Soto's Other Founder-Louis J. Rankin," *De Soto Press*, April 30, May 7, 14, 21, 28, June 4, 1973. Edward H. Fletcher. *Fletcher Family History: The Descendants of Robert Fletcher of Concord, Mass.* Boston, MA, 1881. Obituary, *St. Louis Post-Dispatch*, Aug. 10, 1897. Obituary, *St. Louis Republic*, Aug. 11, 1897. Obituary, *Jefferson Democrat*, Aug. 12, 1897. *History of Franklin, Jefferson, Washington, Crawford, and Gasconade Counties, Missouri.* Chicago, IL, 1888.

William McCune Reading

Colonel, 69 Enrolled MO Militia, Aug. 26, 1862. Dismissed Oct. 13, 1863. Colonel, 69 Enrolled MO Militia, Feb. 11, 1865. Commission vacated March 12, 1865.

Born: June 25, 1828, Pike Co., MO

Died: June 1, 1909, Assumption, IL

Occupation: Dry goods merchant, farmer, and livestock dealer

Miscellaneous: Resided LaGrange, Lewis Co., MO, to 1878; Assumption, Christian Co., IL, after 1878

Buried: Greenwood Cemetery, Assumption, IL

References: *Portrait and Biographical Record of Christian County, Illinois.* Chicago, IL, 1893. Obituary, *Pana Palladium*, June 10, 1909. *History of Lewis, Clark, Knox and Scotland Counties, Missouri.* St. Louis and Chicago, 1887. www.ancestry.com.

John H. Reed

Captain, Co. D, 3 MO Cavalry, Nov. 26, 1861. Taken prisoner, Marks' Mills, AR, April 25, 1864. Confined Camp Ford, Tyler, TX. Escaped Aug. 19, 1864. Returned to regiment, Sept. 21, 1864. Major, 3 MO Cavalry, June 18, 1864. Lieutenant Colonel, 3 MO Cavalry, Sept. 21, 1864. Commanded Separate Cavalry Brigade, 7 Army Corps, Department of Arkansas, April–May 1865. Colonel, 3 MO Cavalry, June 6, 1865. Honorably mustered out, June 14, 1865. Battle honors: Marmaduke's Expedition into Missouri (Chalk Bluff), Advance upon Little Rock (Bayou Fourche), Camden Expedition (Marks' Mills).

Born: April 5, 1823, Berkeley Co., VA (now WV)

Died: Jan. 6, 1894 Fulton, MO

Occupation: Merchant tailor

Miscellaneous: Resided Champaign, Champaign Co., IL, to 1866; Quincy, Adams Co., IL; Macon, Macon Co., MO, 1867–76; and Fulton, Callaway Co., MO, 1876–94

Buried: Oakwood Cemetery, Macon, MO

References: Pension File and Military Service File, National Archives. Henry A. and Mary A. Street. *The Street Genealogy.* Exeter, NH, 1895. Obituary, *Macon Republican*, Jan. 12, 1894. Obituary, *Macon Times*, Jan. 12, 1894. Letters Received, Volunteer Service Branch, Adjutant General's Office, File R246(VS)1867, National Archives. A.W.M. Petty. *A History of the Third Missouri Cavalry: From Its Organization at Palmyra, Missouri, 1861, Up to November Sixth, 1864.* Little Rock, AR, 1865.

Allen Peyton Richardson

Colonel, Cole County Regiment, MO Home Guards, June 17, 1861. Discharged Oct. 1, 1861. *Colonel*, Richardson's Regiment, Six Months MO Militia, Oct. 1, 1861. Honorably mustered out, Dec. 18, 1861. Major, Paymaster, Enrolled MO Militia, July 21, 1863. Colonel, ADC, MO State Militia, Feb. 18, 1864. Commission vacated Jan. 12, 1865.

Born: Nov. 10, 1822 Lawrenceburg, KY

Died: Feb. 15, 1892 Breckenridge, CO

Occupation: Lawyer

Offices/Honors: Missouri Register of Lands, 1849–56. Postmaster, Jefferson City, MO, 1861–67. Missouri Senate, 1862–64. Missouri House of Representatives, 1871–73.

Miscellaneous: Resided Jefferson City, Cole Co., MO, to 1869; Sullivan, Franklin Co., MO (1870); St. Louis, MO, 1873–81; and Breckenridge, Summit Co., CO, after 1881. Brother-in-law of Colonel Austin A. King, Jr. (13 MO Cavalry) and Colonel Walter King (3 MO State Militia Cavalry)

Buried: Woodland-Old City Cemetery, Jefferson City, MO (Lot 40)

References: Obituary, *Jefferson City Daily Tribune*, Feb. 20, 1892. J.T. Pratt. *Pen-Pictures of the Officers and Members of the House of Representatives of the Twenty-Sixth General Assembly of Missouri.* N.p., 1872. Obituary, *St. Louis Post-Dispatch*, Feb. 20, 1892. Albert Griffen. *Biographical Register of the Members of the Twenty-Sixth General Assembly of the State of Missouri.* St. Louis, MO, 1872. Pension File and Military Service File, National Archives.

John Mortimer Richardson

Captain, Company of Spies, Scouts and Messengers, MO Home Guards, June–July 1861. Captain, Co. A, 14 MO State Militia Cavalry, Jan. 24, 1862. Colonel, 14 MO State Militia Cavalry, May 26, 1862. GSW right arm, Neosho, MO, May 31, 1862. Commanded Post of Cassville, District of Southwest Missouri, Department of the Missouri, Nov. 1862. Honorably mustered out, March 5, 1863, upon consolidation of regiment with several other state militia cavalry regiments. Provost Marshal, 4 District of Missouri, March 7, 1864. Resigned Jan. 3, 1865. Battle honors: Carthage, Neosho, Prairie Grove.

Born: Sept. 8, 1820 near Leesburg, Loudoun Co., VA
Died: May 1, 1889, Tucson, AZ
Education: Attended Kenyon College, Gambier, OH
Occupation: Lawyer and newspaper editor
Offices/Honors: Missouri House of Representatives, 1844–46. Secretary of State of Missouri, 1852–56.
Miscellaneous: Resided Springfield, Greene Co., MO, to 1875; Carthage, Jasper Co., MO, 1875–86; and Tucson, Pima Co., AZ, 1886–89
Buried: Park Cemetery, Carthage, MO
References: Malcolm G. McGregor. *The Biographical Record of Jasper County, Missouri.* Chicago, IL, 1901. Marvin L. Van Gilder. *Jasper County: The First Two Hundred Years.* N.p, 1995. Obituary, *Arizona Daily Citizen*, May 1, 1889. Obituary, *Carthage Press*, May 9, 1889. Obituary, *Arizona Daily Star*, May 2, 1889. *History of Jasper County, Missouri.* Des Moines, IA, 1883. *History of Greene County, Missouri.* St. Louis, MO, 1883. Military Service File, National Archives. Letters Received, Volunteer Service Branch, Adjutant General's Office, File R256(VS)1870, National Archives. Jeanette Shiel, "The Life of Hon. John M. Richardson," http://webpages.charter.net/cwnorthandsouth/14thBioA91.html.

Thomas Richeson

Colonel, 6 Enrolled MO Militia, Sept. 24, 1862. Resigned Jan. 21, 1863.

Born: Jan. 1, 1820 Amherst Co., VA
Died: June 18, 1902, St. Louis, MO
Education: Graduated Washington and Lee University, Lexington, VA, 1840
Occupation: White lead and oil manufacturer
Offices/Honors: Treasurer of St. Louis City and County, 1857. President, Merchants' Exchange of St. Louis, 1864.

Thomas Richeson, post-war (Howard L. Conard, editor. *Encyclopedia of the History of Missouri.* New York, Louisville, and St. Louis, 1901).

Miscellaneous: Resided St. Louis, MO
Buried: Bellefontaine Cemetery, St. Louis, MO (Block 54, Lot 2038)
References: Howard L. Conard, editor. *Encyclopedia of the History of Missouri.* New York, Louisville, and St. Louis, 1901. Obituary, *St. Louis Globe-Democrat*, June 19, 1902. Obituary, *St. Louis Republic*, June 19, 1902. Obituary, *St. Louis Post-Dispatch*, June 19, 1902. Logan U. Reavis. *Saint Louis: The Future Great City of the World.* Centennial Edition. St. Louis, MO, 1876. *Catalogue of the Officers and Alumni of Washington and Lee University, Lexington, Virginia, 1749–1888.* Baltimore, MD, 1888. George H. Morgan. *Annual Statement of the Trade and Commerce of Saint Louis, for the Year 1906, Reported to the Merchants' Exchange of St. Louis.* St. Louis, MO, 1907.

George Rinkel, Jr.

Colonel, 15 Enrolled MO Militia, May 14, 1863. Resigned April 21, 1864.

Born: 1838 St. Louis Co., MO
Died: March 24, 1886, St. Louis, MO
Occupation: Saloonkeeper and farmer
Miscellaneous: Resided St. Louis, MO
Buried: Saint Peter's UCC Cemetery, Normandy, St. Louis Co., MO (Old Section, Part 1, Lot 825)
References: www.ancestry.com. www.findagrave.com. "General Order No. 15, Headquarters

First Military District, E.M.M.," *Daily Missouri Democrat*, May 15, 1863. "Special Order No. 6, Headquarters First Military District, E.M.M.," *Daily Missouri Republican*, April 22, 1864. Obituary, *Missouri Republican*, March 26, 1886. J. Thomas Scharf. *History of Saint Louis City and County*. Philadelphia, PA, 1883.

John Francis Ritter

1 Lieutenant, 15 U.S. Infantry, May 14, 1861. Captain, 15 U.S. Infantry, Oct. 24, 1861. Colonel, 1 MO Cavalry, June 18, 1862. Acting AIG and Chief of Staff, Staff of Brig. Gen. Eugene A. Carr, Army of the Southwest, Department of the Missouri, Oct. 1862. Commanded 4 Brigade, 5 Division (District of Memphis), 16 Army Corps, Department of the Tennessee, April–May 1863. Although found guilty by court-martial, July 2, 1863, of "Conduct to the prejudice of good order and military discipline" for openly opposing the arming and enlisting of Negroes and also of "Lying out of his quarters and camp, without leave from his superior officers," he escaped punishment when Major Gen. Stephen A. Hurlbut disapproved the finding and sentence, since "the testimony does not support the specifications." Commanded Reserve Brigade, 1 Cavalry Division, Arkansas Expedition, Department of the Missouri, Aug.–Oct. 1863. Commanded 1 Brigade, Cavalry Division, 7 Army Corps, Department of Arkansas, Jan.–May 1864. Commanded 3 Brigade, 1 Division, 7 Army Corps, Department of Arkansas, July–Sept. 1864. Commanded 2 Brigade, Cavalry Division, 7 Army Corps, Department of Arkansas, Sept.–Nov. 1864. Possibly motivated by the adverse reaction from fellow regimental officers to his retention in command following the expiration of his original term of service, he resigned, Dec. 5, 1864, to resume his position in the 15 U.S. Infantry. Bvt. Major, USA, March 28, 1862, for gallant and meritorious services at the battle of Apache Canyon, NM. Bvt. Lieutenant Colonel, USA, Sept. 10, 1863, for gallant and meritorious services at the capture of Little Rock, AR. Battle honors: Apache Canyon, Glorieta, Advance upon Little Rock (Bayou Meto, Bayou Fourche), Camden Expedition.

Born: Jan. 24, 1836 Reading, PA
Died: Aug. 1, 1872 Catskill, NY
Education: Graduated U.S. Military Academy, West Point, NY, 1856
Occupation: Regular Army (Captain, 8 U.S. Infantry)
Miscellaneous: Resided Reading, Berks Co., PA

John Francis Ritter (Brown's Gallery, Corner of Main & Markham Streets, Little Rock, Arkansas; Roger D. Hunt Collection, USAMHI [RG98S-CWP160.55]).

John Francis Ritter (W.L. Germon's Atelier, No. 702 Chestnut Street, Philadelphia, Pennsylvania; Roger D. Hunt Collection, USAMHI [RG98S-CWP58.95]).

John Francis Ritter (Black & Case, Photographic Artists, Boston & Newport, Rhode Island; author's photograph).

William Perrine Robinson (courtesy Denell Burks).

Buried: Charles Evans Cemetery, Reading, PA (Section E, Lot 99)
References: *Book of Biographies Berks County, Pennsylvania*. Buffalo, NY, 1898. Pension File and Military Service File, National Archives. Obituary, *Reading Daily Eagle*, Aug. 2, 1872. Letters Received, Volunteer Service Branch, Adjutant General's Office, Files R987(VS)1863 and V423(VS)1864, National Archives. Letters Received, Appointment, Commission, and Personal Branch, Adjutant General's Office, File 4858(ACP)1871, National Archives. George W. Cullum. *Biographical Register of the Officers and Graduates of the U.S. Military Academy*. Third Edition. Boston, MA, 1891. Court-martial Case Files, 1809–1894, File NN-0176, National Archives.

William Perrine Robinson

Captain, Co. D, 23 MO Infantry, Sept. 22, 1861. GSW right leg, Shiloh, TN, April 6, 1862. Colonel, 23 MO Infantry, June 7, 1862. Commanded Post of Hudson (Macon Co., MO), Northeastern District of Missouri, Department of the Missouri, Nov. 1862. Commanded Post of Pacific City, District of St. Louis, Department of the Missouri, Dec. 1862–April 1863. Commanded Post of McMinnville (TN), District of Nashville, Department of the Cumberland, Nov. 1863–May 1864. Honorably mustered out, Sept. 22, 1864. Battle honors: Shiloh, Atlanta Campaign (Peach Tree Creek).

William Perrine Robinson, post-war (*History of Harrison and Mercer Counties, Missouri, From the Earliest Time to the Present*. St. Louis and Chicago, 1888).

Born: Feb. 20, 1826 Carlisle, Nicholas Co., KY
Died: June 20, 1904, Manhattan, KS
Education: Attended Wabash College, Crawfordsville, IN
Other Wars: Mexican War (1 Sergeant, Co. E, 3 KY Infantry)
Occupation: Farmer and school teacher before war. Probate judge and county clerk after war.

Offices/Honors: Probate Judge, 1872–78. County Clerk, Harrison Co., MO, 1879–90.

Miscellaneous: Resided Bethany, Harrison Co., MO; Chatham, Sangamon Co., IL, 1861–67; and Manhattan, Riley Co., KS, 1903–04. Father of sixteen children by two wives.

Buried: Miriam Cemetery, Bethany, MO (Original Addition, Block 4, Lot 4)

References: *History of Harrison and Mercer Counties, Missouri, From the Earliest Time to the Present.* St. Louis and Chicago, 1888. Obituary, *Bethany Democrat,* June 29, 1904. Obituary, *Manhattan Nationalist,* June 20, 1904. Obituary, *Manhattan Mercury,* June 21, 1904. Obituary, *Manhattan Republic,* June 23, 1904. Pension File and Military Service File, National Archives.

John B. Rogers

Major, 11 MO State Militia Cavalry, May 7, 1862. Major, 2 MO State Militia Cavalry, Sept. 2, 1862. Colonel, 2 MO State Militia Cavalry, May 26, 1863. Commanded Post of Cape Girardeau, District of Southeastern Missouri, Department of the Missouri, June–Nov. 1863. Commanded Post of Cape Girardeau, District of St. Louis, Department of the Missouri, Dec. 1863–May 1864. A Court of Inquiry convened in June 1864 to examine his official transactions as Post Commander was dissolved in Sept. 1864, with Judge Advocate General Joseph Holt concluding, "Col. Rogers, though guilty perhaps of some carelessness in managing the details of his official duties, especially in his method of dealing with horses captured from the enemy, has satisfactorily cleared himself ... and should be released from arrest and restored to duty." Commanded 2 Sub-District, District of St. Louis, Department of the Missouri, Dec. 1864–Feb. 1865. Honorably mustered out, March 1, 1865. Battle honors: Kirksville.

Born: 1829? NY

Died: Nov. 28, 1868 St. Louis, MO

Occupation: Civil engineer engaged in railroad construction and farmer

Offices/Honors: U.S. Marshal, Eastern District of Missouri, 1866–68

Miscellaneous: Resided Bloomington, Macon Co., MO; Hannibal, Marion Co., MO; and St. Louis, MO

Buried: Riverside Cemetery, Hannibal, MO

References: Pension File and Military Service File, National Archives. Obituary, *Daily Missouri Democrat,* Nov. 30, 1868. Obituary, *Daily Missouri Republican,* Nov. 29, 1868. Obituary, *Palmyra Spectator,* Dec. 4, 1868. Bruce Nichols. *Guerrilla Warfare in Civil War Missouri, Volume IV, September 1864–June 1865.* Jefferson, NC, 2014. *History of Marion County, Missouri.* St. Louis, MO, 1884. Court-martial Case Files, 1809–1894, File LL-2726, National Archives.

William B. Rogers

Sergeant Major, Mercer County Battalion, Six Months MO Militia, Sept. 26, 1861. Honorably mustered out, March 19, 1862. Colonel, 44 Enrolled MO Militia, Aug. 29, 1862. Resigned Sept. 8, 1864. Captain, Co. D, 44 MO Infantry, Sept. 10, 1864. Honorably mustered out, Aug. 15, 1865. Battle honors: Franklin, Nashville, Mobile Campaign (Spanish Fort).

Born: Feb. 8, 1835 Fayette Co., OH

Died: March 22, 1924, Trenton, MO

Education: Attended Grand River College, Edinburg, MO

Occupation: School teacher before war. Newspaper editor and publisher after war.

Offices/Honors: Sheriff, Mercer Co., MO, 1862–64. Postmaster, Ravenna, MO, 1865–68. Missouri Senate, 1869–73.

Miscellaneous: Resided Ravenna, Mercer Co., MO, to 1869; and Trenton, Grundy Co., MO, after 1869

William B. Rogers, post-war (*History of Grundy County, Missouri.* Kansas City, Missouri, 1881).

William B. Rogers, post-war (Walter Williams, editor. *A History of Northwest Missouri*. Chicago and New York, 1915).

Buried: Masonic Cemetery, Trenton, MO
References: Walter Williams, editor. *A History of Northwest Missouri*. Chicago and New York, 1915. Howard L. Conard, editor. *Encyclopedia of the History of Missouri*. New York, Louisville, and St. Louis, 1901. Obituary, *Chillicothe Constitution-Tribune*, March 24, 1924. *The History of Grundy County, Missouri*. Kansas City, MO, 1881. William R. Denslow. *Centennial History of Grundy County, Missouri*. Trenton, MO, 1939. Obituary, *Kansas City Star*, March 23, 1924. Albert Griffen. *Biographical Register of the Members of the Twenty-Sixth General Assembly of the State of Missouri*. St. Louis, MO, 1872. *Rogers' Souvenir History of Mercer County Missouri and Dictionary of Local Data*. Trenton, MO, 1911. Obituary, *King City Chronicle*, March 28, 1924.

Robert Julius Rombauer

Lieutenant Colonel, 1 U.S. Reserve Corps, MO Infantry (3 months), May 7, 1861. Honorably mustered out, Aug. 20, 1861. Colonel, 1 U.S. Reserve Corps, MO Infantry, Sept. 12, 1861. Commanded Post of Pacific City, St. Louis District, Department of the Mississippi, March–May 1862. Commanded 2 Brigade, 3 Division, Army of the Southwest, Department of the Mississippi, July 1862. Commanded 3 Brigade, 3 Division, Army of the Southwest, Department of the Mississippi, Aug.–Sept. 1862. Honorably mustered out, Oct. 6, 1862. *Major*, 5 St. Louis City Guards, Oct. 6, 1864.
Born: Jan. 10, 1830 Podhering, near Munkacs, Hungary
Died: Sept. 25, 1925 St. Louis, MO
Other Wars: Lieutenant of artillery in Honved army during Hungarian War of Independence, 1848–49. Sergeant, Austrian Army, 1849–51.
Occupation: Bank cashier before war. Railroad surveyor after war.
Miscellaneous: Resided St. Louis, MO. Brother-in-law of Colonel John T. Fiala (Additional ADC).
Buried: Bellefontaine Cemetery, St. Louis, MO (Block 24, Lot 2524)
References: Robert J. Rombauer. *Biographical Notes of Robert J. Rombauer, 1917*. St. Louis, MO, 1922. Pension File and Military Service File, National Archives. Istvan Kornel Vida. *Hungarian Emigres in the American Civil War: A History and Biographical Dictionary*. Jefferson, NC, 2012. The Edmund Vasvary Papers, U.S. Army Military History Institute. Robert J. Rombauer. *The Union Cause in St. Louis in 1861: An Historical Sketch*. St. Louis, MO, 1909. Edmund Vasvary. *Lincoln's Hungarian Heroes: The Participation of Hungarians in the Civil War, 1861–1865*. Washington, D.C., 1939. Obituary, *St. Louis Post-Dispatch*, Sept. 26, 1925. "Couple Married 65 Years to Celebrate," *St. Louis Post-Dispatch*, April 20, 1922. Letters Received, Commission Branch, Adjutant General's Office, File R403(CB)1863, National Archives. William C. Winter. *The Civil War in St. Louis: A Guided Tour*. St. Louis, MO, 1994. Eugene Pivany. *Hungarians in the American Civil War*. Cleveland, OH, 1913.

Edward Russell

Colonel, 88 Enrolled MO Militia, July 14, 1864. Commission vacated March 12, 1865.
Born: Jan. 12, 1813 London, England
Died: March 19, 1891, Savannah, MO
Occupation: Tailor, notary public, and farmer
Offices/Honors: Sheriff of Andrew Co., MO. Several terms as Mayor of Savannah, MO.
Miscellaneous: Resided Savannah, Andrew Co., MO
Buried: City Cemetery, Savannah, MO
References: Obituary, *Savannah Reporter*, March 20, 1891. *History of Andrew and DeKalb Counties, Missouri, from the Earliest Time to the Present*. St. Louis and Chicago, 1888.

Otto Schadt

Captain, Co. A, Rifle Battalion, 2 MO Infantry (3 months), April 23, 1861. Honorably mustered out, Aug. 30, 1861. Lieutenant Colonel, 12 MO Infantry, Dec. 10, 1861. Resigned Oct. 2, 1862, "having received and accepted the appointment to organize the above named regiment (34 MO Infantry) as its colonel." Colonel, 34 MO Infantry, Sept. 6, 1862. Regiment did not complete organization. Lieutenant Colonel, 30 MO Infantry, Oct. 29, 1862. Lieutenant Colonel, 6 U.S. Colored Heavy Artillery, Sept. 16, 1863. Declined appointment as Lieutenant Colonel, 6 U.S. Colored Heavy Artillery, Nov. 2, 1863, requesting "to be ordered back for duty to the 30th Regt. MO Vol. Infty." Dishonorably discharged, March 6, 1864, "for offering a bribe to an officer in the service of the United States ... with the object of procuring authority to raise a regiment of Colored Troops with fraudulent intentions in view, and for other reasons involving Conduct unbecoming an officer and a gentleman." Battle honors: Boonville, Chickasaw Bayou, Vicksburg Campaign.

Born: 1828? Prussia
Died: Reported as "deceased" in Chicago newspaper, Sept. 3, 1879
Other Wars: Lieutenant in the Prussian army
Occupation: Artist before war. U.S. Internal Revenue official after war.
Miscellaneous: Resided St. Louis, MO, before war; and Chicago, IL, 1864–70
Buried: Burial place unknown
References: Military Service File, National Archives. Martin W. Ofele. *German-Speaking Officers in the U.S. Colored Troops, 1863–1867*. Gainesville, FL, 2004. Earl J. Hess, "The 12th Missouri Infantry: A Socio-Military Profile of a Union Regiment," *Missouri Historical Review*, Vol. 76, No. 1 (Oct. 1981). "Superior Court, New Suits," *Chicago Daily Inter Ocean*, Sept. 3, 1879. Letters Received, Volunteer Service Branch, Adjutant General's Office, File S1149(VS)1862, National Archives. www.ancestry.com.

Frederick Schaefer

Lieutenant Colonel, 2 MO Infantry (3 months), May 14, 1861. Honorably mustered out, July 30, 1861. Colonel, 2 MO Infantry, Sept. 10, 1861. Commanded 1 Brigade, 2 Division, Army of the Southwest, Department of the Mississippi, Feb.–June 1862. Commanded 1 Brigade, 5 Division, Army of the Mississippi, Aug.–Sept. 1862. Commanded 35 Brigade, 11 Division, 3 Army Corps, Army of the Ohio, Oct.–Nov. 1862. Commanded 2 Brigade, 3 Division, Right Wing, 14 Army Corps, Army of the Cumberland, Nov.–Dec. 1862. GSW Stone's River, TN, Dec. 31, 1862. Battle honors: Boonville, Pea Ridge, Stone's River.

Born: Nov. 11, 1808 Karlsruhe, Baden-Wurttemberg, Germany
Died: Dec. 31, 1862 KIA Stone's River, TN
Other Wars: Mexican War (Captain, Co. F, 1 Regiment, St. Louis Legion, MO Infantry)
Occupation: Brewer
Miscellaneous: Resided Baden-Wurttemberg, Germany; and St. Louis, MO
Buried: Jefferson Barracks National Cemetery, St. Louis, MO (Section OPS1, Grave 2172)
References: J. Thomas Scharf. *History of Saint Louis City and County*. Philadelphia, PA, 1883. Obituary, *Daily Missouri Republican*, Jan. 6, 1863. Henry Boernstein. *Memoirs of a Nobody. The Missouri Years of an Austrian Radical, 1849–1866*. Translated and edited by Steven Rowan. St. Louis, MO, 1997. Philip H. Sheridan. *Personal Memoirs of P.H. Sheridan, General United States Army*. New York City, NY, 1888. Wilhelm Kaufmann. *The Germans in the American Civil War*. Translated by Steven Rowan and edited by Don Heinrich Tolzmann with Werner D. Mueller and Robert E. Ward. Carlisle, PA, 1999. Pension File and Military Service File, National Archives. Letters Received, Volunteer Service Branch, Adjutant General's Office, File G24(VS)1862, National Archives. "Letter from Colonel Laibold," *Daily Missouri Democrat*, Dec. 30, 1863.

Frederick Schaefer (author's photograph).

Nicholas Schittner (also spelled Schuettner)

Colonel, 4 MO Infantry (3 months), May 5, 1861. Honorably mustered out, July 31, 1861. Colonel, 3 Enrolled MO Militia, Sept. 30, 1862. Commission vacated, Oct. 23, 1863.

Born: 1821? Coblenz, Germany
Died: Aug. 2, 1868 St. Louis, MO
Occupation: Carpenter and builder
Offices/Honors: Superintendent in St. Louis city engineer's office, 1864–66
Miscellaneous: Resided St. Louis, MO
Buried: Hillcrest Abbey Mausoleum, St. Louis, MO (Annex, Tier 1, Niche 487)
References: Robert J. Rombauer. *The Union Cause in St. Louis in 1861: An Historical Sketch.* St. Louis, MO, 1909. Pension File and Military Service File, National Archives. Henry Boernstein. *Memoirs of a Nobody. The Missouri Years of an Austrian Radical, 1849–1866.* Translated and edited by Steven Rowan. St. Louis, MO, 1997. Obituary, *Daily Missouri Democrat,* Aug. 3, 1868. Joseph G. Rosengarten. *The German Soldier in the Wars of the United States.* Second edition, revised and enlarged. Philadelphia, PA, 1890. Letters Received, Volunteer Service Branch, Adjutant General's Office, File B3309(VS)1864, National Archives. www.findagrave.com.

Nicholas Schittner (Robert J. Rombauer. *The Union Cause in St. Louis in 1861: An Historical Sketch.* St. Louis, Missouri, 1909).

John Scott (St. Joseph Public Library [V1Pic 27Lozo]).

John Scott

Colonel, 25 Enrolled MO Militia, Sept. 29, 1863. Regiment disbanded, Nov. 1, 1863. Commanded 2 Sub-District, 7 Military District, Department of the Missouri, Nov.–Dec. 1863. Colonel, 81 Enrolled MO Militia, Dec. 8, 1863. Commission vacated, March 12, 1865.

Born: 1812 NC
Died: March 1, 1865, St. Joseph, MO
Occupation: Lawyer
Offices/Honors: City Attorney, St. Joseph, MO, 1852–55. Missouri Senate, 1858–62.
Miscellaneous: Resided St. Joseph, Buchanan Co., MO
Buried: Mount Mora Cemetery, St. Joseph, MO
References: Obituary, *St. Joseph Morning Herald and Daily Tribune,* March 2, 1865. Christian L. Rutt, compiler. *The Daily News' History of Buchanan County and St. Joseph, Missouri, From the Time of the Platte Purchase to the End of the Year 1898.* St. Joseph, MO, 1898. Christian L. Rutt, editor. *History of Buchanan County and the City of St. Joseph and Representative Citizens.* Chicago, IL, 1904. *The History of Buchanan County, Missouri.* St. Joseph, MO, 1881.

Thomas Scott

Colonel, 19 Enrolled MO Militia, April 21, 1863. Commission vacated, April 16, 1864.
Born: Dec. 8, 1816 Shelby Co., KY

Died: Aug. 30, 1887 near Tuscumbia, MO
Occupation: Lawyer and farmer
Offices/Honors: Missouri House of Representatives, 1862–64
Miscellaneous: Resided near Tuscumbia, Miller Co., MO
Buried: Scott Family Cemetery, near Tuscumbia, MO
References: Gerard Schultz. *A History of Miller County, Missouri.* Jefferson City, MO, 1933. *History of Cole, Moniteau, Morgan, Benton, Miller, Maries, and Osage Counties, Missouri, from the Earliest Time to the Present.* Chicago, IL, 1889. www.ancestry.com.

Abraham Jefferson Seay

2 Lieutenant, Co. C, Phelps' Regiment MO Infantry, Sept. 12, 1861. 1 Lieutenant, Co. C, Phelps' Regiment MO Infantry, Dec. 19, 1861. Captain, Co. C, Phelps' Regiment MO Infantry, March 15, 1862. Honorably mustered out, April 8, 1862. Recruiting 2 Lieutenant, 36 MO Infantry, Aug. 28, 1862. Major, 32 MO Infantry, Oct. 20, 1862. Major, Consolidated Battalion, 31 and 32 MO Infantry, Nov. 12, 1864. Lieutenant Colonel, Consolidated Battalion, 31 and 32 MO Infantry, Jan. 14, 1865. *Colonel*, 32 MO Infantry, June 12, 1865. Honorably mustered out, July 18, 1865. Battle honors: Vicksburg Campaign, Dalton, Atlanta Campaign (Dallas, Kenesaw Mountain, Atlanta, Ezra Church, Jonesborough), Savannah Campaign, Campaign of the Carolinas (Bentonville).
Born: Nov. 28, 1832 Amherst Co., VA
Died: Dec. 22, 1915 Long Beach, CA
Occupation: School teacher and lawyer before war. Lawyer, judge and banker after war.
Offices/Honors: Circuit Court Judge, 1875–86. Associate Justice, Oklahoma Territory Supreme Court, 1890–91. Governor of Oklahoma Territory, 1892–93.
Miscellaneous: Resided Steelville, Crawford Co., MO, to 1870; Union, Franklin Co., MO, 1870–90; and Kingfisher, Kingfisher Co., OK, after 1890
Buried: Kingfisher Cemetery, Kingfisher, OK (Block 16, Lot 65)
References: LeRoy H. Fischer, editor. *Oklahoma's Governors, 1890-1907: Territorial Years.* Oklahoma City, OK, 1975. Dan W. Peery, "Autobiography of Governor Abraham Jefferson Seay," *Chronicles of Oklahoma*, Vol. 17, No. 1 (Spring 1939). *The Bench and Bar of St. Louis, Kansas City, Jefferson City, and Other Missouri Cities.*

Abraham Jefferson Seay (courtesy Missouri Historical Society, St. Louis [P0233-2612]).

Abraham Jefferson Seay, post-war (courtesy Missouri Historical Society, St. Louis [P0233-2611]).

St. Louis and Chicago, 1884. "Camm & A.J. Seay: Distinguished Father and Son," *Newsletter, Osage County (MO) Historical Society*, Vol. 7, No. 3 (March 1992). Pension File and Military Service File, National Archives. Obituary, *Morning Tulsa Daily World*, Dec. 24, 1915. Gary L. Scheel. *Rain, Mud & Swamps, 31st Missouri Volunteer Infantry Regiment; Marching Through the South during the Civil War with General William T. Sherman.* Pacific, MO, 1998. Letters Received, Volunteer Service Branch, Adjutant General's Office, File S240(VS)1865, National Archives. Obituary Circular, Whole No. 1197, California MOLLUS.

John Severance

Major, ADC, Staff of Brig. Gen. Benjamin F. Loan, Dec. 15, 1861. Resigned April 12, 1862. Colonel, 25 Enrolled MO Militia, Sept. 8, 1862. Resigned April 22, 1863.

Born: Feb. 25, 1830 Wiscoy, Allegany Co., NY
Died: June 30, 1893, Hutchinson, KS
Occupation: Civil engineer
Offices/Honors: Missouri Senate, 1862–64. City Engineer, St. Joseph, MO, 1866–70. Mayor, St. Joseph, MO, 1870–74. Postmaster, St. Joseph, MO, 1875–76. Commissioner, Industrial Reformatory, Hutchinson, KS, 1885–89. Mayor, Hutchinson, KS, 1890–92.
Miscellaneous: Resided St. Joseph, Buchanan Co., MO, to 1878; Axtell, Marshall Co., KS, 1878–86; and Hutchinson, Reno Co., KS, 1886–93
Buried: East Side Cemetery, Hutchinson, KS (Section 2, Lot 152)
References: Pension File, National Archives. Obituary, *Hutchinson Daily News*, July 1, 1893. Obituary, *St. Joseph Herald*, July 2 and 5, 1893. Obituary, *Axtell Anchor*, July 7, 1893. Christian L. Rutt, compiler. *The Daily News' History of Buchanan County and St. Joseph, Missouri, From the Time of the Platte Purchase to the End of the Year 1898.* St. Joseph, MO, 1898. *The History of Buchanan County, Missouri.* St. Joseph, MO, 1881.

John Henderson Shanklin

Lieutenant Colonel, 3 MO State Militia Cavalry, March 7, 1862. Resigned May 22, 1862. Colonel, 30 Enrolled MO Militia, Aug. 21, 1862. Temporary service as Colonel, 4 Provisional Enrolled MO Militia, Aug. 1, 1864. Commanded Sub-District of Chillicothe, District of North Missouri, Department of the Missouri, Aug. 1864–March 1865. Commission vacated, March 12, 1865. Battle honors: Price's Missouri Expedition.

Born: Nov. 2, 1824 Monroe Co., VA (now WV)
Died: June 14, 1904, Trenton, MO
Other Wars: Mexican War (Private, Co. A, Gilpin's Battalion, MO Infantry)

John Henderson Shanklin, post-war (State Historical Society of Missouri, Photograph Collection [Victoria Branham, P0213, 016676]).

Occupation: Lawyer and banker
Miscellaneous: Resided Trenton, Grundy Co., MO
Buried: Odd Fellows Cemetery, Trenton, MO
References: Henry C. McDougal, "John Henderson Shanklin," *Proceedings of the Twenty-Second Annual Meeting of the Missouri Bar Association.* Columbia, MO, 1905. A.J.D. Stewart, editor. *The History of the Bench and Bar of Missouri.* St. Louis, MO, 1898. Walter Williams, editor. *A History of Northwest Missouri.* Chicago and New York, 1915. *The History of Grundy County, Missouri.* Kansas City, MO, 1881. Howard L. Conard, editor. *Encyclopedia of the History of Missouri.* New York, Louisville, and St. Louis, 1901. Obituary, *Chillicothe Constitution-Tribune*, June 16, 1904. William R. Denslow. *Centennial History of Grundy County, Missouri.* Trenton, MO, 1939. Henry Clay McDougal. *Recollections, 1844–1909.* Kansas City, MO, 1910. Military Service File, National Archives.

William Anderson Shelton

Captain, Co. D, 1 MO State Militia Cavalry, Feb. 19, 1862. Resigned Sept. 10, 1862. Colonel, 45 Enrolled MO Militia, Sept. 27, 1862. Commission vacated, March 12, 1865. Battle honors: Price's Missouri Expedition.

Born: April 15, 1832, Clinton Co., KY
Died: Jan. 25, 1905 Unionville, MO
Occupation: Lawyer and judge
Offices/Honors: Circuit Court Clerk, 1860–66. Missouri Senate, 1867–71. Probate Court Judge, 1880–90.
Miscellaneous: Resided Unionville, Putnam Co., MO
Buried: Unionville Cemetery, Unionville, MO
References: *History of Adair, Sullivan, Putnam and Schuyler Counties, Missouri.* Chicago, IL, 1888. *The United States Biographical Dictionary and Portrait Gallery of Eminent and Self-Made Men.* Missouri Volume. New York, Chicago, St. Louis, and Kansas City, 1878. Pension File and Military Service File, National Archives.

Henry Sheppard

Quartermaster, Greene County Regiment, MO Home Guards, June 11, 1861. Discharged Aug. 17, 1861. Lieutenant Colonel, 72 Enrolled MO Militia, Aug. 16, 1862. Colonel, 72 Enrolled MO Militia, Nov. 11, 1862. Colonel, 6 Provisional Enrolled MO Militia, April 1, 1863. Resigned Sept. 30, 1863. Battle honors: Marmaduke's Expedition into Missouri (Springfield).
Born: Nov. 8, 1821 Bridgeton, NJ
Died: Dec. 19, 1879 New Orleans, LA
Other Wars: Mexican War (Private, Co. H, 3 MO Infantry)
Occupation: Dry goods merchant
Miscellaneous: Resided Springfield, Greene Co., MO
Buried: Maple Park Cemetery, Springfield, MO (Block 36, Lot 15)
References: *History of Greene County, Missouri.* St. Louis, MO, 1883. Howard L. Conard, editor. *Encyclopedia of the History of Missouri.* New York, Louisville, and St. Louis, 1901. Jonathan Fairbanks and Clyde E. Tuck. *Past and Present of Greene County, Missouri.* Indianapolis, IN, 1915. Death notice, *New Orleans Daily Picayune*, Dec. 21, 1879. William K. Hall. *Springfield, Greene County, Missouri Newspaper Abstracts, 1876–1883.* Springfield, MO, 1987.

Albert Sigel

Captain, Co. D, 2 NJ Infantry, May 16, 1861. Honorably discharged, Dec. 14, 1861. Colonel, 13 MO State Militia Cavalry, May 19, 1862. Commanded Post of Waynesville, Rolla Division, District of Missouri, Department of the Mississippi, July–Sept. 1862. Commanded Post of Waynesville, District of Rolla, Department of the Missouri, Sept. 1862–Feb. 1863. Designation of regiment changed to 5 MO State Militia Cavalry, Feb. 2, 1863. Commanded Post (and frequently District) of Rolla, District of Rolla, Department of the Missouri, March–Dec. 1864. Honorably mustered out, Jan. 7, 1865. Battle honors: Price's Missouri Expedition.

Henry Sheppard, post-war (*History of Greene County, Missouri.* St. Louis, Missouri, 1883).

Albert Sigel (Scholten, St. Louis, Missouri; author's photograph).

Albert Sigel, post-war (E.P. Bushnell, Artist, Jefferson City, Missouri; courtesy Dennis Hood, D.V.M.).

Albert Sigel, post-war, with his wife, Rosa, and his daughter, Amalia (author's photograph).

Born: Nov. 15, 1827 Sinsheim, Baden, Germany
Died: March 16, 1884, St. Louis, MO
Education: Attended Karlsruhe (Baden) military school
Other Wars: German Revolution of 1848 (Lieutenant of infantry)
Occupation: Journalist, pension agent, and notary public
Offices/Honors: Recorder of Land Titles, U.S. General Land Office, St. Louis, MO, 1869–71. Adjutant General of Missouri, 1871–73.
Miscellaneous: Resided St. Louis, MO. Brother of Major Gen. Franz Sigel. Author of a small volume of his poetry published under the title *Gedichte* in 1863.
Buried: Gatewood Gardens (formerly New Pickers) Cemetery, St. Louis, MO (Section B3, Lot 158, unmarked)
References: Paul F. Guenther. "Albert Sigel– St. Louis German Poet," *Bulletin of the Missouri Historical Society*, Vol. 36 (April 1980). Carl W. Schlegel. *Schlegel's German-American Families in the United States*. New York Edition. New York City, NY, 1916. Pension File and Military Service File, National Archives. James Grant Wilson and John Fiske, editors. *Appletons' Cyclopedia of American Biography*. New York City, NY, 1888. Adolf E. Zucker, editor. *The Forty-Eighters: Political Refugees of the German Revolution of 1848*. New York City, NY, 1950. Albert Griffen. *Biographical Register of the Members of the Twenty-Sixth General Assembly of the State of Missouri*. St. Louis, MO, 1872. Obituary, *Missouri Republican*, March 18, 1884. Obituary, *St. Louis Post-Dispatch,* March 18, 1884. Obituary, *New York Times*, March 21, 1884.

James Owens Sitton

Colonel, 34 Enrolled MO Militia, Sept. 7, 1862. Ordered into active service as Captain, Co. I, 9 Provisional Enrolled MO Militia, Aug. 4, 1863. Relieved from duty, Nov. 9, 1863. Resigned June 10, 1864.
Born: July 29, 1822, Callaway Co., MO
Died: March 6, 1888, Owensville, MO
Occupation: Physician
Offices/Honors: Missouri House of Representatives, 1854–60. U.S. Marshal, Western District of Missouri, 1861–62. Missouri Senate, 1862–64.
Miscellaneous: Resided Woolam, Third Creek Twp., Gasconade Co., MO
Buried: Sitton Family Cemetery, near Canaan, Clay Twp., Gasconade Co., MO
References: Obituary, *Hermann Advertiser-*

Courier, March 14, 1888. A. Van Doren Honeyman. *The Honeyman Family in Scotland and America, 1548-1908*. Plainfield, NJ, 1909. Enid Wells Sitton. *Sitton and Gibson Genealogy, 1745-1966*. Houston, TX, 1971. www.ancestry.com.

Edwin Jacob Smart

Captain, Co. F, 5 MO State Militia (6 months), Sept. 3, 1861. Honorably mustered out, Feb. 5, 1862. Lieutenant Colonel, 10 MO State Militia Cavalry, April 8, 1862. Colonel, 10 MO State Militia Cavalry, May 5, 1862. Commanded Post of Louisiana (MO), St. Louis Division, District of Missouri, Department of the Mississippi, April–June 1862. Commanded Post of Paris, Northeastern District of Missouri, Department of the Missouri, Nov. 1862. Designation of regiment changed to 3 MO State Militia Cavalry, Feb. 2, 1863. Commanded Post of Patterson, District of St. Louis, Department of the Missouri, April 1863. Suffering from rheumatism and "loss of voice produced by severe laryngitis," he resigned May 23, 1863. Recruiting 2 Lieutenant, Co. E, 49 MO Infantry, Aug. 12, 1864. Major, 49 MO Infantry, Sept. 22, 1864. Commanded Sub-District of Boone, District of North Missouri, Department of the Missouri, Dec. 1864–Jan. 1865. Lieutenant Colonel, 49 MO Infantry, Feb. 9, 1865. Honorably mustered out, Aug. 2, 1865. Battle honors: Marmaduke's Expedition into Missouri (Patterson).

Born: April 19, 1819, Hempstead, NY
Died: Sept. 13, 1883 Moberly, MO
Other Wars: Mexican War (1 Sergeant, 2 U.S. Dragoons)
Occupation: Farmer and Regular Army enlisted man before war. Railroad construction superintendent after war.
Miscellaneous: Resided Louisiana, Pike Co., MO, to 1878; Mexico, Audrain Co., MO, 1878-80; and Moberly, Randolph Co., MO, 1880-83
Buried: St. Mary's Catholic Cemetery, Moberly, MO (Block 5, Lot 15)
References: Pension File and Military Service File, National Archives. Obituary, *Moberly Daily Monitor*, Sept. 14, 1883. Clayton Keith. *Military History of Pike County, Missouri*. Louisiana, MO, 1915. *History of Audrain County, Missouri*. St. Louis, MO, 1884.

Asa G. Smith

Colonel, Stone County Regiment, MO Home Guards, June 6, 1861. Discharged Nov. 6, 1861.
Born: 1812? VA
Died: April 8, 1862, Stone Co., MO (pneumonia)
Occupation: Farmer
Offices/Honors: Sheriff, Dade Co., MO, 1841-42 (absconded with county funds)
Miscellaneous: Resided James Twp., Taney Co., MO; and Galena, Stone Co., MO
Buried: Burial place unknown
References: Pension File, National Archives. *History of Hickory, Polk, Cedar, Dade and Barton Counties, Missouri*. Chicago, IL, 1889. www.ancestry.com.

William John Avery Smith

Colonel, 85 Enrolled MO Militia, May 28, 1864. Commission vacated, March 12, 1865. Battle honors: Price's Missouri Expedition.
Born: March 13, 1835, London, England
Died: April 16, 1911, Los Angeles, CA
Occupation: Farmer (1870), painter (1875), janitor (1880), draftsman (1888), deputy tax collector (1894), and deputy assessor (1900)
Miscellaneous: Resided St. Louis, MO; and Los Angeles, CA, after 1875
Buried: Evergreen Cemetery, Los Angeles, CA (Section D, Lot 1064, unmarked)
References: Obituary, *Los Angeles Times*, April 18, 1911. Pension File, National Archives. www.ancestry.com.

William John Avery Smith (H.L. Bliss, Photographer, 293 & 295 Main St., Buffalo, New York; author's photograph).

Robert Rush Spedden

Colonel, 40 Enrolled MO Militia, Sept. 10, 1862. Resigned June 7, 1864.
Born: Aug. 19, 1822 Easton, MD
Died: May 28, 1891, Pomeroy, WA
Occupation: Physician and farmer
Offices/Honors: County Clerk, Pettis Co., MO, 1853–57. First mayor of Astoria, OR. Twelve years as County Clerk, Clatsop Co., OR. County Clerk, Garfield Co., WA, 1890–91.
Miscellaneous: Resided Georgetown, Pettis Co., MO; Astoria, Clatsop Co., OR, 1868–86; and Pomeroy, Garfield Co., WA, 1886–91. Holder of several patents, including one for an improved ship's anchor.
Buried: IOOF Cemetery, Pomeroy, WA
References: Pension File, National Archives. *Washington Pioneers.* Olympia, WA, 1991. Obituary, *Albany Morning Daily Herald*, June 2, 1891. *History of Pettis County, Missouri.* N.p., 1882. *An Illustrated History of Southeastern Washington Including Walla Walla, Columbia, Garfield and Asotin Counties, Washington.* Spokane, WA, 1906. www.ancestry.com.

Edward Stafford

Colonel, 2 Enrolled MO Militia, Sept. 23, 1862. Commission vacated, March 12, 1865. Battle honors: Price's Missouri Expedition.
Born: Nov. 10, 1826 Chateaugay, NY
Died: July 27, 1897, Monte Vista, CO
Occupation: Lawyer and newspaper editor
Offices/Honors: Major Gen., Mississippi State Militia, 1870–72. Chancellor of District Court, 1872–76.
Miscellaneous: Resided St. Louis, MO, to 1867; Greenville, Washington Co., MS, 1867–84; and Boulder, Boulder Co., CO, 1884–97
Buried: Colorado State Veterans Cemetery, Monte Vista, CO
References: *Portrait and Biographical Record of Denver and Vicinity, Colorado.* Chicago, IL, 1898. Dunbar Rowland, editor. *Encyclopedia of Mississippi History.* Madison, WI, 1907. Mary McRoberts. *Genealogical Abstracts from the Boulder Daily Camera, 1891–1900.* Boulder, CO, 1985. www.ancestry.com.

Charles Gottfried Stifel

Colonel, 5 U.S. Reserve Corps, MO Infantry (3 months), May 11, 1861. Honorably mustered out, Sept. 3, 1861. *Colonel*, 5 U.S. Reserve Corps, MO Infantry, Aug. 28, 1861. Discharged Nov. 1, 1861. *Colonel*, 2 St. Louis City Guards, Oct. 4, 1864. Battle honors: Blue Mills.
Born: Jan. 28, 1819 Neuffen, Wurttemberg, Germany
Died: March 18, 1900, St. Louis, MO

Charles Gottfried Stifel (courtesy Missouri Historical Society, St. Louis [P0233-2851]).

Charles Gottfried Stifel, post-war (Klotter & Scherer, St. Louis, Missouri; Courtesy Missouri Historical Society, St. Louis [P0233-2852]).

Occupation: Brewer
Miscellaneous: Resided St. Louis, MO
Buried: Bellefontaine Cemetery, St. Louis, MO (Block 108, Lot 1435)
References: Obituary Circular, Whole No. 205, Missouri MOLLUS. William Hyde and Howard L. Conard, editors. *Encyclopedia of the History of St. Louis*. New York, Louisville, and St. Louis, 1899. Walter B. Stevens. *St. Louis History of the Fourth City, 1763–1909*. Chicago and St. Louis, 1909. Obituary, *St. Louis Republic*, March 19, 1900. Obituary, *St. Louis Post-Dispatch*, March 19, 1900. Robert J. Rombauer. *The Union Cause in St. Louis in 1861: An Historical Sketch*. St. Louis, MO, 1909. William C. Winter. *The Civil War in St. Louis: A Guided Tour*. St. Louis, MO, 1994. James Cox, editor. *Notable St. Louisans in 1900*. St. Louis, MO, 1900. Military Service File, National Archives.

Philip A. C. Stremmel

Colonel, 20 Enrolled MO Militia, Feb. 5, 1863.
Born: Oct. 29, 1812 Prussia
Died: July 4, 1885, St. Louis, MO
Other Wars: Mexican War (1 Lieutenant, Co. C, Gilpin's Battalion, MO Infantry)
Occupation: Notary Public and Justice of the Peace
Offices/Honors: Judge of St. Louis County Court, 1871–74
Miscellaneous: Resided St. Louis, MO
Buried: Bellefontaine Cemetery, St. Louis, MO (Block 200, Lot 3092)
References: Obituary, *St. Louis Globe-Democrat*, July 7, 1885. Obituary, *St. Louis Post-Dispatch*, July 6, 1885. Pension File, National Archives. J. Thomas Scharf. *History of Saint Louis City and County*. Philadelphia, PA, 1883.

James William Strong

1 Lieutenant, Co. E, 24 IA Infantry, Sept. 17, 1862. Disabled by an attack of acute dysentery, he resigned April 4, 1863. Captain, Co. G, 87 Enrolled MO Militia, April 30, 1864. Lieutenant Colonel, 87 Enrolled MO Militia, July 15, 1864. Colonel, 87 Enrolled MO Militia, Oct. 6, 1864. Commission vacated, March 12, 1865.
Born: Sept. 24, 1834 Danville, KY
Died: June 18, 1886, St. Joseph, MO (murdered by Dr. Samuel A. Richmond)
Occupation: Lawyer and newspaper publisher
Miscellaneous: Resided Jacksonville, Morgan Co., IL; Marengo, Iowa Co., IA; and St. Joseph, Buchanan Co., MO

James William Strong, post-war (Mora, 707 Broadway, New York; courtesy Sandra Sheldon).

Buried: Mount Mora Cemetery, St. Joseph, MO
References: Benjamin W. Dwight. *History of the Descendants of Elder John Strong of Northampton, Massachusetts*. Albany, NY, 1871. Pension File and Military Service File, National Archives. Obituary, *St. Joseph Daily Gazette*, June 19, 1886. Obituary, *St. Joseph Weekly Herald*, June 24, 1886. "A Cold-Blooded Deed," *St. Louis Post-Dispatch*, June 18, 1886. Christian L. Rutt, editor. *History of Buchanan County and the City of St. Joseph and Representative Citizens*. Chicago, IL, 1904.

George Richards Taylor

Colonel, 23 Enrolled MO Militia, Sept. 11, 1862. Commission vacated, April 12, 1864.
Born: Nov. 11, 1818 Alexandria, VA
Died: April 6, 1880, St. Louis, MO
Occupation: Lawyer and railroad president
Miscellaneous: Resided St. Louis, MO
Buried: Bellefontaine Cemetery, St. Louis, MO (Block 104, Lot 478). Cenotaph, St. Paul's Cemetery, Alexandria, VA.
References: Logan U. Reavis. *Saint Louis: The Future Great City of the World*. Biographical Edition. St. Louis, MO, 1875. Richard Edwards and Merna Hopewell. *Edwards's Great West and Her Commercial Metropolis, Embracing a General View of the West, and a Complete History of St. Louis*.

St. Louis, MO, 1860. J. Thomas Scharf. *History of Saint Louis City and County*. Philadelphia, PA, 1883. Obituary, *St. Louis Globe-Democrat*, April 7, 1880. Obituary, *St. Louis Post-Dispatch*, April 6, 1880. Mary B. Cunningham and Jeanne C. Blythe. *The Founding Family of St. Louis*. St. Louis, MO, 1977.

Jacob Torian Tindall

Colonel, 23 MO Infantry, Aug. 26, 1861. GSW heart, Shiloh, TN, April 6, 1862. Battle honors: Shiloh.

Born: April 25, 1826, Christian Co., KY

Died: April 6, 1862, KIA Shiloh, TN

Other Wars: Mexican War (Sergeant Major, Gilpin's Battalion, MO Infantry)

Occupation: Lawyer

Offices/Honors: Missouri House of Representatives, 1850–52

Miscellaneous: Resided Trenton, Grundy Co., MO

Buried: Masonic Cemetery, Trenton, MO

References: *The History of Grundy County, Missouri*. Kansas City, MO, 1881. William V.N. Bay. *Reminiscences of the Bench and Bar of Missouri*. St. Louis, MO, 1878. Obituary, *Daily Missouri Republican*, April 28, 1862. Pension File and Military Service File, National Archives. Letters Received, Volunteer Service Branch, Adjutant General's Office, File R21(VS)1862, National Archives.

George Richards Taylor (pre-war) (Richard Edwards and Merna Hopewell. *Edwards's Great West and Her Commercial Metropolis, Embracing a General View of the West, and a Complete History of St. Louis*. St. Louis, Missouri, 1860).

George Richards Taylor, post-war (Logan U. Reavis. *Saint Louis: The Future Great City of the World*. Biographical Edition. St. Louis, Missouri, 1875).

Jacob Torian Tindall (*History of Grundy County, Missouri*. Kansas City, Missouri, 1881).

Orwin Cullen Tinker

Colonel, 53 Enrolled MO Militia, Oct. 16, 1862. Commission vacated, March 12, 1865.

Born: July 19, 1810, Morristown, VT
Died: July 5, 1893, Louisiana, MO
Occupation: Engaged in harness and saddlery business
Miscellaneous: Resided Lick Creek, Salt River Twp., Ralls Co., MO (1860) and Louisiana, Pike Co., MO
Buried: Riverview Cemetery, Louisiana, MO (Old Cemetery, Lot 4)
References: Obituary, *Pike County News*, July 6, 1893. Obituary, *St. Louis Globe-Democrat*, July 7, 1893. Kathryn H. Campbell. *John Biggs, the Welshman, and His Descendants, 1729–1979.* Dallas, TX, 1981. Obituary, *Chariton Courier*, July 14, 1893. *History of Marion County, Missouri.* St. Louis, MO, 1884.

George Ramsey Todd

Lieutenant Colonel, 10 MO Infantry, Aug. 15, 1861. Colonel, 10 MO Infantry, Dec. 1, 1861. Honorably discharged, April 9, 1862, upon adverse report of a Board of Examination.

Born: Jan. 1, 1825 Vevay, IN
Died: Aug. 28, 1905 Ouray, CO
Occupation: Lawyer
Miscellaneous: Resided Keokuk, Lee Co., IA; Wyandotte, Wyandotte Co., KS; and Ouray, Ouray Co., CO, after 1875
Buried: Cedar Hill Cemetery, Ouray, CO
References: Obituary, *Ouray Herald*, Sept. 1, 1905. Letters Received, Volunteer Service Branch, Adjutant General's Office, Files M445(VS)1862, T297(VS)1862, and T699(VS)1862, National Archives. Military Service File, National Archives. Marcus O. Frost. *Regimental History of the Tenth Missouri Volunteer Infantry.* Topeka, KS, 1892.

Charles Loveland Tucker

Colonel, 17 Enrolled MO Militia, Sept. 17, 1862. Commission vacated, April 12, 1864.

Born: March 2, 1814, Boston, MA
Died: Oct. 26, 1891 Saco, ME
Occupation: Engaged in the grain and commission business, being identified with the Washington Mills and later owning the Pacific Mills
Offices/Honors: President, Merchants' Exchange of St. Louis, 1867
Miscellaneous: Resided St. Louis, MO, to 1874; Logansport, Cass Co., IN, 1874–89; and Saco, York Co., ME, after 1889
Buried: Bellefontaine Cemetery, St. Louis, MO (Block 31, Lot 302)

George Ramsey Todd (courtesy Brad and Donna Pruden).

Charles Loveland Tucker, post-war (George H. Morgan. *Annual Statement of the Trade and Commerce of Saint Louis, for the Year 1906, Reported to the Merchants' Exchange of St. Louis.* St. Louis, Missouri, 1907).

References: Obituary, *St. Louis Globe-Democrat*, Oct. 28, 1891. Ephraim Tucker. *Genealogy of the Tucker Family from Various Authentic Sources*. Worcester, MA, 1895. George H. Morgan. *Annual Statement of the Trade and Commerce of Saint Louis, for the Year 1906, Reported to the Merchants' Exchange of St. Louis*. St. Louis, MO, 1907.

John Fulkerson Tyler

Major, 14 MO Home Guards, Sept. 1, 1861. Taken prisoner, Lexington, MO, Sept. 19, 1861. Paroled Sept. 25, 1861. Discharged Oct. 19, 1861. Major, ADC, Staff of Brig. Gen. John M. Schofield, MO State Militia, Dec. 3, 1861. Lieutenant Colonel, 1 MO State Militia Infantry, April 11, 1862. Colonel, 1 MO State Militia Infantry, March 18, 1863. Commanded Post of Pilot Knob, District of St. Louis, Department of the Missouri, March–April 1863 and April–Aug. 1864. Assistant Provost Marshal, 2 Sub-District (Hannibal, MO), District of North Missouri, Department of the Missouri, Aug.–Dec. 1864. Dishonorably dismissed, Jan. 13, 1865, for "fraudulent conduct in connection with transportation passes, trading in substitutes, and sanctioning the same in employees under his control, he being at the time on duty as Assistant Provost Marshal." His appeal to President Lincoln for revocation of his dismissal was denied upon the recommendation of Judge Advocate General Joseph Holt, who observed, "The Government has suffered so much from substitute brokers, that it should show no mercy to any officer, who has so little regard for his honor, and the dignity of the service, as to engage in or countenance it; and though Colonel Tyler has exhibited great devotion by abandoning his friends and property to espouse the cause of the Union, having forgotten his duty, he should be held to a strict accountability." Battle honors: Lexington.

Born: Sept. 12, 1838 Jonesville, Lee Co., VA
Died: March 2, 1911, St. Joseph, MO
Education: Graduated Virginia Military Institute, Lexington, VA, 1859
Occupation: Lawyer, real estate agent, and insurance agent
Miscellaneous: Resided Lexington, Lafayette Co., MO, before war; and St. Joseph, Buchanan Co., MO, after war
Buried: Mount Mora Cemetery, St. Joseph, MO (Section C, Block 12, Lot 1)
References: *Portrait and Biographical Record of Buchanan and Clinton Counties, Missouri*. Chicago, IL, 1893. Christian L. Rutt, editor. *History of Buchanan County and the City of St. Joseph and Representative Citizens*. Chicago, IL, 1904. *The History of Buchanan County, Missouri*. St. Joseph, MO, 1881. David W. Dillard. *The Union Post Commanders at Pilot Knob, 1861–1865*. Ironton, MO, 2013. Military Service File, National Archives. Letters Received, Volunteer Service Branch, Adjutant General's Office, File M3996(VS)1864, National Archives. Obituary, *St. Joseph Gazette*, March 2, 1911. Obituary, *Kansas City Star*, March 3, 1911. Jennings C. Wise. *The Military History of the Virginia Military Institute from 1839 to 1865*. Lynchburg, VA, 1915. M. Secrist. *Lee County, Virginia: History Revealed Through Biographical and Genealogical Sketches of Its Ancestors*. N.p., 2013.

Henry Frederick Vahlkamp

Captain, Co. H, 3 Enrolled MO Militia, Sept. 24, 1862. Major, 3 Enrolled MO Militia, March 28, 1864. Colonel, 3 Enrolled MO Militia, July 22, 1864. Commission vacated, March 12, 1865. Battle honors: Price's Missouri Expedition.

Born: Jan. 9, 1830 Prussia
Died: Jan. 31, 1873 St. Louis, MO
Occupation: Lumber merchant and sawmill operator
Miscellaneous: Resided St. Louis, MO
Buried: Old Picker Cemetery, 7133 Gravois Road, St. Louis, MO
References: Obituary, *Daily Missouri Republican*, Feb. 2, 1873. Death notice, *Daily Missouri Democrat*, Feb. 1, 1873. www.ancestry.com.

Delos Van Deusen

Captain, Co. H, 6 MO Infantry, June 17, 1861. Lieutenant Colonel, 6 MO Infantry, April 2, 1864. *Colonel, 6 MO Infantry, May 2, 1865.* Honorably mustered out, Aug. 17, 1865. Battle honors: Atlanta Campaign (Resaca, Kenesaw Mountain, Atlanta, Ezra Church, Jonesborough), Savannah Campaign, Campaign of the Carolinas.

Born: Dec. 9, 1823 Allegany Co., NY
Died: Nov. 15, 1905 Litchfield, IL
Occupation: Engaged in the boot, shoe and leather business before war. Bank cashier after war.
Miscellaneous: Resided Litchfield, Montgomery Co., IL
Buried: Elmwood Cemetery, Litchfield, IL (Block 22, Lot 15)

Delos Van Deusen, post-war (State Historical Society of Iowa, Des Moines).

References: Jacob L. Traylor. *Past and Present of Montgomery County, Illinois*. Chicago, IL, 1904. Obituary, *Litchfield Monitor*, Nov. 17, 1905. *Portrait and Biographical Record of Montgomery and Bond Counties, Illinois*. Chicago, IL, 1892. William H. Perrin, editor. *History of Bond and Montgomery Counties, Illinois*. Chicago, IL, 1882. *The Biographical Encyclopedia of Illinois of the Nineteenth Century*. Philadelphia, PA, 1875. Pension File and Military Service File, National Archives.

Philip Riley Van Frank

Captain, Co. A, Washington County Battalion, Six Months MO Militia, Sept. 19, 1861. Honorably mustered out, Jan. 8, 1862. 2 Lieutenant, Battalion Adjutant, 12 MO State Militia Cavalry, May 17, 1862. 1 Lieutenant, RQM, 12 MO State Militia Cavalry, July 30, 1862. Honorably mustered out, March 4, 1863. Colonel, 32 Enrolled MO Militia, April 30, 1864. Resigned Oct. 4, 1864.

Born: Jan. 10, 1829 Cortland Co., NY
Died: April 19, 1915, Kansas City, MO
Occupation: Civil engineer engaged in railroad construction
Miscellaneous: Resided Hopewell, Washington Co., MO, to 1864; Murphysboro, Jackson Co., IL, 1864–69; Cape Girardeau, Cape Girardeau Co., MO, 1869–81; Bismarck, St. Francois Co., MO; Springfield, Greene Co., MO, 1894–1901; and Kansas City, MO. Brother-in-law of Colonel William H. Evens (32 Enrolled MO Militia).

Philip Riley Van Frank (T. H. Fitzgibbon, Photographer, 116 North Fourth Street, St. Louis, Missouri; Ken Turner collection).

Philip Riley Van Frank, post-war (Howard L. Conard, editor. *Encyclopedia of the History of Missouri*. New York, Louisville, St. Louis, 1901).

Buried: Hopewell Cemetery, Hopewell, MO

References: Howard L. Conard, editor. *Encyclopedia of the History of Missouri*. New York, Louisville, and St. Louis, 1901. Obituary, *Potosi Journal*, April 28, 1915. Obituary, *Kansas City Star*, April 20, 1915. Pension File and Military Service File, National Archives.

George E. Waring, Jr.

Major, 39 NY Infantry, June 6, 1861. Resigned Aug. 2, 1861. Major, Fremont Hussars, MO Cavalry, Aug. 2, 1861. Colonel, 4 MO Cavalry, Jan. 9, 1862. Commanded Post of Lebanon (MO), Army of the Southwest, Department of the Mississippi, March 1862. Commanded 2 Brigade, 3 Division, Army of the Southwest, Department of the Mississippi, May 1862. Commanded Cavalry Brigade, Army of Southeast Missouri, Department of the Missouri, Dec. 1862. Commanded Cavalry Division, Army of Southeast Missouri, Department of the Missouri, Jan.–Feb. 1863. Commanded Post of Columbus (KY), District of Columbus, 16 Army Corps, Department of the Tennessee, April–June 1863. Commanded 1 Brigade, 6 Division, 16 Army Corps, Department of the Tennessee, July–Aug. 1863 and Oct.–Dec. 1863. Commanded Detached Brigade, Cavalry Division, 16 Army Corps, Department of the Tennessee, Dec. 1863–Jan. 1864. Commanded 1 Brigade, Cavalry Division, 16 Army Corps, Department of the Tennessee, Feb.–April 1864 and May–June 1864. Commanded Cavalry Division, 16 Army Corps, Department of the Tennessee, April–May 1864. Honorably mustered out, March 25, 1865, to date Oct. 24, 1864, by reason of the reduction of his regiment. Battle honors: First Bull Run, Searcy Landing, Batesville, Lexington (TN), Meridian Expedition (Okolona), Forrest's Expedition into West Tennessee and Kentucky, Brice's Cross Roads.

Born: July 4, 1833, Pound Ridge, NY

Died: Oct. 29, 1898 New York City, NY (contracted yellow fever while conducting a study of the sanitation situation in Cuba)

Occupation: Agriculturist, sanitary engineer, and author

Offices/Honors: Street Commissioner of New York City, 1895–98

Miscellaneous: Resided Stamford, Fairfield Co., CT; and Newport, Newport Co., RI. Although he authored numerous works on agricultural and sanitary topics, perhaps his best known book was *Whip and Spur*, in which he related Civil War experiences highlighted by his affection for favorite horses.

George E. Waring, Jr. (Roger D. Hunt Collection, USAMHI [RG98S-CWP207.26]).

George E. Waring, Jr. (Hoelke & Benecke, Photographers, S.E. Cor., 4th and Market Sts., St. Louis, Missouri; Massachusetts MOLLUS Collection, USAMHI [Vol. 135, p. 6901]).

Buried: Woodland Cemetery, Stamford, CT (Section D, Lot 140)

References: Allen Johnson and Dumas Malone, editors. *Dictionary of American Biography*. New York City, NY, 1964. *The National Cyclopedia of American Biography*. Vol. 6. New York City, NY, 1896. Albert Shaw, "Col. George E. Waring, Jr." *The American Monthly Review of Reviews*, Vol. 18, No. 6 (Dec. 1898). Obituary, *New York Times*, Oct. 30, 1898. Obituary, *Brooklyn Daily Eagle*, Oct. 29, 1898. Michael Bacarella. *Lincoln's Foreign Legion: The 39th New York Infantry, The Garibaldi Guard*. Shippensburg, PA, 1996. Edwin C. Bearss. *Forrest at Brice's Cross Roads and in North Mississippi in 1864*. Dayton, OH, 1979. Military Service File, National Archives. Letters Received, Volunteer Service Branch, Adjutant General's Office, File I507(VS)1862, National Archives. MOLLUS Application Papers, U.S. Army Military History Institute. George E. Waring, Jr. *Whip and Spur*. Boston, MA, 1875.

Isaac Sanders Warmoth

Colonel, 63 Enrolled MO Militia, Oct. 13, 1863. Called into active service as Lieutenant Colonel with five companies of his regiment, Sept. 10, 1864. Relieved from active duty, Dec. 2, 1864. Commission vacated, March 12, 1865.

Born: Oct. 11, 1816 Bedford Co., TN
Died: March 23, 1887, Salem, IL

Other Wars: Mexican War (Sergeant, Co. F, 3 IL Infantry)

Occupation: Harness maker, hotelkeeper, and lawyer

Offices/Honors: Postmaster, Rolla, MO, 1870–73. Several terms as Mayor of Rolla, MO.

Miscellaneous: Resided Fairfield, Wayne Co., IL, to 1856; Xenia, Clay Co., IL (1860); Rolla, Phelps Co., MO, 1862–79; and Salem, Marion Co., IL, after 1879. Father of Henry C. Warmoth, Lieutenant Colonel of the 32 MO Infantry and later Governor of Louisiana.

Buried: East Lawn Cemetery, Salem, IL (Section D, Row B, Lot 4)

References: *The United States Biographical Dictionary and Portrait Gallery of Eminent and Self-Made Men*. Missouri Volume. New York, Chicago, St. Louis, and Kansas City, 1878. Obituary, *Rolla Herald*, March 31, 1887. Obituary, *Chicago Daily Tribune*, March 26, 1887. *History of Wayne and Clay Counties, Illinois*. Chicago, IL, 1884. Pension File and Military Service File, National Archives.

Marinus Willet Warne

Colonel, 16 Enrolled MO Militia, Sept. 17, 1862. Commission vacated, April 12, 1864.

Born: Dec. 7, 1810 New Brunswick, NJ
Died: July 21, 1881, Lawrence, KS

Isaac Sanders Warmoth, post-war (Brady-Handy Photograph Collection, Library of Congress [LC-DIG-cwpbh-05082]).

Marinus Willet Warne (pre-war) (Richard Edwards and Merna Hopewell. *Edwards's Great West and Her Commercial Metropolis, Embracing a General View of the West, and a Complete History of St. Louis*. St. Louis, Missouri, 1860).

Occupation: Merchant dealing in hardware, cutlery and house furnishing goods. Manufactured barbed wire after moving to Lawrence, KS.

Miscellaneous: Resided St. Louis, MO, to 1877; and Lawrence, Douglas Co., KS, after 1877

Buried: Oak Hill Cemetery, Lawrence, KS (Section 6, Lot 12)

References: Richard Edwards and Merna Hopewell. *Edwards's Great West and Her Commercial Metropolis, Embracing a General View of the West, and a Complete History of St. Louis.* St. Louis, MO, 1860. George W. Labaw. *A Genealogy of the Warne Family in America.* New York City, NY, 1911. Obituary, *Lawrence Daily Journal,* July 23, 1881.

David Walker Wear

Major, 52 Enrolled MO Militia, Oct. 1, 1862. ADC, Staff of Brig. Gen. Thomas L. Crawford, Enrolled MO Militia, Nov. 1862–Jan. 1863. Colonel, 52 Enrolled MO Militia, June 10, 1863. Commanded Post of Boonville, District of Central Missouri, Department of the Missouri, Sept. 1863. Temporary service as Captain, Co. D, 9 Provisional Enrolled MO Militia. Lieutenant Colonel, 45 MO Infantry, Sept. 29, 1864. Commanded Post of Jefferson City, District of Central Missouri, Department of the Missouri, Nov. 1864. Resigned April 1, 1865, since "I do not feel competent to pass an examination before the Board to which I am ordered." Battle honors: Shelby's Raid in Arkansas and Missouri (Boonville).

Born: May 31, 1843, Otterville, MO
Died: Oct. 20, 1896 Boonville, MO
Occupation: Lawyer
Offices/Honors: Missouri Senate, 1883–85. Superintendent of Yellowstone National Park, 1885–86. Chief of Southern Division, U.S. Bureau of Pensions, 1887–89.
Miscellaneous: Resided Boonville, Cooper Co., MO; and St. Louis, MO, 1876–87
Buried: Walnut Grove Cemetery, Boonville, MO (Division 7, Lot 136)
References: William Hyde and Howard L. Conard, editors. *Encyclopedia of the History of St. Louis.* New York, Louisville, and St. Louis, 1899. *The Bench and Bar of St. Louis, Kansas City, Jefferson City, and Other Missouri Cities.* St. Louis and Chicago, 1884. Pension File and Military Service File, National Archives. Obituary, *St. Louis Globe-Democrat,* Oct. 21, 1896. Douglas Niermeyer, "Lieutenant Colonel David Walker Wear, 45th Missouri Infantry," http://www.suvcw.org/mollus/art048.htm.

Andrew Jackson Weber (Abraham Lincoln Presidential Library & Museum, [ALPLM]).

Andrew Jackson Weber

Captain, Co. B, 11 MO Infantry, Aug. 3, 1861. Major, 11 MO Infantry, April 21, 1862. Lieutenant Colonel, 11 MO Infantry, Dec. 29, 1862. Colonel, 11 MO Infantry, May 15, 1863. Shell wound head, Young's Point, LA, June 29, 1863. Battle honors: Fredericktown, New Madrid and Island No. 10, Iuka, Corinth, Jackson, Vicksburg Campaign.

Born: Sept. 9, 1840 Springfield, IL
Died: June 30, 1863, DOW Young's Point, LA
Occupation: Farmer
Miscellaneous: Resided Springfield, Sangamon Co., IL
Buried: Oak Ridge Cemetery, Springfield, IL (Block 10, Lot 152)
References: John C. Power. *History of the Early Settlers of Sangamon County, Illinois.* Springfield, IL, 1876. Obituary, *Daily Missouri Democrat,* July 13, 1863. Obituary, *Daily Illinois State Journal,* July 14, 1863. Obituary, *Daily Illinois State Register,* July 11, 1863. Dennis W. Belcher. *The 11th Missouri Volunteer Infantry in the Civil War: A History and Roster.* Jefferson, NC, 2011. Newton Bateman and Paul Selby, editors. *Historical Encyclopedia of Illinois and History of Sangamon County.* Chicago, IL, 1912. Duncan McCall. *Three*

Years in the Service. A Record of the Doings of the 11th Reg. Missouri Vols. Springfield, IL, 1864. Military Service File, National Archives.

Oliver Wells

Major, 33 Enrolled MO Militia, Sept. 15, 1862. AAG and Acting Ordnance Officer, 7 Military District, Department of the Missouri, July–Oct. 1863. Temporary service as Major, 4 Provisional Enrolled MO Militia. 1 Lieutenant, Adjutant, 12 MO Cavalry, Sept. 22, 1863. Lieutenant Colonel, 12 MO Cavalry, Jan. 20, 1864. Colonel, 12 MO Cavalry, March 21, 1864. Commanded 1 Brigade, 1 Division, Cavalry Corps, District of West Tennessee, Department of the Tennessee, Sept.–Oct. 1864. Commanded 1 Brigade, 5 Division, Cavalry Corps, Military Division of the Mississippi, Nov. 1864 and Feb.–April 1865. Commanded 1 Cavalry Brigade, Department of the Missouri, May 1865. Resigned Dec. 2, 1865. Battle honors: Campbellsville, Franklin, Powder River Indian Expedition.
Born: Sept. 20, 1820 Abbotsford, Quebec, Canada
Died: Dec. 14, 1874 St. Joseph, MO
Occupation: Civil engineer before war. Clerk and draftsman after war.
Offices/Honors: Chief Clerk in the office of the U.S. Collector of Internal Revenue, 1867–74
Miscellaneous: Resided St. Joseph, Buchanan Co., MO
Buried: City Cemetery (now known as Sunbridge Cemetery), St. Joseph, MO (unmarked)
References: Albert Welles. *History of the Welles Family in England and Normandy, With the Derivation from Their Progenitors of Some of the Descendants in the United States.* New York City, NY, 1876. Obituary, *St. Joseph Daily Morning Herald*, Dec. 15, 1874. Pension File and Military Service File, National Archives. Obituary, *St. Joseph Daily Gazette,* Dec. 15, 1874. Letters Received, Volunteer Service Branch, Adjutant General's Office, File W2885(VS)1864, National Archives.

Joseph Weydemeyer

Captain of Artillery, Staff of Major Gen. John C. Fremont, Aug. 10, 1861. Discharged Oct. 11, 1861. Lieutenant Colonel, 2 MO Light Artillery, Nov. 8, 1861. Commanded Post of Houston, Rolla Division, District of Missouri, Department of the Mississippi, July 1862. Commanded Post of Salem, Rolla Division, District of Missouri, Department of the Mississippi, Aug.–Oct. 1862. Having been ordered to appear before a Board of Examination, he resigned, Sept. 15, 1863, "considering such an Examination as an humiliating process after more than two years service in the U.S. Army." Lieutenant Colonel, 41 MO Infantry, Sept. 3, 1864. Colonel, 41 MO Infantry, Sept. 17, 1864. Commanded 1 Sub-District, District of St. Louis, Department of the Missouri, Dec. 1864–June 1865. Honorably mustered out, July 11, 1865.
Born: Feb. 2, 1818 Munster, North Rhine-Westphalia, Germany
Died: Aug. 20, 1866 St. Louis, MO
Other Wars: German Revolution of 1848 (Captain of artillery)
Occupation: Journalist, Marxist pioneer, and labor activist
Offices/Honors: St. Louis County auditor, 1866
Miscellaneous: Resided Milwaukee, WI; Chicago, IL; and St. Louis, MO
Buried: Probably Holy Ghost Cemetery (no longer in existence), St. Louis, MO (His widow, Louisa, was buried there in Nov. 1867)

Joseph Weydemeyer (Hoelke & Benecke, Photographers, S.E. Cor., 4th and Market Sts., St. Louis, Missouri; Roger D. Hunt Collection, USAMHI [RG98S-CWP160.59]).

References: Karl Obermann. *Joseph Weydemeyer, Pioneer of American Socialism.* New York City, NY, 1947. Obituary, *Daily Missouri Democrat*, Aug. 22, 1866. Obituary, *New York Times*, Aug. 27, 1866. Obituary, *Daily Missouri Republican*, Aug. 22, 1866. Adolf E. Zucker, editor. *The Forty-Eighters: Political Refugees of the German Revolution of 1848.* New York City, NY, 1950. Military Service File, National Archives. Frank I. Herriott, "The German Conference in the Deutsches Haus, Chicago, May 14–15, 1860," *Transactions of the Illinois State Historical Society for the Year 1928.* Springfield, IL, 1928. George Lipsitz, "Joseph Weydemeyer, St. Louis' Marxist County Auditor," *St. Louis Magazine*, Vol. 16, No. 7 (July 1984). J. Thomas Scharf. *History of Saint Louis City and County.* Philadelphia, PA, 1883. Letters Received, Volunteer Service Branch, Adjutant Generals Office, File I213(VS)1863, National Archives. Joseph P. Weydemeyer Papers, 1861–1865 (A1736). Missouri History Museum Archives, St. Louis.

Robert White (pre-war) (courtesy Missouri Historical Society, St. Louis [P0249-3096]).

Robert White

Lieutenant Colonel, 5 U.S. Reserve Corps, MO Infantry (3 months), May 11, 1861. Honorably mustered out, Sept. 3, 1861. Colonel, 14 MO Home Guards, Sept. 1, 1861. GSW spine, Lexington, MO, Sept. 20, 1861. Taken prisoner, Lexington, MO, Sept. 20, 1861. Discharged Oct. 19, 1861. Exchanged Oct. 26, 1861. Battle honors: Lexington.

Born: Oct. 18, 1821 VA
Died: July 30, 1873, near Carlyle, IL
Occupation: Tinner and plumber before war. Farmer after war.
Offices/Honors: Clerk of the St. Louis Land Court, 1862–65
Miscellaneous: Resided St. Louis, MO, to 1866; and Beaver Creek, Bond Co., IL, after 1866
Buried: Bellefontaine Cemetery, St. Louis, MO (Block 20, Lot 4866)
References: "Memoirs of Colonel Robert White, January 1871," Robert White Papers, 1861–1908 (B648), Missouri History Museum Archives, St. Louis, MO. Larry Wood. *The Siege of Lexington, Missouri: The Battle of the Hemp Bales.* Charleston, SC, 2014. Pension File and Military Service File, National Archives. Obituary, *Daily Missouri Democrat*, Aug. 1, 1873. Michael E. Banasik, editor. *Missouri in 1861: The Civil War Letters of Franc B. Wilkie, Newspaper Correspondent.* Iowa City, IA, 2001. "Col. Robert White," *Daily Missouri Democrat*, March 26, 1862.

Robert White (courtesy Missouri Historical Society, St. Louis [P0249-0985]).

Thomas Jefferson Whitely

Colonel, 32 Enrolled MO Militia, Oct. 17, 1862. Resigned April 1, 1864.

Born: Jan. 25, 1820 Lynchburg, VA
Died: Feb. 26, 1900 St. Louis, MO
Occupation: Boot and shoe salesman
Offices/Honors: Postmaster, Caledonia, MO, 1859–64

Miscellaneous: Resided Caledonia, Washington Co., MO, before war; and St. Louis, MO, after war

Buried: Bellevue Presbyterian Cemetery, Caledonia, MO

References: Obituary, *St. Louis Globe-Democrat*, Feb. 28, 1900. Obituary, *St. Louis Post-Dispatch*, Feb. 27, 1900. B.G. Bakewell, compiler. *The Family Book of Bakewell-Page-Campbell*. Pittsburgh, PA, 1896. www.ancestry.com.

John Freeman Williams

Lieutenant Colonel, 9 MO State Militia Cavalry, May 3, 1862. Commanded Post of Rolla, District of Rolla, Department of the Missouri, Feb.–March 1863. Colonel, 9 MO State Militia Cavalry, July 13, 1863. Commanded 7 Military District, Enrolled MO Militia, Department of the Missouri, July 1863–May 1864. Commanded Post of Macon, District of North Missouri, Department of the Missouri, June 1864. Commanded Sub-District of Macon, District of North Missouri, Department of the Missouri, Jan.–Feb. 1865. Honorably mustered out, Feb. 11, 1865.

Born: April 18, 1828, Lynchburg, VA

Died: Jan. 17, 1892 Macon, MO

Education: Attended Masonic College, near Palmyra, MO. Graduated University of Missouri, Columbia, MO, 1848.

Occupation: Lawyer

Offices/Honors: Missouri House of Representatives (Speaker), 1877–79. Missouri State Insurance Commissioner, 1881–85.

Miscellaneous: Resided Fayette, Howard Co., MO, before war; and Macon, Macon Co., MO, after war

Buried: Oakwood Cemetery, Macon, MO

References: Obituary, *Macon Times*, Jan. 22, 1892. Obituary, *Macon Republican*, Jan. 22, 1892. Obituary, *St. Louis Republic*, Jan. 18, 1892. *The United States Biographical Dictionary and Portrait Gallery of Eminent and Self-Made Men*. Missouri Volume. New York, Chicago, St. Louis, and Kansas City, 1878. *The Bench and Bar of St. Louis, Kansas City, Jefferson City, and Other Missouri Cities*. St. Louis and Chicago, 1884. Pension File and Military Service File, National Archives. Chancy R. Barns, editor. *The Commonwealth of Missouri: A Centennial Record*. St. Louis, MO, 1877. Charles F. Ritter and Jon L. Wakelyn. *American Legislative Leaders, 1850–1910*. Westport, CT, 1989.

Samuel M. Wirt

Private, Co. C, 2 Northeast MO Home Guards, July 15, 1861. Discharged Oct. 7, 1861. Colonel, 50 Enrolled MO Militia, Aug. 29, 1862. Resigned Jan. 18, 1865. Major, 39 MO Infantry, Sept. 8, 1864. Commanded Post of Mexico, District of North Missouri, Department of the Missouri, Oct. 1864. Lieutenant Colonel, 39 MO Infantry, Feb. 2, 1865. Honorably mustered out, July 19, 1865.

John Freeman Williams (courtesy Robert J. Younger).

Samuel M. Wirt (E. Long, Photographer, Benton Barracks, St. Louis, Missouri; author's photograph).

Born: 1817 PA
Died: Oct. 26, 1887 Kansas City, MO
Occupation: Physician
Offices/Honors: Circuit Court Clerk, 1859–66
Miscellaneous: Resided Edina, Knox Co., MO; Nickerson, Reno Co., KS (1880); and Kansas City, MO. Brother-in-law of Bvt. Brig. Gen. David B. Hillis.
Buried: Wildmead Cemetery, Nickerson, KS
References: Pension File and Military Service File, National Archives. *History of Lewis, Clark, Knox and Scotland Counties, Missouri.* St. Louis and Chicago, 1887. www.ancestry.com.

Christian Doerner Wolff

Lieutenant Colonel, 5 MO Infantry (3 months), May 18, 1861. Honorably mustered out, Aug. 26, 1861. Colonel, 4 Enrolled MO Militia, Oct. 18, 1862. Temporary service as Colonel, 10 Provisional Enrolled MO Militia. Brig. Gen., Enrolled MO Militia, Oct. 1, 1864. Commanded Post of Jefferson City, District of Central Missouri, Department of the Missouri, Oct. 1864. Battle honors: Carthage, Price's Missouri Expedition.
Born: June 30, 1822, Elbesheim, Bavaria, Germany
Died: May 21, 1899, Clayton, MO
Other Wars: Mexican War (Sergeant, Co. B, 3 MO Mounted Infantry)
Occupation: Farmer and municipal official
Offices/Honors: Judge of St. Louis Court of Criminal Correction, 1865–70. St. Louis County Public Administrator, 1877–82. Circuit Court Clerk, 1883–89.
Miscellaneous: Resided St. Louis, MO; and Clayton, St. Louis Co., MO
Buried: St. Lucas UCC Cemetery, Sappington, St. Louis Co., MO (Block 5, Lot 4)
References: William Hyde and Howard L. Conard, editors. *Encyclopedia of the History of St. Louis.* New York, Louisville, and St. Louis, 1899. Obituary, *St. Louis Globe-Democrat,* May 22, 1899. Obituary, *St. Louis Post-Dispatch,* May 22, 1899. Military Service File, National Archives.

Richard Goodridge Woodson

Major, 10 MO State Militia Cavalry, May 5, 1862. Designation of regiment changed to 3 MO State Militia Cavalry, Feb. 2, 1863. Colonel, 3 MO State Militia Cavalry, May 25, 1863. Commanded Post of Pilot Knob, District of Southeastern Missouri, Department of the Missouri, Aug.–Oct. 1863. Commanded Post of Pilot Knob, District of St. Louis, Department of the Missouri, Nov. 1863–Feb. 1864. Submitted his resignation to Governor Willard P. Hall, Feb. 19, 1864, since "My private affairs now in great confusion from my long neglect demand my immediate attention and make this step absolutely necessary for my interests." Rather than accepting his resignation, Governor Hall, "upon the recommendation of the Department Commander," vacated his commission as colonel, Feb. 27, 1864, for "insubordinate conduct," the insubordination supposedly referring to "a correspondence between Adjutant General Gray and myself about recruiting out of my regiment, and in which I admit I was disrespectful to him." Battle honors: Marmaduke's Expedition into Missouri (Patterson), Expedition to Pocahontas, Arkansas.
Born: Sept. 6, 1833 Prince Edward Co., VA
Died: March 8, 1911, Dardenne, St. Charles Co., MO
Education: Graduated University of Missouri, Columbia, MO, 1854
Occupation: Lawyer before war; and farmer after war
Miscellaneous: Resided St. Louis, MO, before war; and Dardenne, St. Charles Co., MO, after war. Brother-in-law of Colonel Julian Bates (14 Enrolled MO Militia).
Buried: Dardenne Presbyterian Churchyard, Dardenne, MO
References: Pension File and Military Service File, National Archives. *Portrait and Biographical Record of St. Charles, Lincoln and Warren Counties, Missouri.* Chicago, IL, 1895. David W. Dillard. *The Union Post Commanders at Pilot Knob, 1861–1865.* Ironton, MO, 2013. Obituary, *St. Charles Cosmos-Monitor,* March 15, 1911. *History of St. Charles, Montgomery and Warren Counties, Missouri.* St. Louis, MO, 1885. "Colonel Richard Goodrich Woodson Papers, Fort Davidson Collection," https://mostateparks.com/sites/mostateparks/files/colwoodson4.pdf.

Humphrey Marshall Woodyard

Colonel, 2 Northeast MO Infantry, Oct. 5, 1861. Lieutenant Colonel, 21 MO Infantry, Feb. 1, 1862. Having been elected Judge of the 4th Judicial Circuit Court of Missouri, he resigned Jan. 27, 1864. Battle honors: Shiloh, Siege of Corinth.
Born: 1810? Pendleton Co., KY
Died: April 14, 1864, Memphis, MO (acute inflammation of the bladder)
Occupation: Lawyer
Offices/Honors: Missouri House of Representatives, 1848–50. Circuit Court Judge, 1864.

Humphrey Marshall Woodyard (State Historical Society of Missouri, Photograph Collection [Dr. Leslie Anders, P0365, 020462]).

Miscellaneous: Resided Canton, Lewis Co., MO

Buried: Burial place unknown (originally buried in Family Cemetery near his home)

References: Pension File and Military Service File, National Archives. Leslie Anders. *The Twenty-first Missouri: From Home Guard to Union Regiment*. Westport, CT, 1975. Obituary, *Canton Press*, April 21, 1864. Letters Received, Volunteer Service Branch, Adjutant General's Office, File R21(VS)1862, National Archives. *History of Lewis, Clark, Knox and Scotland Counties, Missouri*. St. Louis and Chicago, 1887. "The Funeral of Judge Woodyard," *Daily Missouri Democrat*, April 27, 1864.

Crafts James Wright

Colonel, 13 MO Infantry, Aug. 3, 1861. Commanded Post of Clarksville, TN, March 1862. Nominated as Brig. Gen., U.S. Volunteers, May 22, 1862. Nomination tabled by U.S. Senate, July 16, 1862. Designation of 13 MO Infantry changed to 22 OH Infantry, July 7, 1862. Commanded 2 Brigade, 2 Division, District of Corinth, Army of West Tennessee, June–July 1862. Responding to several reported instances of insubordination by Wright, Major Gen. Grant on Aug. 10, 1862, endorsed a recommendation for his discharge and commented, "From the day Col. Wright first reported to me for duty, to the present time, he has been the cause of more complaints from his immediate commanders than any six officers of this command. He has constantly raised the question of rank with those immediately over him ... and he is constantly raising points and occupying the time of his superior officers with a correspondence, useless to the service, and to some extent insubordinate." A Board of Examination convened Aug. 23, 1862, recommended that he be discharged on account of physical disability. Meanwhile, suffering from "the effects of two days' constant fighting" at Shiloh and "laying on the ground at night in the rain and mud," he resigned Sept. 9, 1862, since "he is satisfied, in this debilitating climate, thus confined (to his bed), he cannot speedily recover full strength for active duty." Battle honors: Fort Donelson, Shiloh.

Born: July 13, 1808, Troy, NY

Died: July 22, 1883, Chicago, IL

Education: Graduated U.S. Military Academy, West Point, NY, 1828

Occupation: Lawyer, newspaper editor and journalist. After removing to Chicago, he was Superintendent and Steward of the U.S. Marine Hospital there.

Crafts James Wright (Hoag & Quick's Art Palace, No. 100 4th St., Opp. Post Office, Cincinnati, Ohio; Roger D. Hunt Collection, USAMHI [RG98S-CWP207.68]).

Offices/Honors: Secretary of the Washington Peace Conference, February 1861

Miscellaneous: Resided Cincinnati, OH, before war; Glendale, Hamilton Co., OH, 1862–75; and Chicago, IL, 1875–83

Buried: Spring Grove Cemetery, Cincinnati, OH (Section 84, Lot 7)

References: *Fifteenth Annual Reunion of the Association of the Graduates of the U.S. Military Academy at West Point, NY.* East Saginaw, MI, 1884. George W. Cullum. *Biographical Register of the Officers and Graduates of the U.S. Military Academy.* Third Edition. Boston and New York, 1891. Pension File and Military Service File, National Archives. Obituary, *Chicago Daily Tribune*, July 24, 1883. Obituary, *Cincinnati Commercial Gazette*, July 24–25, 1883. *Report of the Proceedings of the Society of the Army of the Tennessee at the Sixteenth Meeting.* Cincinnati, OH, 1885. Letters Received, Volunteer Service Branch, Adjutant General's Office, File M1287(VS)1862, National Archives. John Y. Simon, editor. *The Papers of Ulysses S. Grant.* Vol. 5: April 1–August 31, 1862. Carbondale, IL, 1973.

Thomas Clarkson (aka Clark) Wright

Captain, Co. D, Fremont Battalion, MO Cavalry, July 5, 1861. Major, Fremont Battalion, MO Cavalry, Aug. 23, 1861. Lieutenant Colonel, Fremont Battalion, MO Cavalry, Jan. 9, 1862. Colonel, 6 MO Cavalry, Feb. 14, 1862. Commanded Post of Forsythe (MO), Army of the Southwest, Department of the Mississippi, April–May 1862. Commanded 2 Division, Army of the Frontier, Department of the Missouri, Nov. 1862. Although he received commendation for his energy in scouting and engaging guerrillas, his brief service as division commander (based on seniority) resulted in Brig. Gen. Francis J. Herron effecting his transfer with the explanation to Major Gen. Curtis, "...there are some officers that must be cleared out. They are worse than worthless. It was a narrow escape getting rid of Colonel Wright." Honorably discharged, Sept. 16, 1863, upon adverse report of a Board of Examination, which found that he was "wholly unqualified and totally unfitted for the position which he now holds." Engaged in cotton buying activities in Mississippi after his discharge, he and his associates were convicted by a Military Commission, June 23, 1864, of "Disobedience and defiant violation of Military Orders" in refusing to surrender possession of cotton specifically protected by military authorities, escaping punishment, however, through the leniency of Major Gen. Henry W. Slocum. Battle honors: Wet Glaze, Wilson's Creek, Pea Ridge, Arkansas Post, Vicksburg Campaign.

Born: Aug. 16, 1823 Leesburg, Highland Co., OH

Died: March 2, 1875, Lafayette, IN

Occupation: Farmer and hardware merchant

Miscellaneous: Resided Jackson Twp., Highland Co., OH (1850); Orleans, Jackson Twp., Polk Co., MO (1860); and Lafayette, Tippecanoe Co., IN (1870)

Buried: Greenbush Cemetery, Lafayette, IN (Division 3, Lot 755)

References: Pension File and Military Service File, National Archives. Obituary, *Lafayette Daily Journal*, March 3, 1875. *History of Champaign County, Illinois.* Philadelphia, PA, 1878. Letters Received, Volunteer Service Branch, Adjutant General's Office, File W1745(VS)1863, National Archives. *The War of the Rebellion: A Compilation of the Official Records of the Union and Confederate Armies.*

Thomas Clarkson Wright (G.H. McConnell, Photographer, No. 62 North 4th St., St. Louis, Missouri; courtesy Dennis Hood, D.V.M.).

Thomas Clarkson Wright (left) and Judge Jonas Tebbetts (Wilson's Creek National Battlefield [WICR 31948]).

(Vol. 22, Part 1, p. 105). Washington, D.C., 1888. John Y. Simon, editor. *The Papers of Ulysses S. Grant*. Vol. 9: July 7–December 31, 1863. Carbondale, IL, 1982. William W. Hinshaw. *Encyclopedia of American Quaker Genealogy*. Vol. 5. Baltimore, MD, 1994. Lorand V. Johnson. *The Descendants of William and John Johnson: Colonial Friends of Virginia*. Boston, MA, 1935. Clark Wright Papers, 1861–1863 (R0523), State Historical Society of Missouri, Rolla. Court-martial Case Files, 1809–1894, File NN-2190, National Archives.

Lebbeus Zevely

Colonel, 28 Enrolled MO Militia, Sept. 11, 1862. Commanded 2 Military District, Enrolled MO Militia, Nov. 1864. Commission vacated, March 12, 1865. Battle honors: Price's Missouri Expedition.

Lebbeus Zevely (J.W. Hutchinson, Jefferson City, Missouri; author's photograph).

Born: Aug. 11, 1831 NC
Died: April 14, 1873, Linn, MO
Occupation: Lawyer and newspaper editor
Offices/Honors: Missouri House of Representatives, 1856–58, 1862–64, and 1867–69. Postmaster, Linn, MO, 1860–61.
Miscellaneous: Resided Linn, Osage Co., MO
Buried: Linn Public Cemetery, Linn, MO. Also a modern cenotaph in Pointers Creek Cemetery, Linn, MO.
References: "Col. Lebbeus Zevely and His Role in the Civil War," *Newsletter, Osage County (MO) Historical Society*, Vol. 7, No. 4 (April 1992). Obituary, *The Peoples' Tribune (Jefferson City, MO)*, April 16, 1873. Obituary, *Lexington Weekly Caucasian*, April 19, 1873. Obituary, *Sedalia Democrat*, April 18, 1873. *History of Cole, Moniteau, Morgan, Benton, Miller, Maries, and Osage Counties, Missouri, from the Earliest Time to the Present*. Chicago, IL, 1889.

Arkansas

Regiments

1st Cavalry
M. La Rue Harrison   Aug. 7, 1862   Mustered out Aug. 23, 1865, **Bvt. Brig. Gen., USV**

2nd Cavalry
John E. Phelps   March 18, 1864   Mustered out Aug. 20, 1865, **Bvt. Brig. Gen., USV**

3rd Cavalry
Abraham H. Ryan   Feb. 10, 1864   Mustered out June 30, 1865

4th Cavalry
Lafayette Gregg   Oct. 16, 1864   Mustered out June 30, 1865

1st Infantry
James M. Johnson   March 25, 1863   Mustered out Aug, 10, 1865, **Bvt. Brig. Gen., USV**

2nd Infantry
Marshall L. Stephenson   July 6, 1864   Mustered out Aug. 8, 1865

3rd Infantry (regiment failed to complete organization)
William M. Fishback   Oct. 1, 1863

4th Infantry (regiment failed to complete organization)
Edward J. Brooks   Oct. 4, 1863

4th Mounted Infantry (regiment failed to complete organization)
Elisha Baxter   Oct. 23, 1863   Relieved from duty May 12, 1864

Biographies

Elisha Baxter

Quartermaster, 1 AR Volunteers (30 days), CSA, Nov.–Dec. 1861. Renewing his allegiance to the Federal Government, he was captured and charged by the Confederate authorities with treason in April 1863, but escaped to the Union lines before trial. *Colonel*, 4 AR Mounted Infantry, Oct. 23, 1863. Regiment did not complete organization. Relieved from duty, May 12, 1864, upon election to U.S. Senate.
Born: Sept. 1, 1827 Rutherford Co., NC
Died: May 31, 1899, Batesville, AR
Occupation: Lawyer and judge
Offices/Honors: Arkansas House of Representatives, 1854–56 and 1858–60. Elected to U.S. Senate, 1864, but Congress refused to seat him and others from Southern States. Circuit Court Judge, 1868–73. Governor of Arkansas, 1873–74.
Miscellaneous: Resided Batesville, Independence Co., AR. His election as governor over Joseph Brooks precipitated the Brooks-Baxter War, which claimed about 50 casualties before President Grant acted to restore Baxter to power.
Buried: Oaklawn Cemetery, Batesville, AR

Elisha Baxter (Bankes' Gallery of Photographic Art, S.E. Cor. Main & Markham Sts., Little Rock, Arkansas; courtesy Henry Deeks).

Elisha Baxter, post-war (*Biographical and Historical Memoirs of Northeast Arkansas*. Chicago, Nashville and St. Louis, 1889).

References: John Hallum. *Biographical and Pictorial History of Arkansas.* Albany, NY, 1887. *Biographical and Historical Memoirs of Northeast Arkansas.* Chicago, Nashville and St. Louis, 1889. Fay Hempstead. *A Pictorial History of Arkansas from Earliest Times to the Year 1890.* St. Louis and New York, 1890. Allen Johnson and Dumas Malone, editors. *Dictionary of American Biography.* New York City, NY, 1964. Ted R. Worley, editor, "Elisha Baxter's Autobiography," *Arkansas Historical Quarterly*, Vol. 14, No. 2 (Summer 1955). Nancy A. Williams, editor. *Arkansas Biography: A Collection of Notable Lives.* Fayetteville, AR, 2000. Obituary, *Arkansas Democrat*, June 1, 1899. Obituary, *Daily Arkansas Gazette*, June 2, 1899. Letters Received, Volunteer Service Branch, Adjutant General's Office, File B1141(VS)1864, National Archives. *The National Cyclopedia of American Biography.* Vol. 10. New York City, NY, 1909.

Edward James Brooks

1 Lieutenant, 7 U.S. Infantry, Feb. 26, 1861. Despite being "dropped from the rolls for disloyalty," May 16, 1861, he remained loyal throughout the war. Finally, upon the recommendation of General Grant, July 29, 1868, the order dropping him from the rolls was changed to accept his resignation, effective May 16, 1861. *Colonel*, 4 AR Infantry, Oct. 4, 1863. Regiment did not complete organization.

Born: Oct. 13, 1830 Detroit, MI
Died: Nov. 20, 1897 Denver, CO
Other Wars: Mexican War (Private, Co. I, 7 NY Volunteers)
Occupation: 1 Lieutenant, 7 U.S. Infantry, before war. Wholesale merchant, lawyer, real estate agent, and insurance agent after war.
Offices/Honors: United States Commissioner, Fort Smith, AR, 1870–75. Chief Clerk, Office of the Surveyor General, District of Colorado, 1881–85. Brig. Gen., commanding Colorado National Guard, 1891–97.
Miscellaneous: Resided Washington, D.C., and Fayetteville, Washington Co., AR, before war; Fort Smith, Sebastian Co., AR, 1865–78; and Denver, Arapahoe Co., CO, 1878–97
Buried: Fairmount Cemetery, Denver, CO (Block 3, Lot 41)
References: Obituary, *Rocky Mountain News*, Nov. 21, 1897. Obituary, *Denver Post*, Nov. 22, 1897. Obituary, *Daily Arkansas Gazette*, Nov. 24, 1897. Pension File, National Archives. Letters Received, Commission Branch, Adjutant General's Office, File B406(CB)1868, National Archives. John Y. Simon, editor. *The Papers of Ulysses S. Grant.* Vol. 18: October 1, 1867–June 30, 1868. Carbondale, IL, 1991. *Report of the Adjutant General of Arkansas for the Period of the Late Rebellion, and to November 1, 1866.* Washington, D.C., 1867.

William Meade Fishback

Colonel, 3 AR Infantry (later 4 AR Cavalry), Oct. 1, 1863. Regiment did not complete organization.

Born: Nov. 5, 1831 Jeffersonton, Culpeper Co., VA

Died: Feb. 9, 1903 Fort Smith, AR

Education: Attended University of Virginia, Charlottesville, VA

Occupation: Lawyer

Offices/Honors: Elected to U.S. Senate, 1864, but Congress refused to seat him and others from Southern States. Arkansas House of Representatives, 1877–81 and 1885–87. Governor of Arkansas, 1893–95.

Miscellaneous: Resided Fort Smith, Sebastian Co., AR

Buried: Oak Cemetery, Fort Smith, AR (Section 10, Lot 44)

References: John Hallum. *Biographical and Pictorial History of Arkansas.* Albany, NY, 1887. Allen Johnson and Dumas Malone, editors. *Dictionary of American Biography.* New York City, NY, 1964. Obituary, *Fort Smith Times*, Feb. 9, 1903. Obituary, *Arkansas Democrat*, Feb. 10, 1903. Willis M. Kemper. *Genealogy of the Fishback Family in America.* New York City, NY, 1914. *History of Benton, Washington, Carroll, Madison, Crawford, Franklin, and Sebastian Counties, Arkansas.* Chicago, IL, 1889. *The National Cyclopedia of American Biography.* Vol. 10. New York City, NY, 1909. Powell Clayton. *The Aftermath of the Civil War in Arkansas.* New York City, NY, 1915. Letters Received, Volunteer Service Branch, Adjutant General's Office, File F824(VS)1863, National Archives. *Catalogue of the Delta Kappa Epsilon Fraternity: Biographical and Statistical.* New York City, NY, 1890.

Lafayette Gregg

Colonel, 4 AR Cavalry, Oct. 16, 1864. Honorably mustered out, June 30, 1865.

Born: Feb. 6, 1825 near Moulton, AL

Died: Nov. 1, 1891 Fayetteville, AR

Lafayette Gregg (William Brown, Photographer of the Army of Arkansas; Special Collections, University of Arkansas Libraries, Fayetteville [Gregg Family Papers, MC 1000, Box 3, Folder 7, Item 1]).

William Meade Fishback, post-war (John Hallum. *Biographical and Pictorial History of Arkansas.* Albany, New York, 1887).

Occupation: Lawyer, judge, and banker
Offices/Honors: Arkansas House of Representatives, 1854–55. Associate Justice, Arkansas Supreme Court, 1868–74.
Miscellaneous: Resided Fayetteville, Washington Co., AR. A founder of the University of Arkansas.
Buried: Evergreen Cemetery, Fayetteville, AR (Section II, Lot 1)
References: Nancy A. Williams, editor. *Arkansas Biography: A Collection of Notable Lives.* Fayetteville, AR, 2000. Fay Hempstead. *A Pictorial History of Arkansas from Earliest Times to the Year 1890.* St. Louis and New York, 1890. Obituary, *Arkansas Democrat,* Nov. 2, 1891. Obituary, *Daily Arkansas Gazette,* Nov. 3, 1891. Barbara P. Easley. *Obituaries of Washington County, Arkansas.* Bowie, MD, 1996. Gregg Family Papers (MC 1000), Special Collections, University of Arkansas Libraries, Fayetteville, AR. Military Service File, National Archives.

Abraham Hall Ryan

1 Lieutenant, Co. A, 17 IL Infantry, May 13, 1861. 1 Lieutenant, Adjutant, 17 IL Infantry, May 25, 1861. Acting AAG, Staff of Colonel Leonard F. Ross, 3 Brigade, 1 Division, Army of the Tennessee, April–June 1862. Captain, Co. A, 17 IL Infantry, May 14, 1862. Acting ADC, Staff of Brig. Gen. Leonard F. Ross, District of Jackson, District of Corinth, and District of Eastern Arkansas, Department of the Tennessee, July 1862–July 1863. Acting ADC, Staff of Major Gen. Frederick Steele, Army of Arkansas, Department of the Missouri, Aug. 1863–Feb. 1864. Colonel, 3 AR Cavalry, Feb. 10, 1864. Commanded Post of Lewisburg (AR), District of Little Rock, 7 Army Corps, Department of Arkansas, April–Sept. 1864 and Nov.–Dec. 1864. Commanded 4 Brigade, Cavalry Division, District of Little Rock, 7 Army Corps, Department of Arkansas, Sept.–Oct. 1864. Commanded Post of Lewisburg (AR), 7 Army Corps, Department of Arkansas, Jan.–June 1865. Honorably mustered out, June 30, 1865. Battle honors: Fort Donelson, Shiloh, Siege of Corinth, Iuka, Yazoo Pass Expedition, Advance Upon Little Rock, Operations in Arkansas (Dardanelle).
Born: Feb. 16, 1837 New York City, NY
Died: Dec. 29, 1903 East Orange, NJ
Occupation: Silver plater and bell hanger before war, in partnership with Colonel John N. Cromwell (47 IL Infantry). Saw mill operator, lumber dealer, and banker after war.
Miscellaneous: Resided Peoria, Peoria Co., IL, before war; Little Rock, Pulaski Co., AR, 1865–81; and East Orange, Essex Co., NJ, after 1881
Buried: Oak Grove Cemetery, Falmouth, MA
References: William H. Powell, editor. *Officers of the Army and Navy (Volunteer) Who Served in the Civil War.* Philadelphia, PA, 1893.

Abraham Hall Ryan (courtesy Everitt Bowles).

Abraham Hall Ryan (Bogardus, Photographer, 363 Broadway, New York; Roger D. Hunt Collection, USAMHI [RG98S-CWP26.32]).

Marshall Lovejoy Stephenson

Major, 10 IL Cavalry, Nov. 25, 1861. Assistant Provost Marshal General, Army of the Frontier, Department of the Missouri, Jan.–April 1863. Assistant Provost Marshal General, District of Southwest Missouri, Department of the Missouri, April–Aug. 1863. Detailed to superintend organization of 2 AR Infantry, Aug. 31, 1863. GSW right hip, Jenkins' Ferry, AR, April 30, 1864. Colonel, 2 AR Infantry, July 6, 1864. Commanded 2 Brigade, 2 Division, 7 Army Corps, Department of Arkansas, Sept.–Oct. 1864. Commanded 1 Brigade, Frontier Division, 7 Army Corps, Department of Arkansas, Dec. 1864. Honorably mustered out, Aug. 8, 1865. Battle honors: Camden Expedition (Jenkins' Ferry).

Born: March 28, 1838, Granville, Putnam Co., IL

Died: Sept. 18, 1911 Battle Creek, MI

Occupation: Lawyer, judge, and banker

Offices/Honors: Circuit Court Judge, 1868–72. Associate Justice, Arkansas Supreme Court, 1872–74.

Miscellaneous: Resided Springfield, Sangamon Co., IL, before war; Huntsville, Madison Co., AR, 1867–71; and Helena, Phillips Co., AR, after 1871; except several years in Muskegon, Muskegon Co., MI (1880).

Buried: Oak Hill Cemetery, Battle Creek, MI (Section O, Lot 36)

References: Fay Hempstead. *A Pictorial History of Arkansas from Earliest Times to the Year 1890*. St. Louis and New York, 1890. Obituary, *Daily Arkansas Gazette,* Sept. 19, 1911. Obituary, *Battle Creek Journal*, Sept. 18, 1911. Obituary, *Arkansas Democrat*, Sept. 19, 1911. Pension File and Military Service File, National Archives. Letters Received, Volunteer Service Branch, Adjutant General's Office, File S2053(VS)1864, National Archives. www.ancestry.com.

Abraham Hall Ryan (Roger D. Hunt Collection, USAMHI [RG98S-CWP58.4]).

Charles Morris, editor. *Men of the Century*. Philadelphia, PA, 1896. Obituary Circular, Whole No. 804, New York MOLLUS. *National Cyclopedia of American Biography*. Vol. 5. New York City, NY, 1907. Obituary, *New York Sun*, Dec. 30, 1903. Obituary, *New York Times*, Dec. 30, 1903. Obituary, *Falmouth Enterprise*, Jan. 2, 1904. Henry Whittemore. *The Founders and Builders of the Oranges*. Newark, NJ, 1896. "Col. Abraham H. Ryan," *Daily Arkansas Gazette*, Dec. 2, 1894. Pension File and Military Service File, National Archives. Letters Received, Volunteer Service Branch, Adjutant General's Office, File R156(VS)1864, National Archives.

CALIFORNIA

Regiments

1st Cavalry
David Fergusson	Feb. 9, 1863	Dismissed July 21, 1863
Oscar M. Brown	Dec. 31, 1863	Resigned Dec. 31, 1865
William McCleave	Jan. 6, 1866	Mustered out Oct. 19, 1866

2nd Cavalry
Andrew J. Smith	Oct. 2, 1861	Resigned Nov. 13, 1861, **Brig. Gen., USV**
Columbus Sims	Nov. 13, 1861	Resigned Jan. 31, 1863
George S. Evans	Feb. 1, 1863	Mustered out May 31, 1863, **Bvt. Brig. Gen., USV**
Edward McGarry	Nov. 29, 1864	Mustered out March 31, 1866, **Bvt. Brig. Gen., USV**

1st Infantry
James H. Carleton	Aug. 19, 1861	Promoted **Brig. Gen., USV,** April 28, 1862
Joseph R. West	June 1, 1862	Promoted **Brig. Gen., USV,** Dec. 4, 1862
Edwin A. Rigg	Dec. 4, 1862	Mustered out Sept. 30, 1864

2nd Infantry
Francis J. Lippitt	Sept. 2, 1861	Mustered out Oct. 11, 1864, **Bvt. Brig. Gen., USV**
Thomas F. Wright	Jan. 6, 1865	Mustered out April 16, 1866, **Bvt. Brig. Gen., USV**

3rd Infantry
Patrick E. Connor	Sept. 4, 1861	Promoted **Brig. Gen., USV,** March 30, 1863
Robert Pollock	March 29, 1863	Mustered out Nov. 14, 1864

4th Infantry
Henry M. Judah	Sept. 6, 1861	Resigned Nov. 8, 1861, **Brig. Gen., USV**
Ferris Forman	Nov. 8, 1861	Resigned Aug. 20, 1863
James F. Curtis	May 20, 1864	Mustered out Nov. 30, 1865, **Bvt. Brig. Gen., USV**

5th Infantry
John Kellogg	Sept. 12, 1861	Resigned Nov. 8, 1861
George W. Bowie	Nov. 8, 1861	Mustered out Dec. 14, 1864, **Bvt. Brig. Gen., USV**

6th Infantry
Henry M. Black	Feb. 1, 1863	Mustered out Oct. 27, 1865

7th Infantry
Charles W. Lewis	Jan. 11, 1865	Mustered out May 22, 1866, **Bvt. Brig. Gen., USV**

8th Infantry
Allen L. Anderson	March 7, 1865	Mustered Nov. 10, 1865, **Bvt. Brig. Gen., USV**

Biographies

Henry Moore Black

Captain, 9 U.S. Infantry, Sept. 10, 1856. Commanded Post of Fort Vancouver (WA), District of Oregon, Department of the Pacific, June–Nov. 1861. Commanded Post of Alcatraz Island (CA), Department of the Pacific, Sept. 1862–Jan. 1863. Colonel, 6 CA Infantry, Feb. 1, 1863. Commanded Post of Benicia Barracks (CA), Department of the Pacific, April 1863–Feb. 1864. Major, 7 U.S. Infantry, July 25, 1863. Commanded Military District of Humboldt, Department of the Pacific, Feb.–July 1864. Detached as Commandant of Cadets, U.S. Military Academy, West Point, NY, Sept. 1864–Sept. 1865. Honorably mustered out of volunteer service, Oct. 27, 1865. Bvt. Lieutenant Colonel, USA, and Bvt. Colonel, USA, March 13, 1865, for faithful and meritorious services during the war.

Born: Jan. 15, 1827 Delaware Co., PA
Died: Aug. 5, 1893 Chicago, IL
Education: Graduated U.S. Military Academy, West Point, NY, 1847
Other Wars: Mexican War (2 Lieutenant, 7 U.S. Infantry)
Occupation: Regular Army (Colonel, 23 U.S. Infantry, retired Jan. 15, 1891). Commandant of Cadets, U.S. Military Academy, West Point, NY, 1864–70.
Buried: Post Cemetery, West Point, NY (Section 23, Row A, Grave 9)

Henry Moore Black (National Archives [B-2728]).

Henry Moore Black (Silas Selleck, Photographic Artist, Next Wells Fargo & Co., 415 Montgomery St., San Francisco; Massachusetts MOLLUS Collection, USAMHI [Vol. 126, p. 6452L]).

Henry Moore Black (author's photograph).

References: *Twenty-Fifth Annual Reunion of the Association of the Graduates of the U.S. Military Academy at West Point, NY.* Saginaw, MI, 1894. George W. Cullum. *Biographical Register of the Officers and Graduates of the U.S. Military Academy.* Third Edition. Boston, MA, 1891. Obituary Circular, Whole No. 118, Michigan MOLLUS. Obituary, *Detroit Free Press*, Aug. 6, 1893. Obituary, *Chicago Daily Tribune*, Aug. 8, 1893. Pension File and Military Service File, National Archives. Florence Van Rensselaer, compiler. *The Livingston Family in America and Its Scottish Origins*. New York City, NY, 1949. Fred R. Brown. *History of the Ninth U.S. Infantry, 1799-1909*. Chicago, IL, 1909.

Oscar Monroe Brown

Lieutenant Colonel, 1 CA Cavalry, Feb. 13, 1863. Commanded Post of Camp Union, Sacramento (CA), District of California, Department of the Pacific, Nov.-Dec. 1863. Colonel, 1 CA Cavalry, Dec. 31, 1863. Commanded Post of Fort Craig (NM), Department of New Mexico, June 1864-Feb. 1865. Commanded Post of Fort Marcy (NM), Department of New Mexico, March-Aug. 1865. Commanded Post of Fort Bascom (NM), District of New Mexico, Department of California, Aug.-Oct. 1865. Commanded Post of Los Pinos (NM), District of New Mexico, Department of California, Nov.-Dec. 1865. Resigned Dec. 31, 1865.

Born: Dec. 27, 1827 Petersburg, VA
Died: Oct. 16, 1889 Las Vegas, NM
Other Wars: Mexican War (Sergeant, Co. B, 3 MO Mounted Infantry)
Occupation: Lawyer
Offices/Honors: Post Sutler, Fort Sumner, NM, 1866-68
Miscellaneous: Resided Stockton, San Joaquin Co., CA; San Francisco, CA; Globe, Gila Co., AZ; Dallas, TX; and Las Vegas, San Miguel Co., NM
Buried: Santa Fe National Cemetery, Santa Fe, NM (Section O, Plot 321)
References: Obituary, *Las Vegas Daily Optic*, Oct. 17, 1889. Pension File and Military Service File, National Archives. Darlis A. Miller. *The California Column in New Mexico*. Albuquerque, NM, 1982. Don McDowell. *The Beat of the Drum: The History, Events and People of Drum Barracks, Wilmington, California*. Wilmington, CA, 1993. Letters Received, Volunteer Service Branch, Adjutant General's Office, File A125(VS)1866, National Archives. Letters Received, Commission Branch, Adjutant General's Office, Files W99(CB)1866 and B317(CB)1868, National Archives.

David Fergusson

Major, 1 CA Cavalry, Nov. 21, 1861. Commanded Post of Camp Wright, Oak Grove, CA, District of Southern California, Department of the Pacific, Dec. 1861-Feb. 1862. Commanded Post of Camp Carleton, San Bernardino, CA, District of Southern California, Department of the Pacific, Feb.-March 1862. Chief Commissary of Subsistence and Acting AQM, Staff of Brig. Gen. James H. Carleton, California Column, Department of New Mexico, June-Sept. 1862. Commanded District of Western Arizona, Department of New Mexico, July-Sept. 1862. *Lieutenant Colonel*, 1 CA Cavalry, Nov. 30, 1862. Commanded Post of Mesilla (AZ), Department of New Mexico, Dec. 1862-Jan. 1863. *Colonel*, 1 CA Cavalry, Feb. 9, 1863. Commanded Post of Tucson (AZ), Department of New Mexico, March-May 1863. Complaining that "General Carleton has seen fit to keep me detached, except for six weeks, from my regiment since I was commissioned in it, and performing duties beneath my rank and not appropriate to my arm of the service," and arguing that "I am not properly in the service of the United States, as I have never been mustered in," he "vacated the Office of Colonel," May 25, 1863, and returned to his home in San Francisco. Dishonorably dismissed, July 21, 1863, for "leaving his command without orders or authority," with Major Gen. Henry W. Halleck observing, "Whatever may have been the character of his grievances from his superiors, these could not have justified so grave a military offence."

Born: Sept. 11, 1824 near Blair Atholl, Perthshire, Scotland
Died: July 7, 1918, Los Angeles, CA
Other Wars: Mexican War (Sergeant, Co. B, 1 U.S. Artillery)
Occupation: Regular Army (Sergeant Major, 2 U.S. Infantry), 1848-53, and Chief Clerk, Quartermaster's Department, Department of the Pacific, before war. Mining superintendent, railroad executive, and bank executive after war.
Miscellaneous: Resided San Francisco, CA, before war; and Tepic, Jalisco, Mexico, 1866-72; Mexico City, Mexico, 1872-82; London, England, 1882-83; Washington, D.C., 1883-88; Seattle, King Co., WA, 1888-1903; Berkeley, Alameda Co., CA, 1903-15; and Los Angeles, CA, 1915-18. Author of a scholarly work on the Mexican Inquisition, based on a group of documents collected and translated by him.
Buried: Oak Hill Cemetery, Washington, D.C. (Chapel Hill, Lot 651)
References: James Ferguson and Robert M. Fergusson, editors. *Records of the Clan and Name of Fergusson, Ferguson and Fergus*. Sup-

plement. Edinburgh, Scotland, 1899. Constance Wynn Altshuler. *Cavalry Yellow & Infantry Blue: Army Officers in Arizona Between 1851 and 1886.* Tucson, AZ, 1991. Obituary, *Berkeley Daily Gazette,* July 9, 1918. Death notice, *Los Angeles Times,* July 8, 1918. Military Service File, National Archives. Letters Received, Volunteer Service Branch, Adjutant General's Office, File N320(VS)1863, National Archives. Andrew E. Masich. *The Civil War in Arizona: The Story of the California Volunteers, 1861–1865.* Norman, OK, 2006. David Fergusson. *Trial of Gabriel De Granada by the Inquisition in Mexico, 1642–1645.* Baltimore, MD, 1899. www.findagrave.com.

Ferris Forman

Colonel, 4 CA Infantry, Nov. 8, 1861. Commanded Post of Camp Sigel, near Auburn, CA, Department of the Pacific, Dec. 1861–Jan. 1862. Commanded Post of Camp Union, near Sacramento, CA, Department of the Pacific, Feb.–April 1862. Commanded Post of Camp Latham, near Los Angeles, CA, Department of the Pacific, May–Sept. 1862. Commanded Post of Benicia Barracks, Department of the Pacific, Sept. 1862–March 1863. Commanded District of Southern California, Department of the Pacific, April–July 1863. Resigned Aug. 20, 1863.

Ferris Forman, post-war (*History of Fayette County, Illinois.* Philadelphia, Pennsylvania, 1878).

Born: Aug. 24, 1808 Nichols, Tioga Co., NY
Died: Feb. 11, 1901 Stockton, CA
Education: Attended Oxford (NY) Academy. Graduated Union College, Schenectady, NY, 1832.
Other Wars: Mexican War (Colonel, 3 IL Infantry)
Occupation: Lawyer
Offices/Honors: Illinois Senate, 1844–46. Postmaster, Sacramento, CA, 1853–57. Secretary of State of California, 1858–60.
Miscellaneous: Resided Vandalia, Fayette Co., IL; Sacramento, Sacramento Co., CA, 1849–66; and Stockton, San Joaquin Co., CA, after 1886
Buried: San Joaquin Catholic Cemetery, Stockton, CA (Division H, Section 1, Peters Plot)
References: Newton Bateman, Paul Selby, Robert W. Ross, and John J. Bullington, editors. *Historical Encyclopedia of Illinois and History of Fayette County.* Chicago, IL, 1910. *The United States Biographical Dictionary and Portrait Gallery of Eminent and Self-Made Men.* Illinois Volume. Chicago, Cincinnati, and New York, 1876. *History of Fayette County, Illinois.* Philadelphia, PA, 1878. *The Biographical Encyclopedia of Illinois of the Nineteenth Century.* Philadelphia, PA, 1875. Obituary, *Sacramento Evening Bee,* Feb. 11, 1901. Obituary, *San Francisco Chronicle,* Feb. 12, 1901. Obituary, *Los Angeles Times,* Feb. 12, 1901. Pension File and Military Service File, National Archives. Anne Spottswood Dandridge, compiler. *The Forman Genealogy.* Cleveland, OH, 1903.

John Kellogg

Adjutant, 3 U.S. Artillery, June 17, 1861. Captain, Commissary of Subsistence, USA, Aug. 3, 1861. Colonel, 5 CA Infantry, Sept. 12, 1861. Resigned from volunteer service, Nov. 8, 1861. Major, Commissary of Subsistence, USA, June 29, 1864. Lieutenant Colonel and Chief Commissary of Subsistence, Staff of Major Gen. Philip H. Sheridan, Middle Military Division, Aug. 1864–April 1865. Battle honors: Shenandoah Valley campaign.
Born: Jan. 6, 1826 Shelburne, MA
Died: April 25, 1865, City Point, VA (illness due to exposure in Shenandoah Valley campaign)
Education: Graduated U.S. Military Academy, West Point, NY, 1849
Occupation: Regular Army (Major, Commissary of Subsistence)
Miscellaneous: Resided Shelburne, Franklin Co., MA

John Kellogg (Bradley & Rulofson, Successors to R. H. Vance, Cor. of Montgomery and Sacramento Sts., San Francisco, California; author's photograph).

John Kellogg (J.W. Brown, Winchester, West Virginia; *Greenfield Gazette, Centennial Edition, Greenfield, Mass., Feb. 1, 1892.* Greenfield, Massachusetts, 1892).

Buried: Shelburne Center Cemetery, Shelburne, MA

References: *Greenfield Gazette, Centennial Edition, Greenfield, Mass., Feb. 1, 1892.* Greenfield, MA, 1892. George W. Cullum. *Biographical Register of the Officers and Graduates of the U.S. Military Academy.* Third Edition. Boston, MA, 1891. Timothy Hopkins. *The Kelloggs in the Old World and the New.* San Francisco, CA, 1903. Military Service File, National Archives. Letters Received, Commission Branch, Adjutant General's Office, Files K232(CB)1863, K293(CB)1864, S1317(CB)1864, and M291(CB)1865, National Archives.

William McCleave

Captain, Co. A, 1 CA Cavalry, Aug. 23, 1861. Taken prisoner, Pima Villages, AZ Territory, March 10, 1862. Exchanged July 7, 1862. Commanded Post of Fort West (NM), Department of New Mexico, Feb.–June 1863. Major, 1 CA Cavalry, May 1, 1863. Commanded Post of Las Cruces (NM), Department of New Mexico, Oct. 1863–Jan. 1864. Chief Quartermaster and Chief Commissary of Subsistence, Staff of Colonel George W. Bowie, District of Arizona, Department of New Mexico, Feb.–Sept. 1864. Commanded Post of Fort Sumner (NM), District of New Mexico, Department of California, Feb. 1865–Aug. 1866. *Colonel*, 1 CA Cavalry, Jan. 6, 1866. Honorably mustered out, Oct. 19, 1866. Bvt. Lieutenant Colonel, USV, March 13, 1865, for a successful pursuit of, and gallantry in the engagement with, the Apache Indians. Battle honors: Operations Against Indians in New Mexico (Rio Bonito), Adobe Walls.

Born: June 24, 1823, Benburb, County Tyrone, Ireland

Died: Feb. 3, 1904 Berkeley, CA

Occupation: Regular Army enlisted man (1 Sergeant, Co. K, 1 U.S. Dragoons) and farmer before war. Regular Army (Captain, 8 U.S. Cavalry, retired March 20, 1879).

Miscellaneous: Resided Berkeley, Alameda Co., CA. He refused to draw his pay while a prisoner, March–July 1862, prompting Brig. Gen. James H. Carleton, in a letter to Major Gen. Henry W. Halleck, to praise "the devotion of this noble Irishman," who "possesses all the elements of which heroes and patriots are made." Three of his sons were career military officers.

Buried: San Francisco National Cemetery, San Francisco, CA (Section OS, Plot 55, Grave 5)

William McCleave (courtesy Everitt Bowles).

References: Constance Wynn Altshuler. *Cavalry Yellow & Infantry Blue: Army Officers in Arizona Between 1851 and 1886.* Tucson, AZ, 1991. Lee Myers, "Captain William McCleave, Fighting Cavalryman," *Southwest Heritage,* Vol. 3, No. 2 (March 1969). Al Reck, "California in the Civil War: Cavalryman from Berkeley Outwits Southern Captors," *Oakland Tribune,* March 26, 1961. Obituary, *San Francisco Chronicle,* Feb. 4, 1904. Obituary, *Oakland Tribune,* Feb. 4, 1904. Obituary, *San Francisco Call,* Feb. 4, 1904. Aurora Hunt. *The Army of the Pacific.* Glendale, CA, 1951. Andrew E. Masich. *The Civil War in Arizona: The Story of the California Volunteers, 1861–1865.* Norman, OK, 2006. Pension File and Military Service File, National Archives. Obituary Circular, Whole No. 746, California MOLLUS. *The War of the Rebellion: A Compilation of the Official Records of the Union and Confederate Armies.* (Vol. 50, Part 2, pp.222–223). Washington, DC, 1897. Daniella Thompson, "William McCleave, Civil War Hero, Established a Military Dynasty," http://berkeleyheritage.com/eastbay_then-now/mccleave.html.

Robert Pollock

Major, 1 CA Infantry, Aug. 26, 1861. Major, 3 CA Infantry, Sept. 4, 1861. Lieutenant Colonel, 3 CA Infantry, Dec. 12, 1861. Commanded Post of Camp Hooker, near Stockton (CA), Department of the Pacific, Sept.–Nov. 1862. Commanded Post of Camp Union, near Sacramento (CA), Department of the Pacific, Nov. 1862–April 1863. Colonel, 3 CA Infantry, March 29, 1863. Commanded Post of Camp Douglas (UT), District of Utah, Department of the Pacific, June 1863–Sept. 1864. Honorably mustered out, Nov. 14, 1864. Lieutenant Colonel, 2 CA Infantry, Jan. 7, 1865. Commanded Fort Goodwin (AZ), District of Arizona, Department of California, Nov. 1865–May 1866. Honorably mustered out June 23, 1866. Bvt. Colonel, USV, March 13, 1865, for faithful and meritorious services.

Born: Sept. 17, 1819 Philadelphia, PA
Died: Feb. 24, 1901 Cornelius, OR
Other Wars: Mexican War (2 Lieutenant, Co. H, 1 VA Infantry).
Occupation: Carpenter and mining superintendent before war. Regular Army (Captain, 21 U.S. Infantry, retired Sept. 17, 1883), after war.
Miscellaneous: Resided San Francisco, CA, before war; Portland, Multnomah Co., OR; and Cornelius, Washington Co., OR, after war
Buried: Mountain View Memorial Gardens, Forest Grove, OR

Robert Pollock (Frederick Hill Meserve. Historical Portraits, a Part of the Collection of Americana of Frederick Hill Meserve, New York City, 1913-1915; Courtesy New York State Library, Manuscripts and Special Collections).

Robert Pollock, 1880 (Letters Received, Commission Branch, Adjutant General's Office, File P228(CB)1867, National Archives).

References: Harvey K. Hines. *An Illustrated History of the State of Oregon*. Chicago, IL, 1893. Obituary circular, Whole No. 146, Oregon MOLLUS. Constance Wynn Altshuler. *Cavalry Yellow & Infantry Blue: Army Officers in Arizona Between 1851 and 1886*. Tucson, AZ, 1991. Obituary, *Hillsboro Argus*, Feb. 28, 1901. Obituary, *Portland Morning Oregonian*, Feb. 25, 1901. Pension File and Military Service File, National Archives. Letters Received, Commission Branch, Adjutant General's Office, File P228(CB)1867, National Archives. James F. Varley. *Brigham and the Brigadier: General Patrick Connor and His California Volunteers in Utah and Along the Overland Trail*. Tucson, AZ, 1989.

Edwin Augustus Rigg

Captain, Co. A, 1 CA Infantry, Aug. 15, 1861. Major, 1 CA Infantry, Sept. 5, 1861. Commanded Post of Camp Wright, Oak Grove, CA, District of Southern California, Department of the Pacific, Oct.–Nov. 1861. Commanded Post of Fort Yuma (CA), District of Southern California, Department of the Pacific, Dec. 1861–April 1862. Lieutenant Colonel, 1 CA Infantry, April 28, 1862. Colonel, 1 CA Infantry, Dec. 4, 1862. Commanded Post of Fort Craig (NM), Department of New Mexico, Dec. 1862–April 1864. Commanded Apache Expedition, District of Arizona, Department of New Mexico, May–Aug. 1864. Commanded Fort Goodwin (AZ), Department of New Mexico, June–July 1864. Honorably mustered out, Sept. 30, 1864. Lieutenant Colonel, 1 CA Veteran Infantry, March 24, 1865. Commanded Post of Fort Craig (NM), Department of New Mexico, March–May 1865. Commanded Post of Fort Craig (NM), District of New Mexico, Department of California, July–Aug. 1865. Commanded Post of Los Pinos (NM), District of New Mexico, Department of California, Jan.–May 1866. Honorably mustered out, Oct. 13, 1866. Battle honors: Apache Expedition from Fort Craig (NM) to Fort Goodwin (AZ).

Born: Jan. 15, 1822 Philadelphia, PA
Died: Jan. 27, 1882 Contention City, AZ
Other Wars: Captain, Marion Rifles, California State Militia, 1856–61
Occupation: U.S. Custom House inspector and saloonkeeper before war. Regular Army (1 Lieutenant, 25 U.S. Infantry, honorably mustered out Jan. 1, 1871) and Post Trader, Fort Craig, NM, after war.
Offices/Honors: Postmaster, Fort Craig, NM, 1873–77
Miscellaneous: Resided San Francisco, CA, before war; Philadelphia, PA; Fort Craig, Socorro Co., NM; and Contention City, Cochise Co., AZ, 1880–82
Buried: Contention City Cemetery, Cochise Co., AZ (unmarked)
References: Constance Wynn Altshuler. *Cavalry Yellow & Infantry Blue: Army Officers in Arizona Between 1851 and 1886*. Tucson, AZ, 1991. Jerry D. Thompson. *A Civil War History of the New Mexico Volunteers & Militia*. Albuquerque, NM, 2015. Andrew E. Masich. *The Civil War in Arizona: The Story of the California Volunteers, 1861–1865*. Norman, OK, 2006. Pension File and Military Service File, National Archives. Obituary, *Tombstone Daily Epitaph*, Jan. 29, 1882. Letters Received, Appointment, Commission and Personal Branch, Adjutant General's Office, File 3435(ACP)1872, National Archives. Darlis A. Miller. *The California Column in New Mexico*. Albuquerque, NM, 1982. Letters Received, Volunteer Service Branch, Adjutant General's Office, File 4766(VS)1871, National Archives.

Columbus Sims

Lieutenant Colonel, 2 CA Cavalry, Sept. 19, 1861. Colonel, 2 CA Cavalry, Nov. 13, 1861. Commanded Post of Camp Alert, near San Francisco,

CA, Department of the Pacific, Nov. 1861–July 1862. Upon reports of insubordination and mutiny among the men of his regiment during the march to Fort Churchill, NV, he was suspended from command, Aug. 20, 1862. A Board of Officers convened to investigate the reports, after reviewing numerous accounts of his drunkenness and incompetency, recommended his discharge, concluding that he "is incapacitated to command said regiment and unqualified to act in his present position," since "his conduct during the march ... was exceedingly improper, and he was during said march inefficient as a commander." He resigned Jan. 31, 1863.

Born: 1829? Lancaster Co., SC

Died: Aug. 14, 1869 Hamilton, near Ely, White Pine Co., NV (delirium tremens)

Occupation: Lawyer

Miscellaneous: Resided Los Angeles, CA, before war; Idaho City, ID Territory; and San Francisco, CA, after war

Buried: Place of burial unknown

References: Obituary, *Sacramento Daily Union*, Aug. 20, 1869. Obituary, *Idaho World*, Aug. 26, 1869. Obituary, *Idaho Statesman*, Aug. 24, 1869. Obituary, *San Luis Obispo Tribune*, Aug. 30, 1869. Military Service File, National Archives. Letters Received, Volunteer Service Branch, Adjutant General's Office, File M2368(VS)1862, National Archives. Maurice H. Newmark and Marco R. Newmark. *Sixty Years in Southern California, 1853–1913, Containing the Reminiscences of Harris Newmark.* New York City, NY, 1916. Beatrice M. Doughtie. *The Mackeys and Allied Families.* Decatur, GA, 1957.

Colorado Territory

Regiments

1st Cavalry (designation of regiment changed from 1st CO Infantry, Nov. 1, 1862)
John M. Chivington	April 10, 1862	Mustered out Jan. 6, 1865

2nd Cavalry
James H. Ford	Nov. 5, 1863	Mustered out July 19, 1865, **Bvt. Brig. Gen., USV**

3rd Cavalry
George L. Shoup	Sept. 21, 1864	Mustered out Dec. 28, 1864

1st Infantry (designation of regiment changed to 1st CO Cavalry, Nov. 1, 1862)
John P. Slough	Aug. 26, 1861	Resigned April 9, 1862, **Brig. Gen., USV**
John M. Chivington	April 10, 1862	Mustered out Jan. 6, 1865

1st Mounted Militia
Samuel E. Browne	Feb. 27, 1865	Mustered out April 29, 1865

2nd Infantry
Jesse H. Leavenworth	Feb. 17, 1862	Discharged Sept. 26, 1863

3rd Infantry
William Larimer, Jr.	Aug. 7, 1862	Resigned Dec. 6, 1862

Biographies

Samuel E. Browne

Declined appointment as Captain, 17 U.S. Infantry, Sept. 8, 1861. Colonel, 1 CO Mounted Militia, Feb. 27, 1865. Honorably mustered out, April 29, 1865.

Born: May 12, 1822, Greencastle, Franklin Co., PA

Died: May 29, 1902, Denver, CO

Education: Graduated Marshall College, Mercersburg, PA, 1839

Occupation: Lawyer

Offices/Honors: Ohio House of Representatives, 1860–62. U.S. District Attorney, Colorado Territory, 1862–65.

Miscellaneous: Resided Piqua, Miami Co., OH, before war; and Denver, Arapahoe Co., CO, after war

Buried: Fairmount Cemetery, Denver, CO (Block 4, Lot 100)

References: *History of the City of Denver, Arapahoe County, and Colorado.* Chicago, IL, 1880. Obituary, *Rocky Mountain News*, May 30, 1902. Obituary, *Denver Post*, May 30, 1902. *Representative Men of Colorado in the Nineteenth Century.* Denver, CO, 1902. *Report of the Denver Bar Association.* Denver, CO, 1903. W. Cooper. *Sketches of the Senators and Representatives in the Fifty-Fourth General Assembly of the State of Ohio.* Columbus, OH, 1861. Letters Received, Volunteer Service Branch, Adjutant General's Office, File C1831(VS)1865, National Archives. Letters Received, Adjutant General's Office, File B708(AGO)1861, National Archives. John H.

Nankivell. *History of the Military Organizations of the State of Colorado, 1860–1935.* Denver, CO, 1935. Frank Hall. *History of the State of Colorado.* Chicago, IL, 1889. Jerome C. Smiley, editor. *History of Denver With Outlines of the Earlier History of the Rocky Mountain Country.* Denver, CO, 1901.

Samuel E. Browne, post-war (Frank Hall. *History of the State of Colorado.* Chicago, Illinois, 1889).

Samuel E. Browne, post-war (*Representative Men of Colorado in the Nineteenth Century.* Denver, Colorado, 1902).

John Milton Chivington

Major, 1 CO Infantry, Feb. 21, 1862. Colonel, 1 CO Infantry, April 10, 1862. Commanded Southern Military District of New Mexico, Department of New Mexico, June–Oct. 1862. Designation of regiment changed to 1 CO Cavalry, Nov. 1, 1862. Commanded District of Colorado, Department of the Missouri, Nov. 1862–Dec. 1863. Nominated Brig. Gen., USV, Jan. 19, 1863, to rank from Nov. 29, 1862. Nomination as Brig. Gen., USV, withdrawn, Feb. 12, 1863. Commanded Military District of Colorado, Department of Kansas, Jan.–Dec. 1864. Honorably mustered out, Jan. 6, 1865. Three separate hearings investigating his role in the Sand Creek Massacre failed to produce conclusive evidence of his culpability, but he was nevertheless the object of prolonged attacks in the public press and elsewhere. Battle honors: Apache Canyon, Glorieta, Sand Creek.

Born: Jan. 27, 1821 near Lebanon, Warren Co., OH

Died: Oct. 4, 1894 Denver, CO

Occupation: Methodist clergyman before war. Freighter and newspaper editor after war.

John Milton Chivington (Jerome C. Smiley, editor. *History of Denver with Outlines of the Earlier History of the Rocky Mountain Country.* Denver, Colorado, 1901).

John Milton Chivington (Stevenson & Marshall's Photograph Rooms, 40 Delaware St., Leavenworth, Kansas; Courtesy the author).

John Milton Chivington, post-war (Frank Hall. *History of the State of Colorado*. Chicago, Illinois, 1889).

Miscellaneous: Resided Nebraska City, Otoe Co., NE; Denver, Arapahoe Co., CO, to 1867 and after 1883; Washington, D.C.; Troy, Rensselaer Co., NY; San Diego, CA (1870); and Blanchester, Clinton Co., OH (1880). After his son, Thomas, died by drowning in 1868, he married his son's widow, but she divorced him three years later.

Buried: Fairmount Cemetery, Denver, CO (Block 2, Lot 143)

References: Lori Cox-Paul, "John M. Chivington: The 'Reverend Colonel' 'Marry-Your-Daughter' 'Sand Creek Massacre,'" *Nebraska History*, Vol. 88, No. 4 (Oct. 2007). Reginald S. Craig. *The Fighting Parson: The Biography of Col. John M. Chivington*. Tucson, AZ, 1959. William J. Convery, "John M. Chivington," *Soldiers West: Biographies from the Military Frontier*. Edited by Paul A. Hutton and Durwood Ball. Second Edition. Norman, OK, 2009. Dan L. Thrapp. *Encyclopedia of Frontier Biography*. Glendale, CA, 1988. Jerome C. Smiley, editor. *History of Denver with Outlines of the Earlier History of the Rocky Mountain Country*. Denver, CO, 1901. Frank Hall. *History of the State of Colorado*. Chicago, IL, 1889. Pension File and Military Service File, National Archives. William C. Whitford. *Colorado Volunteers in the Civil War: The New Mexico Campaign in 1862*. Denver, CO, 1906. Ovando J. Hollister. *Boldly They Rode: A History of the First Colorado Regiment of Volunteers*. Lakewood, CO, 1949. Court-martial Case Files, 1809–1894, File MM-2867, National Archives.

William Larimer, Jr.

Colonel, 3 CO Infantry, Aug. 7, 1862. Resigned Dec. 6, 1862. Captain, Co. A, 14 KS Cavalry, Aug. 12, 1863. Honorably mustered out, June 25, 1865.

Born: Oct. 24, 1809 Circleville, Westmoreland Co., PA

Died: May 16, 1875, near Leavenworth, KS

Occupation: Farmer

Offices/Honors: Major Gen., Pennsylvania State Militia, 1852. Nebraska House of Representatives, 1855–56. Kansas Senate, 1869 and 1870.

Miscellaneous: Resided Omaha, NE; Denver, CO; and Leavenworth, Leavenworth Co., KS

Buried: Allegheny Cemetery, Pittsburgh, PA (Section 1, Lot 64). Removed from Mount Muncie Cemetery, Leavenworth, KS, March 17, 1882.

References: Herman S. Davis. *Reminiscences of General William Larimer and of His Son William H.H. Larimer, Two of the Founders of Denver City*. Lancaster, PA, 1918. John N. Boucher. *History of Westmoreland County, Pennsylvania*.

File, National Archives. Blanche V. Adams, "The Second Colorado Cavalry in the Civil War," *Colorado Magazine*, Vol. 8, No. 3 (May 1931). J. Sterling Morton. *Illustrated History of Nebraska: A History of Nebraska From the Earliest Explorations of the Trans-Mississippi Region*. Lincoln, NE, 1911.

Jesse Henry Leavenworth

Colonel, 2 CO Infantry, Feb. 17, 1862. Commanded Post of Fort Larned (KS), District of the Border, Department of the Missouri, July–Sept. 1863. Dishonorably discharged, Sept. 26, 1863, for "irregular and deceptive conduct in organizing his regiment, by giving or countenancing the raising of an artillery company, without the authority of the War Department." His dishonorable discharge was revoked, March 26, 1864, upon the recommendation of Judge Advocate General Joseph Holt, who noted that "in the organization of this company, he was merely adapting his force to the arm which had for some time been attached to his command by his superior officer; and that in preparing the company for the field he received the direct cooperation of the Territorial Governor, and, in the use which he made of it in service, the full approval of Maj. Gen. Blunt." His honorable discharge, effective Sept. 26, 1863, was approved by President Lincoln with the endorsement, "… Col. Leavenworth, under the circumstances, did nothing to censure, and all to commend."

Born: March 29, 1807, Danville, VT
Died: March 12, 1885, Milwaukee, WI
Education: Graduated U.S. Military Academy, West Point, NY, 1830
Other Wars: Black Hawk War (2 Lieutenant, 2 U.S. Infantry)
Occupation: Regular Army (2 Lieutenant, 2 U.S. Infantry, resigned Oct. 31, 1836). Civil engineer and lumber merchant before war. U.S. Indian agent and clerk after war.
Miscellaneous: Resided Chicago, IL; and Milwaukee, WI. Son of Brig. Gen. Henry Leavenworth.
Buried: Forest Home Cemetery, Milwaukee, WI (Section 31, Block 8, Lot 4)
References: William E. Unrau, "The Civil War Career of Jesse Henry Leavenworth," *Montana: The Magazine of Western History*. Vol. 12, No. 2 (Spring 1962). Carolyn T. Foreman, "Col. Jesse H. Leavenworth," *Chronicles of Oklahoma*. Vol. 13, No. 1 (March 1935). Dan L. Thrapp. *Encyclopedia of Frontier Biography*.

William Larimer, Jr. (pre-war, 1852) (John N. Boucher. *History of Westmoreland County, Pennsylvania*. New York and Chicago, 1906).

William Larimer, Jr. (pre-war, 1860) (Herman S. Davis. *Reminiscences of General William Larimer and of His Son William H.H. Larimer, Two of the Founders of Denver City*. Lancaster, Pennsylvania, 1918).

New York and Chicago, 1906. Rachel H.L. Mellon, editor. *The Larimer, McMasters and Allied Families*. Philadelphia, PA, 1903. Obituary, *Leavenworth Times*, May 18, 1875. Obituary, *Pittsburgh Daily Commercial*, May 18, 1875. Military Service

Jesse Henry Leavenworth (courtesy Karl Sundstrom).

Glendale, CA, 1988. Pension File and Military Service File, National Archives. Letters Received, Volunteer Service Branch, Adjutant General's Office, File L6(VS)1863, National Archives. Blanche V. Adams, "The Second Colorado Cavalry in the Civil War," *Colorado Magazine,* Vol. 8, No. 3 (May 1931). George W. Cullum. *Biographical Register of the Officers and Graduates of the U.S. Military Academy.* Third Edition. Boston, MA, 1891. Elias W. Leavenworth. *A Genealogy of the Leavenworth Family in the United States.* Syracuse, NY, 1873. Death notice, *Milwaukee Sentinel,* March 14, 1885.

George Laird Shoup

2 Lieutenant, Co. C, 2 CO Infantry, Dec. 18, 1861. 1 Lieutenant, Co. C, 2 CO Infantry, Nov. 1, 1862. 1 Lieutenant, Co. L, 1 CO Cavalry, April 20, 1863. Honorably mustered out, Sept. 20, 1864. Colonel, 3 CO Cavalry, Sept. 21, 1864. Commanded Camp Elbert (CO), District of Colorado, Department of Kansas, Oct. 1864. Honorably mustered out, Dec. 28, 1864. Battle honors: Sand Creek.
  Born: June 15, 1836, Kittanning, PA
  Died: Dec. 21, 1904 Boise, ID

Jesse Henry Leavenworth (Clifford & Gibson's Art Emporium, No. 126 Wisconsin St., Just Above the P.O., Milwaukee, Wisconsin; author's photograph).

George Laird Shoup (George D. Wakely, Artist, Denver City, Colorado Territory; Colorado State Historical Society [Scan #10031856, History Colorado]).

George Laird Shoup, post-war (William H. Powell, editor. *Officers of the Army and Navy (Volunteer) Who Served in the Civil War.* Philadelphia, Pennsylvania, 1893).

Occupation: Dry goods merchant, mine operator, and livestock raiser

Offices/Honors: U.S. Postmaster, Salmon City, Idaho Territory, 1869–70 and 1872–77. Idaho Territory House of Representatives, 1875–77. Idaho Territory Council, 1879–81. Governor of Idaho Territory, 1889–90. Governor of Idaho, 1890. U.S. Senate, 1890–1901.

Miscellaneous: Resided Galesburg, Knox Co., IL; and Colorado Territory, before war; and Salmon City, Lemhi Co., ID; and Boise, Ada Co., ID, after war

Buried: Pioneer (Masonic) Cemetery, Boise, ID (Block 5, Lot 15)

References: David L. Crowder, "Pioneer Sketch: George Laird Shoup," *Idaho Yesterdays,* Vol. 33, No. 4 (Winter 1990). *An Illustrated History of the State of Idaho.* Chicago, IL, 1899. William H. Powell, editor. *Officers of the Army and Navy (Volunteer) Who Served in the Civil War.* Philadelphia, PA, 1893. Obituary, *Idaho Statesman,* Dec. 22, 1904. *Statue of Hon. George Laird Shoup, Late a Senator from Idaho, Erected in Statuary Hall of the Capitol at Washington.* Washington, D.C., 1910. Obituary Circular, Whole No. 785, California MOLLUS. Pension File and Military Service File, National Archives. Raymond G. Carey, "The 'Bloodless Third' Regiment, Colorado Volunteer Cavalry," *Colorado Magazine,* Vol. 38, No. 4 (Oct. 1961). James L. Harrison, compiler. *Biographical Directory of the American Congress, 1774–1949.* Washington, D.C., 1950.

Kansas

Regiments

2nd Cavalry
Robert B. Mitchell	March 15, 1862	Promoted **Brig. Gen., USV,** April 8, 1862
William F. Cloud	May 26, 1862	Mustered out Jan. 19, 1865
Owen A. Bassett	Jan. 20, 1864	Revoked Feb. 17, 1864

5th Cavalry
Hamilton P. Johnson	Aug. 13, 1861	KIA Sept. 17, 1861
John Ritchie	Sept. 17, 1861	Resigned Dec. 11, 1861, **Bvt. Brig. Gen., USV**
Powell Clayton	March 7, 1862	Promoted **Brig. Gen., USV,** Aug. 1, 1864

6th Cavalry
William R. Judson	Sept. 10, 1861	Mustered out March 11, 1865, **Bvt. Brig. Gen., USV**

7th Cavalry
Charles R. Jennison	Oct. 29, 1861	Resigned May 1, 1862
Albert L. Lee	May 17, 1862	Promoted **Brig. Gen., USV,** Nov. 29, 1862
Thomas P. Herrick	June 1, 1863	Mustered out Feb. 28, 1865
Francis M. Malone	Sept. 1, 1865	Mustered out Sept. 29, 1865

9th Cavalry
Edward Lynde	March 29, 1862	Mustered out Nov. 25, 1864

11th Cavalry
Thomas Ewing, Jr.	Sept. 15, 1862	Promoted **Brig. Gen., USV,** March 13, 1863
Thomas Moonlight	April 25, 1864	Mustered out July 17, 1865, **Bvt. Brig. Gen., USV**
Preston B. Plumb	July 17, 1865	Mustered out Sept. 13, 1865

14th Cavalry
Charles W. Blair	Nov. 20, 1863	Mustered out Aug. 11, 1865, **Bvt. Brig. Gen., USV**

15th Cavalry
Charles R. Jennison	Oct. 17, 1863	Dismissed June 23, 1865
William F. Cloud	July 26, 1865	Mustered out Oct. 19, 1865

16th Cavalry
Werter R. Davis	Oct. 8, 1864	Mustered out Nov. 28, 1865

1st Infantry
George W. Deitzler	June 5, 1861	Promoted **Brig. Gen., USV,** Nov. 29, 1862
William Y. Roberts	June 1, 1863	Mustered out June 17, 1864

1st Indian Home Guards
Robert W. Furnas	May 22, 1862	Resigned Nov. 22, 1862
Stephen H. Wattles	Dec. 26, 1862	Mustered out May 31, 1865

1st State Militia
Samuel A. Drake	Sept. 17, 1863	Promoted BG, KS State Militia, Feb. 29, 1864
Charles H. Robinson	March 19, 1864	

2nd Infantry (3 months)
Robert B. Mitchell	June 20, 1861	Mustered out Oct. 31, 1861, **Brig. Gen., USV**

2nd Indian Home Guards
John Ritchie	June 22, 1862	Mustered out May 31, 1865, **Bvt. Brig. Gen., USV**

2nd State Militia
Warren W.H. Lawrence	Sept. 19, 1863	Resigned Nov. 18, 1863
Reuben A. Randlett	Nov. 30, 1863	Resigned
George W. Veale	May 9, 1864	

3rd Infantry
James Montgomery	July 25, 1861	To 34th USCT March 5, 1863

3rd Indian Home Guards
William A. Phillips	July 11, 1862	Mustered out June 10, 1865

3rd State Militia
Francis B. Swift	Nov. 2, 1863	Resigned
Charles A. Willemsen	Feb. 13, 1864	

4th Infantry (designation of regiment changed to 10th KS Infantry upon consolidation with 3rd KS Infantry, April 3, 1862)
William Weer, Jr.	June 20, 1861	Dismissed Aug. 20, 1864

4th Indian Home Guards
James M. Pomeroy	Dec. 26, 1862	Declined April 26, 1863

4th State Militia
Stephen S. Cooper	Nov. 4, 1863	Superseded Nov. 16, 1864
William D. McCain	Nov. 16, 1864	

5th Indian Home Guards
David B. Corwin	Jan. 11, 1863	Relieved from duty Sept. 15, 1863

5th State Militia
Gustavus A. Colton	Sept. 28, 1863	

6th State Militia
James D. Snoddy	June 13, 1864	Relieved from duty Oct. 16, 1864
James Montgomery	Oct. 15, 1864	

7th State Militia
Peter McFarland   Dec. 9, 1863

8th Infantry
Henry W. Wessells	Sept. 29, 1861	Resigned Feb. 7, 1862, **Brig. Gen., USV**
Robert H. Graham	Feb. 28, 1862	Discharged Sept. 30, 1862
John A. Martin	Nov. 1, 1862	Mustered out Nov. 15, 1864, **Bvt. Brig. Gen., USV**
John Conover	Nov. 21, 1864	Mustered out Nov. 28, 1865

8th State Militia
Samuel N. Wood	Nov. 10, 1863	Promoted BG, KS State Militia, Feb. 29, 1864
William S. Smith	July 4, 1864	

9th Infantry (designation of regiment changed to 2nd KS Cavalry upon consolidation with reorganized 2nd KS Infantry, March 27, 1862)
Robert H. Graham	Nov. 11, 1861	Not mustered
Alson C. Davis	Jan. 9, 1862	Resigned Feb. 20, 1862

9th State Militia
Frank M. Tracy   Feb. 17, 1864

10th Infantry
William F. Cloud	March 27, 1862	To 2nd KS Cavalry May 26, 1862
William Weer, Jr.	June 1, 1862	Dismissed Aug. 20, 1864

10th State Militia
William Pennock   Nov. 18, 1863

11th State Militia
Andrew J. Mitchell   Oct. 28, 1863

12th Infantry
Charles W. Adams   Sept. 30, 1862   Mustered out June 30, 1865, **Bvt. Brig. Gen., USV**

12th State Militia
Levi S. Treat   Dec. 12, 1863

13th Infantry
Thomas M. Bowen   Sept. 20, 1862   Mustered out June 28, 1865, **Bvt. Brig. Gen., USV**

13th State Militia
Julius A. Keeler   Oct. 13, 1863

14th State Militia
David W. Scott	Nov. 9, 1863	Resigned
James M. Harvey	Oct. 19, 1864	

15th State Militia
John T. Price   Nov. 4, 1863

16th State Militia
Frederick W. Potter   Dec. 24, 1863

17th State Militia

Edwin C. Manning	Nov. 14, 1863	

18th State Militia

Perry L. Hubbard	March 7, 1864	Superseded
Matthew Quigg	Sept. 10, 1864	

19th State Militia

Melvin S. Grant	May 13, 1864	Promoted BG, KS State Militia, Aug. 22, 1864
Benjamin F. Akers	Sept. 3, 1864	Superseded
Andrew C. Hogan	Oct. 14, 1864	

20th State Militia

John B. Hubbell	June 28, 1864

21st State Militia

Sandy Lowe	Sept. 23, 1864

22nd State Militia

James P. Taylor	Sept. 7, 1864

23rd State Militia

William Weer, Jr.	Oct. 15, 1864

24th State Militia

Isaac Stadden	Oct. 22, 1864

Biographies

Benjamin Franklin Akers

Captain, Co. A, 19 KS State Militia, June 3, 1864. Colonel, 19 KS State Militia, Sept. 3, 1864. Superseded as colonel by Andrew C. Hogan, Oct. 14, 1864.

Born: Sept. 27, 1829 Swinton, Yorkshire, England

Died: Nov. 19, 1878 Lawrence, KS

Occupation: Livery stable keeper and freighter before war. Stock dealer and breeder of fine horses after war.

Miscellaneous: Resided Leavenworth, Leavenworth Co., KS, to 1872; Lawrence, Douglas Co., KS; and Wakarusa, Douglas Co., KS

Buried: Woodland Cemetery, Cleveland, OH (Section 27, Lot 8)

References: *The United States Biographical Dictionary*. Kansas Volume. Chicago and Kansas City, 1879. Obituary, *Lawrence Daily Journal,* Nov. 20, 1878. Obituary, *Leavenworth Times,* Nov. 20, 1878. Obituary, *Garnett Journal,* Nov. 23, 1878.

Benjamin Franklin Akers (pre-war) (Kansas-Memory.org, Kansas Historical Society, Item No. 210750).

Owen Abbott Bassett

Lieutenant Colonel, 9 KS Infantry, Dec. 30, 1861. Designation of regiment changed to 2 KS Infantry, March 15, 1862. Designation of regiment changed to 2 KS Cavalry, March 27, 1862. Commissioned *Colonel*, 2 KS Cavalry, May 27, 1862, to date April 9, 1862. Brig. Gen. James G. Blunt, commanding the Department of Kansas, refused to allow his muster as colonel, having already ordered the transfer of Colonel William F. Cloud of the 10 KS Infantry to the colonelcy of the 2 KS Cavalry, in response to a War Department directive establishing William Weer of the 4 KS Infantry as colonel of the recently consolidated 10 KS Infantry. Commanded Post of Fort Riley, Department of Kansas, May–June 1862. His efforts to win recognition as colonel finally resulted in his muster in as colonel, Jan. 20, 1864. However, on Feb. 17, 1864, the War Department ordered his muster out as colonel from the date of his muster in, thereby recognizing Colonel Cloud's claim to that position. Commanded 2 Brigade, District of the Frontier, Department of Arkansas, Jan.–Feb. 1864. Commanded Cavalry Brigade, Frontier Division, Department of Arkansas, March 1864. Chief of Staff to Brig. Gen. John M. Thayer, District of the Frontier, Department of Arkansas, May 1864–Jan. 1865. Honorably mustered out, Jan. 6, 1865. Battle honors: Old Fort Wayne, Cane Hill, Prairie Grove, Camden Expedition.

Born: July 16, 1834, Troy, Bradford Co., PA
Died: July 19, 1896, Ellsworth, KS
Education: Attended Denmark Academy, Denmark, IA
Occupation: Lawyer and judge
Offices/Honors: Kansas Territory House of Representatives, 1857–58. Judge of 4th Judicial District of Kansas, 1869–77. Grand Master of the Grand Lodge of Kansas Masons, 1873–74.
Miscellaneous: Resided Lawrence, Douglas Co., KS; and Ellsworth, Ellsworth Co., KS, in later years
Buried: Oak Hill Cemetery, Lawrence, KS (Section 7, Lot 207)
References: *The United States Biographical Dictionary. Kansas Volume.* Chicago and Kansas City, 1879. Alfred T. Andreas. *History of the State of Kansas.* Chicago, IL, 1883. Obituary, *Lawrence Daily Journal*, July 20, 1896. George W. Martin, editor. *Transactions of the Kansas State Historical Society, 1907–08.* Topeka, KS, 1908. William E. Connelley. *A Standard History of Kansas and Kansans.* Chicago and New York, 1918. E.F. Caldwell. *A Souvenir History of Lawrence, Kansas.* Lawrence, KS, 1898. Pension File and Military Service File, National Archives. Letters Received, Volunteer Service Branch, Adjutant General's Office, Files B643(VS)1862 and M1733(VS)1863, National Archives.

Owen Abbott Bassett, post-war (E.F. Caldwell. *A Souvenir History of Lawrence, Kansas.* Lawrence, Kansas, 1898).

William Fletcher Cloud

Major, 2 KS Infantry, May 23, 1861. Colonel, 10 KS Infantry, March 27, 1862. Although transferred to the colonelcy of the 2 KS Cavalry, May 26, 1862, in response to a War Department directive establishing Colonel William Weer of the 4 KS Infantry as colonel of the recently consolidated 10 KS Infantry, he was not mustered as colonel until Feb. 25, 1864, to date from June 1, 1862 (later modified to May 26, 1862). Commanded 3 Brigade, Department of Kansas, Aug.–Oct. 1862. Commanded 3 Brigade, 1 Division, Army of the Frontier, Department of the Missouri, Oct.–Dec. 1862. Commanded 2 Brigade, 1 Division, Army of the Frontier, Department of the Missouri, Jan.–Feb. 1863. Commanded District of Southwestern Missouri, Department of the Missouri, Feb.–July 1863. Commanded 2 Brigade, District of the Frontier, Department of the Missouri, Sept.–Nov. 1863. Acting ADC, Staff of Major Gen. Samuel R. Curtis, Department of Kansas, Oct. 1864. Honorably mustered out, Jan. 19, 1865. Colonel, 15 KS Cavalry, July 26, 1865. Commanded 3 Sub-District, District of the Upper Arkansas, Department of the Missouri, Aug. 1865. Honorably mustered out, Oct. 19, 1865. Battle honors: Wilson's Creek, Shelbina, Old Fort Wayne, Cane Hill, Prairie Grove, Devil's Backbone, Price's Missouri Expedition (Big Blue, Westport, Mine Creek).

Born: March 23, 1825, Champaign Co., OH
Died: March 4, 1905, Kansas City, MO
Other Wars: Mexican War (Sergeant, Co. K, 2 OH Infantry)
Occupation: Merchant tailor before war. Lawyer and real estate agent after war.
Offices/Honors: Missouri House of Representatives, 1871–73. Deputy Collector, U.S. Internal Revenue Service, 1877–85.
Miscellaneous: Resided Emporia, Lyon Co., KS, 1858–67; Carthage, Jasper Co., MO, 1867–94; and Kansas City, MO, 1894–1905. Author of *Church and State or Mexican Politics from Cortez to Diaz* (Kansas City, MO, 1896).
Buried: Park Cemetery, Carthage, MO (Block 13, Lot 24)

William Fletcher Cloud (KansasMemory.org, Kansas Historical Society, Item No. 221223).

William Fletcher Cloud (Parker & Tomlinson, Fort Scott, Kansas; William L. Webb. *Battles and Biographies of Missourians or the Civil War Period of Our State*. Kansas City, Missouri, 1900).

William Fletcher Cloud (A.C. Nichols, Photographist, 62 Delaware St., Leavenworth, Kansas; KansasMemory.org, Kansas Historical Society, Item No. 227434/page 23).

References: *The History of Jasper County, Missouri.* Des Moines, IA, 1883. William L. Webb. *Battles and Biographies of Missourians or the Civil War Period of Our State.* Kansas City, MO, 1900. Marvin L. Van Gilder. *Jasper County: The First Two Hundred Years.* N.p., 1995. Obituary, *Kansas City Star,* March 4, 1905. Obituary, *Carthage Evening Press,* March 6, 1905. Wiley Britton, "A Day With Colonel W.F. Cloud," *Chronicles of Oklahoma,* Vol. 5, No. 3 (September 1927). J.T. Pratt. *Pen-Pictures of the Officers and Members of the House of Representatives of the Twenty-Sixth General Assembly of Missouri.* N.p., 1872. Military Service File, National Archives. Letters Received, Volunteer Service Branch, Adjutant General's Office, Files C1866(VS)1863 and M1733(VS)1863, National Archives.

Gustavus Adolphus Colton

Colonel, 5 KS State Militia, Sept. 28, 1863. Battle honors: Price's Missouri Expedition (Big Blue, Westport).
Born: Oct. 20, 1828 Woodstock, VT
Died: July 26, 1894, Kansas City, MO
Occupation: Lawyer, newspaper editor, and real estate agent

Gustavus Adolphus Colton (pre-war) (Kansas-Memory.org, Kansas Historical Society, Item No. 2366).

Offices/Honors: Kansas Territory House of Representatives, 1859–60 (Speaker 1860). Kansas House of Representatives, 1861. Kansas Senate, 1865.
Miscellaneous: Resided Paola, Miami Co., KS; and Kansas City, MO
Buried: Paola Cemetery, Paola, KS (Oak Grove Addition, Southern Half, Row 6, Lot 11)
References: Charles F. Ritter and Jon L. Wakelyn. *American Legislative Leaders, 1850–1910.* Westport, CT, 1989. Alfred T. Andreas. *History of the State of Kansas.* Chicago, IL, 1883. George W. Colton. *A Genealogical Record of the Descendants of Quartermaster George Colton.* Lancaster, PA, 1912. *The United States Biographical Dictionary.* Kansas Volume. Chicago and Kansas City, 1879. George W. Martin, editor. *Transactions of the Kansas State Historical Society, 1907–08.* Topeka, KS, 1908. Obituary, *Kansas City Star,* July 27, 1894. Obituary, *Osawatomie Graphic,* July 27, 1894.

John Conover

2 Lieutenant, Abernathy's Co., KS Home Guards, July 25, 1861. Honorably mustered out, Aug. 27, 1861. 2 Lieutenant, Co. A, 8 KS Infantry, Aug. 28, 1861. 2 Lieutenant, Co. I, 8 KS Infantry, Oct. 31, 1861. 1 Lieutenant, Co. I, 8 KS Infantry, Dec. 12, 1861. Captain, Co. F, 8 KS Infantry, March 15, 1862. Major, 8 KS Infantry, Aug. 23, 1864. Lieutenant Colonel, 8 KS Infantry, Sept. 30, 1864. *Colonel,* 8 KS Infantry, Nov. 21, 1864. Honorably mustered out, Nov. 28, 1865. Bvt. Colonel, USV, March 13, 1865, for gallant and meritorious services during the war (Declined, "…if they were only given to those deserving them, to officers who have seen service in the field, who did their whole duty in action, then a brevet commission would be valued, and the party receiving it would accept it as an honor, and feel that his government appreciated his services, but how different are these papers issued"). Battle honors: Chickamauga, Chattanooga-Ringgold Campaign (Orchard Knob, Missionary Ridge), Atlanta Campaign, Nashville.
Born: Nov. 27, 1835 near New Brunswick, NJ
Died: Jan. 8, 1914 Kansas City, MO
Occupation: Hardware merchant
Miscellaneous: Resided Leavenworth, Leavenworth Co., KS, to 1875; and Kansas City, MO, 1875–1914
Buried: Elmwood Cemetery, Kansas City, MO (Block B, Lot 5)

John Conover (courtesy Missouri Historical Society, St. Louis [P0232-2990]).

John Conover, post-war (Theodore S. Case, editor. *History of Kansas City, Missouri.* Syracuse, New York, 1888).

References: William E. Connelley. *A Standard History of Kansas and Kansans.* Chicago and New York, 1918. Carrie Westlake Whitney. *Kansas City, Missouri: Its History and Its People, 1808–1908.* Chicago, IL, 1908. Theodore S. Case, editor. *History of Kansas City, Missouri.* Syracuse, NY, 1888. Obituary, *Leavenworth Times,* Jan. 9, 1914. Obituary Circular, Whole No. 390, Kansas MOLLUS. *The United States Biographical Dictionary.* Kansas Volume. Chicago and Kansas City, 1879. Bill McFarland. *Keep the Flag to the Front: The Story of the Eighth Kansas Volunteer Infantry.* Overland Park, KS, 2008. *Society of the Army of the Cumberland. Forty-Second Reunion, Chattanooga, Tenn.* Chattanooga, TN, 1914. Pension File and Military Service File, National Archives. Letters Received, Commission Branch, Adjutant General's Office, File C1285(CB)1866, National Archives.

Stephen Stanley Cooper

Colonel, 4 KS State Militia, Nov. 4, 1863. Superseded as colonel by William D. McCain, Nov. 16, 1864.

Born: Aug. 20, 1826 Mount Carmel, IL

Died: Dec. 4, 1899 Oskaloosa, KS

Education: Attended Indiana Asbury (now DePauw) University, Greencastle, IN. Attended Rush Medical College, Chicago, IL.

Other Wars: Mexican War (Private, Co. K, 15 U.S. Infantry)

Occupation: Physician, dry goods merchant, and hotelkeeper

Offices/Honors: Kansas Territory House of Representatives, 1857–58. Treasurer, Jefferson Co., KS, 1862–64. Kansas Senate, 1867–68. Kansas House of Representatives, 1887.

Miscellaneous: Resided Oskaloosa, Jefferson Co., KS

Buried: Pleasant View Cemetery, Oskaloosa, KS

References: Obituary, *Oskaloosa Independent,* Dec. 8, 1899. Obituary, *Valley Falls New Era,* Dec. 9, 1899. George W. Martin, editor. *Transactions of the Kansas State Historical Society, 1907–08.* Topeka, KS, 1908. Alfred T. Andreas. *History of the State of Kansas.* Chicago, IL, 1883. *The United States Biographical Dictionary.* Kansas Volume. Chicago and Kansas City, 1879. Pension File, National Archives.

David Bruen Corwin

Lieutenant Colonel, 2 Indian Home Guards, KS Infantry, June 22, 1862, Accepted appointment as Colonel, 5 Indian Home Guards, KS Infantry, Jan. 11, 1863. The regiment failing to complete organization, he was mustered out of service to date Jan. 11, 1863, thereby essentially negating his actual service to Sept. 15, 1863, when he was relieved from duty. Official recognition of his service as colonel finally occurred March 19, 1915, in response to a ruling by Judge Advocate General Enoch H. Crowder. Battle honors: Expedition into Indian Territory, Shirley's Ford, Newtonia, Prairie Grove, Van Buren.

Born: Nov. 27, 1839 Dayton, OH
Died: April 9, 1917, Cincinnati, OH
Education: Graduated Cincinnati (OH) Law School, 1866
Occupation: Freighting contractor before war. Lawyer and capitalist after war.
Offices/Honors: Dayton City Solicitor, 1867–71 and 1889–91. Ohio Senate, 1874–76.
Miscellaneous: Resided Dayton, Montgomery Co., OH
Buried: Woodland Cemetery, Dayton, OH (Section 44, Lot 1129)
References: *The National Cyclopedia of American Biography*. Vol. 17. New York City, NY, 1920. Obituary, *Dayton Daily News*, April 10, 1917. Augustus W. Drury. *History of the City of Dayton and Montgomery County, Ohio*. Chicago, IL, 1909. *History of Dayton, Ohio*. Dayton, OH, 1889. Pension File and Military Service File, National Archives. Letters Received, Volunteer Service Branch, Adjutant General's Office, Files C1425(VS)1862 and I581(VS)1862, National Archives. Obituary Circular, Whole No. 1133, Ohio MOLLUS.

David Bruen Corwin, post-war (*The National Cyclopedia of American Biography*. Volume 17. New York City, New York, 1920).

Alson Chapin Davis

Colonel, 9 KS Infantry, Jan. 9, 1862. Resigned Feb. 20, 1862.

Born: Nov. 22, 1830 Yates, Orleans Co., NY
Died: July 12, 1881, Longmeadow, MA
Education: Graduated Union College, Schenectady, NY, 1856. Graduated Albany (NY) Law School, 1856.
Occupation: Lawyer
Offices/Honors: Attorney General, Kansas Territory, 1858–61
Miscellaneous: Resided Wyandotte Co., KS, before war; and Brooklyn, NY, after war. Brother-in-law of Bvt. Brig. Gen. Roy Stone.
Buried: Green-Wood Cemetery, Brooklyn, NY (Section G, Lot 19891)
References: Obituary, *Brooklyn Daily Eagle*, July 14, 1881. Obituary, *Wyandott Herald*, July 21, 1881. Obituary, *New York Herald*, July 14, 1881. George W. Martin, editor. *Transactions of the Kansas State Historical Society, 1907–08*. Topeka, KS, 1908. Obituary, *New York Tribune*, July 14, 1881. Henry C. Johnson, editor. *The Tenth General Catalogue of the Psi Upsilon Fraternity*. Bethlehem, PA, 1888. Leander Hall. *Half Century History of the Class of 1856, Union College*. N.p., 1906. *Wyandotte County and Kansas City, Kansas, Historical and Biographical*. Chicago, IL, 1890. Perl W. Morgan, editor. *History of Wyandotte County, Kansas, and Its People*. Chicago, IL, 1911.

Werter Renick Davis

Chaplain, 12 KS Infantry, Sept. 30, 1862. Resigned Jan. 26, 1864, to accept promotion. Lieutenant Colonel, 16 KS Cavalry, March 10, 1864. Commanded Post of Fort Leavenworth, District of North Kansas, Department of Kansas, Sept. 1864–Jan. 1865. Colonel, 16 KS Cavalry, Oct. 8, 1864. Commanded Post of Fort Leavenworth, District of North Kansas, Department of the Missouri, Jan.–April 1865. Commanded District of North Kansas, Department of the Missouri, April 1865. Commanded Post of Fort Laramie, Dakota Territory, District of the Plains, Department of the Missouri, July–Sept. 1865. Honorably mustered out, Nov. 28, 1865. Battle honors: Price's Missouri Expedition.

Born: April 1, 1815, Circleville, OH
Died: June 22, 1893, Baldwin City, KS
Education: Attended Kenyon College, Gambier OH. M.D., Cincinnati (OH) Medical College, 1858. D.D., Indiana Asbury (now DePauw) University, Greencastle, IN, 1859.

Werter Renick Davis, post-war (Homer K. Ebright. *The History of Baker University*. Baldwin City, Kansas, 1951).

Samuel Adams Drake, post-war (Massachusetts MOLLUS collection, USAMHI [Commandery Series, Vol. 9, p. 379).

Occupation: Methodist clergyman
Offices/Honors: President, Baker University, Baldwin City, KS, 1858–62. Kansas House of Representatives, 1861.
Miscellaneous: Resided Baldwin City, Douglas Co., KS
Buried: Oakwood Cemetery, Baldwin City, KS (East Half Main Section, NE Corner)
References: Homer K. Ebright. *The History of Baker University*. Baldwin City, KS, 1951. Virginia G. Markham. *John Baldwin and Son Milton Come to Kansas: An Early History of Baldwin City, Baker University, and Methodism in Kansas*. Baldwin City, KS, 1982. Obituary, *Lawrence Weekly World*, June 29, 1893. Obituary, *Wyandott Herald*, June 29, 1893. Obituary, *Lawrence Daily Journal*, June 22, 1893. *Alumni Record of Baker University*. Baldwin City, KS, 1917. Alfred T. Andreas. *History of the State of Kansas*. Chicago, IL, 1883. Pension File and Military Service File, National Archives. George W. Martin, editor. *Transactions of the Kansas State Historical Society, 1907–08*. Topeka, KS, 1908. James Grant Wilson and John Fiske, editors. *Appletons' Cyclopedia of American Biography*. New York City, NY, 1888.

Samuel Adams Drake

Colonel, 1 KS State Militia, Sept. 17, 1863. Brig. Gen., 1 Brigade, KS State Militia, Feb. 29, 1864. Lieutenant Colonel, 17 KS Infantry, July 28, 1864. Commanded Post of Paola, District of South Kansas, Department of Kansas, Oct. 1864. Honorably mustered out, Nov. 16, 1864. Battle honors: Price's Missouri Expedition.
Born: Dec. 19, 1833 Boston, MA
Died: Dec. 4, 1905 Kennebunkport, ME
Occupation: Bookseller and stationer before war. Historian after war. Author of twenty-three books, mostly relating to historical events in New England and the Middle West.
Miscellaneous: Resided Boston, MA, and Leavenworth, Leavenworth Co., KS, to 1870; Melrose, Middlesex Co., MA, 1870–86; and Kennebunkport, York Co., ME, 1887–1905. Brother of Bvt. Brig. Gen. George B. Drake.
Buried: Wyoming Cemetery, Melrose, MA
References: Charles H. Pope, "Deaths: Samuel Adams Drake," *The New England Historical and Genealogical Register*, Vol. 60 (July 1906). Allen Johnson and Dumas Malone, editors. *Dictionary of American Biography*. New York City, NY, 1964. *The National Cyclopedia of American*

Biography. Vol. 25. New York City, NY, 1936. Alice S. Thompson. *The Drake Family of New Hampshire: Robert, of Hampton, and Some of His Descendants.* Concord, NH, 1962. Obituary, *Boston Journal,* Dec. 5, 1905. Obituary, *Boston Daily Globe,* Dec. 4, 1905. Pension File and Military Service File, National Archives.

Robert Wilkinson Furnas

Colonel, 1 Indian Home Guards, KS Infantry, May 22, 1862. Commanded Indian Brigade, Department of Kansas, July–Aug. 1862. Claiming that he only accepted the colonelcy of Indian troops "on the representations of my friends … that my presence would not be required longer than about September or October," he submitted his resignation, Sept. 7, 1862, explaining that "I have always doubted the propriety and policy of arming and placing in the field Indians. Five months connection with an Indian regiment only confirms me in the opinion that full-blood Indians cannot be made soldiers, and that to attempt it is a useless waste of both time and money." Major Gen. James G. Blunt would not forward the resignation to the War Department in this form. It was finally forwarded and accepted, Nov. 22, 1862, stating simply, "my domestic and pecuniary affairs are in such a condition as to require my immediate presence." Captain, Co. E, 2 NE Cavalry, Dec. 8, 1862. Colonel, 2 NE Cavalry, March 24, 1863. Honorably mustered out, Dec. 1, 1863. Battle honors: Expedition into Indian Territory, Expedition against Indians in Dakota (White Stone Hill).

Born: May 5, 1824, near Troy, Miami Co., OH
Died: June 1, 1905, Lincoln, NE
Occupation: Newspaper editor and horticulturist
Offices/Honors: Nebraska Territory Council, 1857–61. Governor of Nebraska, 1873–75.
Miscellaneous: Resided Brownville, Nemaha Co., NE
Buried: Walnut Grove Cemetery, Brownville, NE (Lot 298)
References: J. Sterling Morton. *Illustrated History of Nebraska: A History of Nebraska from the Earliest Explorations of the Trans-Mississippi Region.* Lincoln, NE, 1911. *A Biographical and Genealogical History of Southeastern Nebraska.* Chicago and New York, 1904. Allen Johnson and Dumas Malone, editors. *Dictionary of American Biography.* New York City, NY, 1964. Obituary, *Nebraska State Journal,* June 2, 1905. A.C. Edmunds. *Pen Sketches of Nebraskans.* Lincoln, NE, 1871. Alfred T. Andreas. *History of the State of Nebraska.* Chicago, IL, 1882. *Biographical Souvenir of the Counties of Buffalo, Kearney and Phelps, Nebraska.* Chicago, IL, 1890. Robert Sobel and John Raimo, editors. *Biographical Directory of the Governors of the United States, 1789–1978.* Westport, CT, 1988. Thomas W. Tipton. *Forty Years of Nebraska at Home and in Congress.* Lincoln, NE, 1902. Robert C. Farb, "The Military Career of Robert W. Furnas," *Nebraska History,* Vol. 32, No. 1 (March 1951). Obituary Circular, Whole No. 231, Nebraska MOLLUS. Pension File and Military Service File, National Archives. Letters Received, Volunteer Service Branch, Adjutant General's Office, File C533(VS)1867, National Archives. Chris Rein, "The U.S. Army, Indian Agency, and the Path to Assimilation: The First Indian Home Guards in the American Civil War," *Kansas History: A Journal of the Central Plains,* Vol. 36, No. 1 (Spring 2013). M. Jane Johansson, editor. *Albert C. Ellithorpe: The First Indian Home Guards and the Civil War on the Trans-Mississippi Frontier.* Baton Rouge, LA, 2016.

Robert Wilkinson Furnas (pre-war, 1855) (J. Sterling Morton. *Illustrated History of Nebraska: A History of Nebraska from the Earliest Explorations of the Trans-Mississippi Region.* Lincoln, Nebraska, 1911.)

Robert Henry Graham

Robert Wilkinson Furnas (seated leftmost, with Major John Taffe, Lieut. Col. William F. Sapp, Major John W. Pearman, Surgeon Aurelius Bowen, Adjutant Henry M. Atkinson, and Major George Armstrong, left to right) (J. Sterling Morton. *Illustrated History of Nebraska: A History of Nebraska from the Earliest Explorations of the Trans-Mississippi Region*. Lincoln, Nebraska, 1911).

Captain, Graham's Co., MO Cavalry, Aug. 8, 1861. Lieutenant Colonel, 14 MO Home Guards, Sept. 3, 1861. Discharged Oct. 19, 1861. *Colonel*, 9 KS Infantry, Nov. 11, 1861. Colonel, 8 KS Infantry, Feb. 28, 1862, upon the resignation of Colonel Henry W. Wessells of the 8 KS Infantry and the consolidation of the regiment with a battalion raised for service in New Mexico. Provost Marshal General of Kansas, March–May 1862. Honorably discharged, Sept. 30, 1862, on account of physical disability.

Born: 1834 Italy, Yates Co., NY
Died: Nov. 11, 1862 Lima, NY (consumption)
Education: Attended Genesee Wesleyan Seminary and Genesee College, Lima, NY. Graduated Albany (NY) Law School, 1857.
Occupation: Lawyer and newspaper editor
Miscellaneous: Resided Moline, Rock Island Co., IL; and Lima, Livingston Co., NY
Buried: Mount Albion Cemetery, Albion, NY (Chestnut Avenue, Lot 424)

Robert Wilkinson Furnas, post-war (Nebraska State Historical Society [RG4389-03]).

Robert Henry Graham (author's photograph).

References: Pension File and Military Service File, National Archives. Obituary, *Orleans American*, Nov. 20, 1862. Bill McFarland. *Keep the Flag to the Front: The Story of the Eighth Kansas Volunteer Infantry.* Overland Park, KS, 2008. Obituary, *Northern Christian Advocate (Auburn, NY)*, Dec. 17, 1862. Letters Received, Volunteer Service Branch, Adjutant General's Office, File L38(VS)1863, National Archives. *Portrait and Biographical Album of Rock Island County, Illinois.* Chicago, IL, 1885. "From Jefferson City," *Daily Missouri Democrat*, Sept. 23, 1861. www.ancestry.com.

Melvin Seth Grant

Colonel, 19 KS State Militia, May 13, 1864. Brig. Gen., 1 Brigade, KS State Militia, Aug. 22, 1864. Battle honors: Price's Missouri Expedition (Mockbee Farm).

Born: July 9, 1831, Ontario, NY

Died: Oct. 4, 1914 Leavenworth, KS

Occupation: Merchant dealing in groceries and provisions before war. Merchant dealing in agricultural implements after war.

Miscellaneous: Resided Leavenworth, Leavenworth Co., KS

Buried: Mount Muncie Cemetery, Lansing, Leavenworth Co., KS (Section 15, Lot 13)

References: Obituary, *Leavenworth Times*, Oct. 6, 1914. Obituary, *Leavenworth Post*, Oct. 5, 1914. Obituary, *Topeka Daily Capital*, Oct. 7, 1914. Alfred T. Andreas. *History of the State of Kansas.* Chicago, IL, 1883. www.ancestry.com.

James Madison Harvey

Captain, Co. H, 4 KS Infantry, Aug. 7, 1861. Captain, Co. G, 10 KS Infantry, Feb. 20, 1862. Commanded Gratiot Street Military Prison, St. Louis, MO, May–Aug. 1864. Honorably mustered out, Aug. 19, 1864. Colonel, 14 KS State Militia, Oct. 19, 1864. Battle honors: Prairie Grove.

Born: Sept. 21, 1833 Salt Sulphur Springs, Monroe Co., VA (now WV).

Died: April 15, 1894, near Vinton, Riley Co., KS

Occupation: Farmer, surveyor, and civil engineer

Offices/Honors: Kansas House of Representatives, 1865–66. Kansas Senate, 1867–68. Governor of Kansas, 1869–73. U.S. Senate, 1874–77.

Miscellaneous: Resided near Vinton, Riley Co., KS; Lynnhaven, Princess Anne Co., VA, 1884–87; and Richmond, VA, 1887–90

Buried: Highland Cemetery, Junction City, KS (Section 11)

James Madison Harvey (KansasMemory.org, Kansas Historical Society, Item No. 208183).

James Madison Harvey, post-war (New River Side Gallery, Kansas Avenue, Above 5th St., Topeka, Kansas; author's photograph).

References: William E. Connelley. *A Standard History of Kansas and Kansans.* Chicago and New York, 1918. Obituary, *Junction City Weekly Union*, April 21, 1894. Obituary, *Topeka State Journal*, April 16, 1894. *The National Cyclopedia of American Biography.* Vol. 8. New York City, NY, 1900. James Grant Wilson and John Fiske, editors. *Appletons' Cyclopedia of American Biography.* New York City, NY, 1888. James L. Harrison, compiler. *Biographical Directory of the American Congress, 1774-1949.* Washington, D.C., 1950. Alfred T. Andreas. *History of the State of Kansas.* Chicago, IL, 1883. Winifred N. Slagg. *Riley County, Kansas: A Story of Early Settlements, Rich Valleys, Azure Skies and Sunflowers.* Manhattan, KS, 1968. https://www.kshs.org/kansapedia/james-madison-harvey/17032. Pension File and Military Service File, National Archives.

Thomas Peverly Herrick

Captain, Co. A, 7 KS Cavalry, Aug. 31, 1861. Major, 7 KS Cavalry, Oct. 29, 1861. Lieutenant Colonel, 7 KS Cavalry, Sept. 3, 1862. Colonel, 7 KS Cavalry, June 1, 1863. Commanded 1 Brigade, Cavalry Division, 16 Army Corps, Department of the Tennessee, Aug.–Sept. 1863. Commanded 1 Brigade, 1 Division, Cavalry Corps, District of West Tennessee, Department of the Tennessee, July–Sept. 1864. Honorably mustered out, Feb. 28, 1865. Battle honors: Corinth, Operations on the Mississippi Railroad (Coffeeville), Iuka (July 7, 1863), Tupelo, Expedition to Oxford, MS (Hurricane Creek).

Born: Feb. 26, 1833 West Bloomfield, NY
Died: Sept. 9, 1866 Highland, KS (cholera)
Education: Attended Genesee Wesleyan Seminary, Lima, NY. Graduated Amherst (MA) College, 1856.
Occupation: Lawyer and dry goods merchant
Offices/Honors: Kansas House of Representatives, 1861
Miscellaneous: Resided Highland, Doniphan Co., KS
Buried: Highland Cemetery, Highland, KS
References: William L. Montague, editor. *Biographical Record of the Alumni of Amherst College During Its First Half Century, 1821-1871.* Amherst, MA, 1883. Henry C. Graves. *History of the Class of 1856 of Amherst College, 1852-1896.* Boston, MA, 1896. George W. Martin, editor. *Transactions of the Kansas State Historical Society, 1907-08.* Topeka, KS, 1908. Obituary, *White Cloud Kansas Chief*, Sept. 13, 1866. Obituary, *Wyandotte Commercial Gazette*, Sept. 22, 1866. Obituary, *Atchison Daily Champion*, Sept. 14, 1866.

Thomas Peverly Herrick (A.C. Nichols, Photographist, 62 Delaware St., Leavenworth, Kansas; author's photograph).

Thomas Peverly Herrick (A.C. Nichols, Photographist, 62 Delaware St., Leavenworth, Kansas; KansasMemory.org, Kansas Historical Society, Item No. 227434/page 27).

Stephen Z. Starr. *Jennison's Jayhawkers: A Civil War Cavalry Regiment and Its Commander.* Baton Rouge, LA, 1973. Pension File and Military Service File, National Archives. Letters Received, Volunteer Service Branch, Adjutant

General's Office, File H193(VS)1864, National Archives. Simeon M. Fox, "The Story of the Seventh Kansas," *Transactions of the Kansas State Historical Society, 1903-1904.* Topeka, KS, 1904.

Andrew Canard Hogan

Captain, Co. G, 19 KS State Militia, Dec. 8, 1863. Lieutenant Colonel, 19 KS State Militia, Sept. 3, 1864. Colonel, 19 KS State Militia, Oct. 14, 1864. Battle honors: Price's Missouri Expedition (Big Blue, Westport).
Born: Dec. 25, 1821 Bangor, ME
Died: Feb. 9, 1892 Henry Twp., Vernon Co., MO
Occupation: Farmer and blacksmith
Miscellaneous: Resided Leavenworth, Leavenworth Co., KS; and Henry Twp., Vernon Co., MO
Buried: Lawrence Cemetery, near Hume, Vernon Co., MO
References: Obituary, *Nevada News*, Feb. 17, 1892. Obituary, *Leavenworth Times*, Feb. 18, 1892. www.findagrave.com.

Perry Lamb Hubbard

2 Lieutenant, Co. C, 1 MI Infantry, Nov. 30, 1861. Taken prisoner, June 27, 1862, Gaines' Mill, VA. Confined in Libby Prison, Richmond, VA. Exchanged Aug. 12, 1862. 1 Lieutenant, Co. C, 1 MI Infantry, Oct. 13, 1862. Resigned Nov. 1, 1862, "because of continued ill health" due to "chronic diarrhea, hemorrhoids, and tubercular affection of the left lung." Colonel, 18 KS State Militia, March 7, 1864. Superseded as colonel by Matthew Quigg, Sept. 10, 1864. Battle honors: Gaines' Mill.
Born: May 15, 1841, Bridgewater, VT
Died: March 12, 1912, Denver, CO
Education: Attended Dickinson Institute, Romeo, MI
Occupation: School teacher before war (Taught inventor Thomas A. Edison). Lawyer, judge and real estate agent after war.
Offices/Honors: District Court Judge, 1872-77
Miscellaneous: Resided Port Huron, St. Clair Co., MI; Atchison, Atchison Co., KS, 1863-77; Ouray, Ouray Co., CO, 1877-82; and Denver, CO, 1882-1912
Buried: Fairmount Cemetery, Denver, CO (Block 70, Lot 82)

Perry Lamb Hubbard, post-war (*Representative Men of Colorado in the Nineteenth Century*. Denver, Colorado, 1902).

References: Obituary, *Denver Post*, March 12, 1912. Obituary, *Rocky Mountain News*, March 13, 1912. Obituary, *Atchison Daily Champion*, March 12, 1912. *The United States Biographical Dictionary*. Kansas Volume. Chicago and Kansas City, 1879. *Representative Men of Colorado in the Nineteenth Century*. Denver, CO, 1902. Pension File and Military Service File, National Archives. Thomas W. Herringshaw, editor. *Herringshaw's Encyclopedia of American Biography of the Nineteenth Century*. Chicago, IL, 1905.

John Barker Hubbell

Colonel, 20 KS State Militia, June 28, 1864. Battle honors: Price's Missouri Expedition (Westport).
Born: 1820 NY
Died: July 17, 1887, Onaga, KS
Occupation: Hotelkeeper and farmer before war. Farmer and merchant after war.
Offices/Honors: Sheriff, Dodge Co., MN, 1855. Minnesota Territory House of Representatives, 1856-57.
Miscellaneous: Resided Mantorville, Dodge Co., MN; and Burlingame, Shawnee Co., KS, before war; Holton, Jackson Co., KS; and Onaga, Pottawatomie Co., KS, after war
Buried: Onaga Cemetery, Onaga, KS (Block 1, Lot 7)

References: Pension File, National Archives. *History of Winona, Olmsted, and Dodge Counties.* Chicago, IL, 1884. www.findagrave.com. www.ancestry.com.

Charles Ransford Jennison

Lieutenant Colonel, 7 KS Cavalry, Sept. 24, 1861. Colonel, 7 KS Cavalry, Oct. 29, 1861. Refusing to serve under Brigadier Generals James W. Denver and Samuel D. Sturgis, who hated Kansas abolitionists such as him, and incensed by the proposed transfer of his regiment to New Mexico and by the promotion of James G. Blunt to Brigadier General over him, he resigned May 1, 1862. Colonel, 15 KS Cavalry, Oct. 17, 1863. Commanded Post of Fort Leavenworth (KS), District of the Border, Department of the Missouri, Dec. 1863–Jan. 1864. Commanded Post of Fort Leavenworth, District of North Kansas, Department of Kansas, Jan.–July 1864. Commanded 1 Sub-District, District of South Kansas, Department of Kansas, Aug.–Dec. 1864. Commanded 1 Brigade, 1 Division, Army of the Border, Department of Kansas, Oct.–Nov. 1864. Allegations of plundering and vandalism by his regiment during the pursuit of Price resulted in his court martial on charges of "Conduct to the prejudice of good order and military discipline, Gross and wilful neglect of duty, and Defrauding the Government of the United States." Found guilty of all charges, he was dishonorably dismissed, June 23, 1865. Battle honors: Price's Missouri Expedition (Lexington, Little Blue, Big Blue, Westport, Newtonia).

Born: June 6, 1834, Antwerp, Jefferson Co., NY

Died: June 21, 1884, Leavenworth, KS

Occupation: Physician before war. Farmer and stock raiser after war.

Offices/Honors: Kansas House of Representatives, 1866 and 1868. Kansas Senate, 1872.

Miscellaneous: Resided Mound City, Linn Co., KS, before war; and Leavenworth, Leavenworth Co., KS, after war

Buried: Mountain View Cemetery, Oakland, CA (Plot 36, Lot 163, unmarked)

References: *The United States Biographical Dictionary.* Kansas Volume. Chicago and Kansas City, 1879. Stephen Z. Starr. *Jennison's Jayhawkers: A Civil War Cavalry Regiment and Its Commander.* Baton Rouge, LA, 1973. Obituary, *Leavenworth Times,* June 22, 1884. William Ansel Mitchell.

Charles Ransford Jennison (J.P. Marshall & Co., 40 Delaware St., Leavenworth, Kansas; Roger D. Hunt Collection, USAMHI [RG98S-CWP207.17]).

Charles Ransford Jennison (Library of Congress [LC-DIG-cwpb-06810]).

Charles Ransford Jennison (J. A. Scholten, No. 273 South 4th Street, Corner of Convent, St. Louis, Missouri; Roger D. Hunt Collection, USAMHI [RG98S-CWP64.88]).

Charles Ransford Jennison (Wilson's Creek National Battlefield [WICR 31691]).

Charles Ransford Jennison (courtesy William McFarland).

Charles Ransford Jennison (G.R. & J.J. Collins, Leavenworth, Kansas; Wilson's Creek National Battlefield [WICR 31714]).

Linn County, Kansas: A History. Kansas City, MO, 1928. William E. Connelley. *A Standard History of Kansas and Kansans.* Chicago and New York, 1918. Pension File and Military Service File, National Archives. Letters Received, Volunteer Service Branch, Adjutant General's Office, File J92(VS)1862, National Archives. Simeon M. Fox, "The Story of the Seventh Kansas," *Transactions of the Kansas State Historical Society, 1903–1904.* Topeka, KS, 1904. George W. Martin, editor. *Transactions of the Kansas State Historical Society, 1907–08.* Topeka, KS, 1908.

Hamilton P. Johnson

Colonel, 5 KS Cavalry, Aug. 13, 1861. GSW head, Morristown, MO, Sept. 17, 1861. Battle honors: Morristown.
Born: Jan. 27, 1820 St. Clairsville, OH
Died: Sept. 17, 1861 KIA Morristown, MO
Other Wars: Mexican War (1 Lieutenant, Co. I, 3 KY Infantry)
Occupation: Lawyer and politician
Miscellaneous: Resided Leavenworth, Leavenworth Co., KS. His headstrong nature earned him the nickname of "Hog Johnson."
Buried: Mount Muncie Cemetery, Lansing, Leavenworth Co., KS (Section 15, Lot 37, unmarked)

Hamilton P. Johnson (Chicago History Museum [ICHi-68784]).

References: Alice L. Fry. *Following the Fifth Kansas Cavalry: The Letters.* Independence, MO, 1998. H. Miles Moore. *Early History of Leavenworth City and County.* Leavenworth, KS, 1906. "Encounter with the Enemy at Morristown," *White Cloud Kansas Chief,* Sept. 26, 1861. Hugh D. Fisher. *The Gun and the Gospel: Early Kansas and Chaplain Fisher.* Chicago and New York, 1899. Pension File and Military Service File, National Archives.

Julius Augustus Keeler

Private, Co. D, 2 KS Infantry (3 months), June 20, 1861. Honorably mustered out, Oct. 31, 1861. Colonel, 13 KS State Militia, Oct. 13, 1863. Battle honors: Price's Missouri Expedition.
Born: April 28, 1832, Norwalk, OH
Died: April 9, 1920, Garden City, KS
Occupation: Carpenter, builder, and farmer
Miscellaneous: Resided Olathe, Johnson Co., KS, to 1885; and Garden City, Finney Co., KS, 1885–1920
Buried: Valley View Cemetery, Garden City, KS (Weeks Zone, Lot 304)
References: Obituary, *Garden City Telegram,* April 15, 1920. Wesley B. Keeler, compiler. *Keeler Family: Ralph Keeler of Norwalk, CT, and Some of His Descendants.* Baltimore, MD, 1985. Alfred T. Andreas. *History of the State of Kansas.* Chicago, IL, 1883. Pension File, National Archives.

Warren Wirt Henry Lawrence

Captain, AAG, USV, April 14, 1862. Assigned as AAG, Staff of Brig. Gen. Robert B. Mitchell. Resigned Sept. 29, 1862, since "my personal relations with General Mitchell are of such a nature that I cannot consistently serve in the capacity to which I have been assigned under him." Colonel, 2 KS State Militia, Sept. 19, 1863. Resigned Nov. 18, 1863.
Born: Aug. 18, 1827 OH
Died: Aug. 20, 1906 Mentor, OH
Occupation: Lawyer, railroad promoter, and land speculator
Offices/Honors: Kansas House of Representatives, 1861. Kansas Secretary of State, 1863–65.
Miscellaneous: Resided Peoria City, Franklin Co., KS; Topeka, Shawnee Co., KS; and West Mentor, Lake Co., OH
Buried: Mentor Municipal Cemetery, Mentor, OH (Section 3, Lot 62)

Warren Wirt Henry Lawrence (John Goldin & Co., Washington, D.C.; Wilson's Creek National Battlefield [WICR 31929]).

References: Obituary, *Topeka Daily Capital*, Aug. 27, 1906. Obituary, *Wichita Daily Eagle*, Aug. 28, 1906. George W. Martin, editor. *Transactions of the Kansas State Historical Society, 1907–08*. Topeka, KS, 1908. Pension File, National Archives. Letters Received, Commission Branch, Adjutant General's Office, File L74(CB)1863, National Archives.

Sandy Lowe

Private, Co. D, Cass County (MO) Home Guards, June 27, 1861. Captain, Co. D, Cass County (MO) Home Guards, July 17, 1861. Honorably mustered out, Feb. 28, 1862. Private, Co. A, 7 MO State Militia Cavalry, March 8, 1862. 1 Lieutenant, Co. G, 7 MO State Militia Cavalry, April 21, 1862. GSW left hand and left breast, near Warrensburg, MO, June 17, 1862. Resigned Sept. 23, 1862. Colonel, 21 KS State Militia, Sept. 23, 1864. Battle honors: Warrensburg, Price's Missouri Expedition (Big Blue, Westport).

Born: Aug. 12, 1828 Bonhomme, St. Louis Co., MO

Died: Oct. 10, 1902 Sedan, KS
Occupation: Farmer and lumberman
Offices/Honors: Sheriff, Chautauqua Co., KS, 1890–92
Miscellaneous: Resided Wadesburg, Cass Co., MO; Urich, Henry Co., MO; Peru, Chautauqua Co., KS; Olympia, Thurston Co., WA; Baldwin City, Douglas Co., KS; and Sedan, Chautauqua Co., KS
Buried: Greenwood Cemetery, Sedan, KS
References: Pension File and Military Service File, National Archives. Obituary, *Sedan Lance*, Oct. 16, 1902. Tom A. Rafiner. *Caught Between Three Fires: Cass County, MO, Chaos, & Order No. 11, 1860–1865*. Bloomington, IN, 2010. William E. Connelley. *A Standard History of Kansas and Kansans*. Chicago and New York, 1918. www.ancestry.com.

Edward Lynde

Colonel, 9 KS Cavalry, March 29, 1862. Commanded Troops on the Border, District of the Border, Department of the Missouri, Sept.–Dec. 1863. Commanded 3 Brigade, Frontier Division, 7 Army Corps, Department of Arkansas, May–July 1864. Commanded Post of Huntersville (AR), District of Little Rock, 7 Army Corps, Department of Arkansas, July 1864. Honorably mustered out, Jan. 16, 1865, to date Nov. 25, 1864. Battle honors: Newtonia, Prairie Grove.

Edward Lynde (courtesy Henry Deeks).

Edward Lynde, post-war (*The United States Biographical Dictionary and Portrait Gallery of Eminent and Self-Made Men*. **Missouri Volume. New York, Chicago, St. Louis and Kansas City, 1878).**

Born: Oct. 16, 1820 Saybrook, CT
Died: March 27, 1897, Paola, KS
Occupation: Farmer, trader, railroad superintendent, and grain merchant
Offices/Honors: Kansas Territory House of Representatives, 1859–60. Kansas Senate, 1861–62.
Miscellaneous: Resided Valley Falls, Jefferson Co., KS, to 1868; Kansas City, MO; and Paola, Miami Co., KS
Buried: Mount Muncie Cemetery, Lansing, Leavenworth Co., KS (Section 24, Lot 254, unmarked)
References: Obituary, *Kansas City Journal*, March 29, 1897. *The United States Biographical Dictionary and Portrait Gallery of Eminent and Self-Made Men*. Missouri Volume. New York, Chicago, St. Louis and Kansas City, 1878. *The United States Biographical Dictionary*. Kansas Volume. Chicago and Kansas City, 1879. Obituary, *Oskaloosa Times*, April 2, 1897. Obituary, *Kansas City Star*, March 29, 1897. Obituary, *Leavenworth Times*, March 30, 1897. George W. Martin, editor. *Transactions of the Kansas State Historical Society, 1907–08*. Topeka, KS, 1908. Obituary Circular, Whole No. 178, Kansas MOLLUS. Pension File and Military Service File, National Archives. Letters Received, Volunteer Service Branch, Adjutant General's Office, File L115(VS)1865, National Archives.

Francis Marion Malone

Captain, Co. F, 7 KS Cavalry, Sept. 14, 1861. Major, 7 KS Cavalry, Aug. 12, 1863. Lieutenant Colonel, 7 KS Cavalry, Nov. 3, 1864. Honorably mustered out, Nov. 14, 1864. Lieutenant Colonel, 7 KS Cavalry, Nov. 19, 1864. Commanded Post of Pilot Knob (MO), 3 Sub-District, St. Louis District, Department of the Missouri, March–May 1865. Commanded 2 Sub-District, St. Louis District, Department of the Missouri, May–July 1865. Commanded Fort Kearny, Nebraska Territory, Aug. 1865. Colonel, 7 KS Cavalry, Sept. 1, 1865. Honorably mustered out, Sept. 29, 1865. Battle honors: Iuka (July 7, 1863), Chalmers' Raid in West Tennessee and North Mississippi (Wyatt), Expedition from Memphis into Mississippi (Collierville), Tupelo, Price's Missouri Expedition (Independence, Westport).
Born: July 31, 1838, Toronto, Vermilion Co., IN
Died: Feb. 9, 1927 Pana, IL
Occupation: Farmer before war. Livestock commission merchant and railroad freight agent after war.
Miscellaneous: Resided Moweaqua, Shelby Co., IL, to 1866; Pana, Christian Co., IL, 1866–83; Miles City, Custer Co., MT, 1883–1921; and Pana, Christian Co., IL, 1921–27
Buried: Linwood Cemetery, Pana, IL

Francis Marion Malone (Armstead & White, Artists, Corinth, Mississippi; KansasMemory.org, Kansas Historical Society, Item No. 227434/page 1).

References: Tom Stout, editor. *Montana Its Story and Biography.* Chicago and New York, 1921. Helen Fitzgerald Sanders. *A History of Montana.* Chicago and New York, 1913. Obituary, *Pana Palladium*, Feb. 9, 1927. David W. Dillard. *The Union Post Commanders at Pilot Knob, 1861-1865.* Ironton, MO, 2013. Ken Robison. *Montana Territory and the Civil War.* Charleston, SC, 2013. Obituary, *Anaconda Standard,* Feb. 10, 1927. Obituary, *Helena Independent,* Feb. 10, 1927. Pension File and Military Service File, National Archives. Letters Received, Volunteer Service Branch, Adjutant General's Office, File M2800(VS)1865, National Archives. Stephen Z. Starr. *Jennison's Jayhawkers: A Civil War Cavalry Regiment and Its Commander.* Baton Rouge, LA, 1973.

Edwin Cassander Manning

Private, Co. A, 2 KS Cavalry, Nov. 14, 1861. 1 Sergeant, Co. H, 2 KS Cavalry, Jan. 11, 1862. 1 Lieutenant, Co. C, 1 Indian Home Guards, KS Infantry, Sept. 10, 1862. Resigned March 9, 1863, "owing to a protracted disability," due to "orchitis of long standing following gonorrhea." Colonel, 17 KS State Militia, Nov. 14, 1863. Battle honors: Cane Hill.

Born: Nov. 7, 1838 Redford, Clinton Co., NY
Died: Dec. 11, 1915 Winfield, KS

Edwin Cassander Manning, post-war (Edwin C. Manning. *Biographical, Historical and Miscellaneous Selections.* Cedar Rapids, Iowa, 1911).

Occupation: Journalist, lawyer, and civil engineer
Offices/Honors: Postmaster, Marysville, KS, 1861. Kansas Senate, 1863-66. Kansas House of Representatives, 1871, 1873-74, and 1879. Founder of the city of Winfield, KS.
Miscellaneous: Resided Marysville, Marshall Co., KS, to 1866; Manhattan, Riley Co., KS, 1866-68; Winfield, Cowley Co., KS, 1869-80 and 1896-1915; and Washington, D.C., 1882-96
Buried: Highland Cemetery, Winfield, KS
References: Edwin C. Manning. *Biographical, Historical and Miscellaneous Selections.* Cedar Rapids, IA, 1911. Obituary, *Winfield Daily Free Press*, Dec. 11, 1915. *The United States Biographical Dictionary.* Kansas Volume. Chicago and Kansas City, 1879. Obituary Circular, Whole No. 419, Kansas MOLLUS. George W. Martin, editor. *Transactions of the Kansas State Historical Society, 1901-1902.* Topeka, KS, 1902. William E. Connelley. *A Standard History of Kansas and Kansans.* Chicago and New York, 1918. Pension File and Military Service File, National Archives.

William Delana McCain

1 Lieutenant, Co. C, 4 KS State Militia, Sept. 2, 1863. Captain, Co. C, 4 KS State Militia, Dec. 7, 1863. Colonel, 4 KS State Militia, Nov. 16, 1864. Battle honors: Price's Missouri Expedition (Big Blue).

Born: Feb. 26, 1811 Chattanooga, TN
Died: March 16, 1889, Oskaloosa, KS
Occupation: Farmer
Miscellaneous: Resided Leoni, Butler Co., IA, before war; and Perry and Oskaloosa, Jefferson Co., KS, after war
Buried: Chester Cemetery, Williamstown, Jefferson Co., KS
References: Obituary, *Oskaloosa Independent*, March 23, 1889. www.ancestry.com. www.findagrave.com.

Peter McFarland

Captain, Co. C, 1 KS Infantry, May 29, 1861. GSW head, Wilson's Creek, MO, Aug. 10, 1861. Resigned Dec. 10, 1862. Colonel, 7 KS State Militia, Dec. 9, 1863. Battle honors: Wilson's Creek, Price's Missouri Expedition (Westport).

Born: 1833? Ballymore, County Armagh, Ireland
Died: Oct. 6, 1870 Leavenworth, KS
Occupation: Farmer
Offices/Honors: Probate Judge, 1864-66. Kansas Senate, 1867-68. Sheriff, Leavenworth Co., KS, 1867-70.

Miscellaneous: Resided Leavenworth, Leavenworth Co., KS

Buried: Mount Calvary Cemetery, Leavenworth, KS

References: "Col. Peter McFarland," *Leavenworth Times*, Nov. 18, 1870. Obituary, *Leavenworth Times*, Oct. 7, 1870. Obituary, *Atchison Daily Patriot*, Oct. 7, 1870. Obituary, *Daily Kansas Tribune*, Oct. 7, 1870. George W. Martin, editor. *Transactions of the Kansas State Historical Society, 1907-08*. Topeka, KS, 1908. Jesse A. Hall and Leroy T. Hand. *History of Leavenworth County, Kansas*. Topeka, KS, 1921. Military Service File, National Archives.

Andrew Jackson Mitchell

1 Lieutenant, Co. H, 2 KS Infantry (3 months), May 23, 1861. Captain, Co. H, 2 KS Infantry, June 20, 1861. Honorably mustered out, Oct. 31, 1861. Colonel, 11 KS State Militia, Oct. 28, 1863. Battle honors: Wilson's Creek, Price's Missouri Expedition.

Born: March 1, 1814, Tazewell, TN

Died: July 18, 1898, Chanute, KS

Other Wars: Mexican War (Sergeant, Co. F, 3 MO Mounted Infantry)

Occupation: Farmer

Offices/Honors: Probate Judge, Breckenridge Co. (now Lyon Co.), Kansas Territory, 1860-61

Miscellaneous: Resided near Emporia, Lyon Co., KS; Neosho Rapids, Lyon Co., KS; and Chanute, Neosho Co., KS

Buried: Elmwood Cemetery, Chanute, KS (Section 145, Block 5, Lot 8)

References: Obituary, *Chanute Daily Tribune*, July 19, 1898. Pension File, National Archives. www.ancestry.com.

James Montgomery

Colonel, 3 KS Infantry, July 25, 1861. Honorably mustered out, April 3, 1862, upon consolidation of 3 KS Infantry and 4 KS Infantry to form 10 KS Infantry. Colonel, 34 U.S. Colored Infantry, March 5, 1863. Commanded 4 Brigade, 1 Division, U.S. Forces, Morris Island (SC), Department of the South, Aug.-Nov. 1863. Commanded 3 Brigade, 1 Division, 10 Army Corps, U.S. Forces, Morris Island (SC), Department of the South, Nov. 1863-Jan. 1864. Commanded 3 Brigade, 2 Division, District of Florida, Department of the South, Feb.-April 1864. Resigned Sept. 23, 1864, on account of ill health, due to "a hydrocele of the left side of a large size and chronic bronchitis."

James Montgomery (KansasMemory.org, Kansas Historical Society, Item No. 209263).

James Montgomery (KansasMemory.org, Kansas Historical Society, Item No. 499).

Colonel, 6 KS State Militia, Oct. 15, 1864. Battle honors: Dry Wood Creek, Morristown, Jacksonville, Palatka, Darien, Olustee, Price's Missouri Expedition (Big Blue, Westport).

Born: Dec. 22, 1814 Ashtabula Co., OH

Died: Dec. 6, 1871 near Mound City, KS

Occupation: Farmer

Miscellaneous: Resided Mound City, Linn Co., KS. One of the acknowledged leaders of the Free-State movement in Kansas during 1857-61.

Buried: Woodland Cemetery, Mound City, KS (National Cemetery Plot, Grave 76)

References: William Ansel Mitchell. *Linn County, Kansas: A History*. Kansas City, MO, 1928. Allen Johnson and Dumas Malone, editors. *Dictionary of American Biography*. New York City, NY, 1964. Brian R. Dirck, "By the Hand of God: James Montgomery and Redemptive Violence," *Kansas History: A Journal of the Central Plains*, Vol. 27, No. 1-2 (Spring-Summer 2004). Alfred T. Andreas. *History of the State of Kansas*. Chicago, IL, 1883. Frank William Blackmar, editor. *Kansas: A Cyclopedia of State History*. Chicago, IL, 1912. George W. Martin, editor. *Transactions of the Kansas State Historical Society, 1897-1900*. Topeka, KS, 1900. George W. Martin, editor. *Transactions of the Kansas State Historical Society, 1901-1902*. Topeka, KS, 1902. Obituary, *Fort Scott Daily Monitor*, Dec. 9, 1871. Obituary, *Lawrence Republican Daily Journal*, Dec. 10, 1871. William E. Connelley. *A Standard History of Kansas and Kansans*. Chicago and New York, 1918. Pension File and Military Service File, National Archives. Letters Received, Colored Troops Branch, Adjutant General's Office, File W261(CT)1863, National Archives. Russell Duncan, editor. *Blue-Eyed Child of Fortune: The Civil War Letters of Colonel Robert Gould Shaw*. Athens, GA, 1992.

William Pennock

Captain, Co. A, 10 KS State Militia, Sept. 10, 1863. Colonel, 10 KS State Militia, Nov. 18, 1863. Battle honors: Price's Missouri Expedition (Westport).

Born: 1826 Waynesburg, PA

Died: Feb. 4, 1890 near Ottawa, KS

Occupation: Indian trader, dry goods merchant, and farmer

Offices/Honors: Kansas Territory Senate, 1857-58. Postmaster, Minneola, Franklin Co., KS, 1863-65. Kansas House of Representatives, 1866.

Miscellaneous: Resided Centropolis, Franklin Co., KS; and Ottawa, Franklin Co., KS

Buried: Hope Cemetery, Ottawa, KS (Block 9, Lot 12)

References: Obituary, *Ottawa Daily Republican*, Feb. 7, 1890. Obituary, *Ottawa Herald*, Feb. 13, 1890. George W. Martin, editor. *Transactions of the Kansas State Historical Society, 1907-08*. Topeka, KS, 1908.

William Addison Phillips

Captain, Additional ADC, Jan. 29, 1862. Honorably discharged, March 21, 1862. Major, 1 Indian Home Guards, KS Infantry, June 2, 1862. Colonel, 3 Indian Home Guards, KS Infantry, July 11, 1862. Commanded 3 Brigade, 1 Division, Army of the Frontier, Department of the Missouri, Oct. 1862-Jan. 1863. Commanded District of Western Arkansas and Indian Territory, Department of the Missouri, Jan.-May 1863. Commanded Post of Fort Blunt, Cherokee Nation, District of the Frontier, Department of the Missouri, June-July 1863. Commanded 1 Brigade, District of the Frontier, Department of the Missouri, Nov. 1863-Jan. 1864. Commanded 1 Brigade, District of the Frontier, Department of Kansas, Jan.-Feb. 1864. Commanded Indian Brigade, District of the Frontier, Department of Kansas, Feb.-April 1864. Commanded Indian Brigade, District of the Frontier, 7 Army Corps, Department of Arkansas, April-July 1864 and Dec. 1864-Feb. 1865. Commanded 3 Brigade, 3 Division, 7 Army Corps, Department of Arkansas, Feb.-May 1865. Honorably mustered out, June 10, 1865. Battle honors: Expedition into Indian Territory (Bayou Bernard), Newtonia, Old Fort Wayne, Cane Hill, Prairie Grove, Van Buren, Fayetteville, Fort Gibson, Honey Springs.

Born: Jan. 14, 1824 Paisley, Scotland

Died: Nov. 30, 1893 Fort Gibson, OK

Occupation: Lawyer and newspaper correspondent

Offices/Honors: Kansas House of Representatives, 1866. U.S. House of Representatives, 1873-79.

Miscellaneous: Resided Salina, Saline Co., KS

Buried: Gypsum Hill Cemetery, Salina, KS (Block A, Lot 48)

References: Obituary, *Salina Daily Republican*, Dec. 1, 1893. Allen Johnson and Dumas Malone, editors. *Dictionary of American Biography*. New York City, NY, 1964. Alfred T. Andreas. *History of the State of Kansas*. Chicago, IL, 1883. Frank W. Blackmar, editor. *Kansas: A Cyclopedia of State History*. Chicago, IL, 1912. Franklin G. Adams, editor. *Transactions of the Kansas State Historical Society, 1889-96*. Topeka, KS, 1896. William Horatio Barnes. *The American Government: Biographies of Members of the House of Representatives of the Forty-Third Congress*.

William Addison Phillips (KansasMemory.org, Kansas Historical Society, Item No. 3991).

William Addison Phillips, U.S. House of Representatives, 1873 (William Horatio Barnes. *The American Government: Biographies of Members of the House of Representatives of the Forty-Third Congress*. New York City, New York, 1874).

New York City, NY, 1874. Obituary, *Cherokee Advocate*, Dec. 2, 1893. Obituary, *Topeka Daily Capital*, Dec. 1, 1893. Pension File and Military Service File, National Archives. Letters Received, Volunteer Service Branch, Adjutant General's Office, File P292(VS)1866, National Archives. Letters Received, Commission Branch, Adjutant General's Office, File P402(CB)1863, National Archives. Wiley Britton. *The Union Indian Brigade in the Civil War*. Kansas City, MO, 1922. Annie Heloise Abel. *The American Indian as Participant in the Civil War*. Cleveland, OH, 1919. James L. Harrison, compiler. *Biographical Directory of the American Congress, 1774–1949*. Washington, D.C., 1950. Richard Cordley. *A History of Lawrence, Kansas, from the First Settlement to the Close of the Rebellion*. Lawrence, KS, 1895. Samuel Lamborn, compiler. *The Genealogy of the Lamborn Family*. Philadelphia, PA, 1894.

Preston Bierce Plumb

Recruiting 2 Lieutenant, 11 KS Cavalry, Aug. 12, 1862. Captain, Co. C, 11 KS Cavalry, Sept. 10, 1862. Major, 11 KS Cavalry, Sept. 25, 1862. Chief of Staff and Provost Marshal, Staff of Brig. Gen. Thomas Ewing, Jr., District of the Border, Department of the Missouri, June–Sept. 1863. Commanded Post of Humboldt (KS), District of the Border, Department of the Missouri, Dec. 1863. Commanded Post of Humboldt (KS), Troops in Kansas and Missouri, Department of Kansas, Jan.–Feb. 1864. Commanded Post of Humboldt (KS), District of South Kansas, Department of Kansas, March–July 1864. Lieutenant Colonel, 11 KS Cavalry, April 21, 1864. Commanded Post of Olathe (KS), District of South Kansas, Department of Kansas, Aug.–Oct. 1864. Commanded Fort Halleck, Dakota Territory, District of the Plains, June 1865. *Colonel*, 11 KS Cavalry, July 17, 1865. Honorably mustered out, Sept. 13, 1865. Battle honors: Cane Hill, Prairie Grove, Van Buren, Quantrill's Raid into Kansas, Price's Missouri Expedition (Little Blue, Big Blue, Westport), Dry Creek.

Born: Oct. 12, 1837 Berkshire, Delaware Co., OH

Died: Dec. 20, 1891 Washington, D.C.

Occupation: Lawyer and journalist

Offices/Honors: Kansas House of Representatives, 1862, 1867 (Speaker), and 1868. U.S. Senate, 1877–91.

Miscellaneous: Resided Emporia, Lyon Co., KS

Buried: Maplewood Cemetery, Emporia, KS (Section 3, Lot 113)

Preston Bierce Plumb (Brown's Photographic Gallery, Paola, Kansas; Massachusetts MOLLUS collection, USAMHI [Vol. 130, p. 6662]).

Preston Bierce Plumb, post-war (Brady-Handy Photograph Collection, Library of Congress [LC-DIG-cwpbh-04517]).

References: William E. Connelley. *The Life of Preston B. Plumb, 1837–1891.* Chicago, IL, 1913. Allen Johnson and Dumas Malone, editors. *Dictionary of American Biography.* New York City, NY, 1964. Frank William Blackmar, editor. *Kansas: A Cyclopedia of State History.* Chicago, IL, 1912. Obituary, *Emporia Standard*, Dec. 26, 1891. Obituary, *Topeka State Journal*, Dec. 21, 1891. William E. Connelley. *A Standard History of Kansas and Kansans.* Chicago and New York, 1918. Laura M. French. *History of Emporia and Lyon County.* Emporia, KS, 1929. *The United States Biographical Dictionary.* Kansas Volume. Chicago and Kansas City, 1879. *The National Cyclopedia of American Biography.* Vol. 2. New York City, NY, 1921. Alfred T. Andreas. *History of the State of Kansas.* Chicago, IL, 1883. James L. Harrison, compiler. *Biographical Directory of the American Congress, 1774–1949.* Washington, D.C., 1950. Military Service File, National Archives.

James Morgarum Pomeroy

Captain, Co. B, 16 NY Infantry, May 15, 1861. Resigned July 9, 1861, since "a fundamental dis-

Preston Bierce Plumb (Massachusetts MOLLUS Collection, USAMHI [Vol. 130, p. 6662]).

agreement exists between myself and the two other commissioned officers of my company, occasioning on their part a failure to yield the cooperation and support indispensable to the thorough discipline and efficiency of my command." Major, 2 KS Cavalry, Feb. 28, 1862. GSW right thigh, Little Santa Fe, MO, March 22, 1862. Major, 9 KS Cavalry, March 27, 1862. Appointed *Colonel*, 4 Indian Home Guards, KS Infantry, Dec. 26, 1862. Declined appointment, April 26, 1863. Regiment did not complete organization. Honorably mustered out, Jan. 16, 1865. Appointed *Colonel*, U.S. Veteran Volunteers, Feb. 15, 1865. Lieutenant Colonel, 4 U.S. Veteran Volunteers, July 20, 1865. Honorably mustered out, April 27, 1866. Bvt. Colonel, USV, March 13, 1865, for gallant and meritorious services during the war. Battle honors: Little Santa Fe, Newtonia, Fort Gibson.
Born: Aug. 8, 1836 Belleville, NJ
Died: Nov. 27, 1887 St. Louis, MO
Education: Graduated Wesleyan University, Middletown, CT, 1856
Occupation: Lawyer and author
Offices/Honors: Adjutant General of Arkansas, 1877–79
Miscellaneous: Resided Little Rock, Pulaski Co., AR. Author of several works on the Constitution of the State of Arkansas.
Buried: Jefferson Barracks National Cemetery, St. Louis, MO (Section 59, Grave 11579)
References: *Alumni Record of Wesleyan University, Middletown, Connecticut*. Third Edition, 1881–83. Hartford, CT, 1883. Albert A. Pomeroy. *History and Genealogy of the Pomeroy Family*. Toledo, OH, 1912. *Obituary Record of Alumni of Wesleyan University, for the Academic Year Ending June 28, 1888*. Middletown, CT, 1888. Henry C. Johnson, editor. *The Tenth General Catalogue of the Psi Upsilon Fraternity*. Bethlehem, PA, 1888. Pension File and Military Service File, National Archives. Letters Received, Volunteer Service Branch, Adjutant General's Office, File P97(VS)1864, National Archives. Obituary, *Daily Arkansas Gazette*, Dec. 4, 1887.

Frederick Williams Potter

Captain, Co. B, 16 KS State Militia, Oct. 3, 1863. Colonel, 16 KS State Militia, Dec. 24, 1863.
Born: July 18, 1833, Gloucestershire, England
Died: March 18, 1922, San Jose, CA
Occupation: Farmer
Offices/Honors: Kansas House of Representatives, 1862 and 1874. Kansas Senate, 1863–66.
Miscellaneous: Resided Burlington, Coffey Co., KS, to 1892; and San Jose, Santa Clara Co., CA, after 1892
Buried: Cremated Oakland (CA) Crematory and ashes scattered at sea
References: Obituary, *Oakland Tribune*, March 20, 1922. Obituary, *San Jose Mercury News*, March 21, 1922. www.ancestry.com. www.findagrave.com.

John Thomas Price

Colonel, 15 KS State Militia, Nov. 4, 1863.
Born: Feb. 14, 1826 Louisville, KY
Died: Dec. 30, 1900 Milford, KS
Education: Attended Hanover (IN) College
Other Wars: Mexican War (Sergeant, Co. I, 1 U.S. Dragoons, re-enlisted and discharged, July 1, 1854, as Quartermaster Sergeant)
Occupation: Merchant and farmer
Offices/Honors: Sheriff, Riley Co., KS, 1855–56. Postmaster, Fort Riley, KS, 1866–68. Treasurer, Geary Co., KS, 1872–76.
Miscellaneous: Resided Junction City, Davis Co. (now Geary Co.), KS; and Milford, Geary Co., KS
Buried: Highland Cemetery, Junction City, KS (Section 1, Lot 94)
References: Obituary, *Junction City Daily Union*, Jan. 3, 1901. *The United States Biographical Dictionary. Kansas Volume*. Chicago and Kansas City, 1879. Alfred T. Andreas. *History of the State of Kansas*. Chicago, IL, 1883. "Early Day Sheriffs in Riley County," *Kansas Kin*, Vol. 29, No. 2 (May 1991). Pension File, National Archives. George W. Martin, editor. *Collections of the Kansas State Historical Society, 1909–10*. Topeka, KS, 1910. Letters Received, Volunteer Service Branch, Adjutant General's Office, File K394(VS)1864, National Archives. William A. Dobak. *Fort Riley and Its Neighbors*. Norman, OK, 1998.

Matthew Quigg

Captain, Co. B, 4 KS Infantry, July 16, 1861. Captain, Co. B, 10 KS Infantry, April 3, 1862. GSW right hip, Prairie Grove, AR, Dec. 7, 1862. Commanded Post of Fort Leavenworth (KS), District of the Border, Department of the Missouri, Sept.–Nov. 1863. Commanded Provost Guard, Post of St. Louis, Department of the Missouri, June–July 1864. Honorably mustered out, Aug. 19, 1864. Colonel, 18 KS State Militia, Sept. 10, 1864. Battle honors: Prairie Grove, Price's Missouri Expedition (Little Blue).

Born: Jan. 2, 1837 Cass Co., IL
Died: Aug. 20, 1890 Atchison, KS
Occupation: Freighting business before war. Wholesale grocer and railway fuel agent after war.
Miscellaneous: Resided Atchison, Atchison Co., KS
Offices/Honors: Kansas Senate, 1865–66
Buried: Mount Calvary Cemetery, Atchison, KS
References: Obituary, *Atchison Daily Patriot*, Aug. 21, 1890. Obituary, *Atchison Daily Champion*, Aug. 21, 1890. Pension File and Military Service File, National Archives. Alfred T. Andreas. *History of the State of Kansas.* Chicago, IL, 1883. Obituary Circular, Whole No. 72, Kansas MOLLUS.

Reuben Augustus Randlett

2 Lieutenant, Co. A, 5 KS Cavalry, July 16, 1861. GSW right arm, Morristown, MO, Sept. 17, 1861. Resigned, June 11, 1862, on account of disability from "chronic hepatitis with enlargement of the spleen." Captain, Co. B, 2 KS State Militia, Aug. 25, 1863. Lieutenant Colonel, 2 KS State Militia, Sept. 19, 1863. Colonel, 2 KS State Militia, Nov. 30, 1863. Assistant Quartermaster, Staff of Major Gen. George W. Deitzler, KS State Militia, Oct. 1864. Battle honors: Morristown, Price's Missouri Expedition.
Born: Oct. 18, 1837 Bridgewater, NH

Reuben Augustus Randlett (courtesy David D. Finney).

Reuben Augustus Randlett, post-war (Martin, 629 Kansas Ave., Topeka, Kansas; courtesy David D. Finney).

Died: March 7, 1932, Topeka, KS
Occupation: Farmer before war. Carpenter after war.
Miscellaneous: Resided Topeka, Shawnee Co., KS
Buried: Topeka Cemetery, Topeka, KS (Section 50, Lot 36)
References: Pension File and Military Service File, National Archives. Obituary, *Topeka Daily Capital*, March 8, 1932. William E. Connelley. *Quantrill and the Border Wars.* Cedar Rapids, IA, 1910. "Married Fifty Years," *Topeka Daily Capital*, June 30, 1907. "He Was in Topeka on July 4, 1856," *Topeka Daily Capital*, March 11, 1916. www.findagrave.com.

William Young Roberts

Captain, Co. B, 1 KS Infantry, June 3, 1861. Major, 1 KS Infantry, May 12, 1862. Colonel, 1 KS Infantry, June 1, 1863. Honorably mustered out, June 17, 1864. Volunteer ADC, Staff of Major Gen. Samuel R. Curtis, Department of Kansas, Oct. 1864. Battle honors: Wilson's Creek, Caledonia and Pin Hook (LA), Vicksburg Campaign, Price's Missouri Expedition (Big Blue, Westport).
Born: May 5, 1812, Luzerne Twp., Fayette Co., PA
Died: Feb. 9, 1869 near Lawrence, KS
Occupation: Farmer and newspaper editor

Offices/Honors: Pennsylvania House of Representatives, 1851. Active in the Free-State movement in Kansas, he served as Lieutenant Governor, KS Territory, under the Topeka Constitution, 1856. Kansas Territory House of Representatives, 1860.

Miscellaneous: Resided Wyandotte (now Kansas City), Wyandotte Co., KS; and Lawrence, Douglas Co., KS

Buried: Oak Hill Cemetery, Lawrence, KS (Section 2, Lot 114)

References: Obituary, *Daily Kansas Tribune*, Feb. 10, 1869. Obituary, *Daily Kansas State Journal*, Feb. 10, 1869. Obituary, *Wyandotte Commercial Gazette*, Feb. 13, 1869. Obituary, *White Cloud Kansas Chief*, Feb. 11, 1869. Obituary, *Quincy Whig*, Feb. 16, 1869. Perl W. Morgan, editor. *History of Wyandotte County, Kansas, and Its People*. Chicago, IL, 1911. George W. Martin, editor. *Transactions of the Kansas State Historical Society, 1901–1902*. Topeka, KS, 1902. Alfred T. Andreas. *History of the State of Kansas*. Chicago, IL, 1883. Pension File and Military Service File, National Archives. Letters Received, Volunteer Service Branch, Adjutant General's Office, File P972(VS)1864, National Archives.

William Young Roberts (A.G. DaLee, Lawrence, Kansas; author's photograph).

Charles H. Robinson

Colonel, 1 KS State Militia, March 19, 1864.

Born: Dec. 25, 1829 (or 1824) Philadelphia, PA

Died: Sept. 9, 1911 Phoenix, AZ

Occupation: Architect and bridge builder. Insurance agent and bookkeeper in later years.

Offices/Honors: Assistant Assessor, U.S. Internal Revenue, 1869–74. Leavenworth (KS) City Marshal, 1889.

Miscellaneous: Resided Leavenworth, Leavenworth Co., KS; and Phoenix, Maricopa Co., AZ, after 1891

Buried: Masons Cemetery, Phoenix, AZ (Block 21, Lot 1, Grave 7)

References: Obituary, *Arizona Republican*, Sept. 10, 1911. "Funeral Service for C. H. Robinson," *Arizona Republican*, Sept. 12, 1911. www.ancestry.com. www.findagrave.com.

David Wilson Scott

Colonel, 14 KS State Militia, Nov. 9, 1863. Captain, AQM, USV, June 30, 1864. Chief Quartermaster, Staff of Bvt. Brig. Gen. James H. Ford, District of the Upper Arkansas, Department of Kansas, Jan.–April 1865. Honorably mustered out, March 13, 1866.

William Young Roberts (author's photograph).

David Wilson Scott (National Archives [Photographic Prints of Quartermaster Officers]).

Born: Aug. 3, 1819 Fairfax Co., VA
Died: Oct. 28, 1867 Fort Riley, KS
Education: Attended U.S. Military Academy, West Point, NY (Class of 1840)
Other Wars: Mexican War (1 Lieutenant, 16 U.S. Infantry)
Occupation: Wagon and forage master and acting quartermaster, Fort Riley, KS, 1855–63. Post Sutler, Fort Wallace, KS, 1866.
Miscellaneous: Resided Crawfordsville, Montgomery Co., IN; and Ogden, Riley Co., KS, after 1855
Buried: Post Cemetery, Fort Riley, KS (Section D, Grave 96)
References: Obituary, *Junction City Weekly Union*, Nov. 2, 1867. William A. Dobak. *Fort Riley and Its Neighbors.* Norman, OK, 1998. *Reports of Examining Boards as to Qualifications of Quartermaster Officers, 1864–1865*, Record Group 92, Entry 418, National Archives. Letters Received, Commission Branch, Adjutant General's Office, Files S1848(CB)1864 and S787(CB)1866, National Archives.

William Stoddard Smith

Corporal, Co. A, 7 IL Infantry, May 23, 1861. Honorably mustered out, July 25, 1861. 2 Lieutenant, Co. A, 36 IL Infantry, Aug. 20, 1861. Resigned July 9, 1862, due to "feeble health," caused by a spinal affection. Captain, Co. B, 8 KS State Militia, Sept. 16, 1862. Lieutenant Colonel, 8 KS State Militia, Nov. 10, 1863. Colonel, 8 KS State Militia, July 4, 1864. Battle honors: Pea Ridge.
Born: March 5, 1839, Turner, Du Page Co., IL
Died: Jan. 28, 1890 Cottonwood Falls, KS
Occupation: Farmer and merchant
Offices/Honors: Treasurer, Chase Co., KS, 1860–61
Miscellaneous: Resided Cottonwood Falls, Chase Co., KS
Buried: Prairie Grove Cemetery, Cottonwood Falls, KS
References: Obituary, *Chase County Courant*, Jan. 30, 1890. Howel H. Jones. *Chase County Historical Sketches.* N.p., 1940. Obituary, *Chase County Leader*, Jan. 30, 1890. Pension File and Military Service File, National Archives. Lyman G. Bennett and William M. Haigh. *History of the Thirty-Sixth Regiment Illinois Volunteers during the War of the Rebellion.* Aurora, IL, 1876.

James Donaldson Snoddy

1 Lieutenant, Co. C, 7 KS Cavalry, Dec. 22, 1861. 1 Lieutenant, Co. G, 7 KS Cavalry, Aug. 16, 1862. Upon the urgent recommendation of Lt. Col. Thomas P. Herrick, commanding 7 KS Cavalry, he was dishonorably dismissed, Dec. 30, 1862, for "inefficiency, it being impracticable to convene a Board of Examiners, his regiment being continually on the move." His peremptory dismissal "without trial and without notice of pending charges" was revoked, May 7, 1866, upon the recommendation of Lt. Gen. Ulysses S. Grant, and replaced by an honorable discharge as of the date of dismissal. Colonel, 6 KS State Militia, June 13, 1864. Refusing to recognize the authority of Major Gen. James G. Blunt to command the Kansas militia force, he was relieved from command, Oct. 16, 1864, and arrested for "disobedience of orders and mutinous conduct in the face of the enemy."
Born: Sept. 11, 1837 White Deer Valley, Lycoming Co., PA
Died: Oct. 28, 1917 Pleasanton, KS
Education: Graduated University of Michigan, Ann Arbor, MI, 1859
Occupation: Lawyer and newspaper editor
Offices/Honors: Kansas House of Representatives, 1868–70, 1881, and 1883 (Speaker). Kansas Senate, 1871–72.
Miscellaneous: Resided Mound City, Linn

Co., KS, to 1872; La Cygne, Linn Co., KS, 1872–93; and Pleasanton, Linn Co., KS, 1893–1917

Buried: Pleasanton Cemetery, Pleasanton, KS

References: George W. Martin, editor. *Transactions of the Kansas State Historical Society, 1907–08*. Topeka, KS, 1908. Obituary, *Lawrence Daily Gazette*, Nov. 2, 1917. Obituary, *Kansas City Star*, Oct. 31, 1917. Pension File and Military Service File, National Archives. Obituary, *Olathe Mirror*, Nov. 8, 1917. "Snoddy, Fighting Kansan," *Kansas City Star*, Nov. 4, 1917. "A Candidate for United States Senator Who Has No Votes," *Topeka Daily Capital*, Jan. 11, 1903. Charles F. Ritter and Jon L. Wakelyn. *American Legislative Leaders, 1850–1910*. Westport, CT, 1989. Theodore R. Chase. *The Michigan University Book, 1844–1880*. Detroit, MI, 1880. William Ansel Mitchell. *Linn County, Kansas: A History*. Kansas City, MO, 1928. Letters Received, Volunteer Service Branch, Adjutant General's Office, File H1289(VS)1862, National Archives.

Isaac Stadden

1 Lieutenant, Co. B, 6 KS Cavalry, Sept. 10, 1861. 1 Lieutenant, Adjutant, 6 KS Cavalry, March 7, 1862. Honorably discharged, Aug. 15, 1862. Colonel, 24 KS State Militia, Oct. 22, 1864.

Born: March 28, 1834, Newark, OH
Died: April 10, 1888, Fort Scott, KS
Other Wars: Mexican War (Principal Musician, Co. B, 2 OH Infantry)
Occupation: Wholesale grocer
Offices/Honors: Mayor, Fort Scott, KS, 1865. Brig. Gen., Kansas State Militia, 1883–85.
Miscellaneous: Resided Rockford, Bourbon Co., KS, to 1864; and Fort Scott, Bourbon Co., KS, after 1864
Buried: Evergreen Cemetery, Fort Scott, KS (Section 5)
References: Obituary, *Fort Scott Daily Monitor*, April 11, 1888. *The United States Biographical Dictionary*. Kansas Volume. Chicago and Kansas City, 1879. Alfred T. Andreas. *History of the State of Kansas*. Chicago, IL, 1883. Obituary, *Newton Daily Republican*, April 17, 1888. Richard S. Stadden. *Genealogy of the Stadden Family, Descendants and Relatives of Thomas Stadden and Samuel Stadden*. N.p., 1987. Thomas F. Robley. *History of Bourbon County, Kansas, to the Close of 1865*. Fort Scott, KS, 1894. Military Service File, National Archives.

Francis Bowers Swift

Captain, Co. D, 1 KS Infantry, June 3, 1861. GSW left side, Wilson's Creek, MO, Aug. 10, 1861. Resigned May 18, 1862. Colonel, 3 KS State Militia, Nov. 2, 1863. Resigned (date unknown). Captain, Co. E, 3 KS State Militia, Oct. 13, 1864. Battle honors: Wilson's Creek.

Born: Jan. 24, 1834 Brunswick, ME
Died: March 7, 1916, Girard, KS
Occupation: Printer
Offices/Honors: Kansas House of Representatives, 1865
Miscellaneous: Resided Lawrence, Douglas Co., KS, to 1882; Junction City, Geary Co., KS, 1882–84; and Girard, Crawford Co., KS, after 1884
Buried: Greenhill Cemetery, Muskogee, OK
References: Obituary, *Girard Press*, March 16, 1916. George W. Martin, editor. *Transactions of the Kansas State Historical Society, 1907–08*. Topeka, KS, 1908. Pension File and Military Service File, National Archives. Obituary, *Lawrence Daily Gazette*, March 27, 1916.

James Pugh Taylor

1 Lieutenant, Co. C, 16 IL Infantry, May 24, 1861. Resigned July 25, 1861, "owing to my relation with my company." Colonel, 22 KS State Militia, Sept. 7, 1864.

Born: Sept. 23, 1833 Coles Co., IL
Died: April 1, 1905, Seneca, KS
Occupation: Lawyer and real estate agent

James Pugh Taylor, post-war (courtesy of Thomas P. Dixon).

Offices/Honors: Probate Judge, Nemaha Co., KS, 1863
Miscellaneous: Resided Seneca, Nemaha Co., KS
Buried: Seneca City Cemetery, Seneca, KS
References: Obituary, *Seneca Tribune*, April 6, 1905. Alfred T. Andreas. *History of the State of Kansas*. Chicago, IL, 1883. Ralph Tennal. *History of Nemaha County, Kansas*. Lawrence, KS, 1916. Pension File and Military Service File, National Archives.

Frank Maie Tracy

Private, Co. A, 1 KS Infantry, May 30, 1861. GSW right side of chest and right lung, Wilson's Creek, MO, Aug. 10, 1861. 2 Lieutenant, Co. A, 1 KS Infantry, Sept. 1, 1861. 1 Lieutenant, Co. I, 1 KS Infantry, April 13, 1862. Resigned Oct. 29, 1862, "on account of disability occasioned by a gunshot wound." Captain Co. C, 9 KS State Militia, June 20, 1863. Colonel, 9 KS State Militia, Feb. 17, 1864. Battle honors: Wilson's Creek, Corinth.
Born: Jan. 3, 1838 Ralls Co., MO
Died: Feb. 13, 1888 Troy, KS
Occupation: Newspaper publisher and flour miller
Offices/Honors: Treasurer, Doniphan Co., KS, 1864–68. Postmaster, St. Joseph, MO, 1881–85.
Miscellaneous: Resided Elwood, Doniphan Co., KS, 1861–64; Troy, Doniphan Co., KS, 1864–76 and 1885–88; and St. Joseph, Buchanan Co., MO, 1859–61 and 1876–85.
Buried: Mount Olive Cemetery, Troy, KS
References: *Genealogical and Biographical Record of North-Eastern Kansas*. Chicago, IL, 1900. Obituary, *Troy Times*, Feb. 17, 1888. *History of Buchanan County, Missouri*. St. Joseph, MO, 1881. Obituary, *St. Joseph Daily Gazette*, Feb. 14, 1888. Obituary, *Topeka State Journal*, Feb. 13, 1888. Obituary, *Leavenworth Times*, Feb. 14, 1888. Pension File and Military Service File, National Archives. Alfred T. Andreas. *History of the State of Kansas*. Chicago, IL, 1883. R.F. Smith, editor. *Doniphan County, Kansas, History and Directory for 1868–9*. Wathena, KS, 1868.

Levi Stuart Treat

Colonel, 12 KS State Militia, Dec. 12, 1863. Battle honors: Price's Missouri Expedition (Westport).
Born: Jan. 19, 1814 Glastonbury, CT
Died: April 13, 1881, near Atchison, KS
Occupation: Farmer, fruit grower, and real estate speculator
Miscellaneous: Resided Atchison, Atchison Co., KS
Buried: Mount Vernon Cemetery, Atchison, KS
References: Sheffield Ingalls. *History of Atchison County, Kansas*. Lawrence, KS, 1916. John Harvey Treat. *The Treat Family: A Genealogy of Trott, Tratt, and Treat for Fifteen Generations*. Salem, MA, 1893. Obituary, *Atchison Daily Champion*, April 14, 1881. Obituary, *Atchison Daily Patriot*, April 14, 1881.

George Washington Veale

Captain, Co. A, 6 KS Cavalry, July 21, 1861. Major, 6 KS Cavalry, Dec. 1, 1862. Resigned Oct. 10, 1863, due to "the bad health and distressed condition of my family at home, and the loss and sacrifice of all that I have without any immediate attention, owing to the ill health of my partner." Colonel, 2 KS State Militia, May 9, 1864. Battle honors: Price's Missouri Expedition (Big Blue).
Born: May 20, 1833, near Washington, Daviess Co., IN
Died: Nov. 28, 1916 Topeka, KS
Education: Attended Wabash College, Crawfordsville, IN

George Washington Veale, post-war (James W. Steele. *The Battle of the Blue of the Second Regiment, K.S.M., the Fight, the Captivity, the Escape*. Chicago, Illinois, 1896).

Occupation: Dry goods merchant before war. Capitalist after war, being involved in banking, railroad, and real estate enterprises, as well as philanthropic endeavors.
Offices/Honors: Kansas Senate, 1867–68. Kansas House of Representatives, 1871, 1873, 1877, 1883, 1887, 1889, 1895.
Miscellaneous: Resided Topeka, Shawnee Co., KS
Buried: Topeka Cemetery, Topeka, KS (Section 12, Lot 4)
References: Frank W. Blackmar, editor. *Kansas: A Cyclopedia of State History.* Chicago, IL, 1912. William E. Connelley. *A Standard History of Kansas and Kansans.* Chicago and New York, 1918. Obituary, *Topeka Daily Capital*, Nov. 29, 1916. Obituary, *Topeka State Journal*, Nov. 29, 1916. James W. Steele. *The Battle of the Blue of the Second Regiment, K.S.M., October 22, 1864, the Fight, the Captivity, the Escape.* Chicago, IL, 1896. Alfred T. Andreas. *History of the State of Kansas.* Chicago, IL, 1883. *The United States Biographical Dictionary.* Kansas Volume. Chicago and Kansas City, 1879. "The Grand Old Man of Topeka," *Topeka Daily Capital*, June 25, 1916. Pension File and Military Service File, National Archives. Letters Received, Volunteer Service Branch, Adjutant General's Office, File C343(VS)1863, National Archives.

Stephen Howard Wattles

Lieutenant Colonel, 1 Indian Home Guards, KS Infantry, May 22, 1862. Facing charges of "embezzlement of money belonging to the employees and interpreters," preferred by Major Albert C. Ellithorpe, Dec. 3, 1862, he avoided prosecution when Ellithorpe dropped the charges upon payment of the money by Wattles and his unkept promise to resign. Colonel, 1 Indian Home Guards, KS Infantry, Dec. 26, 1862. Commanded Indian Brigade, District of the Frontier, 7 Army Corps, Department of Arkansas, July–Dec. 1864. Upon resuming command of the Indian Brigade, Jan. 16, 1865, Colonel William A. Phillips reported to Major Gen. Francis J. Herron, "frightful revelations implicating Colonel Wattles ... in the habit of throwing persons in a wretched prison and blackmailing them." Although placed under arrest, March 15, 1865, Wattles somehow avoided prosecution. Honorably mustered out, May 31, 1865. Battle honors: Locust Grove, Prairie Grove, Operations about Fort Gibson (Greenleaf Prairie), Honey Springs.
Born: July 29, 1824, Silver Creek, NY
Died: March 28, 1899, Kalamazoo, MI
Occupation: Livery operator, real estate speculator, and hotel proprietor
Offices/Honors: Nebraska Territory House of Representatives, 1858 and 1861. Sheriff, Sarpy Co., Nebraska Territory, 1860.

Stephen Howard Wattles (author's photograph).

Stephen Howard Wattles (National Archives [BA-211]).

Stephen Howard Wattles (*Portrait and Biographical Record of Kalamazoo, Allegan and Van Buren Counties, Michigan.* Chicago, Illinois, 1892).

Miscellaneous: Resided Bellevue, Sarpy Co., Nebraska Territory, before war; and Kalamazoo, Kalamazoo Co., MI, after war

Buried: Mountain Home Cemetery, Kalamazoo, MI (Section 3, Lot 10)

References: *Portrait and Biographical Record of Kalamazoo, Allegan and Van Buren Counties, Michigan.* Chicago, IL, 1892. Obituary, *Kalamazoo Morning Gazette*, March 29, 1899. Pension File and Military Service File, National Archives. Letters Received, Volunteer Service Branch, Adjutant General's Office, File W307(VS)1863, National Archives. J. Sterling Morton. *Illustrated History of Nebraska: A History of Nebraska from the Earliest Explorations of the Trans-Mississippi Region.* Lincoln, NE 1911. Chris Rein, "The U.S. Army, Indian Agency, and the Path to Assimilation: The First Indian Home Guards in the American Civil War," *Kansas History: A Journal of the Central Plains*, Vol. 36, No. 1 (Spring 2013). M. Jane Johansson, editor. *Albert C. Ellithorpe: The First Indian Home Guards and the Civil War on the Trans-Mississippi Frontier.* Baton Rouge, LA, 2016. *The War of the Rebellion: A Compilation of the Official Records of the Union and Confederate Armies.* (Series 1, Vol. 48, Part 1, p. 542). Washington, D.C., 1896. Wiley Britton. *The Union Indian Brigade in the Civil War.* Kansas City, MO, 1922.

William Weer, Jr.

Colonel, 4 KS Infantry, June 20, 1861. Colonel, 10 KS Infantry, June 1, 1862, upon consolidation of 3 KS Infantry and 4 KS Infantry. Commanded Indian Expedition, Department of Kansas, June–July 1862. Described as "a man abusive and violent in his intercourse with his fellow-officers, notoriously intemperate in habits, entirely disregarding military usages and discipline, always rash in speech, act, and orders, refusing to inferior officers and their reports that consideration which is due an officer of the U.S. Army," he was arrested, July 18, 1862, and relieved of command of the Indian expedition by Colonel Frederick Salomon, who further elaborated, "I could but conclude that the man was either insane, premeditated treachery to his troops, or perhaps that his grossly intemperate habits long continued had produced idiocy or monomania." Commanded 2 Brigade, Department of Kansas, Aug.–Oct. 1862. Commanded 2 Brigade, 1 Division, Army of the Frontier, Department of the Missouri, Oct.–Dec. 1862. Commanded 1 Division, Army of the Frontier, Department of the Missouri, Dec. 1862–April 1863. Acting AIG, Staff of Major Gen. John M. Schofield, Department of the Missouri, July 1863. Commanded Alton (IL) Military Prison, Jan.–April 1864. Dishonorably dismissed Aug. 20, 1864, for "Drunkenness on duty, Conduct to the prejudice of good order and military discipline, and Conduct unbecoming an officer and a gentleman" while commanding the Alton Military Prison. Colonel, 23 KS State Militia, Oct. 15, 1864. He appealed his dismissal directly to President Lincoln, who although lacking the authority to reverse the findings of the Court Martial, issued an order, Dec. 20, 1864, removing the disability to re-enter service, against the recommendation of Judge Advocate General Joseph Holt. Battle honors: Dry Wood Creek, Locust Grove, Newtonia, Old Fort Wayne, Cane Hill, Prairie Grove, Shelby's Raid in Arkansas and Missouri.

Born: Dec. 20, 1824 Philadelphia, PA
Died: Feb. 28, 1867 Wyandotte, KS
Education: Graduated McKendree College, Lebanon, IL, 1841
Occupation: Lawyer
Offices/Honors: Probate Judge, Macoupin Co., IL, 1851–53. Attorney General, Kansas Territory, 1857–58. Kansas Senate, 1865–66.
Miscellaneous: Resided Carlinville, Macoupin Co., IL, to 1856; and Wyandotte, Wyandotte

Co., KS, after 1856. Described by a sutler with the Army of the Frontier as "a bold, bluff, brave man, notorious, even to recklessness, so far as he himself is concerned, with a big head, bushy whiskers, and a well knit form, with the endurance of a mule and the heart of a lion."

Buried: Probably Carlinville City Cemetery, Carlinville, IL (unmarked, with his wife, Gloriana, who died in 1854)

References: Joseph Guandolo, editor. *Centennial McKendree College With St. Clair County History.* Lebanon, IL, 1928. Charles A. Walker, editor. *History of Macoupin County, Illinois: Biographical and Pictorial.* Chicago, IL, 1911. Military Service File, National Archives. Letters Received, Volunteer Service Branch, Adjutant General's Office, Files K198(VS)1862, L428(VS)1862, and O306(VS)1864, National Archives. Obituary, *Wyandotte Commercial Gazette,* March 2, 1867. Obituary, *Atchison Daily Champion,* March 7, 1867. Death Notice, *Alton Daily Democrat,* March 2, 1867. *The War of the Rebellion: A Compilation of the Official Records of the Union and Confederate Armies.* (Vol. 13, pp. 476, 484–485). Washington, D.C., 1885. Court-martial Case Files, 1809–1894, File NN-2369, National Archives. M. Jane Johansson, editor. *Albert C. Ellithorpe: The First Indian Home Guards and the Civil War on the Trans-Mississippi Frontier.* Baton Rouge, LA, 2016. Michael E. Banasik, editor. *Reluctant Cannoneer: The Diary of Robert T. McMahan of the Twenty-Fifth Independent Ohio Light Artillery.* Iowa City, IA, 2000. "From the Army of the Frontier," *Daily Missouri Republican,* March 3, 1863. "The Alton Democrat on Col. Weer," *Alton Telegraph,* Sept. 2, 1864. "Colonel Weer," *Daily Missouri Republican,* Sept. 3, 1864. H. Miles Moore. *Early History of Leavenworth City and County.* Leavenworth, KS, 1906.

Charles August Willemsen

Colonel, 3 KS State Militia, Feb. 13, 1864.
Born: Dec. 3, 1831 Langenberg, Germany
Died: March 27, 1910, St. Louis, MO
Occupation: Tanner and dealer in hides and leather to 1887; and President of Willemsen Belting Co. after 1887
Miscellaneous: Resided Lawrence, Douglas Co., KS, to 1873; and St. Louis, MO, after 1873
Buried: St. Matthew Cemetery, St. Louis, MO (Block 10, Lot 12). Removed to Valhalla Cemetery, Normandy, MO, Aug. 4, 1927.

References: Obituary, *Lawrence Daily World,* March 30, 1910. Death notice, *St. Louis Post-Dispatch,* March 28, 1910. Death notice, *St. Louis Globe-Democrat,* March 29, 1910. www.ancestry.com.

Samuel Newitt Wood

Captain, Co. I, 2 KS Infantry, June 20, 1861. Captain, Co. G, 6 MO Cavalry, Oct. 28, 1861. Lieutenant Colonel, 6 MO Cavalry, Feb. 14, 1862. Facing court martial on multiple charges, he resigned, Aug. 12, 1862, since "I am worn out, sick, and must have rest or die." Brigade commander, Robert J. Rombauer, forwarded the resignation with the recommendation, "There appears to be no harmony between Col. [Clark] Wright and Lt. Col. Wood, none between Lt. Col. Wood and Major [Henry] Hawkins, and likewise there is the same lack of mutual support between Lt. Col. Wood and several of the company officers highly to the detriment of the service." Colonel, 8 KS State Militia, Nov. 10, 1863. Brig. Gen., 5 Brigade, KS State Militia, Feb. 29, 1864. Battle honors: Wilson's Creek, Spring River, Price's Missouri Expedition.

Born: Dec. 30, 1825 Mount Gilead, OH

Samuel Newitt Wood, post-war (Leonard & Martin, Topeka, Kansas; KansasMemory.org, Kansas Historical Society, Item No. 90676).

Samuel Newitt Wood, post-war (*The United States Biographical Dictionary*. Kansas Volume. Chicago and Kansas City, 1879).

Died: June 23, 1891, Hugoton, Stevens Co., KS (assassinated while attending court during a contentious county-seat struggle)

Occupation: Lawyer, newspaper editor, and farmer

Offices/Honors: Kansas Territory House of Representatives, 1859–60. Kansas Senate, 1861–62 and 1867. Kansas House of Representatives, 1864, 1866, 1876, and 1877 (Speaker).

Miscellaneous: Resided Cottonwood Falls, Chase Co., KS; Council Grove, Morris Co., KS; and Woodsdale, Stevens Co., KS

Buried: Prairie Grove Cemetery, Cottonwood Falls, KS

References: Margaret L. Wood. *Memorial of Samuel N. Wood*. Kansas City, MO, 1892. Howel H. Jones. *Chase County Historical Sketches*. N.p., 1940. Obituary, *Topeka Daily Capital*, June 24, 1891. Obituary, *Cottonwood Falls Reveille*, June 25, 1891. *The United States Biographical Dictionary*. Kansas Volume. Chicago and Kansas City, 1879. Charles F. Ritter and Jon L. Wakelyn. *American Legislative Leaders, 1850–1910*. Westport, CT, 1989. Alfred T. Andreas. *History of the State of Kansas*. Chicago, IL, 1883. George W. Martin, editor. *Transactions of the Kansas State Historical Society, 1907–08*. Topeka, KS, 1908. William E. Connelley. *A Standard History of Kansas and Kansans*. Chicago and New York, 1918. Pension File and Military Service File, National Archives. Letters Received, Volunteer Service Branch, Adjutant General's Office, File P269(VS)1862, National Archives.

Louisiana

Regiments

1st Cavalry
Harai Robinson	Jan. 14, 1864	Mustered out Sept. 1, 1865

2nd Cavalry
Daniel J. Keily	Sept. 6, 1864	Mustered out Aug. 20, 1865, **Bvt. Brig. Gen., USV**

1st Infantry
Richard E. Holcomb	Aug. 18, 1862	KIA June 14, 1863
William O. Fiske	Aug. 18, 1863	Mustered out July 12, 1865, **Bvt. Brig. Gen., USV**

1st New Orleans Infantry
Curtis W. Killborn	Sept. 28, 1863	Mustered as Major Aug. 4, 1864
Sheldon Sturgeon	April 25, 1865	Mustered out Aug. 15, 1865

2nd Infantry
Charles J. Paine	Oct. 23, 1862	Discharged March 8, 1864, **Brig. Gen., USV**
Charles Everett	April 1, 1864	Mustered out Sept. 11, 1865, **Bvt. Brig. Gen., USV**

2nd New Orleans Infantry (regiment failed to complete organization)
Robert B. Brown	Sept. 28, 1863

5th Infantry (regiment failed to complete organization)
Alexander Warner	June 30, 1863

6th Infantry (Colored)
Robert W.B. Des Anges	July 4, 1863	Mustered out Oct. 15, 1863

7th Infantry (Colored)
Mardon W. Plumly	July 10, 1863	Mustered out Sept. 7, 1863

Biographies

Robert B. Brown

Captain, Co. E, 30 MA Infantry, Jan. 1, 1862. Provost Marshal, Jefferson Parish, LA, Sept. 1862–Sept. 1864. Detailed as *Colonel*, 2 New Orleans Infantry, Sept. 28, 1863. Regiment failed to complete organization; incomplete regiment consolidated with 1 New Orleans Infantry. Staff of Brig. Gen. Thomas W. Sherman, Defenses of New Orleans, Sept. 1864–Jan. 1865. Honorably mustered out, Jan. 18, 1865. Battle honors: Baton Rouge.

Born: Dec. 14, 1825 Glasgow, Scotland
Died: March 9, 1881, Boston, MA
Education: Attended Comer's Commercial College, Boston, MA
Occupation: Clothing merchant
Miscellaneous: Resided Melrose, Middlesex Co., MA; and Boston, MA
Buried: Mount Hope Cemetery, Mattapan, MA (Landon Walk, Lot 260, unmarked)

Robert B. Brown (E. Jacobs, Photographic Gallery, 93 Camp Street, New Orleans, Louisiana; Massachusetts MOLLUS Collection, USAMHI [Vol. 104, p.5367L]).

Robert B. Brown (Massachusetts MOLLUS Collection, USAMHI [Vol. 104, p. 5366]).

References: Obituary, *Boston Post*, March 10, 1881. Obituary, *Boston Herald*, March 12, 1881. Obituary, *Boston Evening Transcript*, March 9, 1881. Pension File, National Archives. Letters Received, Volunteer Service Branch, Adjutant General's Office, File B505(VS)1870, National Archives. Thomas W. Bicknell, editor. *History and Genealogy of the Bicknell Family and Some Collateral Lines of Normandy, Great Britain and America.* Providence, RI, 1913. *The War of the Rebellion: A Compilation of the Official Records of the Union and Confederate Armies.* (Vol. 26, Part 1, p. 741). Washington, D.C., 1889.

Robert William Burdett Des Anges

Captain, Co. A, 81 U.S. Colored Infantry, March 28, 1863. Acting ADC, Staff of Brig. Gen. Daniel Ullmann, Corps d'Afrique, Department of the Gulf, April–July 1863. Detailed as Colonel, 6 LA (Colored) Infantry, July 4, 1863. Honorably mustered out as colonel, Oct. 15, 1863. Acting AAG, Staff of Brig. Gen. Daniel Ullmann, 1 Division, Corps d'Afrique, Department of the Gulf, Sept. 1863–April 1864. Major, AAG, USV, April 7, 1864. AAG, Staff of Brig. Gen. Daniel Ullmann, 1 Division, Corps d'Afrique, Department of the Gulf, May–July 1864. AAG, District of Baton Rouge, Northern Division of Louisiana, Department of the Gulf, Feb.–April 1865. AAG, Staff of Major Gen. Edward R.S. Canby, Department of the Gulf, June–Nov. 1865. Honorably mustered out, Jan. 20, 1866.

Born: May 10, 1835, Marylebone, London, England

Died: Jan. 14, 1894 New York City, NY

Other Wars: Described by a fellow officer in the 81 USCT as "a soldier of fortune. He had served two years in India, was at the siege of Delhi, at the siege of Sebastopol, and was commendably proud of his medals and orders for brilliant services." At his 1875 trial for complicity in smuggling it was revealed that he actually served in the English army as a Paymaster's Clerk and fled to America in 1863 due to a deficiency in his accounts.

Occupation: Broker and U.S. Customs inspector

Offices/Honors: Chief clerk, Warehouse Department, NY Custom House, 1871–73. Deputy Collector of Customs, Port of New York, 1873–75.

Miscellaneous: Resided New York City, NY. Convicted Nov. 9, 1875 of complicity in smuggling silks through the Customs Appraiser's Office at an undervaluation and sentenced to imprisonment for two years. With four months remaining in his sentence, he was pardoned by President Rutherford B. Hayes.

Buried: Fair View Cemetery, Fairview, Monmouth Co., NJ (Section V, Lot 509, unmarked)

References: Pension File and Military Service File, National Archives. Letters Received, Appointment, Commission and Personal Branch, Adjutant General's Office, File 2718(ACP)1875, National Archives. Andrew Wender Cohen. *Contraband: Smuggling and the Birth of the American Century.* New York and London, 2015. Andrew Wender Cohen, "Smuggling, Globalization, and America's Outward State, 1870–1909," *The Journal of American History*, Vol. 97, No. 2 (September 2010). Isaac S. Bangs, "The Ullmann Brigade," *War Papers Read Before the Commandery of the State of Maine MOLLUS*. Vol. 2. Portland, ME, 1902. "The Silk Smugglers," *Washington National Republican*, Nov. 11, 1875. "Col. Des Anges Convicted," *New York Times,* Nov. 10, 1875. "The Case of Col. Des Anges," *New York Times*, Nov. 28, 1875. "Pardoned by Hayes," *New York Sun*, Aug. 4, 1877. www.ancestry.com.

Richard Erskine Holcomb

1 Lieutenant, RQM, 3 CT Infantry (3 months), May 14, 1861. Honorably mustered out, Aug. 12, 1861. Major, 13 CT Infantry, Dec. 22, 1861. Colonel, 1 LA Infantry, Aug. 18, 1862. Commanded Post of Donaldsonville (LA), Department of the Gulf, Jan.–Feb. 1863. GSW leg, Port Hudson, LA, May 27, 1863. Commanded 1 Brigade, 4 Division, 19 Army Corps, Department of the Gulf, June 14, 1863. GSW head, Port Hudson, LA, June 14, 1863. Battle honors: First Bull Run, Operations in West Louisiana (Indian Bend, Irish Bend, Bayou Vermillion), Port Hudson.

    Born: Sept. 28, 1824 Granby, CT
    Died: June 14, 1863, KIA Port Hudson, LA
    Occupation: Railroad contractor and farmer
    Miscellaneous: Resided East Granby, Hartford Co., CT
    Buried: Granby Cemetery, Granby, CT
    References: Carol Laun. *The Holcomb Collection.* Granby, CT, 1998. Jesse M. Seaver. *The Holcomb(e) Genealogy: A Genealogy, History and Directory of the Holcomb(e)s of the World.* Philadelphia, PA, 1925. Elizabeth Weir McPherson. *The Holcombes, Nation Builders.* Washington, DC, 1947. Homer B. Sprague. *History of the 13th Infantry Regiment of Connecticut Volunteers, During the Great Rebellion.* Hartford, CT, 1867. David C. Edmonds. *The Guns of Port Hudson: The Investment, Siege and Reduction.* Lafayette, LA, 1984. Letters Received, Volunteer Service Branch, Adjutant General's Office, File H468(VS)1869, National Archives. Pension File and Military Service File, National Archives. William A. Croffut and John M. Morris. *The Military and Civil History of Connecticut During the War of 1861-65.* New York City, NY, 1868. *The Connecticut War Record.* Vol. 1, No. 9 (April 1864).

Richard Erskine Holcomb (Jesse M. Seaver. *The Holcomb(e) Genealogy: A Genealogy, History and Directory of the Holcomb(e)s of the World.* Philadelphia, Pennsylvania, 1925).

Curtis Williams Killborn

1 Lieutenant, Adjutant, 6 MI Infantry, Aug. 20, 1861. Provost Marshal, Baton Rouge, LA, May–July 1862. Provost Marshal, New Orleans, LA, Aug. 1862–Jan. 1864. Designation of regiment changed to 1 MI Heavy Artillery, July 28, 1863. Detailed as *Colonel*, 1 New Orleans Infantry, Sept. 28, 1863. Commissary of Prisoners, Department of the Gulf, Feb.–Aug. 1864. The regiment never attaining full strength, he accepted muster in as Major, 1 New Orleans Infantry, Aug. 4, 1864. Commanded Camp of Distribution, New Orleans, LA, Dec. 1864–May 1866. Honorably mustered out, June 1, 1866. Battle honors: Baton Rouge.

Curtis Williams Killborn (author's photograph).

Born: Aug. 1827 NY
Died: Oct. 31, 1901 New Orleans, LA
Occupation: Clerk, U.S. Internal Revenue Assessor, and railroad baggage master
Miscellaneous: Resided Kalamazoo, Kalamazoo Co., MI, before war; and New Orleans, LA, after war
Buried: Metairie Cemetery, New Orleans, LA (Section 57, Lot 34)
References: Pension File and Military Service File, National Archives. Letters Received, Volunteer Service Branch, Adjutant General's Office, Files M2772(VS)1863 and K654(VS)1864, National Archives. "Deposition of Col. C.W. Killborn, Nov. 21, 1874," U.S. Southern Claims Commission, Disallowed and Barred Claims, 1871–1880, National Archives. Death notice, *New Orleans Times-Picayune*, Nov. 3, 1901. *The War of the Rebellion: A Compilation of the Official Records of the Union and Confederate Armies.* (Vol. 26, Part 1, p. 741). Washington, D.C., 1889.

Mardon Wilson Plumly

Private, Co. I, 71 PA Infantry, June 28, 1861. 2 Lieutenant, Co. D, 40 NY Infantry, July 1, 1862. GSW left breast, 2nd Bull Run, VA, Aug. 29, 1862. Resigned Nov. 23, 1862, "having been afflicted with chronic diarrhea for the past year, which has rendered me totally unfit for duty most of that time." Colonel, 7 LA (Colored) Infantry, July 10, 1863. Honorably mustered out, Sept. 7, 1863. Colonel, 86 U.S. Colored Infantry, Sept. 7, 1863. Commanded 1 Brigade, District of West Florida, Department of the Gulf, Feb. 1864. Resigned Aug. 8, 1864, since "I feel that.... I shall not be able to pass so rigorous an examination in all branches of education as is required by the General Order requiring my appearance before the Board of Examination." Private, Co. K, 1 LA Cavalry, Dec. 29, 1864. Sergeant, Co. K, 1 LA Cavalry, Dec. 31, 1864. 1 Sergeant, Co. K, 1 LA Cavalry, Feb. 26, 1865. Reduced to Private. June 13, 1865. Honorably mustered out, Aug. 28, 1865. Battle honors: Ball's Bluff, Fair Oaks, 2nd Bull Run.
Born: Dec. 12, 1841 Trenton, NJ
Died: Nov. 5, 1889 near Fort Ross, Sonoma Co., CA
Education: Attended Jefferson Medical College, Philadelphia, PA
Occupation: Medical student before war. Laborer after war.
Miscellaneous: Resided San Francisco, CA; and Sea View, Sonoma Co., CA. Brother-in-law of Bvt. Brig. Gen. John W. Ames (6 U.S. Colored Infantry).
Buried: Sea View Cemetery, Sea View, CA (unmarked)
References: Pension File and Military Service File, National Archives. Letters Received, Colored Troops Branch, Adjutant General's Office, File 371(CT)1879, National Archives. Obituary, *Sonoma Democrat*, Nov. 16, 1889. www.ancestry.com.

Harai Robinson

Volunteer ADC, Staff of Brig. Gen. Andrew J. Hamilton, Military Governor of Texas, Dec. 13, 1862. Major, 1 LA Cavalry, Jan. 20, 1863. Chief of Cavalry, Staff of Major Gen. Nathaniel P. Banks, Department of the Gulf, Feb.–May 1863. Lieutenant Colonel, 1 LA Cavalry, Aug. 4, 1863. Colonel, 1 LA Cavalry, Jan. 14, 1864. Commanded 3 Brigade, Cavalry Division, Department of the Gulf, Jan.–April 1864. GSW right hip, Sabine Cross Roads, LA, April 8, 1864. Provost Marshal General, Department of the Gulf, Aug. 1864–Feb. 1865. Acting in collusion with Major Gen. Stephen A. Hurlbut in "the acceptance of bribes from citizens for the performance of official acts," he was arrested, Feb. 13, 1865, and held in confinement but never brought before a military tribunal. After being honorably mustered out,

Sept. 1, 1865, he was finally prosecuted in the U.S. Circuit Court, which decided that it had no jurisdiction in the case and dismissed all charges, March 15, 1866. Battle honors: Port Hudson, Operations in West Louisiana, Operations in the Teche Country (Bayou Bourbeau, Camp Pratt, Bayou Portage), Red River Campaign (Wilson's Farm, Sabine Cross Roads).

Born: Aug. 1, 1828 New York City, NY
Died: Dec. 16, 1886 Gorgona, Panama
Occupation: Merchant before war. After war engaged as railroad freight clerk in San Francisco and civil engineer in the employ of the Panama Canal Co.
Miscellaneous: Resided New Orleans, LA; Barranquilla, Colombia; San Francisco, CA; and Gorgona, Panama
Buried: Place of burial unknown
References: Pension File and Military Service File, National Archives. Letters Received, Volunteer Service Branch, Adjutant General's Office, Files O399(VS)1862 and R407(VS)1865, National Archives. Obituary, *New Orleans Daily Picayune*, Jan. 14, 1887. "Recent Deaths: Colonel Harai Robinson," *United States Army and Navy Journal*. Feb. 12, 1887. David C. Edmonds. *Yankee Autumn in Acadiana: A Narrative of the Great Texas Overland Expedition Through Southwestern Louisiana, October-December 1863*. Lafayette, LA, 1979. Jeffrey N. Lash. *A Politician Turned General: The Civil War Career of Stephen Augustus Hurlbut*. Kent, OH, 2003. Dispatches from U.S. Consuls in Panama City, Panama, 1823–1906 (Record Group 59), National Archives. John Y. Simon, editor. *The Papers of Ulysses S. Grant*. Vol. 15: May 1–December 31, 1865. Carbondale, IL, 1988. Harai Robinson Papers, 1861–1889, Mss. 488, Louisiana and Lower Mississippi Valley Collections, Louisiana State University Libraries, Baton Rouge, LA.

Sheldon Sturgeon

2 Lieutenant, 1 U.S. Infantry, May 6, 1861. 1 Lieutenant, 1 U.S. Infantry, June 24, 1861. Captain, 1 U.S. Infantry, April 25, 1862. Chief Mustering Officer, Military Division of West Mississippi, Nov. 1864–Aug. 1865. Colonel, 1 New Orleans Infantry, April 25, 1865. Honorably mustered out of volunteer service, Aug. 15, 1865. Chief Mustering Officer, Military Division of the Gulf, Oct. 1865–June 1866. Bvt. Major and Bvt. Lieutenant Colonel, USA, March 13, 1865, for gallant and meritorious services during the war. Battle honors: First Bull Run.

Sheldon Sturgeon, West Point Cadet, Class of May 1861 (USAMHI [RG25S-West Point Album-1861]).

Sheldon Sturgeon (P.S. du Pont Longwood Photograph Collection, Hagley Museum and Library, Wilmington, Delaware [1969_2_PA7_04].

Sheldon Sturgeon, post-war (William H. Powell and Edward Shippen, editors. *Officers of the Army and Navy (Regular) Who Served in the Civil War*. Philadelphia, Pennsylvania, 1892).

Born: Feb. 7, 1838 Sparta, Livingston Co., NY
Died: July 22, 1892, Hagerstown, MD
Education: Graduated U.S. Military Academy, West Point, NY, May 1861
Occupation: Regular Army (Captain, 6 U.S. Cavalry, retired May 17, 1876)
Miscellaneous: Resided Nunda, Livingston Co., NY; and Dansville, Livingston Co., NY
Buried: Greenmount Cemetery, Dansville, NY (Section R, Lot 20)
References: William H. Powell and Edward Shippen, editors. *Officers of the Army and Navy (Regular) Who Served in the Civil War*. Philadelphia, PA, 1892. George W. Cullum. *Biographical Register of the Officers and Graduates of the U.S. Military Academy*. Third Edition. Boston, MA, 1891. Mary Elizabeth Sergent. *They Lie Forgotten: The United States Military Academy, 1856–1861, Together with a Class Album for the Class of May 1861*. Middletown, NY, 1986. Obituary, *Dansville Express*, July 28, 1892. Obituary, *Hagerstown Daily Mail*, July 22, 1892. Obituary, *Buffalo Morning Express*, July 28, 1892. *Twenty-Fourth Annual Reunion of the Association of the Graduates of the U.S. Military Academy*. Saginaw, MI, 1893. Letters Received, Appointment, Commission and Personal Branch, Adjutant General's Office, File 80(ACP)1873, National Archives. Letters Received, Volunteer Service Branch, Adjutant General's Office, Files S3393(VS)1864 and S2304(VS)1865, National Archives. Military Service File, National Archives.

Alexander Warner

Major, 3 CT Infantry (3 months), May 14, 1861. Honorably mustered out, Aug. 12, 1861. Lieutenant Colonel, 13 CT Infantry, Jan. 15, 1862. Detached as *Colonel*, 5 LA Infantry, June 30, 1863. Regiment failed to complete organization. Resigned Aug. 12, 1863. Battle honors: 1st Bull Run, Operations in West Louisiana (Irish Bend).
Born: Jan. 10, 1827 Smithfield, RI
Died: Sept. 7, 1914 Point Pleasant, NJ
Education: Attended Woodstock (CT) Academy and Wesleyan Academy, Wilbraham, MA
Occupation: Cotton twine manufacturer before war. Cotton planter, farmer, and banker after war.

Alexander Warner (with wife, Mary, and son, Benjamin) (Filley & Gilbert, 337 Chapel Street, New Haven, Connecticut; Courtesy of Steve Meadow).

Alexander Warner, post-war (*Companions of the Military Order of the Loyal Legion of the United States.* New York City, New York, 1901).

Offices/Honors: Mississippi Senate, 1870–76. Major General, Mississippi State Militia, 1875–76. Treasurer of Connecticut, 1887–89. Kansas House of Representatives, 1893 and 1895.

Miscellaneous: Resided Woodstock, Windham Co, CT, before war; Calhoun Station, Madison Co., MS, 1866–70; Jackson, Hinds Co., MS, 1870–77; Pomfret, Windham Co., CT, 1877–90; Baxter Springs, Cherokee Co., KS, 1890–1900; Salisbury, Wicomico Co., MD, 1900–02; and Ridgefield, Fairfield Co., CT. Upon the failure of the Baxter Springs (KS) Bank in 1897, he was convicted of violating the state banking law.

Buried: Woodstock Hill Cemetery, Woodstock, CT

References: Richard M. Bayles. *History of Windham County, Connecticut.* New York City, NY, 1889. John A. Spalding, compiler. *Illustrated Popular Biography of Connecticut.* Hartford, CT, 1891. Cleveland Abbe and Josephine Genung Nichols. *Abbe-Abbey Genealogy: In Memory of John Abbe and His Descendants.* New Haven, CT, 1916. Obituary, *Hartford Courant*, Sept. 9, 1914. Obituary, *New York Tribune*, Sept. 8, 1914. Obituary, *Norwich Bulletin*, Sept. 11, 1914. Clarence W. Bowen. *The History of Woodstock, Connecticut.* Norwood, MA, 1926. *Companions of the Military Order of the Loyal Legion of the United States.* New York City, NY, 1901. Pension File and Military Service File, National Archives. Letters Received, Volunteer Service Branch, Adjutant General's Office, File L605(VS)1863, National Archives. Homer B. Sprague. *History of the 13th Infantry Regiment of Connecticut Volunteers, During the Great Rebellion.* Hartford, CT, 1867. "A Prominent Kansan Charged With Embezzlement," *Topeka Mail and Breeze*, June 11, 1897. "Hon. A. Warner," *Canton American Citizen*, March 20, 1875.

Nebraska Territory

Regiments

1st Cavalry
John M. Thayer	July 21, 1861	Promoted **Brig. Gen., USV,** Oct. 4, 1862
Robert R. Livingston	Oct. 4, 1862	Mustered out July 10, 1865, **Bvt. Brig. Gen., USV**

2nd Cavalry
Robert W. Furnas	March 24, 1863	Mustered out Dec. 1, 1863

1st Volunteer Militia
Oliver P. Mason	Aug. 11, 1864

Biographies

Robert Wilkinson Furnas

Colonel, 1 Indian Home Guards, KS Infantry, May 22, 1862. Commanded Indian Brigade, Department of Kansas, July–Aug. 1862. Claiming that he only accepted the colonelcy of Indian troops "on the representations of my friends ... that my presence would not be required longer than about September or October," he submitted his resignation, Sept. 7, 1862, explaining that "I have always doubted the propriety and policy of arming and placing in the field Indians. Five months connection with an Indian regiment only confirms me in the opinion that full-blood Indians cannot be made soldiers, and that to attempt it is a useless waste of both time and money." Major Gen. James G. Blunt would not forward the resignation to the War Department in this form. It was finally forwarded and accepted, Nov. 22, 1862, stating simply, "my domestic and pecuniary affairs are in such a condition as to require my immediate presence." Captain, Co. E, 2 NE Cavalry, Dec. 8, 1862. Colonel, 2 NE Cavalry, March 24, 1863. Honorably mustered out, Dec. 1, 1863. Battle honors: Expedition into Indian Territory, Expedition against Indians in Dakota (White Stone Hill).

Born: May 5, 1824, near Troy, Miami Co., OH
Died: June 1, 1905, Lincoln, NE

Robert Wilkinson Furnas (pre-war, 1855) (J. Sterling Morton. *Illustrated History of Nebraska: A History of Nebraska from the Earliest Explorations of the Trans-Mississippi Region.* Lincoln, Nebraska, 1911).

Robert Wilkinson Furnas (seated leftmost, with Major John Taffe, Lieut. Col. William F. Sapp, Major John W. Pearman, Surgeon Aurelius Bowen, Adjutant Henry M. Atkinson, and Major George Armstrong, left to right) (J. Sterling Morton. *Illustrated History of Nebraska: A History of Nebraska from the Earliest Explorations of the Trans-Mississippi Region*. Lincoln, Nebraska, 1911).

Robert Wilkinson Furnas, post-war (Nebraska State Historical Society [RG4389-03]).

Occupation: Newspaper editor and horticulturist
Offices/Honors: Nebraska Territory Council, 1857–61. Governor of Nebraska, 1873–75.
Miscellaneous: Resided Brownville, Nemaha Co., NE
Buried: Walnut Grove Cemetery, Brownville, NE (Lot 298)
References: J. Sterling Morton. *Illustrated History of Nebraska: A History of Nebraska from the Earliest Explorations of the Trans-Mississippi Region*. Lincoln, NE, 1911. *A Biographical and Genealogical History of Southeastern Nebraska*. Chicago and New York, 1904. Allen Johnson and Dumas Malone, editors. *Dictionary of American Biography*. New York City, NY, 1964. Obituary, *Nebraska State Journal*, June 2, 1905. A.C. Edmunds. *Pen Sketches of Nebraskans*. Lincoln, NE, 1871. Alfred T. Andreas. *History of the State of Nebraska*. Chicago, IL, 1882. *Biographical Souvenir of the Counties of Buffalo, Kearney and Phelps, Nebraska*. Chicago, IL, 1890. Robert Sobel and John Raimo, editors. *Biographical Directory of the Governors of the United States, 1789–1978*. Westport, CT, 1988. Thomas W. Tipton. *Forty Years of Nebraska at Home and in Congress*. Lincoln, NE, 1902. Robert C. Farb, "The Military Career of Robert W. Furnas," *Nebraska History*, Vol. 32, No. 1 (March 1951). Obituary Circular, Whole No. 231, Nebraska MOLLUS. Pension File and Military Service File, National Archives. Letters Received, Volunteer Service Branch, Adjutant General's Office, File C533(VS)1867, National Archives. Chris Rein, "The U.S. Army, Indian Agency, and the Path to Assimilation: The First Indian Home Guards in the American Civil War," *Kansas History: A Journal of the Central Plains*, Vol. 36, No. 1 (Spring 2013). M. Jane Johansson, editor. *Albert C. Ellithorpe: The First Indian Home Guards and the Civil War on the Trans-Mississippi Frontier*. Baton Rouge, LA, 2016.

Oliver Perry Mason

Colonel, 1 NE Volunteer Militia, Aug. 11, 1864.
Born: May 13, 1829, Brookfield, Madison Co., NY

Oliver Perry Mason (J. Sterling Morton. *Illustrated History of Nebraska: A History of Nebraska from the Earliest Explorations of the Trans-Mississippi Region*. Lincoln, Nebraska, 1911).

Died: Aug. 18, 1891 Lincoln, NE
Education: Graduated New York State Normal School, Albany, NY, 1850
Occupation: Lawyer
Offices/Honors: Nebraska Territory House of Representatives, 1858–59. Nebraska Territory Council, 1864–66 (President, 1865–66). Chief Justice, Nebraska Supreme Court, 1866–73.
Miscellaneous: Resided Nebraska City, Otoe Co., NE, 1855–74; Lincoln, Lancaster Co., NE, after 1874
Buried: Wyuka Cemetery, Nebraska City, NE (Original Ground, Lot 590)
References: J. Sterling Morton. *Illustrated History of Nebraska: A History of Nebraska from the Earliest Explorations of the Trans-Mississippi Region*. Lincoln, NE 1911. A.C. Edmunds. *Pen Sketches of Nebraskans*. Lincoln, NE, 1871. Alfred T. Andreas. *History of the State of Nebraska*. Chicago, IL, 1882. Obituary, *Nebraska State Journal*, Aug. 19, 1891. Obituary, *Lincoln Evening News*, Aug. 18, 1891. Obituary Circular, Whole No. 81, Nebraska MOLLUS. Letters Received, Volunteer Service Branch, Adjutant General's Office, File N259(VS)1866, National Archives. *The National Cyclopedia of American Biography*. Vol. 5. New York City, NY, 1907.

NEVADA TERRITORY

Regiments

1st Infantry

Daniel E. Hungerford	Date unknown	Resigned (date unknown)
Charles A. Sumner	March 9, 1864	Regiment disbanded May 19, 1864

Biographies

Daniel Elihu Hungerford

Lieutenant Colonel, 36 NY Infantry, Sept. 17, 1861. Resigned July 6, 1862, "as well for my own self-respect as for the honor of the military profession." *Colonel*, 1 NV Infantry, date unknown. Resigned in response to accusations of gambling and squandering money subscribed for raising the regiment. Battle honors: Fair Oaks.

Daniel Elihu Hungerford, post-war (author's photograph).

Born: April 14, 1821, Frankfort, Herkimer Co., NY
Died: July 20, 1896, Rome, Italy
Other Wars: Mexican War (Captain, Co. G, 1 NY Vols.)
Occupation: Barber and hairdresser in early life. Druggist, physician, and railroad president in later life.
Miscellaneous: Resided New York City, NY; Downieville, Sierra Co., CA; San Francisco, CA; and Rome, Italy
Buried: Green-Wood Cemetery, Brooklyn, NY (Section 125, Lot 29275)
References: Ignatius I. Murphy. *Life of Colonel Daniel E. Hungerford.* Hartford, CT, 1891. Obituary, *Los Angeles Times*, July 25, 1896. F. Phelps Leach. *Additions and Corrections for Thomas Hungerford of Hartford and New London, Conn., and His Descendants in America.* East Highgate, VT, 1932. Obituary, *Santa Cruz Evening Sentinel*, July 21, 1896. Obituary, *Brooklyn Daily Eagle*, July 20, 1896. Oscar T. Shuck, editor. *Sketches of Leading and Representative Men of San Francisco.* London, New York, and San Francisco, 1875. "Washington's Birthday in Downieville," *Sacramento Daily Union*, Feb. 27, 1861. Pension File and Military Service File, National Archives. Letters Received, Volunteer Service Branch, Adjutant General's Office, File S1078(VS)1865, National Archives.

Charles Allen Sumner

Captain, AQM, USV, Nov. 26, 1862. Quartermaster, Fort Churchill, NV Territory. Resigned March 30, 1864. *Colonel*, 1 NV Infantry, March 9, 1864. Regiment did not complete organization, its recruitment being discontinued, May 19, 1864, and its enlisted companies consolidated into a battalion.

Charles Allen Sumner, post-war (Charles A. Sumner. *Shorthand and Reporting: A Lecture.* New Edition. New York City, New York, 1882).

Born: Aug. 2, 1835 Great Barrington, MA
Died: Jan. 31, 1903 San Francisco, CA
Education: Attended Trinity College, Hartford, CT
Occupation: Lawyer, newspaper editor, and stenographic reporter
Offices/Honors: Nevada Senate, 1865–68. U.S. House of Representatives, 1883–85.
Miscellaneous: Resided San Francisco, CA; and Virginia City, Storey Co., NV, 1865–68
Buried: San Francisco National Cemetery, San Francisco, CA (George H. Thomas Post, Grave 298)
References: Charles A. Sumner. *Shorthand and Reporting: A Lecture.* New Edition. New York City, NY, 1882. Obituary Circular, Whole No. 697, California MOLLUS. Obituary, *San Francisco Call*, Feb. 2, 1903. Obituary, *Sacramento Evening Bee*, Feb. 2, 1903. Pension File, National Archives. Obituary, *San Francisco Chronicle*, Feb. 2, 1903. Letters Received, Volunteer Service Branch, Adjutant General's Office, File S1078(VS)1865, National Archives. James L. Harrison, compiler. *Biographical Directory of the American Congress, 1774–1949.* Washington, D.C., 1950. Stuart Murray. *A Time of War: A Northern Chronicle of the Civil War.* Lee, MA, 2001.

NEW MEXICO TERRITORY

Regiments

1st Cavalry (organized by consolidation of 1st, 2nd, 4th and 5th NM Infantry, May 31, 1862)
Christopher Carson	Sept. 20, 1861	Mustered out Oct. 8, 1866, **Bvt. Brig. Gen., USV**

1st Infantry (consolidated with 2nd, 4th and 5th NM Infantry to form 1st NM Cavalry, May 31, 1862)
Ceran St. Vrain	Aug. 13, 1861	Resigned Sept. 20, 1861
Christopher Carson	Sept. 20, 1861	To 1st NM Cavalry, **Bvt. Brig. Gen., USV**

1st Infantry (New Organization)
Henry R. Selden	April 25, 1864	Died Feb. 2, 1865
Francisco P. Abreu	Feb. 3, 1865	Mustered out Sept. 1, 1866

1st Militia
Juan C. Armijo	Date unknown

2nd Infantry (consolidated with 1st, 4th and 5th NM Infantry to form 1st NM Cavalry, May 31, 1862)
Miguel E. Pino	Aug. 19, 1861	Mustered out May 31, 1862

2nd Militia
Nicolas Pino	Feb. 15, 1862

3rd Militia
Robert H. Stapleton	Dec. 6, 1861

3rd Mounted Infantry
Jose G. Gallegos	Sept. 27, 1861	Mustered out March 6, 1862

4th Infantry (consolidated with 1st, 2nd and 5th NM Infantry to form 1st NM Cavalry, May 31, 1862)
Gabriel R. Paul	Dec. 9, 1861	Mustered out May 31, 1862, **Brig. Gen., USV**

5th Infantry (consolidated with 1st, 2nd and 4th NM Infantry to form 1st NM Cavalry, May 31, 1862)
Benjamin S. Roberts	Dec. 9, 1861	Mustered out May 31, 1862, **Brig. Gen., USV**

Biographies

Francisco Paula Abreu

Captain, Co. C, 1 NM Infantry, July 3, 1861. Captain, Co. A, 1 NM Cavalry, May 10, 1862. Commanded Post of Fort Stanton (NM), Department of New Mexico, March 1863. Major, 1 NM Cavalry, Sept. 14, 1863. Commanded Post of Fort Canby (NM), Department of New Mexico, Sept.–Nov. 1863. Resigned Dec. 14, 1863. Lieutenant Colonel, 1 NM Infantry, Jan. 11, 1864. Commanded Post of Fort Union (NM), Department of New Mexico, April–Aug. 1864. Commanded Post of Fort Bascom (NM), Department of New Mexico, Oct.–Dec. 1864. Commanded Post of Fort Union (NM), Department of New Mexico, Feb.–July 1865. Colonel, 1 NM Infantry, Feb. 3, 1865. Commanded Post of Fort Craig (NM), Department of New Mexico, Oct. 1865–July 1866. Honorably mustered out, Sept. 1, 1866. Battle honors: Valverde, Navajo Expedition, Adobe Walls.

Born: Aug. 18, 1831 Santa Fe, NM
Died: July 25, 1879, Anton Chico, NM
Occupation: Merchant
Offices/Honors: New Mexico Territory House of Representatives (Speaker), 1867–68. New Mexico Territory Council, 1873–77.
Miscellaneous: Resided Santa Fe, NM, before war; and Chaperito, San Miguel Co., NM, after war
Buried: Masonic Cemetery, Las Vegas, NM
References: Charles F. Ritter and Jon L. Wakelyn. *American Legislative Leaders, 1850–1910.* Westport, CT, 1989. Obituary, *New Mexico Herald*, July 30, 1879. Obituary, *Santa Fe Weekly New Mexican*, Aug. 2, 1879. Jerry D. Thompson. *A Civil War History of the New Mexico Volunteers & Militia.* Albuquerque, NM, 2015. Military Service File, National Archives.

Juan Cristobal Armijo

Colonel, 1 NM Militia, date unknown.
Born: 1810 Albuquerque, NM
Died: Dec. 27, 1884 Albuquerque, NM
Occupation: Merchant
Miscellaneous: Resided Albuquerque, Bernalillo Co., NM
Buried: Mount Calvary Cemetery, Albuquerque, NM
References: *History of New Mexico: Its Resources and Its People.* Los Angeles, Chicago, and New York, 1907. *An Illustrated History of New Mexico.* Chicago, IL, 1895. Obituary, *Las Cruces Sun-News*, Jan. 3, 1885. Ralph E. Twitchell. *The Leading Facts of New Mexican History.* Cedar Rapids, IA, 1912. Jerry D. Thompson. *A Civil War History of the New Mexico Volunteers & Militia.* Albuquerque, NM, 2015. www.findagrave.com.

Jose Guadalupe Gallegos

Colonel, 3 NM Mounted Infantry, Sept. 27, 1861. Honorably mustered out, March 6, 1862. Battle honors: Valverde.

Born: April 13, 1828, San Jose, San Miguel Co., NM
Died: May 18, 1867, near Las Colonias, NM (Drowned in Pecos River)
Occupation: Rancher and freighter
Offices/Honors: New Mexico Territory House of Representatives, 1855–56 and 1858–59 (Speaker). Sheriff, San Miguel Co., NM, 1857–58. New Mexico Territory Council, 1859–61 (President). A founding member of the Historical Society of New Mexico, 1859.
Miscellaneous: Resided San Jose, San Miguel Co., NM; and Las Colonias, Guadalupe Co., NM
Buried: Anton Chico, Guadalupe Co., NM
References: https://gallegosartistry.wordpress.com/jose-guadalupe-gallegos/. Pension File and Military Service File, National Archives. Charles F. Ritter and Jon L. Wakelyn. *American Legislative Leaders, 1850–1910.* Westport, CT, 1989. Jerry D. Thompson. *A Civil War History of the New Mexico Volunteers & Militia.* Albuquerque, NM, 2015.

Miguel Estanislado Pino

Colonel, 2 NM Infantry, Aug. 19, 1861. Honorably mustered out, May 31, 1862. Battle honors: Valverde, Glorieta.

Born: May 6, 1821, Santa Fe, NM
Died: June 20, 1867, Santa Fe, NM
Occupation: Farmer
Offices/Honors: New Mexico Territory House of Representatives, 1860–61 and 1862–63. New Mexico Territory Council (President), 1865–67.
Miscellaneous: Resided Santa Fe, NM. Brother of Colonel Nicolas Pino (1 NM Militia).
Buried: Rosario Cemetery, Santa Fe, NM (unmarked)
References: Pension File and Military Service File, National Archives. Jerry D. Thompson. *A Civil War History of the New Mexico Volunteers & Militia.* Albuquerque, NM, 2015. Ralph E. Twitchell. *The History of the Military Occupation of the Territory of New Mexico from 1846 to 1851.* Denver, CO, 1909. Letters Received, Adjutant General's Office, File P489(AGO)1861, National Archives. www.ancestry.com.

Nicolas de Jesus Pino, post-war (Ralph E. Twitchell. *The History of the Military Occupation of the Territory of New Mexico from 1846 to 1851.* Denver, Colorado, 1909).

Henry Raymond Selden (Chicago History Museum [ICHi-68788]).

Nicolas de Jesus Pino

Brig. Gen., 1 Brigade, 2 Division, NM Militia, Sept. 9, 1861. Colonel, 2 NM Militia, Feb. 15, 1862. Taken prisoner, Socorro, NM, Feb. 24, 1862. Exchanged Jan. 10, 1863. Battle honors: Socorro.
 Born: Dec. 4, 1819 Santa Fe, NM
 Died: Nov. 14, 1896 Galisteo, NM
 Occupation: Rancher
 Offices/Honors: New Mexico Territory Council, 1869–71 (President), 1873–75, and 1878–80
 Miscellaneous: Resided Santa Fe, NM; and Galisteo, Santa Fe, Co., NM. Brother of Colonel Miguel E. Pino (2 NM Infantry).
 Buried: Village Cemetery, Galisteo, NM (unmarked?)
 References: Obituary, *Santa Fe Daily New Mexican,* Nov. 16, 1896. Ralph E. Twitchell. *The History of the Military Occupation of the Territory of New Mexico from 1846 to 1851.* Denver, CO, 1909. Letters Received, Volunteer Service Branch, Adjutant General's Office, Files N81(VS)1861) and P319(VS)1868, National Archives. Benjamin M. Read. *Illustrated History of New Mexico.* Santa Fe, NM, 1912. Ralph E. Twitchell. *The Leading Facts of New Mexican History.* Cedar Rapids, IA, 1911. Jerry D. Thompson. *A Civil War History of the New Mexico Volunteers & Militia.* Albuquerque, NM, 2015. www.ancestry.net.

Henry Raymond Selden

Captain, 5 U.S. Infantry, Oct. 18, 1855. Commanded Post of Fort Marcy (NM), Department of New Mexico, May–Sept. 1863. Major, 13 U.S. Infantry, July 1, 1863. Colonel, 1 NM Infantry, April 25, 1864. Commanded Post of Fort Union (NM), Department of New Mexico, Sept. 1864–Feb. 1865. Battle honors: Valverde, Glorieta.
 Born: March 14, 1821, Bennington, VT
 Died: Feb. 2, 1865 Fort Union, NM (congestion of the brain)
 Education: Graduated U.S. Military Academy, West Point, NY, 1843
 Other Wars: Mexican War (1 Lieutenant, 5 U.S. Infantry)
 Occupation: Regular Army (Major, 13 U.S. Infantry)
 Miscellaneous: Resided Bennington, Bennington Co., VT
 Buried: Santa Fe National Cemetery, Santa Fe, NM (Section C, Plot 497). Cenotaph, Old First Cemetery, Bennington, VT.
 References: George W. Cullum. *Biographical Register of the Officers and Graduates of the U.S. Military Academy.* Third Edition. Boston, MA, 1891. Letters Received, Appointment, Commission and Personal Branch, Adjutant General's Office, File 4812(ACP)1877, National Archives. Pension File and Military Service File, National Archives. Jerry D. Thompson. *A Civil War His-*

tory of the New Mexico Volunteers & Militia. Albuquerque, NM, 2015.

Robert Hay Stapleton

Colonel, 3 NM Militia, Dec. 6, 1861. Lieutenant Colonel, 3 NM Militia, Jan. 1, 1862. Honorably discharged, April 1, 1862. Battle honors: Valverde.

Born: 1828? Ireland
Died: About July 10, 1889, Socorro, NM
Other Wars: Corporal, Co. K, 2 U.S. Dragoons, 1849–54
Occupation: Dry goods merchant and lumber manufacturer
Miscellaneous: Resided Socorro, Socorro Co., NM
Buried: Probably San Miguel Cemetery, Socorro, NM
References: Pension File, National Archives. Jerry D. Thompson. *A Civil War History of the New Mexico Volunteers & Militia*. Albuquerque, NM, 2015. Obituary, *Sierra County Advocate*, July 19, 1889. "Honorable Mention," *Santa Fe Daily New Mexican*, July 21, 1891.

Ceran St. Vrain

Colonel, 1 NM Infantry, Aug. 13, 1861. Resigned Sept. 20, 1861, since "a multiplicity of private business prevents me from devoting that attention to my command which the service requires and demands."

Born: May 5, 1802, near St. Louis, MO
Died: Oct. 28, 1870 Mora, NM
Occupation: Fur trader and merchant
Miscellaneous: Resided Taos, Taos Co., NM; Pueblo, Pueblo Co., CO; and Mora, Mora Co., NM
Buried: St. Vrain Cemetery, Mora, NM
References: Edward H. Broadhead. *Ceran St. Vrain, 1802–1870*. Second Edition. Pueblo, CO, 1987. Allen Johnson and Dumas Malone, editors. *Dictionary of American Biography*. New York City, NY, 1964. Dan L. Thrapp. *Encyclopedia of Frontier Biography*. Glendale, CA, 1988. LeRoy R. Hafen, editor. *Mountain Men and Fur Traders of the Far West: Eighteen Biographical Sketches*. Selected by Harvey L. Carter. Lincoln, NE, 1982. Nolie Mumey, "Black Beard: Ceran St. Vrain, Frontiersman, Indian Trader, Territorial and Political Leader, and Pioneer Businessman," *The Denver Westerners Monthly Roundup*, Vol. 14, No. 1 (January 1958). Nolie Mumey. *Old Forts and Trading Posts of the West: Bent's Old Fort and Bent's New Fort on the Arkansas River*. Denver, CO, 1956. Edwin L. Sabin. *Kit Carson Days, 1809–1868: "Adventures in the Path of Empire."* Revised Edition. New York City, NY, 1935. Benjamin M. Read. *Illustrated History of New Mexico*. Santa Fe, NM, 1912. Obituary, *Santa Fe Daily New Mexican,* Oct. 29, 1870. Military Service File, National Archives.

Ceran St. Vrain (Edwin L. Sabin. *Kit Carson Days (1809-1868)*. Chicago, Illinois, 1914).

Ceran St. Vrain (Benjamin M. Read. *Illustrated History of New Mexico*. Santa Fe, New Mexico, 1912).

OREGON

Regiments

1st Cavalry
Thomas R. Cornelius	Nov. 7, 1861	Resigned July 17, 1862
Reuben F. Maury	March 30, 1863	Mustered out July 18, 1865

1st Infantry
George B. Currey	June 24, 1865	Mustered out Nov. 20, 1865

Biographies

Thomas Ramsey Cornelius

Colonel, 1 OR Cavalry, Nov. 7, 1861. Commanded Post of Fort Walla Walla (WA), District of Oregon, Department of the Pacific, June 1862. Resigned July 15, 1862.

Born: Nov. 15, 1827 Howard Co., MO

Thomas Ramsey Cornelius, post-war (Elwood Evans. *History of the Pacific Northwest: Oregon and Washington.* Portland, Oregon, 1889).

Died: June 24, 1899, Cornelius, OR
Other Wars: Yakima Indian War, 1855-56 (Colonel, Oregon Mounted Volunteers)
Occupation: Farmer and grain merchant
Offices/Honors: Oregon Territory Council, 1856-58. Oregon Senate, 1859-62 and 1864-76 (President, 1866-67).
Miscellaneous: Resided Cornelius, Washington Co., OR
Buried: Cornelius Methodist Cemetery, Cornelius, OR
References: Elwood Evans. *History of the Pacific Northwest: Oregon and Washington.* Portland, OR, 1889. *Portrait and Biographical Record of Western Oregon.* Chicago, IL, 1904. Obituary, *Hillsboro Argus,* June 29, 1899. Obituary, *Portland Sunday Oregonian,* June 25, 1899. Obituary, *Salem Daily Capital Journal,* June 26, 1899. Harvey K. Hines. *An Illustrated History of the State of Oregon.* Chicago, IL, 1893. Pension File and Military Service File, National Archives. Herbert O. Lang, editor. *History of the Willamette Valley.* Portland, OR, 1885. Charles H. Carey. *A General History of Oregon Prior to 1861.* Portland, OR, 1935. Charles S. Cornelius, compiler. *History of the Cornelius Family in America. Historical, Genealogical, Biographical.* Grand Rapids, MI, 1926.

George Byron Currey

1 Lieutenant, Co. E, 1 OR Cavalry, Jan. 1, 1862. Captain, Co. E, 1 OR Cavalry, March 20, 1862. Commanded Post of Fort Walla Walla (WA), District of Oregon, Department of the

Pacific, Jan. 1864. Commanded Post of Fort Dalles (OR), District of Oregon, Department of the Pacific, Nov. 1864. Commanded Post of Fort Hoskins (OR), District of Oregon, Department of the Pacific, Jan.–March 1865. Discharged, March 3, 1865, to accept promotion. Lieutenant Colonel, 1 OR Infantry, March 22, 1865. Commanded Post of Fort Walla Walla (WA), District of Oregon, Department of the Pacific, April–June 1865. Colonel, 1 OR Infantry, June 24, 1865. Commanded District of Oregon, Department of the Columbia, July 1865. Commanded Department of the Columbia, Aug.–Nov. 1865. Honorably mustered out, Nov. 20, 1865. Battle honors: Grande Ronde Prairie, Expedition to Southeastern Oregon.

Born: April 4, 1833, Crawfordsville, IN
Died: March 2, 1906, LaGrande, OR
Education: Attended Wabash College, Crawfordsville, IN
Other Wars: Rogue River Indian War (2 Lieutenant, 2 OR Mounted Volunteers)
Occupation: Lawyer, farmer, and newspaper editor
Offices/Honors: Receiver, U.S. Land Office, LaGrande, OR, 1883–85
Miscellaneous: Resided The Dalles, Wasco Co., OR (1860); Salem, Marion Co., OR, 1866–68; LaFayette, Yamhill Co., OR, 1868–72; Canyon City, Grant Co., OR, 1872–80; and LaGrande, Union Co., OR
Buried: Grandview Cemetery, LaGrande, OR (Block 116, Lot 3)
References: Obituary, *LaGrande Evening Observer*, March 2 and March 5, 1906. Howard M. Corning, editor. *Dictionary of Oregon History*. Second Edition. Portland, OR, 1989. Pension File and Military Service File, National Archives. Priscilla Knuth, editor, "Cavalry in the Indian Country, 1864," *Oregon Historical Quarterly*, Vol. 65, No. 1 (March 1964). Charles H. Carey. *A General History of Oregon Prior to 1861*. Portland, OR, 1935. Frances Fuller Victor, "The First Oregon Cavalry," *Oregon Historical Quarterly*, Vol. 3, No. 2 (June 1902). Elwood Evans. *History of the Pacific Northwest: Oregon and Washington*. Portland, OR, 1889. Obituary, *Portland Morning Oregonian*, March 3, 1906. Letters Received, Volunteer Service Branch, Adjutant General's Office, File C672(VS)1865, National Archives. Gregory Michno. *The Deadliest Indian War in the West: The Snake Conflict, 1864–1868*. Caldwell, ID, 2007.

Reuben Fry Maury

Lieutenant Colonel, 1 OR Cavalry, Nov. 7, 1861. Colonel, 1 OR Cavalry, March 30, 1863. Commanded Post of Fort Dalles (OR), District of Oregon, Department of the Pacific, Nov. 1863–April 1864. Commanded Post of Fort Boise (ID), District of Oregon, Department of the Pacific, June–Oct. 1864. Commanded Post of Fort Vancouver (WA), District of Oregon, Department of the Pacific, Dec. 1864–Feb. 1865. Commanded District of Oregon, Department of the Pacific, March–July 1865. Honorably mustered out, July 18, 1865. Battle honors: Expedition Against the Snake Indians in Idaho (1862), Expedition Against the Snake Indians in Idaho (1863).

Born: May 23, 1821, near Owingsville, Bath Co., KY
Died: Feb. 20, 1906 near Jacksonville, OR
Education: Attended U.S. Military Academy, West Point, NY (Class of 1841)
Other Wars: Mexican War (2 Lieutenant, Co. A, 1 KY Infantry)
Occupation: Freighter and merchant before war. Miner, farmer, and stock raiser after war.
Miscellaneous: Resided Sacramento, CA, 1850–52; Jacksonville, Jackson Co., OR, after 1852

George Byron Currey (Oregon Historical Society Library [CN-020568]).

Reuben Fry Maury (Oregon Historical Society Library [CN-017814]).

Reuben Fry Maury, post-war (*Portrait and Biographical Record of Western Oregon*. Chicago, Illinois, 1904).

Buried: Jacksonville Cemetery, Jacksonville, OR

References: *Portrait and Biographical Record of Western Oregon*. Chicago, IL, 1904. Obituary, *Medford Mail*, Feb. 23, 1906. Pension File and Military Service File, National Archives. L.C. Merriam, Jr., editor, "The First Oregon Cavalry and the Oregon Central Military Road Survey of 1865," *Oregon Historical Quarterly*, Vol. 60, No. 1 (March 1959). Priscilla Knuth, editor, "Cavalry in the Indian Country, 1864," *Oregon Historical Quarterly*, Vol. 65, No. 1 (March 1964). *History of Southern Oregon, Comprising Jackson, Josephine, Douglas, Curry and Coos Counties*. Portland, OR, 1884. Sue Crabtree West, compiler. *The Maury Family Tree, Descendants of Mary Anne Fontaine (1690–1755) and Matthew Maury (1686–1752)*. Birmingham, AL, 1971. Gregory Michno. *The Deadliest Indian War in the West: The Snake Conflict, 1864–1868*. Caldwell, ID, 2007.

Texas

Regiments

1st Cavalry
Edmund J. Davis	Oct. 26, 1862	Promoted **Brig. Gen., USV,** Nov. 10, 1864
John L. Haynes	May 20, 1865	Mustered out Oct. 31, 1865

2nd Cavalry (consolidated with 1st TX Cavalry, Sept. 10, 1864)
John L. Haynes	Nov. 5, 1863	To 1st TX Cavalry Oct. 5, 1864

Biographies

John Leal Haynes

Colonel of Cavalry, Staff of Brig. Gen. Andrew J. Hamilton, Military Governor of Texas, Nov. 24, 1862. Colonel, 2 TX Cavalry, Nov. 5, 1863. Commanded Cavalry Brigade, 2 Division, 13 Army Corps, Department of the Gulf, April–June 1864. Lieutenant Colonel, 1 TX Cavalry, Oct. 5, 1864, upon consolidation of 2 TX Cavalry with 1 TX Cavalry. Colonel, 1 TX Cavalry, May 20, 1865. Honorably mustered out, Oct. 31, 1865. Battle honors: Expedition from Morganza to Bayou Sara, LA (Bayou Sara).

Born: July 3, 1821, Liberty, Bedford Co., VA
Died: April 2, 1888, Laredo, TX
Other Wars: Mexican War (probably Sergeant, Co. E, 1 TN Infantry, although biographies claim service as 1 Lieutenant, 1 MS Infantry)
Occupation: Merchant, lawyer, newspaper editor, and Republican politician
Offices/Honors: Texas House of Representatives, 1857–61. U.S. Assessor of Internal Revenue, Austin, TX, 1865–68. U.S. Collector of Customs, Galveston, TX, 1869–70. U.S. Collector of Customs, Brownsville, TX, 1872–84.
Miscellaneous: Resided Rio Grande City, Starr Co., TX; Austin, Travis Co., TX; Brownsville, Cameron Co., TX; and Laredo, Webb Co., TX
Buried: Oakwood Cemetery, Austin, TX (Swisher Plot, Section 1, Lot 34)

John Leal Haynes (E. Jacobs, Photographic Gallery, 93 Camp Street, New Orleans, Louisiana; UTSA Special Collections-Institute of Texan Cultures, University of Texas at San Antonio, Texas [General Photograph Collection, 076-0555]).

John Leal Haynes (and his wife, Angelica Irene) (The New Orleans Photographic Co., 57 Camp Street, New Orleans, Louisiana; DeGolyer Library, Southern Methodist University, Lawrence T. Jones III Texas Photography Collection [Ag2008.0005]).

References: Walter P. Webb, editor. *The Handbook of Texas.* Austin, TX, 1952. Eldon S. Branda, editor. *The Handbook of Texas, A Supplement, Volume 3.* Austin, TX, 1976. Obituary, *Dallas Morning News,* April 7, 1888. Obituary, *Galveston Daily News,* April 3, 1888. Pension File and Military Service File, National Archives. William DeRyee and R.E. Moore. *The Texas Album of the Eighth Legislature, 1860.* Austin, TX, 1860. Jerry D. Thompson. *Mexican Texans in the Union Army.* El Paso, TX, 1986. James Marten, "Texans in the U.S. Army: True to the Union," *North & South,* Vol. 3, No. 1 (Nov. 1999). Letters Received, Volunteer Service Branch, Adjutant General's Office, Files H882(VS)1863 and H1298(VS)1865, National Archives. Jerry D. Thompson and Lawrence T. Jones III. *Civil War & Revolution on the Rio Grande Frontier: A Narrative and Photographic History.* Austin, TX, 2004. James A. Mundie, Jr., Dean E. Letzring, Bruce S. Allardice, and John H. Luckey. *Texas Burial Sites of Civil War Notables: A Biographical and Pictorial Field Guide.* Hillsboro, TX, 2002. http://www.haynesfamily.com/John1821.htm.

Washington Territory

Regiments

1st Infantry

Justus D. Steinberger	Oct. 19, 1861	Mustered out Jan. 13, 1864
Justus D. Steinberger	July 9, 1864	Mustered out March 18, 1865

Biographies

Justus Dunott Steinberger

Captain, AAG, USV, Sept. 28, 1861. AAG, Staff of Brig. Gen. Thomas W. Sherman. Resigned Oct. 10, 1861, to accept promotion. Colonel, 1 WA Territory Infantry, Oct. 19, 1861. Commanded District of Oregon, Department of the Pacific, May–July 1862. Commanded Fort Walla Walla (WA), District of Oregon, Department of the Pacific, Aug. 1862–March 1863, June–Dec. 1863, and Sept. 1864–Feb. 1865. Commanded Fort Lapwai (WA), District of Oregon, Department of the Pacific, April–June 1863. Suspected of pro–Southern sympathies, he was mustered out, Jan. 13, 1864, "in consequence of his regiment being below the required standard number of enlisted men." Backed by numerous expressions of support, including from his long-time friend, General Ulysses S. Grant, he was reinstated as Colonel, 1 WA Territory Infantry, July 9, 1864. Honorably mustered out, March 18, 1865.

Born: Sept. 23, 1825 Montgomery Co., PA

Died: Oct. 13, 1870 Helena, MT (thrown from a horse)

Education: Attended Dickinson College, Carlisle, PA. M. D., University of Pennsylvania Medical School, Philadelphia, PA, 1846.

Occupation: Physician and express company agent before war. Major, Paymaster, USA, after war.

Miscellaneous: Resided Marysville, Yuba Co., CA; Portland, Multnomah Co., OR; New York City, NY; and Helena, Lewis and Clark Co., MT

Justus Dunott Steinberger (USAMHI [RG98S-CWP76.77]).

Buried: Custer Battlefield National Cemetery, Crow Agency, MT (Section A, Grave 747)

References: Obituary, *New York Daily Tribune*, Oct. 15, 1870. *The American Annual Cyclopedia and Register of Important Events of the Year 1870.* New York City, NY, 1871. Edmond S. Meany. *History of the State of Washington.* New York City, NY, 1909. Obituary, *Washington Standard.*

Oct. 22, 1870. Letters Received, Commission Branch, Adjutant General's Office, File S1263 (CB)1866, National Archives. Letters Received, Volunteer Service Branch, Adjutant General's Office, File W2192(VS)1863, National Archives. Military Service File, National Archives. Letters Received, Adjutant General's Office, File S1030(AGO)1861, National Archives. Frank A. Kittredge, Ashmun N. Brown, and George W. Easterbrook, "Washington Territory in the War Between the States," *Washington Historical Quarterly*, Vol. 2, No. 1 (Oct. 1907). Priscilla Knuth, editor, "Cavalry in the Indian Country, 1864," *Oregon Historical Quarterly*, Vol. 65, No. 1 (March 1964). Guy V. Henry. *Military Record of Civilian Appointments in the United States Army*. Vol. 2. New York City, NY, 1873. John Y. Simon, editor. *The Papers of Ulysses S. Grant*. Vol. 10: January 1–May 31, 1864. Carbondale, IL, 1982. John Y. Simon, editor. *The Papers of Ulysses S. Grant*. Vol. 17: January 1–September 30, 1867. Carbondale, IL, 1991.

Justus Dunott Steinberger (Edmond S. Meany. *History of the State of Washington.* **New York City, New York, 1909).**

Bibliography

Books

Abbe, Cleveland, and Josephine Genung Nichols. *Abbe-Abbey Genealogy: In Memory of John Abbe and His Descendants*. New Haven, CT: Tuttle, Morehouse & Taylor Co., 1916.

Abel, Annie Heloise. *The American Indian as Participant in the Civil War*. Cleveland, OH: Arthur H. Clark Co., 1919.

Adams, Andrew N., ed. *A Genealogical History of Henry Adams of Braintree, Mass., and His Descendants*. Rutland, VT: Tuttle Co., 1898.

Adams, Franklin G., ed. *Transactions of the Kansas State Historical Society, 1889–96*. Topeka, KS: J.K. Hudson, State Printer, 1896.

Album of Genealogy and Biography Cook County, Illinois. Chicago: La Salle Book Co., 1900.

Allendorf, Donald. *Long Road to Liberty: The Odyssey of a German Regiment in the Yankee Army, the 15th Missouri Volunteer Infantry*. Kent, OH: Kent State University Press, 2006.

Altshuler, Constance Wynn. *Cavalry Yellow & Infantry Blue: Army Officers in Arizona Between 1851 and 1886*. Tucson, AZ: Arizona Historical Society, 1991.

Alumni Record of Baker University. Baldwin City, KS: Baker University, 1917.

Alumni Record of Wesleyan University, Middletown, Connecticut. Third Edition, 1881–83. Hartford, CT: Case, Lockwood & Brainard Co., 1883.

The American Annual Cyclopedia and Register of Important Events of the Year 1867. New York City: D. Appleton & Co., 1868.

The American Annual Cyclopedia and Register of Important Events of the Year 1870. New York City: D. Appleton & Co., 1871.

The American Annual Cyclopedia and Register of Important Events of the Year 1872. New York City: D. Appleton & Co., 1873.

American Biography: A New Cyclopedia. Vol. 10. New York City: American Historical Society, 1922.

Anders, Leslie. *The Eighteenth Missouri*. Indianapolis, IN: Bobbs-Merrill Co., 1968.

_____. *The Twenty-first Missouri: From Home Guard to Union Regiment*. Westport, CT: Greenwood Press, 1975.

Andreas, Alfred T. *History of the State of Kansas*. Chicago: A.T. Andreas, 1883.

_____. *History of the State of Nebraska*. Chicago: Western Historical Co., 1882.

Annual Report of the Adjutant General of Missouri for the Year Ending December 31, 1865. Jefferson City, MO: Emory S. Foster, 1866.

Annual Report of the Adjutant General of the State of Missouri, December 31, 1863. Jefferson City, MO: W.A. Curry, 1864.

The Association of the Graduates of the United States Military Academy. Annual Reunion, June 17th, 1871. New York City: Waldron & Payne, 1871.

Aubin, J. Harris, comp. *Register of the Military Order of the Loyal Legion of the United States*. Boston: Massachusetts Commandery, 1906.

Bacarella, Michael. *Lincoln's Foreign Legion: The 39th New York Infantry, The Garibaldi Guard*. Shippensburg, PA: White Mane Publishing Co., 1996.

Bakewell, B.G., comp. *The Family Book of Bakewell-Page-Campbell*. Pittsburgh, PA: Wm. G. Johnston & Co., 1896.

Banasik, Michael E., ed. *Missouri in 1861: The Civil War Letters of Franc B. Wilkie, Newspaper Correspondent*. Iowa City, IA: Camp Pope Bookshop, 2001.

_____, ed. *Reluctant Cannoneer: The Diary of Robert T. McMahan of the Twenty-Fifth Independent Ohio Light Artillery*. Iowa City, IA: Camp Pope Bookshop, 2000.

Bangs, Isaac S., "The Ullmann Brigade," *War Papers Read Before the Commandery of the State of Maine MOLLUS*. Vol. 2. Portland, ME: Lefavor-Tower Co., 1902.

Barker, Lorenzo A. *Military History (Michigan Boys) Company D, 66th Illinois, Birge's Western Sharpshooters in the Civil War, 1861–1865*. Huntington, WV: Blue Acorn Press, 1994.

Barnes, William H. *The Fortieth Congress of the United States: Historical and Biographical*. New York City: George E. Perine, 1870.

Barnes, William Horatio. *The American Government. Biographies of Members of the House of Representatives of the Forty-Third Congress*. New York City: Nelson & Phillips, 1874.

_____. *History of Congress: The Fortieth Congress of the United States, 1867–1869*. New York City: W.H. Barnes & Co., 1871.

_____. *History of Congress. The Forty-First Congress of the United States, 1869–1871*. New York City: W.H. Barnes & Co., 1872.

Barns, Chancy R., ed. *The Commonwealth of Missouri: A Centennial Record*. St. Louis: Bryan, Brand & Co., 1877.

Bateman, Newton, and Paul Selby, eds. *Historical Encyclopedia of Illinois and History of Sangamon County*. Chicago: Munsell Publishing Co., 1912.

Bateman, Newton, Paul Selby, Robert W. Ross, and John J. Bullington, eds. *Historical Encyclopedia of Illinois and History of Fayette County*. Chicago: Munsell Publishing Co., 1910.

Bay, William V.N. *Reminiscences of the Bench and Bar of Missouri*. St. Louis: F.H. Thomas & Co., 1878.

Bayles, John C., and G. H. Bayles. *Jesse Bayles: A Partial List of his Descendants*. Morgantown, WV: John C. Bayles, 1944.

Bayles, Richard M. *History of Windham County, Connecticut*. New York City: W.W. Preston, 1889.

Bearss, Edwin C. *Forrest at Brice's Cross Roads and in North Mississippi in 1864*. Dayton, OH: Morningside Bookshop, 1979.

Belcher, Dennis W. *The 11th Missouri Volunteer Infantry in the Civil War: A History and Roster*. Jefferson, NC: McFarland, 2011.

The Bench and Bar of St. Louis, Kansas City, Jefferson City, and Other Missouri Cities. St. Louis and Chicago: American Biographical Publishing Co., 1884.

Bennett, Lyman G., and William M. Haigh. *History of the Thirty-Sixth Regiment Illinois Volunteers during the War of the Rebellion*. Aurora, IL: Knickerbocker & Hodder, Printers, 1876.

Bibliography

Bicknell, Thomas W., ed. *History and Genealogy of the Bicknell Family and Some Collateral Lines of Normandy, Great Britain and America.* Providence, RI: T.W. Bicknell, 1913.

A Biographical and Genealogical History of Southeastern Nebraska. Chicago and New York: Lewis Publishing Co., 1904.

Biographical and Historical Catalogue of Washington and Jefferson College. Cincinnati: Elm Street Printing Co., 1889.

Biographical and Historical Memoirs of Northeast Arkansas. Chicago, Nashville and St. Louis: Goodspeed Publishing Co., 1889.

Biographical and Historical Memoirs of Pulaski, Jefferson, Lonoke, Faulkner, Grant, Saline, Perry, Garland and Hot Spring Counties, Arkansas. Chicago, Nashville and St. Louis: Goodspeed Publishing Co., 1889.

The Biographical Dictionary and Portrait Gallery of Representative Men of Chicago, St. Louis and the World's Columbian Exposition. Chicago and New York: American Biographical Publishing Co., 1893.

The Biographical Encyclopedia of Illinois of the Nineteenth Century. Philadelphia: Galaxy Publishing Co., 1875.

Biographical Souvenir of the Counties of Buffalo, Kearney and Phelps, Nebraska. Chicago: F.A. Battey & Co., 1890.

Biographies and Engravings of Grand Masters, Grand Treasurers and Grand Secretaries of the Grand Lodge of Missouri. St. Louis: A.R. Fleming Printing Co., 1901.

Blackmar, Frank William, ed. *Kansas: A Cyclopedia of State History.* Chicago: Standard Publishing Co., 1912.

Blodgett, Edwin A. *Ten Generations of Blodgetts in America.* Barre, VT: Modern Printing Co., 1969.

Boernstein, Henry. *Memoirs of a Nobody: The Missouri Years of an Austrian Radical, 1849–1866.* Translated and edited by Steven Rowan. St. Louis: Missouri Historical Society Press, 1997.

Book of Biographies Berks County, Pennsylvania. Buffalo, NY: Biographical Publishing Co., 1898.

Boucher, John N. *History of Westmoreland County, Pennsylvania.* New York and Chicago: Lewis Publishing Co., 1906.

Bowen, Clarence W. *The History of Woodstock, Connecticut.* Norwood, MA: Plimpton Press, 1926.

Boyle, John, comp. *Boyle Genealogy: John Boyle of Virginia and Kentucky.* St. Louis: Perrin & Smith Printing Co., 1909.

Branch, Benjamin H., Jr. *The Branch, Harris, Jarvis and Chinn Book: A Family Outline.* Ann Arbor, MI: Benjamin H. Branch, 1963.

Branda, Eldon S., ed. *The Handbook of Texas, a Supplement, Volume 3.* Austin, TX: Texas State Historical Association, 1976.

Britton, Wiley. *The Union Indian Brigade in the Civil War.* Kansas City, MO: Franklin Hudson Publishing Co., 1922.

Broadhead, Edward H. *Ceran St. Vrain, 1802–1870.* Second Edition. Pueblo, CO: Pueblo County Historical Society, 1987.

Brown, Fred R. *History of the Ninth U.S. Infantry, 1799–1909.* Chicago: R.R. Donnelley & Sons, 1909.

Buresh, Lumir F. *October 25th and the Battle of Mine Creek.* Kansas City, MO: Lowell Press, 1977.

Busbey, T.A., ed. *The Biographical Directory of the Railway Officials of America.* Chicago: Lakeside Press, 1893.

Caldwell, E.F. *A Souvenir History of Lawrence, Kansas.* Lawrence, KS: E.F. Caldwell, 1898.

Campbell, Kathryn H. *John Biggs, the Welshman, and His Descendants, 1729–1979.* Dallas, TX: K.H. Campbell, 1981.

Carey, Charles H. *A General History of Oregon Prior to 1861.* Portland, OR: Metropolitan Press, 1935.

Case, Theodore S., ed. *History of Kansas City, Missouri.* Syracuse, NY: D. Mason & Co., 1888.

Casto, David E. *Arkansas Late in the Civil War: The 8th Missouri Volunteer Cavalry, April 1864–July 1865.* Charleston, SC: History Press, 2013.

Catalogue of the Delta Kappa Epsilon Fraternity: Biographical and Statistical. New York City: Council Publishing Co., 1890.

Catalogue of the Officers and Alumni of Washington and Lee University, Lexington, Virginia, 1749–1888. Baltimore, MD: John Murphy & Co., 1888.

Cathcart, William, ed. *The Baptist Encyclopaedia.* Philadelphia: Louis H. Everts, 1881.

The Centennial History of Perry County, Missouri, 1821–1921. Perryville, MO: Perry County Historical Society, 1984.

Chase, Theodore R. *The Michigan University Book, 1844–1880.* Detroit, MI: Richmond, Backus & Co., 1880.

Christensen, Lawrence O., William E. Foley, Gary R. Kremer, and Kenneth H. Winn, eds. *Dictionary of Missouri Biography.* Columbia, MO: University of Missouri Press, 1999.

Clayton, Powell. *The Aftermath of the Civil War in Arkansas.* New York City: Neale Publishing Co., 1915.

Cohen, Andrew Wender. *Contraband: Smuggling and the Birth of the American Century.* New York and London: W.W. Norton & Co., 2015.

Colton, George W. *A Genealogical Record of the Descendants of Quartermaster George Colton.* Lancaster, PA: Wickersham Printing Co., 1912.

Commemorative Biographical Encyclopedia of the Juniata Valley, Comprising the Counties of Huntingdon, Mifflin, Juniata, and Perry, Pennsylvania. Chambersburg, PA: J.M. Runk & Co., 1897.

Companions of the Military Order of the Loyal Legion of the United States. New York City: L.R. Hamersly Co., 1901.

Conard, Howard L., ed. *Encyclopedia of the History of Missouri.* New York, Louisville, and St. Louis: Southern History Co., 1901.

Connelley, William E. *The Life of Preston B. Plumb, 1837–1891.* Chicago: Browne & Howell Co., 1913.

_____. *Quantrill and the Border Wars.* Cedar Rapids, IA: The Torch Press, 1910.

_____. *A Standard History of Kansas and Kansans.* Chicago and New York: Lewis Publishing Co., 1918.

Convery, William J., "John M. Chivington," *Soldiers West: Biographies from the Military Frontier.* Edited by Paul A. Hutton and Durwood Ball. Second Edition. Norman, OK: University of Oklahoma Press, 2009.

Cooper, Edward S. *John McDonald and the Whiskey Ring: From Thug to Grant's Inner Circle.* Madison, NJ: Fairleigh Dickinson University Press, 2017.

Cooper, Martha L. *The Civil War and Nodaway County, Missouri: A Border County in a Border State.* Signal Mountain, TN: Mountain Press, 1989.

Cooper, W. *Sketches of the Senators and Representatives in the Fifty-Fourth General Assembly of the State of Ohio.* Columbus, OH: W. Cooper, 1861.

Cordley, Richard. *A History of Lawrence, Kansas, from the First Settlement to the Close of the Rebellion.* Lawrence, KS: Lawrence Journal Press, 1895.

Cornelius, Charles S., comp. *History of the Cornelius Family in America. Historical, Genealogical, Biographical.* Grand Rapids, MI: C.S. Cornelius, 1926.

Corning, Howard M., ed. *Dictionary of Oregon History.* Second Edition. Portland, OR: Binford & Mort Publishing, 1989.

Cornwell, Charles H. *St. Louis Mayors Brief Biographies.* St. Louis: St. Louis Public Library, 1965.

Cox, James, ed. *Notable St. Louisans in 1900.* St. Louis: Benesch Art Publishing Co., 1900.

Craig, Reginald S. *The Fighting Parson: The Biography of Col. John M. Chivington.* Tucson, AZ: Westernlore Press, 1959.

Crissey, William E. *Warrensburg: A History with Folk Lore.* N.p.: W.E. Crissey, 1924.

Croffut, William A., and John M. Morris. *The Military and Civil History of Connecticut During the War of 1861-65.* New York City: Ledyard Bill, 1868.

Cullum, George W. *Biographical Register of the Officers and Graduates of the U.S. Military Academy.* Third Edition. Boston: Houghton, Mifflin & Co., 1891.

Cunningham, Mary B., and Jeanne C. Blythe. *The Founding Family of St. Louis.* St. Louis: Midwest Technical Publications, 1977.

Current, Richard N. *Lincoln's Loyalists: Union Soldiers from the Confederacy.* Boston: Northeastern University Press, 1992.

Dandridge, Anne Spottswood, comp. *The Forman Genealogy.* Cleveland, OH: Forman-Bassett-Hatch Co., 1903.

Davis, Herman S. *Reminiscences of General William Larimer and of His Son William H.H. Larimer, Two of the Founders of Denver City.* Lancaster, PA: New Era Printing Co., 1918.

Davis, Walter B., and Daniel S. Durrie. *An Illustrated History of Missouri.* St. Louis: A.J. Hall & Co., 1876.

Dawson, Charles. *Pioneer Tales of the Oregon Trail and of Jefferson County.* Topeka, KS: Crane & Co., 1912.

Dean, Benjamin D. *Recollections of the 26th Missouri Infantry in the War for the Union.* Lamar, MO: Southwest Missourian Office, 1892.

Dearinger, David B., ed. *Paintings and Sculpture in the Collection of the National Academy of Design.* Volume 1, 1826-1925. Manchester, VT: Hudson Hills Press, 2004.

Denslow, Ray V. *Civil War and Masonry in Missouri.* St. Louis: Grand Lodge, A.F. & A.M., State of Missouri, 1930.

Denslow, William R. *Centennial History of Grundy County, Missouri.* Trenton, MO: W.R. Denslow, 1939.

DeRyee, William, and R.E. Moore. *The Texas Album of the Eighth Legislature, 1860.* Austin, TX: Miner, Lambert & Perry, 1860.

Descendants of Thomas Canfield and Matthew Camfield. Hillsboro, KS: Canfield Family Association, 2006.

Diehl, Harry A. *The Diehl-Deal-Dill-Dale Families of America.* Volume 1. *Diehl Families of York and Adams Counties, Pennsylvania.* Wilmington, DE: H.A. Diehl, 1989.

Dillard, David W. *The Union Post Commanders at Pilot Knob, 1861-1865.* Ironton, MO: Arcadia Valley Career Technology Center, 2013.

Dobak, William A. *Fort Riley and Its Neighbors.* Norman, OK: University of Oklahoma Press, 1998.

Dobbs, Hugh J. *History of Gage County, Nebraska.* Lincoln, NE: Western Publishing & Engraving Co., 1918.

Donald, David, ed. *Inside Lincoln's Cabinet: The Civil War Diaries of Salmon P. Chase.* New York, London, and Toronto: Longmans, Green and Co., 1954.

Doughtie, Beatrice M. *The Mackeys and Allied Families.* Decatur, GA: Bowen Press, 1957.

Douglass, Robert S. *History of Southeast Missouri.* Chicago and New York: Lewis Publishing Co., 1912.

Drury, Augustus W. *History of the City of Dayton and Montgomery County, Ohio.* Chicago: S.J. Clarke Publishing Co., 1909.

Duncan, Russell, ed. *Blue-Eyed Child of Fortune: The Civil War Letters of Colonel Robert Gould Shaw.* Athens, GA: University of Georgia Press, 1992.

Dunham, Niles J. *A History of Jerauld County, South Dakota.* Wessington Springs, SD: N.J. Dunham, 1910.

Dwight, Benjamin W. *The History of the Descendants of Elder John Strong of Northampton, Massachusetts.* Albany, NY: Joel Munsell, 1871.

_____. *The History of the Descendants of John Dwight of Dedham, Massachusetts.* New York City: John F. Trow & Son, 1874.

Dyer, David P. *Autobiography and Reminiscences.* St. Louis: William Harvey Miner Co., 1922.

Easley, Barbara P. *Obituaries of Washington County, Arkansas.* Bowie, MD: Heritage Books, 1996.

Ebright, Homer K. *The History of Baker University.* Baldwin City, KS: H.K. Ebright, 1951.

Edmonds, David C. *The Guns of Port Hudson: The Investment, Siege and Reduction.* Lafayette, LA: Acadiana Press, 1984.

_____. *Yankee Autumn in Acadiana: A Narrative of the Great Texas Overland Expedition Through Southwestern Louisiana, October-December 1863.* Lafayette, LA: Acadiana Press, 1979.

Edmunds, A.C. *Pen Sketches of Nebraskans.* Lincoln, NE: R. & J. Wilbur, Stationers, 1871.

Edwards, Richard, and Merna Hopewell. *Edwards's Great West and Her Commercial Metropolis, Embracing a General View of the West, and a Complete History of St. Louis.* St. Louis: Richard Edwards, 1860.

Eleventh Annual Reunion of the Association of the Graduates of the U.S. Military Academy at West Point, NY. East Saginaw, MI: E.W. Lyon, 1880.

Ellinghouse, Cletis R. *Old Wayne: A Brit's Memoir.* Philadelphia: Xlibris, 2010.

Ellis, William A., ed. *History of Norwich University, 1819-1911, Her History, Her Graduates, Her Roll of Honor.* Montpelier, VT: Capital City Press, 1911.

Evans, Elwood. *History of the Pacific Northwest: Oregon and Washington.* Portland, OR: North Pacific History Co., 1889.

Fairbanks, Jonathan, and Clyde E. Tuck. *Past and Present of Greene County, Missouri.* Indianapolis, IN: A.W. Bowen & Co., 1915.

Ferguson, James, and Robert M. Fergusson, eds. *Records of the Clan and Name of Fergusson, Ferguson and Fergus.* Supplement. Edinburgh, Scotland: David Douglas, 1899.

Fergusson, David. *Trial of Gabriel De Granada by the Inquisition in Mexico, 1642-1645.* Baltimore, MD: Press of the Friedenwald Co., 1899.

Fifteenth Annual Reunion of the Association of the Graduates of the U.S. Military Academy at West Point, NY. East Saginaw, MI: Courier Printing Co., 1884.

Fifty-third Annual Report of the Association of Graduates of the United States Military Academy. Saginaw, MI: Seemann & Peters, 1922.

First Fifty Years of Cazenovia Seminary, 1825-1875. Cazenovia, NY: Nelson & Phillips, 1877.

Fischer, LeRoy H., ed. *Oklahoma's Governors, 1890-1907: Territorial Years.* Oklahoma City, OK: Oklahoma Historical Society, 1975.

Fisher, Hugh D. *The Gun and the Gospel: Early Kansas and Chaplain Fisher.* Chicago and New York: Medical Century Co., 1899.

Fitch, George W. *Past and Present of Fayette County, Iowa.* Indianapolis, IN: B.F. Bowen & Co., 1910.

Fletcher, Edward H. *Fletcher Family History: The Descendants of Robert Fletcher of Concord, Mass.* Boston: Rand, Avery, & Co., 1881.

Fox, Simeon M., "The Story of the Seventh Kansas," *Transactions of the Kansas State Historical Society, 1903-1904.* Topeka, KS: George A. Clark, State Printer, 1904.

French, Laura M. *History of Emporia and Lyon County.* Emporia, KS: Emporia Gazette Print, 1929.

Frost, Marcus O. *Regimental History of the Tenth Missouri Volunteer Infantry.* Topeka, KS: M.O. Frost, 1892.

Fry, Alice L. *Following the Fifth Kansas Cavalry: The Letters.* Independence, MO: Two Trails Publishing, 1998.

Gabriel, Mary. *Notorious Victoria: The Life of Victoria Woodhull, Uncensored.* Chapel Hill, NC: Algonquin Books, 1998.

Genealogical and Biographical Annals of Northumberland County, Pennsylvania. Chicago: J.L. Floyd & Co., 1911.

Genealogical and Biographical Record of North-Eastern Kansas. Chicago: Lewis Publishing Co., 1900.

General Catalogue of Bowdoin College and the Medical School of Maine: A Biographical Record of Alumni and Officers, 1794-1950. Brunswick, ME: Bowdoin College, 1950.

Gentry, North Todd. *The Bench and Bar of Boone County, Missouri.* Columbia, MO: N.T. Gentry, 1916.

Gerteis, Louis S. *The Civil War in Missouri: A Military History.* Columbia, MO: University of Missouri Press, 2012.

Gorman, Nettie W. *Obituaries from The Marshfield Chronicle, Marshfield, Missouri.* Marshfield, MO: N.W. Gorman, 1991.

Graves, Henry C. *History of the Class of 1856 of Amherst College, 1852-1896.* Boston: C.H. Simonds & Co., 1896.

Greenfield Gazette, Centennial Edition, Greenfield, Mass., Feb. 1, 1892. Greenfield, MA: Greenfield Gazette, 1892.

Griffen, Albert. *Biographical Register of the Members of the Twenty-Sixth General Assembly of the State of Missouri.* St. Louis: Albert Griffen, 1872.

Groce, George C., and David H. Wallace. *The New-York Historical Society's Dictionary of Artists in America, 1564-1860.* New Haven and London: Yale University Press, 1957.

Guandolo, Joseph, ed. *Centennial McKendree College with St. Clair County History.* Lebanon, IL: McKendree College, 1928.

Gue, Benjamin F. *History of Iowa from the Earliest Times to the Beginning of the Twentieth Century.* New York City: Century History Co., 1903.

Guinn, James M. *History of the State of California and Biographical Record of the Sacramento Valley, California.* Chicago: Chapman Publishing Co., 1906.

Hafen, LeRoy R., ed. *Mountain Men and Fur Traders of the Far West: Eighteen Biographical Sketches.* Selected by Harvey L. Carter. Lincoln, NE: University of Nebraska Press, 1982.

Hall, Frank. *History of the State of Colorado.* Chicago: Blakely Printing Co., 1889.

Hall, Henry, ed. *America's Successful Men of Affairs.* New York City: New York Tribune, 1895.

Hall, Jesse A., and Leroy T. Hand. *History of Leavenworth County, Kansas.* Topeka, KS: Historical Publishing Co., 1921.

Hall, Leander. *Half Century History of the Class of 1856, Union College.* N.p.: Union College, 1906.

Hall, William K. *Springfield, Greene County, Missouri Newspaper Abstracts, 1876-1883.* Springfield, MO: Ozarks Genealogical Society, 1987.

Hallum, John. *Biographical and Pictorial History of Arkansas.* Albany, NY: Weed, Parsons & Co., 1887.

Harris, Roger Deane. *The Story of the Bloods.* Boston: Roger D. Harris, 1960.

Harrison, James L., comp. *Biographical Directory of the American Congress, 1774-1949.* Washington, D.C.: Government Printing Office, 1950.

Heidgerd, William. *The American Descendants of Chretien Du Bois of Wicres, France.* Part 7. New Paltz, NY: Huguenot Historical Society, 1973.

Heitman, Francis B. *Historical Register and Dictionary of the United States Army.* Washington, D.C.: Government Printing Office, 1903.

Hempstead, Fay. *Historical Review of Arkansas: Its Commerce, Industry and Modern Affairs.* Chicago: Lewis Publishing Co., 1911.

———. *A Pictorial History of Arkansas from Earliest Times to the Year 1890.* St. Louis and New York: N.D. Thompson Publishing Co., 1890.

Henderson, Thomas J. *Official Report of the Trial of the Hon. Albert Jackson, Judge of the Fifteenth Judicial Circuit, Before the Senate, Composing the High Court of Impeachment of the State of Missouri.* Jefferson City, MO: W.G. Cheeney, 1859.

Henry, Guy V. *Military Record of Civilian Appointments in the United States Army.* Vol. 2. New York City: D. Van Nostrand, 1873.

Herr, Pamela, and Mary Lee Spence, eds. *The Letters of Jessie Benton Fremont.* Urbana, IL: University of Illinois Press, 1993.

Herringshaw, Thomas W., ed. *Herringshaw's Encyclopedia of American Biography of the Nineteenth Century.* Chicago: American Publishers' Association, 1905.

Hickok, Charles N. *The Hickok Genealogy: Descendants of William Hickocks of Farmington, Connecticut.* Rutland, VT: Tuttle Publishing Co., 1938.

Higginson, Thomas W. *Harvard Memorial Biographies.* Cambridge, MA: Sever and Francis, 1866.

Hill, Sarah J.F. *Mrs. Hill's Journal—Civil War Reminiscences.* Edited by Mark M. Krug. Chicago: R.R. Donnelley, 1980.

Hines, Harvey K. *An Illustrated History of the State of Oregon.* Chicago: Lewis Publishing Co., 1893.

Hinshaw, William W. *Encyclopedia of American Quaker Genealogy.* Vol. 5. Baltimore, MD: Genealogical Publishing Co., 1994.

History and Families Wright County, Missouri, 1841-1991. Paducah, KY: Turner Publishing Co., 1993.

History of Adair, Sullivan, Putnam, and Schuyler Counties, Missouri. Chicago: Goodspeed Publishing Co., 1888.

History of Andrew and DeKalb Counties, Missouri, from the Earliest Time to the Present. St. Louis and Chicago: Goodspeed Publishing Co., 1888.

History of Audrain County, Missouri. St. Louis: National Historical Co., 1884.

History of Benton, Washington, Carroll, Madison, Crawford, Franklin, and Sebastian Counties, Arkansas. Chicago: Goodspeed Publishing Co., 1889.

History of Boone County, Missouri. St. Louis: Western Historical Co., 1882.

The History of Buchanan County, Missouri. St. Joseph, MO: Union Historical Co., 1881.

History of Carroll County, Missouri. St. Louis: Missouri Historical Co., 1881.

History of Champaign County, Illinois. Philadelphia: Brink, McDonough & Co., 1878.

History of Clay and Platte Counties, Missouri. St. Louis: National Historical Co., 1885.

The History of Clinton County, Ohio. Chicago: W.H. Beers & Co., 1882.

History of Cole, Moniteau, Morgan, Benton, Miller, Maries, and Osage Counties, Missouri, from the Earliest Time to the Present. Chicago: Goodspeed Publishing Co., 1889.

History of Cumberland and Adams Counties, Pennsylvania. Chicago: Warner, Beers & Co., 1886.

History of Daviess County, Missouri. Kansas City, MO: Birdsall & Dean, 1882.

History of Dayton, Ohio. Dayton, OH: United Brethren Publishing House, 1889.

History of Fayette County, Illinois. Philadelphia: Brink, McDonough & Co., 1878.

History of Franklin, Jefferson, Washington, Crawford & Gasconade Counties, Missouri. Chicago: Goodspeed Publishing Co., 1888.

History of Greene County, Missouri. St. Louis: Western Historical Co., 1883.

The History of Grundy County, Missouri. Kansas City, MO: Birdsall & Dean, 1881.

History of Harrison and Mercer Counties, Missouri, From

the Earliest Time to the Present. St. Louis and Chicago: Goodspeed Publishing Co., 1888.

The History of Henry and St. Clair Counties, Missouri. St. Joseph, MO: National Historical Co., 1883.

History of Hickory, Polk, Cedar, Dade and Barton Counties, Missouri. Chicago: Goodspeed Publishing Co., 1889.

History of Jasper County, Missouri. Des Moines, IA: Mills & Co., 1883.

The History of Johnson County, Missouri. Kansas City, MO: Kansas City Historical Co., 1881.

History of Laclede, Camden, Dallas, Webster, Wright, Texas, Pulaski, Phelps and Dent Counties, Missouri. Chicago: Goodspeed Publishing Co., 1889.

History of Lafayette County, Missouri. St. Louis: Missouri Historical Co., 1881.

History of Lewis, Clark, Knox and Scotland Counties, Missouri. St. Louis and Chicago: Goodspeed Publishing Co., 1887.

History of Lincoln County, Missouri, From the Earliest Time to the Present. Chicago: Goodspeed Publishing Co., 1888.

History of Lorain County, Ohio. Philadelphia: Williams Brothers, 1879.

History of Marion County, Missouri. St. Louis: E.F. Perkins, 1884.

History of New Mexico: Its Resources and Its People. Los Angeles, Chicago, and New York: Pacific States Publishing Co., 1907.

History of Newton, Lawrence, Barry and McDonald Counties, Missouri. Chicago: Goodspeed Publishing Co., 1888.

The History of Nodaway County, Missouri. St. Joseph, MO: National Historical Co., 1882.

History of Penobscot County, Maine. Cleveland, OH: Williams, Chase & Co., 1882.

History of Pettis County, Missouri. N.p., 1882.

The History of Pike County, Missouri. Des Moines, IA: Mills & Co., 1883.

History of Randolph and Macon Counties, Missouri. St. Louis: National Historical Co., 1884.

History of Ray County, Missouri. St. Louis: Missouri Historical Co., 1881.

History of Southeast Missouri. Chicago: Goodspeed Publishing Co., 1888.

History of Southern Oregon, Comprising Jackson, Josephine, Douglas, Curry and Coos Counties. Portland, OR: A.G. Walling, 1884.

History of St. Charles, Montgomery and Warren Counties, Missouri. St. Louis: National Historical Co., 1885.

History of Taylor County, Iowa. Des Moines, IA: State Historical Co., 1881.

History of the Arkansas Valley, Colorado. Chicago: O.L. Baskin & Co., 1881.

History of the City of Denver, Arapahoe County, and Colorado. Chicago: O.L. Baskin & Co., 1880.

History of the St. Louis Medical College. St. Louis: T.G. Waterman, 1898.

History of Wayne and Clay Counties, Illinois. Chicago: Globe Publishing Co., 1884.

History of Winona, Olmsted, and Dodge Counties. Chicago: H.H. Hill & Co., 1884.

Hodges, Frances B.S., comp. *The Neville Family of England and the United States.* Wichita Falls, TX: W.E.N. Wilson, 1964.

Holland, Mary A. Gardner, comp. *Our Army Nurses.* Boston: B. Wilkins & Co., 1895.

Holli, Melvin G., and Peter d'Alroy Jones, eds. *Biographical Dictionary of American Mayors, 1820-1980.* Westport, CT: Greenwood Press, 1981.

Hollister, Ovando J. *Boldly They Rode: A History of the First Colorado Regiment of Volunteers.* Lakewood, CO: Golden Press, 1949.

Holtzclaw, B.C. *The Genealogy of the Holtzclaw Family, 1540-1935.* Richmond, VA: Old Dominion Press, 1936.

Honeyman, A. Van Doren. *The Honeyman Family in Scotland and America, 1548-1908.* Plainfield, NJ: Honeyman's Publishing House, 1909.

Hooker, Edward. *The Descendants of Rev. Thomas Hooker, Hartford, Connecticut, 1586-1908.* Rochester, NY: Margaret H. Hooker, 1909.

Hopkins, Timothy. *The Kelloggs in the Old World and the New.* San Francisco, CA: Sunset Press & Photo Engraving Co., 1903.

Houp, J. Randall. *The 24th Missouri Volunteer Infantry: Lyon Legion.* Alma, AR: J. Randall Houp, 1997.

Hunt, Aurora. *The Army of the Pacific.* Glendale, CA: Arthur H. Clark Co., 1951.

Hyde, William, and Howard L. Conard, eds. *Encyclopedia of the History of St. Louis.* New York, Louisville, and St. Louis: Southern History Co., 1899.

The Illinois College Alumni Fund Association: Book of Memorial Memberships. Centennial Edition, 1829-1929. Jacksonville, IL: Alumni Fund Association, 1929.

An Illustrated Historical Atlas Map of Greene County, Missouri. Philadelphia: Brink, McDonough & Co., 1876.

An Illustrated Historical Atlas of Warren County, Missouri. Philadelphia: Edwards Brothers, 1877.

An Illustrated History of New Mexico. Chicago: Lewis Publishing Co., 1895.

An Illustrated History of Southeastern Washington Including Walla Walla, Columbia, Garfield and Asotin Counties, Washington. Spokane, WA: Western Historical Publishing Co., 1906.

An Illustrated History of the State of Idaho. Chicago: Lewis Publishing Co., 1899.

Ingalls, Sheffield. *History of Atchison County, Kansas.* Lawrence, KS: Standard Publishing Co., 1916.

Isbell, Timothy T. *Shiloh and Corinth Sentinels of Stone.* Jackson, MS: University Press of Mississippi, 2007.

Jameson, Ephraim O. *The Jamesons in America, 1647-1900. Genealogical Records and Memoranda.* Concord, NH: Rumford Press, 1901.

Johansson, M. Jane, ed. *Albert C. Ellithorpe: The First Indian Home Guards and the Civil War on the Trans-Mississippi Frontier.* Baton Rouge, LA: Louisiana State University Press, 2016.

Johnson, Allen, and Dumas Malone, eds. *Dictionary of American Biography.* New York City: Charles Scribner's Sons, 1964.

Johnson, Henry C., ed. *The Tenth General Catalogue of the Psi Upsilon Fraternity.* Bethlehem, PA: Comenius Press, 1888.

Johnson, Lorand V. *The Descendants of William and John Johnson: Colonial Friends of Virginia.* Boston: L.V. Johnson, 1935.

Johnson, William F. *History of Cooper County, Missouri.* Topeka and Cleveland: Historical Publishing Co., 1919.

Jones, Howel H. *Chase County Historical Sketches.* N.p.: Chase County Historical Society, 1940.

Jordan, Ewing, comp. *University of Pennsylvania Men Who Served in the Civil War, 1861-1865: Department of Medicine, Classes 1816-1862.* Philadelphia: University of Pennsylvania, 1915.

Jordan, Tristram F. *Leighton Genealogy. An Account of the Descendants of Capt. William Leighton of Kittery, Maine.* Albany, NY: Joel Munsell's Sons, 1885.

Juern, Joan M. *More Than the Sum of His Parts: Arnold Krekel.* Augusta, MO: Mallinckrodt Communications Research, 1999.

Kaufmann, Wilhelm. *The Germans in the American Civil War.* Translated by Steven Rowan and edited by Don Heinrich Tolzmann with Werner D. Mueller and Robert E. Ward. Carlisle, PA: John Kallmann, 1999.

Keeler, Wesley B., comp. *Keeler Family: Ralph Keeler of Norwalk, CT, and Some of His Descendants*. Baltimore, MD: Gateway Press, 1985.

Keith, Clayton. *Military History of Pike County, Missouri*. Louisiana, MO: Press-Journal Print, 1915.

Kemper, Willis M. *Genealogy of the Fishback Family in America*. New York City: Thomas Madison Taylor, 1914.

Kiel, Herman G., comp. *The Centennial Biographical Directory of Franklin County, Missouri*. Washington, D.C.: H.G. Kiel, 1925.

Kilby, William H., comp. *Eastport and Passamaquoddy: A Collection of Historical and Biographical Sketches*. Eastport, ME: Edward E. Shead & Co., 1888.

Kilgo, Dolores A. *Likeness and Landscape: Thomas M. Easterly and the Art of the Daguerreotype*. St. Louis: Missouri Historical Society Press, 1994.

Klein, Margaret C. *Joseph Gravely of Leatherwood*. Palm Coast, FL: M.C. Klein, 1984.

Labaw, George W. *A Genealogy of the Warne Family in America*. New York City: Frank Allaben Genealogical Co., 1911.

Lamborn, Samuel, comp. *The Genealogy of the Lamborn Family*. Philadelphia: Press of M.L. Marion, 1894.

Lang, Herbert O., ed. *History of the Willamette Valley*. Portland, OR: George H. Himes, Book & Job Printer, 1885.

Larsen, Lawrence H. *Federal Justice in Western Missouri: The Judges, the Cases, the Times*. Columbia, MO: University of Missouri Press, 1994.

Lash, Jeffrey N. *A Politician Turned General: The Civil War Career of Stephen Augustus Hurlbut*. Kent, OH: Kent State University Press, 2003.

Laun, Carol. *The Holcomb Collection*. Granby, CT: Salmon Brook Historical Society, 1998.

Lause, Mark A. *Price's Lost Campaign: The 1864 Invasion of Missouri*. Columbia, MO: University of Missouri Press, 2011.

Leach, F. Phelps. *Additions and Corrections for Thomas Hungerford of Hartford and New London, Conn., and His Descendants in America*. East Highgate, VT: F.P. Leach, 1932.

Leake, Paul. *History of Detroit: Chronicle of Its Progress, Its Industries, Its Institutions, and the People of the Fair City of the Straits*. Chicago and New York: Lewis Publishing Co., 1912.

Leavenworth, Elias W. *A Genealogy of the Leavenworth Family in the United States*. Syracuse, NY: S.G. Hitchcock & Co., 1873.

Leonard, John W., ed. *The Book of St. Louisans*. St. Louis: St. Louis Republic, 1906.

Lingenfelter, Richard E. *Death Valley & the Amargosa: A Land of Illusion*. Berkeley, CA: University of California Press, 1986.

Lowry, Thomas P. *Tarnished Eagles: The Courts-Martial of Fifty Union Colonels and Lieutenant Colonels*. Mechanicsburg, PA: Stackpole Books, 1997.

Lozier, Ralph F., "Memorial of John B. Hale," *Proceedings of the Twenty-Third Annual Meeting of the Missouri Bar Association*. Columbia, MO: E.W. Stephens Publishing Co., 1905.

Lyon, Sidney E., ed. *Lyon Memorial: Families of Connecticut and New Jersey*. Detroit: William Graham Printing Co., 1907.

Manning, Edwin C. *Biographical, Historical and Miscellaneous Selections*. Cedar Rapids, IA: E.C. Manning, 1911.

Markham, Virginia G. *John Baldwin and Son Milton Come to Kansas: An Early History of Baldwin City, Baker University, and Methodism in Kansas*. Baldwin City, KS: Baker University, 1982.

Marston, Nathan W., comp. *The Marston Genealogy in Two Parts*. South Lubec, ME: N.W. Marston, 1888.

Martin, George W., ed. *Collections of the Kansas State Historical Society, 1909–10*. Topeka, KS: State Printing Office, 1910.

_____, ed. *Transactions of the Kansas State Historical Society, 1897–1900*. Topeka, KS: W.Y. Morgan, State Printer, 1900.

_____, ed. *Transactions of the Kansas State Historical Society, 1901–1902*. Topeka, KS: W.Y. Morgan, State Printer, 1902.

_____, ed. *Transactions of the Kansas State Historical Society, 1907–08*. Topeka, KS: State Printing Office, 1908.

Marvin, Abijah P. *History of Worcester in the War of the Rebellion*. Worcester, MA: Abijah P. Marvin, 1870.

Marvin, George F., and William T.R. Marvin. *Descendants of Reinold and Matthew Marvin of Hartford, CT, 1638 and 1635, Sons of Edward Marvin of Great Bentley, England*. Boston: T.R. Marvin & Son, 1904.

Masich, Andrew E. *The Civil War in Arizona: The Story of the California Volunteers, 1861–1865*. Norman, OK: University of Oklahoma Press, 2006.

Maxwell, W.J., comp. *General Alumni Catalogue of the University of Pennsylvania*. Philadelphia: Alumni Association of the University, 1917.

May, Samuel P. *The Descendants of Richard Sares (Sears) of Yarmouth, Mass., 1638–1888*. Albany, NY: Joel Munsell's Sons, 1890.

McCall, Duncan. *Three Years in the Service. A Record of the Doings of the 11th Reg. Missouri Vols*. Springfield, IL: Baker & Phillips, 1864.

McDougal, Henry Clay. *Recollections, 1844–1909*. Kansas City, MO: Franklin Hudson Publishing Co., 1910.

McDowell, Don. *The Beat of the Drum: The History, Events and People of Drum Barracks, Wilmington, California*. Wilmington, CA: Drum Barracks Civil War Museum, 1993.

McFarland, Bill. *Keep the Flag to the Front: The Story of the Eighth Kansas Volunteer Infantry*. Overland Park, KS: Leathers Publishing, 2008.

McGregor, Malcolm G. *The Biographical Record of Jasper County, Missouri*. Chicago: Lewis Publishing Co., 1901.

McLean, William E. *The Forty-Third Regiment of Indiana Volunteers. An Historic Sketch of Its Career and Services*. Terre Haute, IN: C.W. Brown, 1903.

McPherson, Elizabeth Weir. *The Holcombes, Nation Builders*. Washington, D.C.: E.W. McPherson, 1947.

McRoberts, Mary. *Genealogical Abstracts from the Boulder Daily Camera, 1891–1900*. Boulder, CO: Mary McRoberts, 1985.

Meany, Edmond S. *History of the State of Washington*. New York City: Macmillan Co., 1909.

Mellon, Rachel H.L., ed. *The Larimer, McMasters and Allied Families*. Philadelphia: J.B. Lippincott Co., 1903.

Memorials of Deceased Companions of the Commandery of the State of Illinois MOLLUS, from Jan. 1, 1912 to Dec. 31, 1922. Chicago: Illinois Commandery MOLLUS, 1923.

Merrill, Georgia D., ed. *History of Androscoggin County, Maine*. Boston: W.S. Fergusson & Co., 1891.

Michno, Gregory. *The Deadliest Indian War in the West: The Snake Conflict, 1864–1868*. Caldwell, ID: Caxton Press, 2007.

Miles, Kathleen W., comp. *Annals of Henry County, Vol. 1, 1885–1900*. Clinton, MO: The Printery, 1973.

_____. *Bitter Ground: The Civil War in Missouri's Golden Valley, Benton, Henry and St. Clair Counties*. Clinton, MO: The Printery, 1971.

Miller, Darlis A. *The California Column in New Mexico*. Albuquerque, NM: University of New Mexico Press, 1982.

Miller, Joaquin. *An Illustrated History of the State of Montana*. Chicago: Lewis Publishing Co., 1894.

Mills, Charles K. *Harvest of Barren Regrets: The Army Ca-*

reer of Frederick William Benteen, 1834–1898. Glendale, CA: A.H. Clark Co., 1985.

The Miscellaneous Documents of the House of Representatives for the First Session of the Fortieth Congress, 1867. Washington, D.C.: Government Printing Office, 1868.

Mitchell, William Ansel. *Linn County, Kansas: A History.* Kansas City, MO: Campbell-Gates, 1928.

Montague, William L., ed. *Biographical Record of the Alumni of Amherst College During Its First Half Century, 1821–1871.* Amherst, MA: Press of J.E. Williams, 1883.

Moore, H. Miles. *Early History of Leavenworth City and County.* Leavenworth, KS: Samuel Dodsworth Book Co., 1906.

Morgan, George H. *Annual Statement of the Trade and Commerce of Saint Louis, for the Year 1906, Reported to the Merchants' Exchange of St. Louis.* St. Louis: R.P. Studley & Co., 1907.

Morgan, Perl W., ed. *History of Wyandotte County, Kansas, and Its People.* Chicago: Lewis Publishing Co., 1911.

Morris, Charles, ed. *Men of the Century.* Philadelphia: L.R. Hamersly & Co., 1896.

Morrison, Leonard A. *History of the Alison or Allison Family in Europe and America.* Boston: Damrell & Upham, 1893.

Morton, J. Sterling. *Illustrated History of Nebraska: A History of Nebraska from the Earliest Explorations of the Trans-Mississippi Region.* Lincoln, NE: Western Publishing and Engraving Co., 1911.

Mullins, Michael A. *The Fremont Rifles: A History of the 37th Illinois Veteran Volunteer Infantry.* Wilmington, NC: Broadfoot Publishing Co., 1990.

Mumey, Nolie. *Old Forts and Trading Posts of the West: Bent's Old Fort and Bent's New Fort on the Arkansas River.* Denver, CO: Artcraft Press, 1956.

Mundie, James A., Jr., Dean E. Letzring, Bruce S. Allardice, and John H. Luckey. *Texas Burial Sites of Civil War Notables: A Biographical and Pictorial Field Guide.* Hillsboro, TX: Hill College Press, 2002.

Murphy, Ignatius I. *Life of Colonel Daniel E. Hungerford.* Hartford, CT: Case, Lockwood & Brainard Co., 1891.

Murray, Stuart. *A Time of War: A Northern Chronicle of the Civil War.* Lee, MA: Berkshire House, 2001.

Nankivell, John H. *History of the Military Organizations of the State of Colorado, 1860–1935.* Denver, CO: W.H. Kistler Stationery Co., 1935.

The National Cyclopedia of American Biography. New York City: James T. White, 1898–1926.

Neal, William A. *An Illustrated History of the Missouri Engineer and the 25th Infantry Regiments.* Chicago: Donohue and Henneberry, 1889.

Newmark, Maurice H., and Marco R. Newmark. *Sixty Years in Southern California, 1853–1913, Containing the Reminiscences of Harris Newmark.* New York City: Knickerbocker Press, 1916.

Nichols, Bruce. *Guerrilla Warfare in Civil War Missouri, Volume IV, September 1864–June 1865.* Jefferson, NC: McFarland & Co., 2014.

Obermann, Karl. *Joseph Weydemeyer, Pioneer of American Socialism.* New York City: International Publishers Co., 1947.

Obituary Record of Alumni of Wesleyan University, for the Academic Year Ending June 28, 1888. Middletown, CT: Wesleyan University, 1888.

Ofele, Martin W. *German-Speaking Officers in the U.S. Colored Troops, 1863–1867.* Gainesville, FL: University Press of Florida, 2004.

Official Army Register of the Volunteer Force of the United States Army for the Years 1861, '62, '63, '64, '65. 8 Vol. Washington, D.C.: Government Printing Office, 1865–1867.

Organization and Status of Missouri Troops (Union and Confederate) in Service During the Civil War. Washington, D.C.: Government Printing Office, 1902.

O'Rourke, Timothy J. *Maryland Catholics on the Frontier: The Missouri and Texas Settlements.* Parsons, KS: Brefney Press, 1980.

Past and Present: A History of Iron County, Missouri, 1857–1994. Marceline, MO: Heritage House Publishing, 1995.

Pattison, John W., comp. *Biographical Sketches of the Officers and Members of the Twenty-Seventh General Assembly of Missouri.* Jefferson City, MO: Regan & Carter, 1874.

Paxton, William M. *Annals of Platte County, Missouri, from Its Exploration Down to June 1, 1897.* Kansas City, MO: Hudson-Kimberly Publishing Co., 1897.

_____. *The Marshall Family.* Cincinnati: Robert Clarke, 1885.

Peabody, Selim H., comp. *Peabody (Paybody, Pabody, Pabodie) Genealogy.* Boston: Charles H. Pope, 1909.

Peck, William F. *Landmarks of Monroe County, New York.* Boston: Boston History Co., 1895.

Peckham, Stephen F. *Peckham Genealogy: The English Ancestors and American Descendants of John Peckham of Newport, Rhode Island, 1630.* New York City: National Historical Co., 1922.

Penick, Lyman W. *The Penick Family: Descendants of Edward Penick/Penix/Pinix of St. Peter's Parish, New Kent County, Virginia.* Verona, VA: McClure Printing Co., 1982.

Perrin, William H., ed. *History of Alexander, Union, and Pulaski Counties, Illinois.* Chicago: O.L. Baskin & Co., 1883.

_____, ed. *History of Bond and Montgomery Counties, Illinois.* Chicago: O.L. Baskin & Co., 1882.

Peterson, Norma L. *Freedom and Franchise: The Political Career of B. Gratz Brown.* Columbia, MO: University of Missouri Press, 1965.

Petty, A.W.M. *A History of the Third Missouri Cavalry: From Its Organization at Palmyra, Missouri, 1861, Up to November Sixth, 1864.* Little Rock, AR: J. Wm. Demby, 1865.

Pictorial and Genealogical Record of Greene County, Missouri. Chicago: Goodspeed Publishing Co., 1893.

Pierce, Frederick Clifton. *Foster Genealogy: Being the Record of the Posterity of Reginald Foster.* Chicago: W.B. Conkey Co., 1899.

Pioneer Trails and Trials: Madison County, 1863–1920. Great Falls, MT: Madison County History Association, 1976.

Piston, William Garrett, and Thomas P. Sweeney. *Portraits of Conflict: A Photographic History of Missouri in the Civil War.* Fayetteville, AR: University of Arkansas Press, 2009.

Pivany, Eugene. *Hungarians in the American Civil War.* Cleveland, OH: E. Pivany, 1913.

Pixley, Edward E., and Franklin Hanford. *William Pixley of Hadley, Northampton, and Westfield, Mass. and Some of His Descendants.* Buffalo, NY: E.D. Strickland, 1908.

Pomeroy, Albert A. *History and Genealogy of the Pomeroy Family.* Toledo, OH: Franklin Printing & Engraving Co., 1912.

Pope, Charles H. *A History of the Dorchester Pope Family, 1634–1888.* Boston: C.H. Pope, 1888.

Porter, Joseph W. *A Genealogy of the Descendants of Richard Porter, Who Settled at Weymouth, Mass., 1635, and Allied Families: Also, Some Account of the Descendants of John Porter, Who Settled at Hingham, Mass., 1635, and Salem (Danvers) Mass., 1644.* Bangor, ME: Burr & Robinson, 1878.

Portrait and Biographical Album of Rock Island County, Illinois. Chicago: Biographical Publishing Co., 1885.

Portrait and Biographical Record of Buchanan and Clinton Counties, Missouri. Chicago: Chapman Bros., 1893.

Portrait and Biographical Record of Christian County, Illinois. Chicago: Lake City Publishing Co., 1893.

Portrait and Biographical Record of Denver and Vicinity, Colorado. Chicago: Chapman Publishing Co., 1898.

Portrait and Biographical Record of Johnson and Pettis Counties, Missouri. Chicago: Chapman Publishing Co., 1895.

Portrait and Biographical Record of Kalamazoo, Allegan and Van Buren Counties, Michigan. Chicago: Chapman Bros., 1892.

Portrait and Biographical Record of Marion, Ralls and Pike Counties, Missouri. Chicago: C.O. Owen & Co., 1895.

Portrait and Biographical Record of Montgomery and Bond Counties, Illinois. Chicago: Chapman Bros., 1892.

Portrait and Biographical Record of St. Charles, Lincoln and Warren Counties, Missouri. Chicago: Chapman Publishing Co., 1895.

Portrait and Biographical Record of Western Oregon. Chicago: Chapman Publishing Co., 1904.

Powell, Betty F. *History of Mississippi County, Missouri, Beginning Through 1972.* Independence, MO: BNL Library Service, 1975.

Powell, William H., ed. *Officers of the Army and Navy (Volunteer) Who Served in the Civil War.* Philadelphia: L.R. Hamersly & Co., 1893.

_____, and Edward Shippen, eds. *Officers of the Army and Navy (Regular) Who Served in the Civil War.* Philadelphia: L.R. Hamersly & Co., 1892.

Power, John C. *History of the Early Settlers of Sangamon County, Illinois.* Springfield, IL: Edwin A. Wilson & Co., 1876.

Pratt, J.T. *Pen-Pictures of the Officers and Members of the House of Representatives of the Twenty-Sixth General Assembly of Missouri.* N.p.: J.T. Pratt, 1872.

Purmort, Charles H. *Purmort Genealogy, Consisting of Nineteen Generations, Nine in England, Ten in America.* Des Moines, IA: Homestead Co., 1907.

Quinby, Henry C. *Genealogical History of the Quinby (Quimby) Family in England and America.* New York City: H.C. Quinby, 1915.

Rafiner, Tom A. *Caught Between Three Fires: Cass County, MO, Chaos, & Order No. 11, 1860-1865.* Bloomington, IN: Xlibris, 2010.

Raymond, Marcius D. *Gray Genealogy, Being a Genealogical Record and History of the Descendants of John Gray, of Beverly Mass.* Tarrytown, NY: M.D. Raymond, 1887.

Read, Benjamin M. *Illustrated History of New Mexico.* Santa Fe, NM: B.M. Read, 1912.

Reamy, Martha & William, comps. *Index to the Roll of Honor.* Baltimore, MD: Genealogical Publishing Co., 1995.

Reavis, Logan U. *Saint Louis: The Future Great City of the World.* Biographical Edition. St. Louis: Gray, Baker & Co., 1875.

_____. *Saint Louis: The Future Great City of the World.* Centennial Edition. St. Louis: C.R. Barns, 1876.

Reed, Laura C., ed. *In Memoriam: Sarah Walter Chandler Coates.* Kansas City, MO: Hudson-Kimberly Publishing Co., 1898.

Reed, William F. *The Descendants of Thomas Durfee of Portsmouth, Rhode Island.* Washington, D.C.: Press of Gibson Brothers, 1905.

Report of the Adjutant General of Arkansas, for the Period of the Late Rebellion, and to November 1, 1866. Washington, D.C.: Government Printing Office, 1867.

Report of the Adjutant General of the State of Kansas, 1861-'65. Vol. 1. Topeka, KS: Kansas State Printing Co., 1896.

Report of the Adjutant General of the State of Kansas, for the Year 1864. Leavenworth, KS: P.H. Hubbell & Co., 1865.

Report of the Adjutant General State of Missouri, 1915-1916. Jefferson City, MO: Hugh Stephens Co., 1916.

Report of the Denver Bar Association. Denver, CO: Smith-Brooks Printing Co., 1903.

Report of the Proceedings of the Society of the Army of the Tennessee, at the Fourth Annual Meeting. Cincinnati: Press of F.W. Freeman, 1877.

Report of the Proceedings of the Society of the Army of the Tennessee, at the Twentieth Meeting. Cincinnati: Society of the Army of the Tennessee, 1893.

Report of the Proceedings of the Society of the Army of the Tennessee, at the Twenty-Eighth Meeting. Cincinnati: Press of F.W. Freeman, 1897.

Report of the Proceedings of the Society of the Army of the Tennessee, at the Twenty-First Meeting. Cincinnati: Society of the Army of the Tennessee, 1893.

Report of the Proceedings of the Society of the Army of the Tennessee at the Sixteenth Meeting. Cincinnati: Press of F.W. Freeman, 1885.

Report of the Proceedings of the Society of the Army of the Tennessee at the Thirty-First Meeting. Cincinnati: Press of F.W. Freeman, 1900.

Report of the Proceedings of the Society of the Army of the Tennessee at the Thirty-Third Meeting. Cincinnati: Press of F.W. Freeman, 1902.

Representative Men of Colorado in the Nineteenth Century. Denver, CO: Rowell Art Publishing Co., 1902.

Ritter, Charles F., and Jon L. Wakelyn. *American Legislative Leaders, 1850-1910.* Westport, CT: Greenwood Press, 1989.

Roberts, Oliver A. *History of the Military Company of the Massachusetts Now Called the Ancient and Honorable Artillery Company of Massachusetts, 1637-1888.* Vol. 3. Boston: Alfred Mudge & Son, 1898.

Robertson, Carmeta P. *Gentry County, MO, the Civil War, 1861-1865: Fighters & Survivors.* Ozark, MO: C.P. Robertson, 1994.

Robison, Ken. *Montana Territory and the Civil War.* Charleston, SC: The History Press, 2013.

Robley, Thomas F. *History of Bourbon County, Kansas, to the Close of 1865.* Fort Scott, KS: Press of Monitor Book & Printing Co., 1894.

Rogers' Souvenir History of Mercer County Missouri and Dictionary of Local Data. Trenton, MO: W.B. Rogers Printing Co., 1911.

Rombauer, Robert J. *Biographical Notes of Robert J. Rombauer, 1917.* St. Louis: R.J. Rombauer, 1922.

_____. *The Union Cause in St. Louis in 1861: An Historical Sketch.* St. Louis: Nixon-Jones Printing Co., 1909.

Rosengarten, Joseph G. *The German Soldier in the Wars of the United States.* Second edition, revised and enlarged. Philadelphia: J.B. Lippincott Co., 1890.

Roster and By-Laws of Col. Hassendeubel Post, No. 13, Department of Missouri, GAR. St. Louis: Col. Hassendeubel Post, 1911.

Rowland, Dunbar, ed. *Encyclopedia of Mississippi History.* Madison, WI: Selwyn A. Brant, 1907.

Rutt, Christian L., comp. *The Daily News' History of Buchanan County and St. Joseph, Missouri, From the Time of the Platte Purchase to the End of the Year 1898.* St. Joseph, MO: St. Joseph Publishing Co., 1898.

_____, ed. *History of Buchanan County and the City of St. Joseph and Representative Citizens.* Chicago: Biographical Publishing Co., 1904.

Sabin, Edwin L. *Kit Carson Days, 1809-1868: "Adventures in the Path of Empire."* Revised Edition. New York City: Press of the Pioneers, 1935.

Sachs, Emanie N. *The Terrible Siren: Victoria Woodhull, 1838-1927.* New York City: Harper & Brothers, 1928.

St. Louis The Fourth City Pictorial and Biographical Deluxe

Supplement. St. Louis and Chicago: S.J. Clarke Publishing Co., 1909.

Sanders, Helen Fitzgerald. *A History of Montana*. Chicago and New York: Lewis Publishing Co., 1913.

Sandy, Wilda. *Here Lies Kansas City*. Kansas City, MO: Bennett Schneider, 1984.

Scharf, J. Thomas. *History of Saint Louis City and County*. Philadelphia: Louis H. Everts & Co., 1883.

Scheel, Gary L. *Rain, Mud & Swamps: 31st Missouri Volunteer Infantry Regiment: Marching Through the South During the Civil War with General William T. Sherman*. Pacific, MO: G.L. Scheel, 1998.

Schlegel, Carl W. *Schlegel's German-American Families in the United States*. New York Edition. New York City: American Historical Society, 1916.

Schrantz, Ward L., comp. *Jasper County, Missouri, in the Civil War*. Carthage, MO: Carthage Press, 1923.

Schultz, Gerard. *A History of Miller County, Missouri*. Jefferson City, MO: Midland Printing Co., 1933.

Seaver, Jesse M. *The Holcomb(e) Genealogy: A Genealogy, History and Directory of the Holcomb(e)s of the World*. Philadelphia: American Historical-Genealogical Society, 1925.

Secrist, M. *Lee County, Virginia: History Revealed Through Biographical and Genealogical Sketches of Its Ancestors*. N.p.: M. Secrist, 2013.

Sergent, Mary Elizabeth. *They Lie Forgotten: The United States Military Academy, 1856-1861, Together with a Class Album for the Class of May 1861*. Middletown, NY: Prior King Press, 1986.

Sheridan, Philip H. *Personal Memoirs of P.H. Sheridan, General United States Army*. New York City: Charles L. Webster & Co., 1888.

Shuck, Oscar T., ed. *Sketches of Leading and Representative Men of San Francisco*. London, New York, and San Francisco: London and New York Publishing Co., 1875.

Simon, John Y., ed. *The Papers of Ulysses S. Grant*. Vol. 5: April 1–August 31, 1862. Carbondale, IL: Southern Illinois University Press, 1973.

_____, ed. *The Papers of Ulysses S. Grant*. Vol. 7: December 9, 1862–March 31, 1863. Carbondale, IL: Southern Illinois University Press, 1979.

_____, ed. *The Papers of Ulysses S. Grant*. Vol. 8: April 1–July 6, 1863. Carbondale, IL: Southern Illinois University Press, 1979.

_____, ed. *The Papers of Ulysses S. Grant*. Vol. 9: July 7–December 31, 1863. Carbondale, IL: Southern Illinois University Press, 1982.

_____, ed. *The Papers of Ulysses S. Grant*. Vol. 10: January 1–May 31, 1864. Carbondale, IL: Southern Illinois University Press, 1982.

_____, ed. *The Papers of Ulysses S. Grant*. Vol. 15: May 1–December 31, 1865. Carbondale, IL: Southern Illinois University Press, 1988.

_____, ed. *The Papers of Ulysses S. Grant*. Vol. 17: January 1–September 30, 1867. Carbondale, IL: Southern Illinois University Press, 1991.

_____, ed. *The Papers of Ulysses S. Grant*. Vol. 18: October 1, 1867–June 30, 1868. Carbondale, IL: Southern Illinois University Press, 1991.

Sitton, Enid Wells. *Sitton and Gibson Genealogy, 1745–1966*. Houston, TX: E.W. Sitton, 1971.

Sixteenth Annual Reunion of the Association of the Graduates of the U.S. Military Academy at West Point, NY. East Saginaw, MI: Evening News, 1885.

Slagg, Winifred N. *Riley County, Kansas: A Story of Early Settlements, Rich Valleys, Azure Skies and Sunflowers*. Manhattan, KS: W.N. Slagg, 1968.

Smiley, Jerome C., ed. *History of Denver with Outlines of the Earlier History of the Rocky Mountain Country*. Denver, CO: Times-Sun Publishing Co., 1901.

Smith, Albert. *History of the Town of Peterborough, Hillsborough County, New Hampshire*. Boston: Press of George H. Ellis, 1876.

Smith, Carlton L. *Peabody at Shiloh: A Short Study of Courage and Injustice*. Harvard, MA: C.L. Smith, 1983.

Smith, Myron J., Jr. *Civil War Biographies from the Western Waters*. Jefferson, NC: McFarland & Company, 2015.

Smith, R.F., ed. *Doniphan County, Kansas, History and Directory for 1868-9*. Wathena, KS: Smith, Vaughan & Co., 1868.

Sobel, Robert, and John Raimo, eds. *Biographical Directory of the Governors of the United States, 1789-1978*. Westport, CT: Meckler Books, 1988.

Society of the Army of the Cumberland. Forty-Second Reunion, Chattanooga, Tenn. Chattanooga, TN: MacGowan-Cooke Printing Co., 1914.

Spalding, John A., comp. *Illustrated Popular Biography of Connecticut*. Hartford, CT: Case, Lockwood & Brainard Co., 1891.

Sprague, Homer B. *History of the 13th Infantry Regiment of Connecticut Volunteers, During the Great Rebellion*. Hartford, CT: Case, Lockwood & Co., 1867.

Stadden, Richard S. *Genealogy of the Stadden Family, Descendants and Relatives of Thomas Stadden and Samuel Stadden*. N.p.: R.S. Stadden, 1987.

Starr, Stephen Z. *Jennison's Jayhawkers: A Civil War Cavalry Regiment and Its Commander*. Baton Rouge, LA: Louisiana State University Press, 1973.

Statue of Hon. George Laird Shoup, Late a Senator from Idaho, Erected in Statuary Hall of the Capitol at Washington. Washington, D.C.: Government Printing Office, 1910.

Steele, James W. *The Battle of the Blue of the Second Regiment, K.S.M., October 22, 1864, the Fight, the Captivity, the Escape*. Chicago: Women's Temperance Publishing Association, 1896.

Stevens, Walter B. *Missouri: The Center State, 1821-1915*. Chicago and St. Louis: S.J. Clarke Publishing Co., 1915.

_____. *St. Louis the Fourth City, 1764–1909*. St. Louis and Chicago: S.J. Clarke Publishing Co., 1909.

Stewart, A.J.D., ed. *The History of the Bench and Bar of Missouri*. St. Louis: Legal Publishing Co., 1898.

Stiles, Henry R., ed. *The Civil, Political, Professional and Ecclesiastical History and Commercial and Industrial Record of the County of Kings and the City of Brooklyn, N.Y*. New York City: W.W. Munsell & Co., 1884.

Stinchfield, John C. *History of the Town of Leeds, Androscoggin County, Maine, From Its Settlement, June 10, 1780*. Lewiston, ME: Lewiston Journal, 1901.

Stone, Mary Amelia. *Memoir of George Boardman Boomer*. Boston: Press of Geo. C. Rand & Avery, 1864.

Stout, Tom, ed. *Montana Its Story and Biography*. Chicago and New York: American Historical Society, 1921.

Street, Henry A. and Mary A. *The Street Genealogy*. Exeter, NH: News-Letter Press, 1895.

Sullivan, John L., comp. *Official Manual of the State of Missouri for the Years 1919–1920*. Jefferson City, MO: Hugh Stephens Co., 1920.

Sumner, Charles A. *Shorthand and Reporting: A Lecture*. New Edition. New York City: Andrew J. Graham, 1882.

Sword, Wiley. *Shiloh: Bloody April*. New York City: William Morrow & Co., 1974.

Tennal, Ralph. *History of Nemaha County, Kansas*. Lawrence, KS: Standard Publishing Co., 1916.

Thompson, Alice S. *The Drake Family of New Hampshire: Robert, of Hampton, and Some of His Descendants*. Concord, NH: New Hampshire Historical Society, 1962.

Thompson, Jerry D. *A Civil War History of the New Mexico Volunteers & Militia*. Albuquerque, NM: University of New Mexico Press, 2015.

_____. *Mexican Texans in the Union Army.* El Paso, TX: Texas Western Press, 1986.

_____, and Lawrence T. Jones III. *Civil War & Revolution on the Rio Grande Frontier: A Narrative and Photographic History.* Austin, TX: Texas State Historical Association, 2004.

Thrapp, Dan L. *Encyclopedia of Frontier Biography.* Glendale, CA: Arthur H. Clark Co., 1988.

Tipton, Thomas W. *Forty Years of Nebraska at Home and in Congress.* Lincoln, NE: State Journal Co., 1902.

Traylor, Jacob L. *Past and Present of Montgomery County, Illinois.* Chicago: S.J. Clarke Publishing Co., 1904.

Treat, John Harvey. *The Treat Family: A Genealogy of Trott, Tratt, and Treat for Fifteen Generations.* Salem, MA: Salem Press Publishing & Printing Co., 1893.

Tucker, Ephraim. *Genealogy of the Tucker Family from Various Authentic Sources.* Worcester, MA: Ephraim Tucker, 1895.

Twenty-Fifth Annual Reunion of the Association of the Graduates of the U.S. Military Academy at West Point, NY. Saginaw, MI: Seemann & Peters, 1894.

Twenty-Fourth Annual Reunion of the Association of the Graduates of the U.S. Military Academy. Saginaw, MI: Seemann & Peters, 1893.

Twitchell, Ralph E. *The History of the Military Occupation of the Territory of New Mexico from 1846 to 1851.* Denver, CO: Smith-Brooks Co., 1909.

_____. *The Leading Facts of New Mexican History.* Cedar Rapids, IA: Torch Press, 1912.

The Union Army. Illinois Edition. Vol. 8. Madison, WI: Federal Publishing Co., 1908.

The United States Biographical Dictionary. Kansas Volume. Chicago and Kansas City: S. Lewis & Co., 1879.

The United States Biographical Dictionary and Portrait Gallery of Eminent and Self-Made Men. Illinois Volume. Chicago, Cincinnati, and New York: American Biographical Publishing Co., 1876.

The United States Biographical Dictionary and Portrait Gallery of Eminent and Self-Made Men. Missouri Volume. New York, Chicago, St. Louis, and Kansas City: United States Biographical Publishing Co., 1878.

Van Gilder, Marvin L. *Jasper County: The First Two Hundred Years.* N.p., M.L. Van Gilder, 1995.

Van Rensselaer, Florence, comp. *The Livingston Family in America and Its Scottish Origins.* New York City: F. Van Rensselaer, 1949.

Varley, James F. *Brigham and the Brigadier: General Patrick Connor and His California Volunteers in Utah and Along the Overland Trail.* Tucson, AZ: Westernlore Press, 1989.

Vasvary, Edmund. *Lincoln's Hungarian Heroes: The Participation of Hungarians in the Civil War, 1861–1865.* Washington, D.C.: Hungarian Reformed Federation of America, 1939.

Vida, Istvan Kornel. *Hungarian Emigres in the American Civil War: A History and Biographical Dictionary.* Jefferson, NC: McFarland & Company, 2012.

Wagner, Allen E. *Good Order and Safety: A History of the St. Louis Metropolitan Police, 1861–1906.* St. Louis: Missouri History Museum, 2008.

Walker, Charles A., ed. *History of Macoupin County, Illinois: Biographical and Pictorial.* Chicago: S.J. Clarke Publishing Co., 1911.

Wanamaker, George W. *History of Harrison County, Missouri.* Topeka and Indianapolis: Historical Publishing Co., 1921.

The War of the Rebellion: A Compilation of the Official Records of the Union and Confederate Armies. 128 Vol. Washington, D.C.: Government Printing Office, 1880–1901.

Ward, William H., ed. *Records of Members of the Grand Army of the Republic With a Complete Account of the Twentieth National Encampment.* San Francisco: H.S. Crocker & Co., 1886.

Waring, George E., Jr. *Whip and Spur.* Boston: James R. Osgood & Co., 1875.

Washington Pioneers. Olympia, WA: Washington State Genealogical Society, 1991.

Watkins, Albert. *History of Nebraska from the Earliest Explorations to the Present Time.* Lincoln, NE: Western Publishing & Engraving Co., 1913.

Webb, Walter P., ed. *The Handbook of Texas.* Austin, TX: Texas State Historical Association, 1952.

Webb, William L. *Battles and Biographies of Missourians or the Civil War Period of Our State.* Kansas City, MO: Hudson-Kimberly Publishing Co., 1900.

Welles, Albert. *History of the Welles Family in England and Normandy, With the Derivation from Their Progenitors of Some of the Descendants in the United States.* New York City: Albert Welles, 1876.

West, Sue Crabtree, comp. *The Maury Family Tree, Descendants of Mary Anne Fontaine (1690–1755) and Matthew Maury (1686–1752).* Birmingham, AL: S.C. West, 1971.

Wheeler, Alma J. Enloe, comp. *Montgomery County, Missouri, Newspaper Records for the Year 1904.* Shelbyville, MO: Wilham Genealogical Research & Publishing, 1996.

Whitford, William C. *Colorado Volunteers in the Civil War: The New Mexico Campaign in 1862.* Denver, CO: State Historical and Natural History Society, 1906.

Whitney, Carrie Westlake. *Kansas City, Missouri: Its History and Its People, 1808–1908.* Chicago: S.J. Clarke Publishing Co., 1908.

Whittemore, Henry. *The Founders and Builders of the Oranges.* Newark, NJ: L.J. Hardham, 1896.

Williams, Nancy A., ed. *Arkansas Biography: A Collection of Notable Lives.* Fayetteville, AR: University of Arkansas Press, 2000.

Williams, Walter, ed. *A History of Northwest Missouri.* Chicago and New York: Lewis Publishing Co., 1915.

Wilson, James Grant, and John Fiske, eds. *Appleton's Cyclopedia of American Biography.* New York City: D. Appleton & Co., 1888.

Winter, William C. *The Civil War in St. Louis: A Guided Tour.* St. Louis: Missouri Historical Society Press, 1994.

Wise, Jennings C. *The Military History of the Virginia Military Institute from 1839 to 1865.* Lynchburg, VA: J.P. Bell Co., 1915.

Wood, Larry. *The Siege of Lexington, Missouri: The Battle of the Hemp Bales.* Charleston, SC: The History Press, 2014.

Wood, Margaret L. *Memorial of Samuel N. Wood.* Kansas City, MO: Hudson-Kimberly Publishing Co., 1892.

Wyandotte County and Kansas City, Kansas, Historical and Biographical. Chicago: Goodspeed Publishing Co., 1890.

Zucker, Adolf E., ed. *The Forty-Eighters: Political Refugees of the German Revolution of 1848.* New York City: Columbia University Press, 1950.

Articles in Periodicals and Newspapers

"Aaron Brown's Wives," *St. Louis Post-Dispatch,* March 5, 1875.

Adams, Blanche V., "The Second Colorado Cavalry in the Civil War," *Colorado Magazine,* Vol. 8, No. 3 (May 1931).

"Administrator's Sale," *Doniphan Prospect,* Aug. 13, 1875.

"Adolph E. Hugo Insane," *New York Times,* July 6, 1885.

"The Alton Democrat on Col. Weer," *Alton Telegraph,* Sept. 2, 1864.

"The Best Governor of Missouri Since the War is Said to be Dying," *Springfield Republican,* Jan. 18, 1900.

"Biographical Notes: Col. Amos W. Maupin," *Franklin County Tribune*, July 23, 1897.
Britton, Wiley, "A Day With Colonel W.F. Cloud," *Chronicles of Oklahoma*, Vol. 5, No. 3 (September 1927).
Brown, Clark, "Incidents in the Life of Col. David Murphy," *Franklin County Tribune*, April 21, 1916.
"Camm & A.J. Seay: Distinguished Father and Son," *Newsletter, Osage County (MO) Historical Society*, Vol. 7, No. 3 (March 1992).
Canan, Howard V., "The Missouri Paw Paw Militia of 1863–1864," *Missouri Historical Review*, Vol. 62, No. 4 (July 1968).
"A Candidate for United States Senator Who Has No Votes," *Topeka Daily Capital*, Jan. 11, 1903.
Carey, Raymond G., "The 'Bloodless Third' Regiment, Colorado Volunteer Cavalry," *Colorado Magazine*, Vol. 38, No. 4 (Oct. 1961).
"The Case of Col. Des Anges," *New York Times*, Nov. 28, 1875.
Cohen, Andrew Wender, "Smuggling, Globalization, and America's Outward State, 1870–1909," *The Journal of American History*, Vol. 97, No. 2 (September 2010).
"Col. Abraham H. Ryan," *Daily Arkansas Gazette*, Dec. 2, 1894.
"Col. Des Anges Convicted," *New York Times*, Nov. 10, 1875.
"Col. Kimball Killed by the Indians," *St. Joseph Morning Herald and Daily Tribune*, Nov. 26, 1865.
"Col. Lebbeus Zevely and His Role in the Civil War," *Newsletter, Osage County (MO) Historical Society*, Vol. 7, No. 4 (April 1992).
"Col. Peter McFarland," *Leavenworth Times*, Nov. 18, 1870.
"Col. Ramming," *Davenport Der Demokrat*, Dec. 24, 1863.
"Col. Robert White," *Daily Missouri Democrat*, March 26, 1862.
"A Cold-Blooded Deed," *St. Louis Post-Dispatch*, June 18, 1886.
"Colonel John F. McMahan," *The Missouri Historical Review*, Vol. 29, No. 1 (Oct. 1934).
"Colonel Ramming," *Davenport Daily Democrat and News*, Sept. 11, 1861.
"Colonel Weer," *Daily Missouri Republican*, Sept. 3, 1864.
"Communication from Officers of the 13th E.M.M.," *Daily Missouri Democrat*, April 4, 1865.
The Connecticut War Record, Vol. 1, No. 9 (April 1864).
"Couple Married 65 Years to Celebrate," *St. Louis Post-Dispatch*, April 20, 1922.
Cox-Paul, Lori, "John M. Chivington: The 'Reverend Colonel' 'Marry-Your-Daughter' 'Sand Creek Massacre,'" *Nebraska History*, Vol. 88, No. 4 (Oct. 2007).
Crowder, David L., "Pioneer Sketch: George Laird Shoup," *Idaho Yesterdays*, Vol. 33, No. 4 (Winter 1990).
"Daniel Q. Gale, Washington's First Lawyer," *Washington Historical Society Newsletter*, Vol. 3, No. 16 (March 1994).
Darlington, Jane E., "Burials, 1870–1892, St. Paul's Episcopal Church, Indianapolis, IN," *The Hoosier Genealogist*, Vol. 35, No. 1 (March 1995).
"De Ahna's Disgrace," *Daily Illinois State Register*, Oct. 11, 1878.
"The Death of Colonel Cornyn," *Daily Missouri Republican*, Aug. 17, 1863.
"Death of Wm. G. Lewis, Action of the Gallatin Bar," *Gallatin North Missourian*, March 18, 1869.
Dirck, Brian R., "By the Hand of God: James Montgomery and Redemptive Violence," *Kansas History: A Journal of the Central Plains*, Vol. 27, No. 1–2 (Spring-Summer 2004).
"Early Day Sheriffs in Riley County," *Kansas Kin*, Vol. 29, No. 2 (May 1991).
"Encounter with the Enemy at Morristown," *White Cloud Kansas Chief*, Sept. 26, 1861.
"Estate of A. Krumsick," *Franklin County Record*, Sept. 2, 1875.
Farb, Robert C., "The Military Career of Robert W. Furnas," *Nebraska History*, Vol. 32, No. 1 (March 1951).
Foreman, Carolyn T., "Col. Jesse H. Leavenworth," *Chronicles of Oklahoma*. Vol. 13, No. 1 (March 1935).
"From Jefferson City," *Daily Missouri Democrat*, Sept. 23, 1861.
"From the Army of the Frontier," *Daily Missouri Republican*, March 3, 1863.
"Funeral of Gen. Boomer," *Massachusetts Weekly Spy*, July 1, 1863.
"The Funeral of Judge Woodyard," *Daily Missouri Democrat*, April 27, 1864.
"Funeral Service for C. H. Robinson," *Arizona Republican*, Sept. 12, 1911.
"Gen. Boomer," *Worcester National Aegis*, July 4, 1863.
"General Order No. 15, Headquarters First Military District, E.M.M.," *Daily Missouri Democrat*, May 15, 1863.
"General Order No. 26, Headquarters 1st Military District, E.M.M.," *Daily Missouri Republican*, Jan. 1, 1865.
Gentry, North T., "General Odon Guitar," *Missouri Historical Review*, Vol. 22, No. 4 (July 1928).
"The Grand Old Man of Topeka," *Topeka Daily Capital*, June 25, 1916.
Grover, George S., "Civil War in Missouri," *Missouri Historical Review*, Vol. 8, No. 1 (Oct. 1913).
Guenther, Paul F. "Albert Sigel—St. Louis German Poet," *Bulletin of the Missouri Historical Society*, Vol. 36 (April 1980).
Hayden, Horace E., "The Oliver Family of New York, Delaware, and Pennsylvania," *New York Genealogical and Biographical Record*, Vol. 20, No. 1 (Jan. 1889).
"He Was in Topeka on July 4, 1856," *Topeka Daily Capital*, March 11, 1916.
Herriott, Frank I., "The German Conference in the Deutsches Haus, Chicago, May 14–15, 1860," *Transactions of the Illinois State Historical Society for the Year 1928*. Springfield, IL: Phillips Bros., 1928.
Hess, Earl J., "The 12th Missouri Infantry: A Socio-Military Profile of a Union Regiment," *Missouri Historical Review*, Vol. 76, No. 1 (Oct. 1981).
"Hon. A. Warner," *Canton American Citizen*, March 20, 1875.
"Indian Murders on the Yellowstone," *The Montana Post* (Virginia City, MT), Sept. 2, 1865.
John D. Crawford Obituary, *Missouri Historical Review*. Vol. 3, No. 3 (April 1909).
"The Killing of Colonel Cornyn," *Daily Missouri Democrat*, Aug. 19, 1863.
Kittredge, Frank A., Ashmun N. Brown, and George W. Easterbrook, "Washington Territory in the War Between the States," *Washington Historical Quarterly*, Vol. 2, No. 1 (Oct. 1907).
Knuth, Priscilla, ed., "Cavalry in the Indian Country, 1864," *Oregon Historical Quarterly*, Vol. 65, No. 1 (March 1964).
"The Late General John B. Gray," *Railway Age*, Vol. 22, No. 1 (July 3, 1896).
"The Late Hon. Marcus Boyd," *Daily Missouri Republican*, Dec. 22, 1866.
"The Late Lieut. Col. James Peckham," *Daily Missouri Democrat*, June 8, 1869.
"Letter from Colonel Laibold," *Daily Missouri Democrat*, Dec. 30, 1863.
"Lieut. Col. Samuel H. Melcher, M.D., Physician, Patriot, Pioneer—A Worthy Son of the Granite State," *The Granite Monthly*, Vol. 48 (New Series, Vol. 11), 1916.
Lipsitz, George, "Joseph Weydemeyer, St. Louis' Marxist County Auditor," *St. Louis Magazine*, Vol. 16, No. 7 (July 1984).

Bibliography

Lobdell, Jared C., ed., "The Civil War Journal and Letters of Colonel John Van Deusen Du Bois, April 12, 1861 to October 16, 1862," *Missouri Historical Review*, Vol. 60, No. 4 (July 1966) and Vol. 61, No. 1 (Oct. 1966).

"Looking Back. The Neglected Grave of Supreme Judge Lovelace Near Montgomery County's Capitol," *Montgomery Tribune*, Nov. 16, 1900.

"Married Fifty Years," *Topeka Daily Capital*, June 30, 1907.

Marten, James, "Texans in the U.S. Army: True to the Union," *North & South*, Vol. 3, No. 1 (Nov. 1999).

McDougal, Henry C., "John Henderson Shanklin," *Proceedings of the Twenty-Second Annual Meeting of the Missouri Bar Association*. Columbia, MO: Press of E.W. Stephens, 1905.

Merriam, L.C., Jr., ed., "The First Oregon Cavalry and the Oregon Central Military Road Survey of 1865," *Oregon Historical Quarterly*, Vol. 60, No. 1 (March 1959).

Miller, Eddie, "De Soto's Other Founder-Louis J. Rankin," *De Soto Press*, April 30, May 7, 14, 21, 28, June 4, 1973.

"Missouri Twins Oldest in America," *St. Louis Post-Dispatch*, May 21, 1902.

Monnett, Howard N., ed., "A Yankee Cavalryman Views the Battle of Prairie Grove," *Arkansas Historical Quarterly*, Vol. 21, No. 4 (Winter 1962).

Morrow, Lynn, "Joseph Washington McClurg: Entrepreneur, Politician, Citizen," *Missouri Historical Review*, Vol. 78, No. 2 (Jan. 1984).

Mumey, Nolie, "Black Beard: Ceran St. Vrain, Frontiersman, Indian Trader, Territorial and Political Leader, and Pioneer Businessman," *The Denver Westerners Monthly Roundup*, Vol. 14, No. 1 (January 1958).

Myers, Lee, "Captain William McCleave, Fighting Cavalryman," *Southwest Heritage*, Vol. 3, No. 2 (March 1969).

Norton, Henry L., "The Travels of the Marstons," *Journal of the Illinois State Historical Society*, Vol. 58, No. 3 (Autumn 1965).

"Obsequies of Col. Everett Peabody," *Springfield Daily Republican*, May 19, 1862.

"Obsequies of Colonel Hassendeubel," *Daily Missouri Democrat*, July 31, 1863.

"Old Aaron Brown: The Story of His Checkered Life Told by One of his Wives," *Rolla Weekly Herald*, March 11, 1875.

"The Oldest Twins," *Hazleton Plain Speaker*, Nov. 21, 1900.

"Pardoned by Hayes," *New York Sun*, Aug. 4, 1877.

"Partners of Many Years," *St. Louis Globe-Democrat*, Nov. 13, 1902.

Peery, Dan W., "Autobiography of Governor Abraham Jefferson Seay," *Chronicles of Oklahoma*, Vol. 17, No. 1 (Spring 1939).

"Philips, History Maker: Jurist Who Died Yesterday Helped Keep Missouri in Union," *Kansas City Star*, March 14, 1919.

Piston, William Garrett, "The Bishops and the Black Hawks: Ambition and Family in Raising a Volunteer Regiment in Civil War Missouri," *Missouri Historical Review*, Vol. 110, No. 3 (April 2016).

Pope, Charles H., "Deaths: Samuel Adams Drake," *The New England Historical and Genealogical Register*, Vol. 60 (July 1906).

Price, James A., "Circular to the Citizens of Platte County, Missouri," *Weston Border Times*, Oct. 14, 1864.

"A Prominent Kansan Charged With Embezzlement," *Topeka Mail and Breeze*, June 11, 1897.

"Recent Deaths: Colonel Harai Robinson," *United States Army and Navy Journal*. Feb. 12, 1887.

Reck, Al, "California in the Civil War: Cavalryman from Berkeley Outwits Southern Captors," *Oakland Tribune*, March 26, 1961.

Rein, Chris, "The U.S. Army, Indian Agency, and the Path to Assimilation: The First Indian Home Guards in the American Civil War," *Kansas History: A Journal of the Central Plains*, Vol. 36, No. 1 (Spring 2013).

"Report No. 124 (Colonel H.C. De Ahna), June 21, 1864," *Reports of Committees of the House of Representatives, Made During the First Session Thirty-Eighth Congress, 1863–64*. Washington, D.C., 1864.

Robinson, H.E., "Two Missouri Historians," *Missouri Historical Review*, Vol. 5, No. 3 (April 1911).

Shaw, Albert, "Col. George E. Waring, Jr.," *The American Monthly Review of Reviews*, Vol. 18, No. 6 (Dec. 1898).

"Short History of David Murphy," *St. Louis Post-Dispatch*, Jan. 18, 1896.

"The Silk Smugglers," *Washington National Republican*, Nov. 11, 1875.

Smith, Carlton L., "A Promising Son is Lost," *Civil War Times Illustrated*, Vol. 24, No.1 (March 1985).

"Snoddy, Fighting Kansan," *Kansas City Star*, Nov. 4, 1917.

"Special Order No. 6, Headquarters First Military District, E.M.M.," *Daily Missouri Republican*, April 22, 1864.

"Successor to Judge Lovelace," *Daily Missouri Republican*, Oct. 17, 1866.

"Sudden Departure of the City Auditor for South America," *Daily Missouri Republican*, June 25, 1866.

"Superior Court, New Suits," *Chicago Daily Inter Ocean*, Sept. 3, 1879.

Thomas, James B., "Down Through the Years in Elyria," *Elyria Chronicle Telegram*, July 24, 1951.

Thorpe, Burton Lee, "In Memoriam Dr. James Albert Price," *Western Dental Journal*, Vol. 30, No. 10 (Oct. 1916).

"Union Colonel James Peckham Describes the Sacking of Jackson, Mississippi, Following Operations Against Vicksburg," *Blue & Gray Magazine*, Vol. 21, Issue 3 (Spring 2004).

Unrau, William E., "The Civil War Career of Jesse Henry Leavenworth," *Montana: The Magazine of Western History*, Vol. 12, No. 2 (Spring 1962).

Vagts, Alfred, "Heinrich Boernstein, Ex- and Repatriate," *Bulletin of the Missouri Historical Society*, Vol. 12, No. 2 (Jan. 1956).

Victor, Frances Fuller, "The First Oregon Cavalry," *Oregon Historical Quarterly*, Vol. 3, No. 2 (June 1902).

von Sahler, L. Hasbrouck, "The Dwights of Stockbridge," *The New York Genealogical and Biographical Record*, Vol. 33, No. 1 (Jan. 1902).

"Washington's Birthday in Downieville," *Sacramento Daily Union*, Feb. 27, 1861.

"William Henry Pulsifer," *Transactions of the Academy of Science of St. Louis*. Vol. 15 (January–December 1905). St. Louis: Nixon-Jones Printing Co., 1905.

Worley, Ted R., ed., "Elisha Baxter's Autobiography," *Arkansas Historical Quarterly*, Vol. 14, No. 2 (Summer 1955).

Internet Sources

https://americangallery19th.wordpress.com/category/boyle-ferdinand-t-l/.

"Amos W. Maupin (1827 MO-1900 MO) Colonel of the 47th MO Infy USV," http://home.usmo.com/~momollus/FranCoCW/Maupin_a.htm.

http://www.ancestry.com

"A Brief Autobiography of Thomas Harbine" (written in 1879), http://www.ancestry.com.

"Colonel Richard Goodrich Woodson Papers, Fort Davidson Collection," https://mostateparks.com/sites/mostateparks/files/colwoodson4.pdf.

"Colonel Robert Hundhausen (Gasconade County)," http://home.usmo.com/~momollus/GascCoCW/HunR.htm.

http://www.findagrave.com.
https://gallegosartistry.wordpress.com/jose-guadalupe-gallegos/.
http://www.haynesfamily.com/John1821.htm.
Hinderberger, Philip R. "Colonel Franz Hassendeubel," http://www.17thmissouri.com/bio_hassendeubel.html.
http://list.genealogy.net/mm/archiv/hannover-l/2007-03/msg00354.html.
"James Alpheus Matthews (Gasconade County)," http://home.usmo.com/~momollus/GascCoCW/Matt.htm.
https://www.kshs.org/kansapedia/james-madison-harvey/17032.
"Missing in Action, the Memoirs of Charles Woodbury Melcher, as told by Thomas P. Doherty," http://copland.udel.edu/~tdoherty/MissingInAction.pdf.
"The Niederwieser Family," http://niederwieser-anton.blogspot.com/.
Niermeyer, Douglas. "Colonel Austin Augustus King, Jr., 13th Missouri Cavalry," http://www.suvcw.org/mollus/art051.htm.
_____. "Colonel Henry Flad, 1st MO Eng. USV," http://home.usmo.com/~momollus/CiCmtg/Flad.htm.
_____. "Lieutenant Colonel David Walker Wear, 45th Missouri Infantry," http://www.suvcw.org/mollus/art048.htm.
Shiel, Jeanette. "The Life of Hon. John M. Richardson," http://webpages.charter.net/cwnorthandsouth/14thBioA91.html.
Thompson, Daniella. "William McCleave, Civil War Hero, Established a Military Dynasty," http://berkeleyheritage.com/eastbay_then-now/mccleave.html.

Manuscript Sources

Abraham Lincoln Presidential Library, Springfield, IL.
- Taylor, James E., *Portrait Gallery Officers of the Union & Confederate Armies. 1861–65.*

Chicago History Museum.
- Taylor, James E., *Portrait Gallery of Union Generals & Colonels That Fell by the Bullet and Disease in the Civil War* (1986.0480 PPL).

Louisiana and Lower Mississippi Valley Collections, Louisiana State University Libraries, Baton Rouge, LA
- Harai Robinson Papers, 1861–1889 (Mss. 488)

Military Order of the Loyal Legion of the United States (MOLLUS)
- Obituary Circulars of various State Commanderies

Missouri History Museum Archives, St. Louis, MO
- Henry Almstedt Papers, 1846–1939 (A0022)
- Herman T. Hesse Papers, 1851–1901 (A0692)
- Joseph P. Weydemeyer Papers, 1861–1865 (A1736)
- Robert White Papers, 1861–1908 (B648)

National Archives
- Card Records of Headstones Provided for Deceased Union Civil War Veterans, 1879–1903 (Record Group 92).
- Court-martial Case Files, 1809–1894 (Record Group 153).
- Dispatches from U.S. Consuls in Panama City, Panama, 1823–1906 (Record Group 59).
- Historical Register of National Homes for Disabled Volunteer Soldiers, 1866–1938 (Record Group 15).
- Letters Received, Adjutant General's Office (Record Group 94).
- Letters Received, Appointment, Commission, and Personal Branch, Adjutant General's Office (Record Group 94).
- Letters Received, Commission Branch, Adjutant General's Office (Record Group 94).
- Letters Received, Colored Troops Branch, Adjutant General's Office (Record Group 94).
- Letters Received by the Secretary of War, Irregular Series, 1861–1866 (Record Group 107).
- Letters Received, Volunteer Service Branch, Adjutant General's Office (Record Group 94).
- Military Service Files (Record Group 94).
- Pension Files (Record Group 15).
- Records of the Commandery of Pennsylvania, MOLLUS, 1865–1935, Vol. 16, Microfilm Series LM047 (Record Group 200)
- Register of Enlistments in the United States Army, 1798–1914 (Record Group 94).
- Regular Army Enlistment Papers, 1798–1912 (Record Group 94).
- Reports of Examining Boards as to Qualifications of Quartermaster Officers, 1864–1865 (Record Group 92)
- U.S. Census Records (Record Group 29).
- U.S. Military Academy Cadet Application Papers, 1805–1866 (Record Group 94).
- U.S. Southern Claims Commission, Disallowed and Barred Claims, 1871–1880 (Record Group 56).

State Historical Society of Missouri-Columbia
- William Bishop Papers, 1839–1891 (C3894)
- William L. Catherwood Papers, 1859–1873 (C3799)
- Odon Guitar Collection, 1836–1906 (C1007)
- William H. McLane Papers, 1836–1893 (C1020)

State Historical Society of Missouri-Rolla
- Clark Wright Papers, 1861–1863 (R0523)

University of Arkansas Libraries, Special Collections, Fayetteville, AR
- Gregg Family Papers (MC 1000)

U.S. Army Military History Institute
- The Edmund Vasvary Papers.
- MOLLUS Application Papers, George E. Waring, Jr.

U.S. Military Academy Library, West Point, NY
- Cullum File.

Vermont Vital Records Through 1870.

Newspapers

Albany (MO) Ledger
Albany (OR) Morning Daily Herald
Alton (IL) Daily Democrat
Anaconda (MT) Standard
Arizona Daily Citizen (Tucson)
Arizona Daily Star (Tucson)
Arizona Republican (Phoenix)
Arkansas Democrat (Little Rock, AR)
Atchison (KS) Daily Champion
Atchison (KS) Daily Patriot
Axtell (KS) Anchor
Baltimore (MD) Sun
Barber County (KS) Index
Batavia (NY) Republican Advocate
Battle Creek (MI) Journal
Berkeley (CA) Daily Gazette
Bethany (MO) Democrat
Bethany (MO) Republican
Boston (MA) Daily Globe
Boston (MA) Evening Transcript
Boston (MA) Herald
Boston (MA) Journal
Boston (MA) Post
Bremerton (WA) Daily News Searchlight
Brooklyn (NY) Daily Eagle
Buffalo (NY) Morning Express
Burlington (NJ) Daily Enterprise
Canton (MO) Press
Carthage (MO) Evening Press
Carthage (MO) Press
Chanute (KS) Daily Tribune

Bibliography

Chariton (MO) Courier
Charleston (MO) Daily Enterprise
Chase County (KS) Courant
Chase County (KS) Leader
Cherokee Advocate (Tahlequah, OK)
Chicago (IL) Daily Tribune
Chicago (IL) Inter Ocean
Chillicothe (MO) Constitution-Tribune
Cincinnati (OH) Commercial Gazette
Cincinnati (OH) Enquirer
Clark County (MO) Democrat
Clinton (MO) Daily Democrat
Colorado Springs (CO) Gazette
Cottonwood Falls (KS) Reveille
Daily Arkansas Gazette (Little Rock)
Daily Davenport (IA) Democrat
Daily Illinois State Journal (Springfield)
Daily Illinois State Register (Springfield)
Daily Kansas State Journal (Lawrence)
Daily Kansas Tribune (Lawrence)
Daily Missouri Democrat (St. Louis)
Daily Missouri Republican (St. Louis)
Dallas (TX) Morning News
Dansville (NY) Express
Dayton (OH) Daily News
De Soto (MO) Press
Denver (CO) Post
Detroit (MI) Free Press
Detroit (MI) News
Detroit (MI) News Tribune
Elyria (OH) Independent Democrat
Emporia (KS) Standard
Falmouth (MA) Enterprise
Fort Scott (KS) Daily Monitor
Fort Smith (AR) Times
Franklin County (MO) Tribune
Gallatin (MO) North Missourian
Galveston (TX) Daily News
Garden City (KS) Telegram
Garnett (KS) Journal
Girard (KS) Press
Hagerstown (MD) Daily Mail
Hartford (CT) Courant
Helena (MT) Independent
Hermann (MO Advertiser-Courier
Hermitage (MO) Index
Hillsboro (OR) Argus
Hutchinson (KS) Daily News
Idaho Statesman (Boise, ID)
Idaho World (Idaho City, ID)
Indianapolis (IN) Daily Sentinel
Indianapolis (IN) Journal
Indianapolis (IN) News
Iron County (MO) Register
Jefferson (MO) Democrat
Jefferson City (MO) Daily Tribune
Jefferson City (MO) Tribune
Jonesboro (IL) Gazette
Junction City (KS) Daily Union
Junction City (KS) Weekly Union
Kalamazoo (MI) Morning Gazette
Kansas City (MO) Journal
Kansas City (MO) Star
Kansas City (MO) Times
King City (MO) Chronicle
Knob Noster (MO) Gem
Lafayette (IN) Daily Journal
LaGrande (OR) Evening Observer
LaGrange (MO) Weekly Indicator
Lamar (MO) Democrat

Las Cruces (NM) Sun-News
Las Vegas (NM) Daily Optic
Lawrence (KS) Daily Gazette
Lawrence (KS) Daily Journal
Lawrence (KS) Daily World
Lawrence (KS) Republican Daily Journal
Lawrence (KS) Weekly World
Leavenworth (KS) Post
Leavenworth (KS) Times
Lexington (MO) Weekly Caucasian
Lexington (MO) Weekly Intelligencer
Liberty (MO) Tribune
Lincoln (NE) Evening News
Litchfield (IL) Monitor
Los Angeles (CA) Herald
Los Angeles (CA) Times
Macon (MO) Republican
Macon (MO) Times
Manhattan (KS) Mercury
Manhattan (KS) Nationalist
Manhattan (KS) Republic
Marion County (MO) Herald
Massachusetts Weekly Spy (Worcester)
Medford (OR) Mail
Medicine Lodge (KS) Cresset
Memphis (MO) Reveille
Mexico (MO) Intelligencer
Mexico (MO) Weekly Ledger
Milwaukee (WI) Sentinel
Missouri Herald (Columbia)
Missouri Republican (St. Louis)
Missouri Weekly Patriot (Springfield)
Moberly (MO) Daily Monitor
Moberly (MO) Evening Democrat
Mobile (AL) Register
Montgomery (MO) Standard
Morning Tulsa (OK) Daily World
Morristown (NJ) Daily Record
Mount Vernon (MO) Fountain & Journal
Natchez (MS) Democrat
Nebraska State Journal (Lincoln)
Neosho (MO) Times
Nevada (MO) News
New Mexico Herald (Las Vegas)
New Orleans (LA) Daily Picayune
New York (NY) Daily Tribune
New York (NY) Herald
New York (NY) Sun
New York (NY) Times
New York (NY) Tribune
Newton (KS) Daily Republican
Nodaway Democrat (Maryville, MO)
Northern Christian Advocate (Auburn, NY)
Norwich (CT) Bulletin
Oakland (CA) Tribune
Oconomowoc (WI) Free Press
Olathe (KS) Mirror
Orleans (NY) American
Osawatomie (KS) Graphic
Oskaloosa (KS) Independent
Oskaloosa (KS) Times
Ottawa (KS) Daily Republican
Ottawa (KS) Herald
Ouray (CO) Herald
Palmyra (MO) Spectator
Pana (IL) Palladium
The Peoples' Tribune (Jefferson City, MO)
Peterborough (NH) Transcript
Pike County (MO) News
Pittsburgh (PA) Daily Commercial

Pittsburgh (PA) Daily Post
Pittsburgh (PA) Dispatch
Portland (OR) Morning Oregonian
Portland (OR) Sunday Oregonian
Potosi (MO) Independent-Journal
Potosi (MO) Journal
Poughkeepsie (NY) Daily Eagle
Quincy (IL) Daily Journal
Quincy (IL) Herald
Quincy (IL) Whig
Reading (PA) Daily Eagle
Richmond (MO) Democrat
Rochester (NY) Democrat and Chronicle
Rocky Mountain News (Denver, CO)
Rolla (MO) Herald
Sacramento (CA) Daily Union
Sacramento (CA) Evening Bee
St. Charles (MO) Cosmos
St. Charles (MO) Cosmos-Monitor
St. Joseph (MO) Daily Gazette
St. Joseph (MO) Daily Morning Herald
St. Joseph (MO) Gazette
St. Joseph (MO) Herald
St. Joseph (MO) Morning Herald and Daily Tribune
St. Joseph (MO) Weekly Gazette
St. Joseph (MO) Weekly Herald
St. Louis (MO) Globe-Democrat
St. Louis (MO) Post-Dispatch
St. Louis (MO) Republic
St. Louis (MO) Republican
Ste. Genevieve (MO) Fair Play
Salem (OR) Daily Capital Journal
Salina (KS) Daily Republican
San Diego (CA) Union
San Francisco (CA) Call
San Francisco (CA) Chronicle
San Jose (CA) Mercury News
San Luis Obispo (CA) Tribune
Santa Cruz (CA) Evening Sentinel
Santa Fe (NM) Daily New Mexican
Santa Fe (NM) Weekly New Mexican
Savannah (MO) Reporter
Sedalia (MO) Daily Capital
Sedalia (MO) Daily Democrat
Sedalia (MO) Democrat
Sedan (KS) Lance
Seneca (KS) Tribune
Shelby County (MO) Herald
Sierra County Advocate (Hillsborough, NM)
Sonoma Democrat (Santa Rosa, CA)
Springfield (MO) Daily Leader
Springfield (MO) Leader
Springfield (MO) Leader-Democrat
Springfield (MO) Republican
The Stanberry (MO) Headlight
Tacoma (WA) Daily Ledger
Tombstone (AZ) Daily Epitaph
Topeka (KS) Daily Capital
Topeka (KS) State Journal
Troy (KS) Times
Union (MO) Tribune-Republican
Valley Falls (KS) New Era
Warrensburg (MO) Journal-Democrat
Warrensburg (MO) Standard
Warrenton (MO) Banner
Warrenton (MO) Herald
Warsaw (IL) Public Record
Washington (DC) Post
Washington Standard (Olympia)
White Cloud (KS) Kansas Chief
Wichita (KS) Daily Eagle
Winfield (KS) Daily Free Press
Wyandott (KS) Herald
Wyandotte (KS) Commercial Gazette

Index

Numbers in ***bold italics*** indicate pages with illustrations

Abreu, Francisco Paula 209, 210
Adams, Charles W. 164
Akers, Benjamin Franklin *165*
Allen, John Daugherty 6, 9, 17, 18
Almstedt, Henry 6, 7, 18, *19*
Ames, John W. 200
Anderson, Allen L. 148
Anderson, George Washington 4, 15, 19
Armijo, Juan Cristobal 209, 210
Armstrong, George *173*, *205*
Asboth, Alexander 69
Atkinson, Henry M. *173*, *205*

Bailey, Robert, Jr. 17, 19
Bailey, William 10, 20
Banks, Nathaniel P. 200
Barnum, William Lewis 10, *20*
Barr, Adam Johnston 16, *21*
Bartholow, Thomas Jeremiah 15, *21*
Bassett, Owen Abbott 162, *166*
Bates, Edward 22
Bates, Julian 11, 22, 139
Baxter, Elisha 143, *144*
Baxter, Hiram *83*
Bayles, David 10, 22
Bayles, Jesse 22
Benton, Thomas Hart 31
Best, Joseph Gibson 12, 22, *23*
Bickett, William Joseph Winterton 4, 14, 23
Bishop, William 3, 6, *23*
Bissell, George P. 24
Bissell, Josiah Wolcott 6, *24*
Black, Henry Moore 148, *149*
Blair, Charles W. 162
Blair, Francis P., Jr. 6, 31, 106
Bland, Peter Edward 9, 25
Blodgett, Wells Howard 15, *25*, *26*
Blood, James Harvey 9, 25, *26*, *27*
Blunt, James G. 159, 166, 172, 177, 190, 204
Boernstein, Henry 7, *27*, *28*
Boomer, George Boardman 12, *28*
Bowen, Aurelius *173*, *205*
Bowen, Thomas M. 164
Bowen, William D. 42
Bowie, George W. 148, 152
Bowyer, Eli 10
Boyd, Marcus 17, 29, 30
Boyd, Sempronius Hamilton 12, *29*, *30*, 87
Boyle, Ferdinand Thomas Lee 8, 30
Bradshaw, Robert C. 15, 18
Branch, Harrison Bell 14, 31
Brawner, Milton Hale 4, *31*, *32*, 76
Brayman, Mason 20
Brewer, Robert Milton 16, 32

Brooks, Edward James 143, 144
Brooks, Joseph 143
Brown, Aaron 12, 32
Brown, Benjamin Gratz 8, *33*
Brown, Egbert B. 25
Brown, John Mason 34
Brown, Oscar Monroe 148, 150
Brown, Richard Hardy 6, *34*
Brown, Robert B. 197, *198*
Brown, William Smith 13, 35
Browne, Samuel E. 156, *157*
Brutsche, John D. 15, *35*
Buffington, Adelbert Rinaldo 12, 35, *36*
Burke, Patrick Emmet 11, 36, *37*

Canby, Edward R.S. 198
Canfield, Cornelius H. 17, 37
Carleton, James H. 148, 150, 152
Carr, Eugene A. 50, 116
Carson, Christopher 209
Catherwood, Edwin Church 5, 6, *38*, 39
Catherwood, Henry Hamilton 10, 38, 39
Catherwood, William Lane 9, 38
Cavender, John S. 13
Chivington, John Milton 156, *157*, *158*
Clapp, William H. *74*
Clayton, Powell 162
Cloud, William Fletcher 162, 164, 166, *167*
Coates, Kersey 17, *39*
Coff, James 10, 39
Cole, Nelson 6, *40*
Coleman, David Crockett 9, 40, *41*
Colman, Norman Jay 3, 41, *42*
Colton, Gustavus Adolphus 163, *168*
Connor, Patrick E. 148
Conover, John 164, 168, *169*
Conrad, Joseph 11
Cooper, Stephen Stanley 163, 169
Cornelius, Thomas Ramsey 213
Cornyn, Florence M. 5, *42*, *43*
Corwin, David Bruen 163, 169, *170*
Cramer, John Frederick 11, 43
Cranor, Manlove 3, 9, 13, 43
Crawford, John Daniel 14, 43, *44*
Crawford, Thomas L. 10, 14, 44, 135
Crittenden, John J. 99
Cromwell, John N. 146
Crowder, Enoch H. 170
Cuddy, William 10, 44
Curley, Thomas 12
Currey, George Byron 213, *214*
Curtis, James F. 148
Curtis, Samuel R. 50, 77, 141, 166, 188

Davis, Alson Chapin 164, 170
Davis, Berryman Kenchin 14, 44
Davis, Edmund J. 216
Davis, John E. 16, 44
Davis, Werter Renick 162, 170, *171*
De Ahna, Henry Charles 3, 45
Deal, Henry J. 17, *45*
Dean, Benjamin Devor 12, *46*
Deimling, Francis Christopher 10, *47*
Deitzler, George W. 162, 188
De Narcy, John Bardorman 10, 47
Denver, James W. 177
Des Anges, Robert William Burdett 197, 198
Dickens, Charles 31
Dodge, Grenville M. 40, 49
Douglass, Joseph Beeler 7, 16, *48*
Drake, George B. 171
Drake, Samuel Adams 163, *171*
DuBois, John Van Deusen 6, 48, *49*
Duestrow, Louis 8, *49*
Dwight, Charles C. 50
Dwight, James Fowler 5, *50*
Dyer, David Patterson 15, *51*

Eads, James B. 55
Eads, James Douglas 3, 52, 80
Eberman, Reuben Jacob 16, 52
Edison, Thomas A. 176
Edwards, William Brewer 3, 52
Ellis, Calvin A. 4, 52, *53*
Ellis, Mary A. 53
Ellithorpe, Albert C. 193
Emerson, John Wesley 17, *53*
Emmons, Benjamin, Jr. 12, 54
Evans, George S. 148
Evens, William Henry 13, *54*, 132
Everett, Charles 197
Ewing, Thomas, Jr. 100, 162, 185

Fagg, Thomas James Clark 9, 54, *55*
Farrar, Bernard G. 13
Fenn, William P. 6, 55
Fergusson, David 148, 150
Fiala, John T. 119
Fishback, William Meade 143, *145*
Fisk, Clinton B. 13, 50, 78
Fiske, William O. 197
Flad, Henry 6, 55, *56*
Flesh, Matthew Martin 14, 56
Fletcher, Thomas C. 13, 15, 47, 76, 114
Forbes, William 14, *57*
Ford, James H. 156, 189
Forman, Ferris 148, *151*
Foster, John Daniel 12, 18, 57
Foster, Samuel Augustus 8, 14, 57, *58*

237

Index

Frantz, John H. *74*
Fremont, John C. 22, 45, 57, 136
Fritz, Charles Augustus 7, 8, 58
Furnas, Robert Wilkinson 163, *172, 173, 204, 205*
Fyan, Robert Washington 15, 59

Gage, Joseph S. 13
Gale, Daniel Quinby 16, 59
Gallegos, Jose Guadalupe 209, 210
Gamble, Hamilton R. 74, 86
Garibaldi, Giuseppe 45
Geiger, Washington Franklin 5, 59, *60*
Gilmour, James W. 32
Glover, John Montgomery 4, *60, 61*
Graham, Robert Henry 164, *173*
Grant, Melvin S. 165, 174
Grant, Nathaniel 18, 61
Grant, Ulysses S. 24, 29, 31, 53, 79, 140, 144, 190, 218
Gravely, Joseph Jackson 5, 61, *62*
Gray, John Burritt 7, *62*, 139
Green, Clark Hall 15, 63
Gregg, Lafayette 143, *145*
Guitar, Odon 5, *63, 64*

Hagen, Oscar *74*
Hale, John Blackwell 8, 17, 64
Hall, George Henry 5, 64, *65*
Hall, Willard P. 64, 97, 139
Halleck, Henry W. 45, 48, 52, 97, 150, 152
Hamilton, Andrew J. 200, 216
Hamilton, Charles S. 86
Hampton, Noah H. 4, 65
Harbine, Thomas 18, *65*
Harding, Chester, Jr. 10, 12, 15, 82
Harrington, Eugene Clarence 8, 66
Harrison, M. La Rue 143
Harvey, James Madison 164, *174*
Hassendeubel, Franz Philipp 11, *66*
Hawkins, Henry 195
Hayes, Rutherford B. 198
Haynes, John Leal *216, 217*
Hayward, John Thornton Kirkland 14, 67
Heaston, David Jackson 16, *67*
Heath, William Henry 13, *68*
Heren, William 8, 14, 68
Herrick, Thomas Peverly 162, *175*, 190
Herron, Francis J. 40, 141, 193
Hesse, Herman Theodor 8, *69*
Hickox, Franklin Whiting 15, 69
Hildenbrand, Henry 10, 70
Hill, Eben Marvin 6, *70*
Hillis, David B. 139
Hogan, Andrew Canard 165, 176
Holcomb, Richard Erskine 197, *199*
Holland, Colley Blondville 17, 70, *71*
Holmes, Samuel Allison 10, 14, *71*
Holt, Joseph 25, 118, 131, 159, 194
Howland, James T. 17, 71
Hubbard, Perry Lamb 165, *176*
Hubbell, John Barker 165, 176
Hugo, Adolph E. 7, 72
Hundhausen, Robert 8, *72*
Hungerford, Daniel Elihu *207*

Hurlbut, Stephen A. 42, 86, 116, 200
Huston, Daniel, Jr. 5, *73, 74*
Hutton, John Edward 16, 74

Imhauser, Henry 3, 74

Jackson, Albert 6, 74
Jameson, D.R. 65
Jameson, Ephraim Hall Emery 10, *75*
Jennison, Charles Ransford 162, *177, 178*
Johnson, Hamilton P. 162, *179*
Johnson, James M. 143
Johnson, James W. 11, 12, 75
Joliat, Francis Joseph 11, 75
Jones, Fidelio Sharp 9, 17, *76*
Joslyn, John Jay 4, 31, 76
Judah, Henry M. 148
Judson, William R. 162

Kallmann, Herrmann F. 7, *77*
Keeler, Julius Augustus 164, 179
Keily, Daniel J. 197
Kellogg, John 148, 151, *152*
Kelly, Thompson J. 15, 77
Kelton, John C. 10
Kettle, James Gibson 17, 77, *78*
Killborn, Curtis Williams 197, 199, *200*
Kimball, Thomas Fox 3, 78
King, Austin A. 78, 79
King, Austin Augustus, Jr. 6, 78, 79, 114
King, Walter 4, 78, 79, 114
Kleinschmidt, Henry Frederick Conrad 9, 79
Knapp, John 9, 10, 79, *80*
Knaus, Jacob 3, 80
Kossuth, Louis 101
Krekel, Arnold 12, 80, *81*
Krum, John Marshall 10, *81, 82*
Krumsick, August 16, 82
Krumsick, George 16, 82
Kutzner, Edward Augustus 7, 13, 14, 82, *83*

Laibold, Bernard 7, 83, *84*
Larimer, William, Jr. 156, 158, *159*
Latham, Milton S. 45
Lawrence, Warren Wirt Henry 163, 179, *180*
Lawson, William 17, 84
Leavenworth, Franklin 17, 84
Leavenworth, Henry 159
Leavenworth, Jesse Henry 156, 159, *160*
Lee, Albert L. 162
Lee, Robert E. 90
Leighton, George Eliot 9, *85*
Lewis, Charles W. 148
Lewis, William Grigsby 16, 85
Lincoln, Abraham 25, 74, 131, 194
Lindsay, James 17, 85, *86*
Lippitt, Francis J. 148
Lipscomb, Henry Stapleton 5, 86
Livingston, Robert R. 87, 204
Loan, Benjamin F. 123
Logan, John A. 68

Lothrop, Warren Lane 6, 86, *87*
Lovelace, Walter L. 17, 87
Lowe, Sandy 165, 180
Ludlow, Benjamin Chambers *50*
Lynde, Edward 162, *180, 181*
Lyon, James Jerome 12, 87, *88*

Malone, Francis Marion 162, *181*
Manning, Edwin Cassander 165, *182*
Manter, Francis Howe 13, 88, *89*
Marshall, Louis Henry 3, 89, *90*
Marston, Henry Charles 9, 90
Martin, James C. 3, 90
Martin, John A. 164
Marvin, Asa Crosby 16, 90
Mason, Oliver Perry 204, 205, *206*
Massey, Hervey A. 15, 91
Matthews, James Alpheus 3, 8, 91
Maupin, Amos W. 15, 16, 91, *92*
Maury, Reuben Fry 213, 214, *215*
McCain, William Delana 163, 169, 182
McCleave, William 148, 152, *153*
McClernand, John A. 68
McClurg, Alexander C. 92
McClurg, Joseph Washington 4, 5, *92, 93*
McFarland, Peter 164, 182
McFerran, James Hamilton Bowles 4, *93*
McGarry, Edward 148
McLane, William H. 10, 16, 94
McMahan, John Foster 6, *94*
McNeil, John 4, 8, 52
Melcher, Samuel Henry 13, *95*
Merrill, Lewis 4
Meumann, Theodore 8, *96*
Meyers, George Frederick 9, 96
Miller, Lewis P. 16, 96, *97*
Miller, Madison 11, 97, 114
Miller, Thomas, Jr. 12, 97
Million, Brainard M. 10, 97
Mills, James K. 12
Mitchell, Adam Clark 12, 97
Mitchell, Andrew Jackson 164, 183
Mitchell, Robert B. 162, 163, 179
Moberly, William Edward 14, 97
Montgomery, James 163, *183*
Moonlight, Thomas 162
Moore, David 7, 12, 16, 22
Morgan, William James 11, 97, *98*
Morrison, Edward 10, 98
Morsey, Frederick 16, 98, *99*
Moss, James Hugh 15, 18, *99*
Mower, Joseph A. 10
Murphy, David 15, 99, *100*

Neill, Henry 9, 17, *101*
Nemett, Joseph 5, 101
Nevill, Henry O'Bannon 3, 101, 102
Nevill, James Morgan 16, 102
Newcomb, Carman Adams 18, *102, 103*
Newgent, Andrew Gray 3, *103*
Niederwieser, Tony 9, 104

Okeson, William Black 17, 104
Oliver, Paul A. 104
Oliver, William Stockley 9, 104

Osterhaus, Peter J. 10
Owens, James William 3, 100, 104, *105*

Paine, Charles J. 197
Palmer, Ratcliff Boone 17, 105
Parker, Charles Wheeler 14, 105
Paul, Gabriel R. 209
Peabody, Everett 11, 12, *105*, *106*
Pearman, John W. *173*, *205*
Peckham, James 13, 106
Penick, William Ridgeway 5, *107*
Penney, Joseph 78
Pennock, William 164, 184
Phelps, John E. 143
Phelps, John S. 4, 17
Philips, John Finis 5, 101, 107, *108*
Phillips, Oliver P. 17, 108
Phillips, William Addison 163, 184, *185*, 193
Pike, Bennett 8, 16, *109*
Pike, Edward C. 9, *109*, *110*
Pile, William A. 13
Pino, Miguel Estanislado 209, 210, 211
Pino, Nicolas de Jesus 209, 210, *211*
Pleasanton, Alfred 40, 93, 95
Plumb, Preston Bierce 162, 185, *186*
Plumly, Mardon Wilson 197, 200
Plummer, Joseph B. 10, 22
Pollock, Robert 148, *153*, *154*
Pomeroy, James M. 163, 186
Pope, John 49, 86, 89, 90
Pope, William 16, 110
Porter, John Cooper 18, *110*
Poser, Rudolph von 13, 110
Poten, August Hero 8, *111*
Potter, Frederick Williams 164, 187
Pound, John 14, 111
Price, James Albert 14, *112*
Price, John Thomas 164, 187
Price, Thomas L. 111
Pulsifer, William Henry 18, 112
Purmort, William Wallace 13, *113*

Quigg, Matthew 165, 176, 187

Ramming, Henry 8, 113
Randlett, Reuben Augustus 163, *188*
Rankin, Louis James 18, 113
Reading, William McCune 17, 114
Reed, John H. 4, 114
Reynolds, Joseph J. 31
Richardson, Allen Peyton 3, 4, 78, 79, 114
Richardson, John Mortimer 6, 115
Richeson, Thomas 9, *115*
Richmond, Samuel A. 128
Rigg, Edwin Augustus 148, 154
Rinkel, George, Jr. 11, 115
Ritchie, John 162, 163
Ritter, John Francis 4, *116*, *117*
Roberts, Benjamin S. 209
Roberts, William Young 162, 188, *189*

Robinson, Charles H. 163, 189
Robinson, Harai 197, 200
Robinson, William Perrine 12, *117*
Rogers, John B. 4, 118
Rogers, William B. 15, *118*, *119*
Rombauer, Robert Julius 7, 119, 195
Rosecrans, William S. 33, 40, 49, 50, 86, 95
Ross, Leonard F. 146
Russell, Edward 18, 119
Ryan, Abraham Hall 143, *146*, *147*

St. Vrain, Ceran 209, *212*
Salomon, Charles E. 8
Salomon, Frederick 58, 194
Sanborn, John B. 35, 78
Sapp, William F. *173*, *205*
Saxton, Rufus 22
Schadt, Otto 13, 120
Schaefer, Frederick 7, *120*
Schittner, Nicholas 7, 8, *121*
Schofield, John M. 40, 49, 50, 62, 95, 131, 194
Scott, David Wilson 164, 189, *190*
Scott, John 12, 18, *121*
Scott, Thomas 11, 121
Seay, Abraham Jefferson 13, *122*
Selden, Henry Raymond 209, *211*
Severance, John 12, 123
Shanklin, John Henderson 8, 13, *123*
Sheldon, Charles S. 11
Shelton, William Anderson 15, 123
Shepard, Isaac F. 8
Sheppard, Henry 9, 17, *124*
Sheridan, Philip H. 151
Sherman, Thomas W. 197, 218
Shoup, George Laird 156, *160*, *161*
Sigel, Albert 5, 6, *124*, *125*
Sigel, Franz 7, 125
Sims, Columbus 148, 154
Sitton, James Owens 13, 125
Slocum, Henry W. 141
Slough, John P. 156
Smart, Edwin Jacob 4, 5, 126
Smith, Andrew J. 87, 88, 148
Smith, Asa G. 4, 126
Smith, Giles A. 9
Smith, Morgan L. 9, 40
Smith, William John Avery 18, *126*
Smith, William Stoddard 164, 190
Snoddy, James Donaldson 163, 190
Spedden, Robert Rush 14, 127
Stadden, Isaac 165, 191
Stafford, Edward 7, 127
Stapleton, Robert Hay 209, 212
Steele, Frederick 88, 89, 146
Steinberger, Justus Dunott *218*, *219*
Stephenson, Marshall Lovejoy 143, 147
Stevenson, John D. 9
Stifel, Charles Gottfried 7, 9, *127*
Stone, Roy 170
Stremmel, Philip A. C. 11, 128
Strong, James William 18, *128*

Sturgeon, Sheldon 197, *201*, *202*
Sturgis, Samuel D. 177
Sumner, Charles Allen 207, *208*
Swift, Francis Bowers 163, 191
Sykes, George 57

Taffe, John *173*, *205*
Taylor, George Richards 12, 128, *129*
Taylor, James Pugh 165, *191*
Tebbetts, Jonas *142*
Thayer, John M. 166, 204
Tindall, Jacob Torian 12, *129*
Tinker, Orwin Cullen 16, 130
Todd, George Ramsey 10, *130*
Tracy, Frank Maie 164, 192
Treat, Levi Stuart 164, 192
Tucker, Charles Loveland 11, *130*
Tyler, John Fulkerson 7, 131

Ullmann, Daniel 198

Vahlkamp, Henry Frederick 7, 131
Van Deusen, Delos 9, 131, *132*
Van Frank, Philip Riley 13, 54, *132*
Veale, George Washington 163, *192*

Wangelin, Hugo 10
Waring, George E., Jr. 4, *133*
Warmoth, Henry C. 134
Warmoth, Isaac Sanders 16, *134*
Warne, Marinus Willet 11, *134*
Warner, Alexander 197, *202*, *203*
Wattles, Stephen Howard 163, *193*, *194*
Wear, David Walker 16, 135
Weber, Andrew Jackson 10, *135*
Webster, Daniel 94
Weer, William, Jr. 163, 164, 165, 166, 194
Wells, Oliver 6, 136
Wessells, Henry W. 164, 173
West, Joseph R. 50, 76, 148
Weydemeyer, Joseph 14, *136*
White, Robert 11, *137*
Whitely, Thomas Jefferson 13, 137
Willemsen, Charles August 163, 195
Williams, John Freeman 5, *138*
Wirt, Samuel M. 15, *83*, *138*
Wolff, Christian Doerner 8, 10, 139
Wood, Samuel Newitt 164, *195*, *196*
Wood, William D. 5
Woodhull, Victoria Claflin 26
Woodson, Richard Goodridge 4, 22, 139
Woodyard, Humphrey Marshall 7, 139, *140*
Wright, Crafts James 11, *140*
Wright, Thomas Clarkson 5, *141*, *142*, 195
Wright, Thomas F. 148

Zakrzewski, Herman 77
Zevely, Lebbeus 13, *142*

www.ingramcontent.com/pod-product-compliance
Lightning Source LLC
Chambersburg PA
CBHW060340010526
44117CB00017B/2901